# Pop Culture Places

# Pop Culture Places

## AN ENCYCLOPEDIA OF PLACES IN AMERICAN POPULAR CULTURE

Volume 1: A–F

**Gladys L. Knight**

GREENWOOD

AN IMPRINT OF ABC-CLIO, LLC
Santa Barbara, California • Denver, Colorado • Oxford, England

**Library of Congress Cataloging-in-Publication Data**

Knight, Gladys L., 1974–
Pop culture places : an encyclopedia of places in American popular culture / Gladys L. Knight.
pages cm
Includes bibliographical references and index.
ISBN 978-0-313-39882-7 (hardcopy : alk. paper) — ISBN 978-0-313-39883-4 (ebook)
1. Historic sites—United States—Encyclopedias. 2. Popular culture—United States—Encyclopedias. 3. United States—Civilization—Encyclopedias. I. Title.
E159.K65 2014
973.03—dc23 2014002595

ISBN: 978-0-313-39882-7
EISBN: 978-0-313-39883-4

18 17 16 15 14 1 2 3 4 5

This book is also available on the World Wide Web as an eBook.
Visit www.abc-clio.com for details.

Greenwood
An Imprint of ABC-CLIO, LLC

ABC-CLIO, LLC
130 Cremona Drive, P.O. Box 1911
Santa Barbara, California 93116-1911

This book is printed on acid-free paper ∞

Manufactured in the United States of America

# Contents

# Alphabetical List of Entries

# Topical List of Entries

## Cities and Towns



## Civil Rights Movement and Counterculture Places



## Corporate Spaces



## Covert and Mysterious Places

## Early American Places



## Entertainment Spectacles



## Ethnic Neighborhoods



## Fairs and Festivals



## Film Industry and Hollywood



## Government Places



## Halls of Fame



## Homes and Estates

## Hotels



## Infamous and Tragic Places



## Islands



## Libraries and Archives



## Memorials and Monuments

## Military Institutions and Places



## Museums



## Native American Spaces



## Natural Wonders and Landscapes



## Neighborhoods and Communities

Greenwich Village
Harlem
Little Italy
Mobile Homes and Trailer Parks
Off-Grid
Spanish Harlem
Suburbia
Tent Cities

## Nightclubs

Billy Bob's Texas
CBGB
Cotton Club
Gilley's
Studio 54

## Nostalgic Americana

American Diner
Barbershops
Barns
Coney Island
Drive-In Movie Theater
Main Street
Roller-Skating Rinks
Soda Fountain
Summer Camp
U.S. Route 66
Woolworth's

## Parks and National Parks

Adirondacks
Central Park
Muscle Beach
Olympic National Park
Redwood National and State Parks
Skateparks
State and National Parks
Yellowstone National Park
Yosemite National Park

## Parties and Celebrations

Bar Mitzvah/Bat Mitzvah
Quinceañera
Rave
Weddings

## Prisons and Internment Camps

Alcatraz
Attica
Folsom State Prison
Manzanar

## Regions

Adirondacks
Amish Country
Appalachia
Cajun Country
Everglades
Great Lakes
Great Plains
Great Smoky Mountains
Mississippi Delta
Mojave Desert
Napa Valley
Okefenokee Swamp
Silicon Valley

## Restaurants and Bars

American Diner
The Brown Derby
McDonald's
Saloons, Bars, and Taverns
Soda Fountain
Starbucks

## Roadside Attractions



## Schools, Colleges, and Universities



## Shops and Retail Spaces



## Sporting and Competitive Events



## Sporting Venues



## States

## Streets and Districts



## Theaters



## Trails and Highways



## Transportation



## Vacation Spots



## Virtual Places



## The Wild West

## Youth Culture Places



## Zoos and Aquariums

# Preface

Simply defined, places are the spaces where people congregate as well as the experiences that happen within that space at a particular moment in time. Places can be contrived and human-made, natural, symbolic, or inextricably bound to an event or a particular group. Places can be sacred or secular, formal or casual, and even virtual.

In any form, places are replete with extraordinary significance and meaning. Places shed light on culture, identity, values, and trends. Places shape and are shaped, define and are defined by the societies that create and use them. Places embody the narrative of the human story, its past and present. They tell the story of the nation's history, development, and transformation from its earliest into contemporary times. If one is disposed to look, places reveal the issues, challenges, and triumphs of civilization.

Places transcend physical boundaries because they are influenced by people, time, and events; they reflect the local community and the nation at large. Places unite people in a common heritage, experience, and reality, and this shared association inevitably influences popular culture.

Popular culture refers to activities, objects, and media forms (such as newspapers, printed matter, film, television, advertising, and ephemera) that reflect the tastes, sensibilities, interests, customs, and folkways of the general population at a given time. Thus, countless places, large and small, across America have been repositories of popular culture throughout its history.

## Scope

In *Pop Culture Places: An Encyclopedia of Places in American Popular Culture*, places—a vast and varied array of them—stand front and center. Each place—more than 350 in all—is listed as a main entry. The selection process aimed to include places that reflect a full-bodied assortment of spaces that are iconic, popular, historically or culturally significant, and in some way representative of the American experience.

Places can be categorized in a variety of ways. Some, such as raves (a gathering that takes place within a physical structure), man caves, Tiffany & Company, and megachurches, are traditionally exclusive to various segments of the population based on gender, age, economic class, or religious belief. Other places, such as malls, museums, and monuments, are inclusive to the general public of any age and background. Most places included in these volumes exist in specific localities. However, some places, such as Main Street and barber shops, exist in recognizable forms across the country.

### More on the Types of Places

It must be stressed that this work includes an immense assortment of places, covering a broad array of spaces. Included are colleges and universities such as all-women's institutions, historically black colleges and universities, the prestigious Ivy League institutions, and military academies. The corporate and technological world is represented by entries such as Silicon Valley, Microsoft, and Apple Inc. The Civil Rights Movement is covered with entries for places such as the 16th Street Baptist Church, where a horrific bombing killed African American youth, generated worldwide sympathy, and propelled activism and change within American society. Entries such as those on Gettysburg and Little Bighorn introduce readers to major war campaigns in the United States. Places which reflect the religious diversity in America and the role religion plays in public life are represented by entries on Amish Country, Eldridge Street Synagogue, and Temple Square.

Major cities, ghost towns, islands, and ethnic enclaves are featured. Readers will find famous streets, popular events, fairs, music venues, and places where people go to eat and drink such as the soda fountain, the American Diner, McDonald's, and Starbucks. The homes of famous people such as George Washington and Jesse James are examined alongside infamous prisons such as Alcatraz and Folsom State Prison. Places that speak to specific epochs in American history, such as the Old West, are included due to its enduring allure in the national imagination. Curious readers are advised to take the time to peruse the topic list to see for themselves how the entries are related.

### Purpose

The purpose of this reference work is to enlighten and educate readers about what it is that attracts the general public to a specific place through highly readable and digestible entries arranged in an A–Y encyclopedic format. In some cases, the information contained in these entries will enhance the readers' existing knowledge. In many cases however, the information will be completely new to them. In both cases, entries explore critical issues, such as how a place came to be, the events that have occurred there, and the role the place has played (or indeed continues to play) in the lives of the people who lived in or visited it. Critically, the entries also examine the ways in which a place has been portrayed in popular media and consider why it has secured a position in the cannon of American popular culture.

Readers will enjoy the fact that many places they experience in their own lives are included in this work. This is a significant and intentional circumstance that demonstrates how even seemingly insignificant, everyday places, like the mall or dormitories, play a role in the nation's sweeping and diverse narrative and help to define American popular culture.

### Audience

This book is intended to be a helpful and insightful resource for high school and college students as well as adults. Readers will find information that is relevant to their personal lives and should approach this text as an invitation to explore the American experience.

### Arrangement and Format

This book is presented in a user-friendly format. The introduction places the entries within the context of American history by adopting a chronological order. More than 200 sidebars are incorporated throughout the text to provide additional information on pertinent topics and people, along with examples of popular culture forms such as music, television, film, and literature.

A topical list of entries organizes the entries by subject matter. In this way, readers can see at a glance the many types of places that appear within a given subject. It is thus possible, for topical research purposes, to read the book by thematic subject. The entries, presented in alphabetical order, form the heart of the book. A select bibliography has been included along with an index in order to facilitate further investigation of topics.

### Notable Features

What makes this reference work unique is that the entries are not simple summaries of historical events, but rather they include sections that also provide detailed narratives and examples of references to the subject in popular culture, as well as provide practical information for visitors. The entries feature subheadings that direct the flow of information in an easy-to-follow style. As much as possible, uniform subheadings (Historical Perspectives, Contemporary Perspectives, Images in Popular Culture, and For Visitors) are used throughout, which allows the reader to quickly understand the significance of the information being presented. Virtually all the entries include information on "historical perspectives" in order to situate the subject in the context of America's cultural history. The most up-to-date information available, which generally covers the late 20th and 21st centuries, is included under the Contemporary Perspectives subheading. The subheading Images in Popular Culture highlights appearances of the subject in popular media such as literature, television, and film. Other subheadings focus on the people who have been associated with a particular place. For example, the Adirondacks region has been visited by waves of people with different interests and backgrounds such as artists, philosophers, and the moneyed families of the gilded age. Subheadings for issues or controversies have been included where relevant. The entry on Facebook, for example, features an issues section that discusses how technology has challenged society in terms of information overload and risks in such areas as personal safety, employment security, and bullying.

The For Visitors section includes fun and informative tidbits designed to give readers an idea of what they can expect when visiting the places referenced. Sidebars elaborate on interesting topics, while suggestions for further reading follow each entry.

### What the Reader Will Gain

Whether the reader reads the book from cover to cover or simply reads entries by topic for purposes of research, this book will reveal a treasure trove of unusual information. Readers will gain an understanding of why a place has entered the nation's collective imagination, why it has remained a salient image in American cultural life, or indeed, why, in some cases, a place's time in the national spotlight has ended.

Most of all, readers will learn about America, about its fascinating past and present and the diverse peoples, inventions, technologies, businesses, institutions, and developments that helped shape the country and its culture. Through an examination of hallowed places such as the sundry memorials showcased on the National Mall in Washington, D.C., patriotic places such as Plymouth Colony, the Alamo, and the Statue of Liberty, and places associated with tragedy such as Ground Zero, Wounded Knee, and Columbine High School, readers will be able to grasp the full spectrum of the American experience.

Some themes appear frequently in this work: westward expansion, civil rights, economic and industrial development, diversity, and environmentalism. Through such themes, readers will deepen their understanding of how the world around them came to be. They will make connections between individual experiences of a place and the broader social context. Entries on trendy places such as man caves, cubicles in office spaces, cruise ships, Costco, Walmart, and Cyberspace will challenge readers to expand their conception of place and look at the modern world from a different perspective, for such places yield interesting insights into American identities, cultures, and lifestyles that define the present era.

Some entries explore the zany or kitschy side of American life. Lucy the Elephant, the Coral Castle, Wall Drug, and Graceland fit this fun-loving category. On the other end of the spectrum, Jefferson's dignified and elegant Monticello, Frank Lloyd Wright's incomparable Fallingwater, and the soaring majesty of the Empire State Building bear witness to America's enduring love of architectural beauty and sophistication, both public and private. Entries that touch on strange, reputedly paranormal, or conspiratorial topics, such as Area 51 and the Winchester Mystery House, are evidence of yet another, more unusual aspect of American life.

**Special Note**

Please note that the information included herein is specific to the purpose of this reference work. The entries in this book were written to provide key highlights as to the subject's historical and cultural significance, not as an exhaustive and detailed treatment of each place. Each entry could, if explored to its full potential, fill numerous chapters of a single work. Nonetheless, the Further Reading section that is included at the end of each entry as well as the Select Bibliography at the back of the book offer readers stepping stones to further explore these pop culture places in all their rich and immense detail.

It is my hope that readers will enjoy the many poignant and compelling individual stories within *Pop Culture Places: An Encyclopedia of Places in American Popular Culture*. Together they form an epic narrative about the places that most exemplify the American experience.

# Introduction

Collectively, the entries of *Pop Culture Places: An Encyclopedia of Places in American Popular Culture* tell the riveting story of America's growth. In the beginning of the nation's history, which starts in the 17th century, the areas in which people lived, worked, and carried on with their daily lives were Spartan settlements that gradually grew into neatly laid-out towns comprising homes, churches, and a few buildings for specific trades. Into the 18th century and beyond, the number and complexity of brick and mortar places increased. Places built for amusement, recreation, and entertainment, reflecting the influence of Europe and American ingenuity, proliferated. Other places such as natural spaces and museums, memorials, and historical areas reflected America's efforts to preserve and celebrate the national memory and to create areas for reflection amid the vortex of everyday hustle and bustle.

If the story of America were told in terms of its physical spaces, the narrative would at first appear sparse and simple, progressively becoming more and more congested and sophisticated. Following is a chronological narrative that illustrated how some of the notable places that are featured in this book fit into the context of America's soaring rise from colonial times to the present.

### Precontact

To best contrast America's evolution, a depiction of the New World before the arrival of the Europeans is in order. Though evidence exists of early intercontinental voyages, such as the explorations helmed by Norse explorer Leif Ericson 500 years before Christopher Columbus sailed to America in 1492, the indigenous population of Native American tribes exerted total control of their environment. Migrating to disparate regions of the present-day nation at will, the Native tribes adapted to various environments, constructing dwellings and designated spaces for specific functions as they saw fit.

In the northeast and northwest, Native American tribes built their homes out of timber. In the Great Plains region, the nomadic tribes commonly built teepees, made out of animal hides, which were easily taken down and reconstructed as the tribes migrated with herds such as the buffalo. In the desert regions of the Southwest, homes were typically carved out of the side of cliffs or made of adobe, a material comprising such materials as mud and straw.

With the exception of these domiciles, special lodges for ceremonial and social gatherings, and structures such as totem poles, the New World was a virtually pristine wilderness. The continent was panoply of primordial forests, deserts, mountainous areas, and grasslands crossed with rivers, lakes, and streams. Within this vast land, the tribes designated areas for sacred burial grounds, hunting grounds, and fishing areas. Places such as mountains, caves, canyons, and lakes were believed to be as sacred, some of which were believed to be endowed with healing properties.

### European Contact

Christopher Columbus, sailing for Spain, is credited with discovering America in the late 15th century. Whether or not this event was truly a discovery, there is no doubt that his arrival ushered forth a new era for the New World. Columbus was followed by explorer John Cabot, who sailed for England and arrived in 1497, and Amerigo Vespucci, who explored the coast of South America in 1501. "Amerigo" is the source of the name "America," by which the continent was thereinafter known.

The first major wave of European exploration in America was conducted by the Spanish. Their early contributions to the emergence of new places in America consisted primarily of missions that were built in the American South and Southwest in such present-day states as Florida, Texas, New Mexico, and California. These missions were originally used to convert the Native American population to Catholicism. Later, many of the missions were used as military forts or turned over to private ownership. Cities and towns emerged in the areas surrounding these missions.

### Colonial Times and American Revolution

The monumental moment when English colonists set foot on American soil occurred in 1607. In that year, Jamestown, Virginia, was established. Jamestown endures as a place of importance because this was the first permanent English colony in the New World. The Jamestown colonists endured difficult times, most grimly during the winter of 1609 and 1610 known as the Starving Time, when a mere 60 out of 500 colonists survived starvation. Jamestown went on to become the capital of the colony of Virginia, the first of the original 13 American colonies.

Modern Americans also hold dear the place known as Plymouth Rock, where the pilgrims of the Plymouth colony purportedly landed in 1620 after traveling on the ship known as the *Mayflower.* Though it lasted only until 1681, the Plymouth Colony had a lasting impact on the nation with the legendary first Thanksgiving celebration.

The last of the 13 colonies, Georgia, was founded in 1732. All 13 colonies, divided into the northern, middle, and southern colonies, were located along the eastern coast of the continent. Though they exported many goods back to England, tapping into the tremendous resources of the continent, they were largely self-sufficient. Important institutions were established during the colonial period, such as seven of the nine Ivy League institutions, Harvard, Yale, Princeton, Penn, Columbia, Brown, and Dartmouth.

The colonial period was punctuated by strife. The French and Indian Wars (1688–1763) resulted from territorial conflicts. In 1691, the residents of Salem, Massachusetts, embarked on a hunt for alleged witches; the town would forever be associated with the infamous Salem Witch Trials. In the mid-18th century, the colonies were vexed by increased taxes and oppressive rule imposed by the British. They lashed out with protests, riots, and political action. The most well-known protest was known as the Boston Tea Party.

The Boston Tea Party involved Massachusetts patriots seizing 342 chests of tea from three ships and tossing them into the Boston Harbor on December 16, 1773. In 1774, the First Continental Congress, an assembly of delegates from the 13 colonies, gathered in Philadelphia, Pennsylvania, a place of great historical import. Many of the gatherings that led to the formation and early development of the new nation were held in Philadelphia. Tensions fomented and the American Revolution began in 1775.

In that same year, George Washington was elected commander in chief of the Continental Army. In 1776, the famed Declaration of Independence was signed in Philadelphia. The war ended in 1783, following the British surrender at Yorktown, one of the settlements comprising the Historic Triangle. This term refers to the three living museums located at the historic settlements of Jamestown, Williamsburg, and Yorktown.

### New Nation

In 1789, Washington was elected the first president of the United States. At the time, there were only 13 states (the 13 original colonies) in the nation. During the first of his two terms, Washington selected a mostly barren parcel of land near the Potomac River, some 15 miles away from his beautiful estate, Mount Vernon, to be the permanent site of the nation's capital.

Construction on the Presidential Palace began in 1792. In 1800, John Adams became the first president to live there. After the War of 1812, people began to refer to the residence as the White House, a tradition that was made official in 1901. Renovations and expansions continued into the 20th century. This trend set the tone for the overall development of Washington, D.C.

The cornerstone of the U.S. Capitol was laid in 1793. Though Congress, the Supreme Court, the Library of Congress, and the courts of the District of Columbia moved into the building in 1800, construction and renovations continued through the next two centuries. The Washington Monument, one of the area's most distinguished landmarks commemorating a U.S. President, was constructed from 1848 to 1884. Other presidential memorials followed, including the Lincoln Memorial, completed in 1922 and the Thomas Jefferson Memorial, completed in 1943.

Washington, D.C. would also become the home of stunning war memorials such as the Iwo Jima Memorial, completed in 1954; the first part of the Vietnam Veterans Memorial, completed in 1982; the Korean War Veterans Memorial, completed in 1995; and the National World War II Memorial, completed in 2004.

Today, visitors to the capital witness a bustling and fully developed region laden with breathtaking architecture, federal buildings, memorials, and historic neighborhoods.

### Slavery

Slavery was once a part of the culture in all 13 colonies. However, between 1783 and 1804, eight of those colonies—Vermont, Pennsylvania, Massachusetts, New Hampshire, Connecticut, Rhode Island, New York, and New Jersey—officially abolished the vile practice. In the other five southern colonies, slavery persisted into statehood and was expanded by the addition of newly established states in the region.

Abolitionism, the movement that advocated the end of slavery, emerged during this period. Abolitionism consisted primarily of lecturing and the dissemination of antislavery literature. One extreme form of slave protest was staged by John Brown, who led a raid on Harpers Ferry in 1859. The raid ended disastrously for him and the men who fought alongside him. Harpers Ferry stands today as a memorial to that raid and to the long fight for equal rights.

### Civil War

At the onset of the Civil War, which began on April 12, 1861, America was divided by a line that separated the 23 states that remained loyal to the Union and the 11 states that succeeded from the Union, becoming the Confederate states.

Many places associated with this era are well-known destinations today. Under the slave system that produced lucrative crops such as cotton and tobacco, landowners built lavish plantation homes.

Critical Union victories, resulting in horrendous loss of life, occurred on the battlefields of Antietam in 1862 and Gettysburg in 1863.

### Westward Expansion

America's migration westward gathered steam after President Thomas Jefferson acquired the Louisiana Territory from France in 1803. Commissioned by Jefferson, Meriwether Lewis and William Clark's expedition reached the Pacific Ocean in 1805. Westward expansion was guided by explorers and fur traders who were no strangers to the vast lands to the west of the Mississippi River, the storied waterway which drew a lively assortment of characters and along which many river towns sprouted.

In the 1830s, a dramatic relocation of Native Americans took place. In 1838, thousands of Cherokee died on the Trail of Tears. The survivors would go on to establish the Cherokee Nation with headquarters in Tahlequah, Oklahoma. Many other tribes suffered on reservations, where they were prohibited from speaking their languages or observing their cultural and religious traditions.

As Native Americans steadily lost their lands, America continued to expand. The large area of Texas was obtained after the Texas Revolution (1835–1836). The Battle of the Alamo, which was the revolution's most famous battle, ended disastrously for the Americans but functioned as a rallying symbol that propelled the Americans to victory in 1836. Texas became an independent Republic and, in 1845, a state. After the Mexican–American War, which occurred from 1846 to 1848, America acquired the states of California, Arizona, Nevada, and Utah.

For many, the West symbolized new beginnings, adventure, and opportunity. Though fraught with danger and hardship, endless streams of individuals and families made the journey West beginning in the mid-19th century. They traveled primarily on famous trails such as the Oregon Trail, the Santa Fe Trail, the California Trail, and the Mormon Trail. In modern days, these trails and the history and culture of frontier travel are memorialized in the National Frontier Trails Museum in Independence, Missouri. People headed West for many reasons, such as to homestead, establish cattle ranches, to flee religious persecution, and—the most popular reason—to prospect gold or silver.

The era of the Old West that followed was one of the most popular periods in American history. This era saw the development of notorious and famous towns with sensational names like Deadwood, Tombstone, and Virginia City. Images and tales of cowboys, lawless drifters and daring lawmen, saloons, and open plains continue to captivate the national imagination just as they once did the general public. The lives of many immigrants and ethnic groups from faraway places were also interwoven in the gripping narrative of the American West.

By the end of the second half of the 19th century, the days of the sensational American West, as well as the traditional way of life for Native Americans, had faded. Historians assert that the invention and widespread use of fences to delineate private lands put an end to cow herding by cowboys. The Transcontinental Railroad brought many more people to the West and prompted the civilization of the region.

Though the Native Americans of the West fought the decimation of their way of life and the loss of their lands from the 1870s to the 1890s, they ultimately lost the fight and were relegated to reservations. The near decimation of the buffalo on the Great Plains by commercial hunters and the U.S. Army was another sign that the way of life of the Old West had ended.

### Gilded Age

The so-called Gilded Age, which pertained mostly to American cities, was a period that lasted from the 1870s to the 1890s. During this period, America began to experience remarkable growth and urbanization along with the rise of extraordinarily wealthy families. Powerful tycoons, such as Andrew Carnegie, who maintained an enormous steel empire, John D. Rockefeller, who owned Standard Oil Company, and William Henry Vanderbilt, a railroad baron, lived in opulence.

Such men and their descendants built mansions to live in as well as exclusive wilderness lodges in places such as the Adirondacks. They contributed to the intellectual, cultural, and artistic life in American society by building venues for the arts, particularly in major city centers, such as New York and Chicago. Carnegie Hall, a concert venue established by Andrew Carnegie, was completed in 1891. Rockefeller contributed money to establish the University of Chicago. He founded the Rockefeller Foundation in 1913, a program that has supported numerous institutions and programs. Vanderbilt helped make possible the YMCA, an organization dedicated to supporting young men transitioning into city life and the Metropolitan Opera.

Other prestigious American tycoons established luxurious hotels. The Waldorf Hotel, opened in 1893, and the Astoria Hotel, opened in 1897, were the creations of cousins William Waldorf Astor and John Jacob Astor IV. The hotels later merged; today, the famous and celebrated hotel is known as the Waldorf Astoria.

The advent of the skyscraper in the late 20th century heralded a new modern age in architecture. The first skyscraper, the Home Insurance Building, was established in 1885 in Chicago, followed by other skyscrapers, such as the Flat Iron building in New York City. Other popular excursions in New York included strolls and rides on carousels in Central Park and shopping at upscale retail stores like Bloomingdale's.

### Progressive Era

The period known as the Progressive Era occurred from 1890 to 1919. During this period, American cities underwent rapid urbanization and population growth. Urbanization brought forth more skyscrapers, factories, the magic of electricity, and amusement parks with thrilling mechanical rides. But overcrowding became a problem as large waves of European immigrants, most of them arriving by way of Ellis Island in New York City, and people leaving their farms in the country converged on the metropolitan areas seeking excitement and employment.

American cities experienced a crisis. Poverty, ramshackle and overly crowded tenements and slums, labor abuses and abominable working conditions, crime, and pollution prompted the wealthy to move out to the suburbs. Individuals such as Jane Addams, who founded a settlement house known as Hull House in Chicago in 1889, stepped forward to address the needs of immigrants. She also campaigned to end child labor and participated in the playground movement to establish playing areas for children.

Another development that occurred during this period, one that reflected the nation's conscious efforts to protect its pristine areas from development and exploitation, was the establishment of national parks. For example, the breathtaking Yosemite, the nation's third national park, opened in 1890.

### Early 20th Century

America continued to undergo sweeping transformation during the 20th century. The invention of the automobile and the creation of the film industry changed the course of everyday American life. Automobiles made Americans more mobile. The 1920s saw the development of Hollywood as a playground for glamorous celebrities. In this same decade, American cities reeled under the influence of mob violence that was exacerbated by Prohibition, which made it unlawful to sell and distribute alcohol.

Alcohol continued to be imbibed in speakeasies and nightclubs, such as the 21 Club and Harlem's Cotton Club, where patrons danced the night away to the lively big band music of the era. In the 1930s, Americans endured the Great Depression. But progress continued unchecked, illustrated by the epic construction of Hoover Dam in 1931. In the same year, New York's Empire State Building, which was the largest structure in the world at the time, was opened.

### Mid-20th Century

In 1941, Pearl Harbor in Hawaii was attacked by the Japanese. World War II had been raging since 1939, but after the attack on Pearl Harbor, President Franklin D. Roosevelt entered America into the conflict. As the war progressed, Americans learned about the atrocities of the Holocaust, the mass killings of Jews by Adolf Hitler's Nazi regime. But for many years, they knew nothing about the Los Alamos National Laboratory in New Mexico that was founded in 1943. There, workers contributed to the creation of atomic weapons. In 1945, atomic bombs were dropped on Hiroshima and Nagasaki. The war ended in victory for the Allied forces, though much of Europe and Japan lay in ruins.

In the aftermath of the war, America underwent a succession of dramatic changes. In the 1950s, the emergence of the middle class, the mainstreaming of the automobile, and the development of the interstate highway system resulted in the development of new spaces such as shopping malls, roadside attractions, suburban sprawl, and drive-in theaters and restaurants such as McDonald's.

The atomic age and Cold War tensions between the Soviet Union and America generated a degree of anxiety among the American people. One result of this was that in the late 1950s, America aggressively pursued space exploration. In 1958, the National Aeronautics and Space Administration (NASA) was founded. This organization was followed by the building of places such as the Lyndon B. Johnson Space Center, founded in 1961, and the John F. Kennedy Space Center, founded in 1962.

Notable leaders, such as John F. Kennedy, Martin Luther King Jr., and Robert F. Kennedy, were victims of violence during the tumultuous 1960s. John F. Kennedy was president at the time when he was assassinated at Dealey Plaza in Dallas, Texas, on November 22, 1963. King, who was the face of the civil rights movement, was assassinated at the Lorraine Motel in Memphis, Texas, on March 29, 1968. Kennedy's brother Robert was assassinated at the Ambassador Hotel in Los Angeles, California, on June 5, 1968.

### Contemporary Times

Into the late 20th century and the beginning of the 21st century, the nation had reached a point where it looked nothing like it had in times past. Small–town, early- and mid-20th-century life, with its charming soda fountains, diners, Main Streets, barbershops, and nostalgic stores, was regarded as a bygone era. Many such historic places, symbols of the past, were memorialized in museums, preserved as tourist sites, and remembered by landmarks and statues.

Nuclear power emerged as viable source of energy, though the public expressed some concern regarding nuclear energy following incidents such as the Three Mile Island accident that occurred in 1979.

Modern life increasingly comprised advanced technology, much of which emerged out of Silicon Valley. Diversions, such as casinos, museums, cruises, and trips to national and state parks, that had been considered upper-class amusements became mainstream pursuits. Cities, towns, and suburbs were linked by an elaborate system of highways. In most cities, towns, and suburbs, shopping centers, big-box retailers like Costco, fast-food chains, and sundry retail chains were constructed.

As the nation becomes increasingly sophisticated, efforts to incorporate a more natural and environmentally friendly lifestyle have spawned subcultural trends based on alternative power sources, community gardens, and off-grid living. Tragedies, such as the shooting incident at Columbine High School in 1999 and the terrorist attacks on the World Trade Center and the Pentagon in 2001, horrified the nation and reflected challenges of the new century.

### In Conclusion

The history of America seen through the lenses of popular places is a remarkable journey. As a writer, the process brought depth and richness to my understanding of America, a country in which I was born, raised, and I live. Learning about such places gave new meaning to such memories as roller-skating rinks, the local Piggly Wiggly and Woolworth's, and present-day excursions to the Olympic National Forest and the National Mall. Everywhere you, the reader, look are places that you experience on a daily or intermittent basis or on special occasions. Or, you hear about a variety of places through popular mediums such as television, film, the Internet, and literature. The morning coffee at Starbucks, the road trip on the highway to the Grand Canyon, the field trip to a local museum, the stop through the drive-thru at McDonald's, the suburbs where you live, and the images of Washington, D.C. on the local news channel are places that have histories and are connected to fascinating events, people, and experiences. Your own personal interaction within such spaces adds to this story, as well as the specialness of places in American popular culture.

# A

## Academy Awards (Oscars)

The Academy Awards are star-studded annual events at which the Academy of Motion Picture Arts and Sciences (AMPAS) recognizes excellence in actors, directors, screenwriters, and other individuals within the film industry. Winners of various categories, such as Best Actor in a Leading Role and Best Picture, receive gold-plated statuettes, the illustrious Academy Award of Merit, otherwise known as the Oscar. Academy Awards ceremonies, or the Oscars, as the events are frequently called, started in 1929, and in 1953 were televised for the first time. The Oscars are one of the longest running and most popular televised programs of their kind, occurring generally in February, March, or April. The Oscars is also the forerunner of other popular awards shows, such as the Emmy Awards for television and the Grammy Awards for music.

Prominent features of the Academy Awards include celebrities adorned in glitzy designer gowns, the red carpet, and big-budget production numbers. During the ceremony, celebrities announce the nominations and winners in some two dozen categories. Nominations are given to films released in the United States during the previous calendar year. Special tributes are commonly made, and musical groups and dancers perform the five songs nominated for Best Original Song. While past ceremonies have lasted from one hour to four hours, most telecasts now run between three and four hours. Some critics blast this affair as stereotypical Hollywood excess, materialism, and exclusivity, but a great many, in contrast, are drawn to the Academy Awards for those same reasons.

### Hollywood's Most Famous Statuette

The Oscar statuette, officially known as the Academy Award of Merit, is awarded by the Academy of Motion Picture Arts and Sciences to actors and other professionals in the film industry. The gold-plated statuette depicts the figure of a knight standing on a film reel holding a crusader's sword and is Hollywood's ultimate symbol of recognition. The film reel comprises five spokes, which represent the original branches of the industry: actors, directors, producers, technicians, and writers.

The idea for the statuette was conceived at a dinner in the Crystal Ballroom of the Biltmore Hotel in Los Angeles, California, shortly after the Academy of Motion Picture Arts and Sciences was founded in 1927. Metro-Goldwyn-Mayer (MGM) art director Cedric Gibbons was selected to design the statuette, and George Stanley was chosen to sculpt it. When completed, the statuette stood 13 inches tall and weighed 8 1/2 pounds. No one knows for sure how the statuette received its nickname of "Oscar," though it is said that Margaret Herrick, who was then an Academy librarian, remarked that the statuette looked like her Uncle Oscar.

The first Oscar was awarded at the first Academy Awards ceremony, which was held on May 16, 1929, in the Blossom Room at the Hollywood Roosevelt Hotel.

### Historical Perspectives

The Academy Awards ceremony was the brainchild of an organization (AMPAS) founded by influential leaders in America's burgeoning film industry based in California. In 1927, Louis B. Mayer, a studio head of the prominent film company, Metro-Goldwyn-Mayer, also known as MGM, met with film professionals to address criticism from media watchdogs who deemed some films inappropriate for the American public. This meeting was followed by a gathering of 36 industry professionals, culminating in the birth of AMPAS. Originally, the organization was established to help censure films and better manage the operation of the industry and labor disputes.

AMPAS's mission expanded over the years. In 1929, AMPAS put on its first Academy Awards ceremony. Then, as now, winners were selected through a voting process by members of AMPAS, who were culled from individuals within the film industry by the Board of Governors of AMPAS. Current categories include Best Actor in a Leading Role, Best Actor in a Supporting Role, Best Actress in a Leading Role, Best Actress in a Supporting Role, Best Costume Design, Best Documentary Feature, Best Director, Best Film Editing, Best Foreign Language Film, Best Original Score, Best Picture, and Best Writing.

AMPAS also operates other lesser-known projects and programs. For example, it hosts the Governors Awards, the Sci-Tech Awards, and the Student Academy Awards. Other projects include book publication, film training, fellowships and grants, public lectures, a visiting artists program, film screenings, exhibits, and the maintenance of library holdings and motion picture collections. By and large, the organization's most prestigious event is the Academy Awards.

### Evolution

The Academy Awards ceremony has morphed considerably since its conception, particularly in terms of locale. In 1929, the first Academy Awards was a private affair that took place at the Hotel Roosevelt in Hollywood. Some 270 celebrities attended. As is still the case, these celebrities were by invitation only; winners received the covetous Oscar, and attendees participated in a post-awards party. In those days, winners were announced three months prior to the Academy Awards ceremony; nowadays, the winners' names are not revealed to the public or the winners until the day of the show. In the Academy Awards' first year, *Wings* (1927) won Best Picture; Emil Jennings won Best Actor in Leading Role for *The Last Command* (1928) and *The Way of All Flesh* (1927), and Janet Gaynor won Best Actress in Leading Role for *Seventh Heaven* (1927), *Street Angel* (1928), and *Sunrise: A Song of Two Humans* (1927).

For the next several decades, the Academy Awards had no permanent home. Venues included the Ambassador Hotel, the Biltmore Hotel, Grauman's Chinese Theatre, the Shrine Civic Auditorium, the Academy Award Theater, the RKO Pantages Theatre, the Santa Monica Civic Auditorium, and the Dorothy Chandler Pavilion. Since 2002, the ceremony has been held at the Kodak Theatre, which is now known as the Dolby Theatre.

Another significant change in the Academy Awards occurred in 1953 when the general public caught the first glimpse of the previously exclusive and glamorous world of the Oscars with the advent of television. The 25th Oscars, viewed by a staggering 40 million people, marked the beginning of a new era for the Academy Awards. The telecast fueled the public's fascination with beautiful stars and glamour and appealed to American values of good old-fashioned competition. This show set many traditions that continue to this day, including celebrity hosts and multiple presenters and performers. Among the winners revealed to television viewers were Best Picture *The Greatest Show on Earth* (1952), Best Actor in a Leading Role Gary Cooper in *High Noon* (1952), and Best Actress in a Leading Role Shirley Booth in *Come Back, Little Sheba* (1952).

The Academy Awards today are engulfed in extraneous activities and copious amounts of press coverage. The Academy Awards are covered by assorted media sources, such as local news stations, gossip and reputable magazines, newspapers, talk shows, online websites, blogs, and social network sites. Pre-events include interviews, talk about possible nominations, prediction of winners, past Academy Awards happenings, and speculation about who will host the show. In the hours before the main event, the paparazzi cover the red carpet, where celebrities model tuxedos and gowns designed by legendary names in the fashion industry. The ceremony is followed by parties such as the Governor's Ball, the official after-party of the Academy Awards, more interviews, and television specials. The Internet and gossip magazines are ablaze with fashion shots and critiques, acceptance speeches, and reprises of newsworthy incidents. One such unforgettable incident occurred in 1974 when a man ran naked across the stage. In 2003, actor Adrien Brody created a memorable Oscars moment when he passionately kissed actress Halle Barry.

### Milestones

Over its 80-plus history, the Academy Awards has attained memorable and controversial moments, which continues, to this day, to make unprecedented, if gradual, milestones. For example, only four African American males have won Best Actor in Leading Role since the Academy Awards first began; the first winner was Sidney Poitier for his role in *Lilies of the Field* (1963). Only one African American woman, HalleBerry for her role in *Monster Ball* (2001), has received Best Actress in a Leading Role. The first African American to win any Oscar was Hattie McDaniel in 1939 when she won Best Actress in a Supporting Role in *Gone with the Wind* (1939). Finally, in 2010, Kathryn Bigelow became the first woman to win Best Director in Academy Awards history.

Into the new millennium, the Academy Awards remains the premier American awards show, one of the few remaining events in the country where glamour, pomp, and circumstance rule the day.

***See also*** California; Grauman's Chinese Theatre; Hollywood

### Further Reading

"The Academy of Motion Picture Arts and Sciences." *Oscars*. http://www.oscars.org.

Cosgrave, Bronwyn. 2007. *Made for Each Other: Fashion and the Academy Awards*. New York: Bloomsbury USA.

Mapp, Edward. 2008. *African Americans and the Oscar: Decades of Struggle and Achievement*. Lanham, Maryland: Scarecrow Press.

Osborne, Robert A. 2008. *80 Years of the Oscar: The Official History of the Academy Awards*. New York: Abbeville Press.

Pawlak, Debra Ann. 2011. *Bringing Up Oscar: The Story of Men and Women Who Founded the Academy*. New York: Pegasus Books.

## Adirondacks

"The Adirondacks" is shorthand for a region in Upstate New York, more formally known as the Adirondack Park (or the Adirondack State Park) that was created in 1892. The term also refers to the Adirondack Mountains—a roughly circular range that boasts the highest peaks in the state—which are wholly contained within the park's 6.1 million acres. A little less than half the land is a protected forest preserve that includes peaks, wilderness, and wild forest; the rest is private property comprising villages and small towns. Some 135,000 people live on private lands; other private lands are used for forestry, agriculture, and recreation. The term *Adirondack* originates from the Iroquois word for "bark-eater," a derisive term used by the Iroquois to refer to a neighboring Native American tribe, the Algonquin.

View of Lake Placid from Whiteface Mountain in the Adirondacks of New York State, September 3, 2012. (Dreamstime.com)

The ruggedly beautiful Adirondacks are, however, nothing to sneer about. Not only does the park have numerous year-round residents, it is a noted oasis for vacationers, tourists, and outdoor adventurers. Millions of visitors journey to the region each year to camp, canoe, hike, hunt, ski, and visit the countless historical and scenic sites. Despite an ever-present controversy between preservationists and proponents of development, the Adirondacks remain a thriving vestige of America's rugged outdoor and pioneer heritage, small town community life, and wild open spaces.

**Historical Perspectives**

Before the advent of tranquil villages, busy lumber mills, and ski slopes, the Adirondack region was an uninhabited mountain wilderness, known only to the Native Americans who populated the continent from East Coast to West. The nearest residents were the Algonquin and Iroquois, who favored the Adirondacks for hunting, fishing, and gathering of plants, herbs, and berries, and who passed through the area when they journeyed from one location to another, often traveling along the waterways for which the region is famous. According to contemporary statistics, the region boasts over 2,300 lakes and ponds, 1,500 miles of rivers, and 30,000 miles of brooks and streams. There are more than 60 fish species, more than 50 animal species, and more than 200 bird species—bountiful resources for indigenous communities before the arrival of the Europeans.

The first recorded non-Native American to set foot upon the Adirondack Mountains is believed to have been Samuel de Champlain, a French explorer who traveled to the region in 1609. In the mid-1600s, French fur trappers and traders were lured to the Adirondacks in pursuit of the high profits afforded by the fur industry. (Fur was all the rage among the fashionable elite of Europe, fueling the demand for fur from North America.) Missionaries soon followed, Christianizing a significant portion of the indigenous population.

Life in the Adirondack Mountains at this time was precarious at best. Swashbuckling wilderness men, trappers, and traders lived off the land, trudging as best they could through the hazardous terrain before the trails were cleared. They endured bitter cold winters and the constant threat of attack by wild animals such as black bear, bobcat, and coyote, as well as violent human confrontations. Territorial disputes between the French and British and their respective Native American allies exacerbated tensions in the region and culminated in the French and Indian War (1754–1763). Following seven years of conflict, several waves of groups spread across the region. Some exploited the region's extensive natural resources; others sought solace from urbanization; and many arrived in search of adventure or vacation homes in wild spaces.

**Mining and Logging**

In the 18th century, mining and logging replaced fur trading as the leading industries in the region. Men—married or not—came alone to the Adirondacks to make their fortunes. They toiled solemnly and doggedly, mining iron ore and other minerals or cutting down the seemingly endless supply of massive primeval trees—spruce, pine, and hemlock—sending them down the rivers and streams to the sawmills where they would be processed. In time, the land thus cleared by the loggers opened the way for new settlements, for the increasing numbers of men who wanted to bring their wives and children to the region necessitated the establishment of new communities. Towns like St. Regis and Old Forge were born.

To the working class, the chance to make a living off the land through raw grit and physical labor was practical and appealing. But to East Coast high society and intellectuals, who had access to wealth and indulged in leisurely activities, the Adirondacks presented an altogether different opportunity.

### Influences: Philosophers and Artists

In the first half of the 19th century, New York City was a bustling, ever-expanding, urbanized place at the vanguard of both fashion and technology. However, some individuals saw that the development of city streets, cars, factories, large populations, and towering buildings brought with it a host of environmental issues, such as pollution, constant noise, and eradication of natural landscapes. Philosophers like Henry David Thoreau, who spent two years on Walden Pond, criticized modern-day living and espoused the benefits of getting back to nature. Thoreau and other philosophers constructed and regularly escaped to philosophers' camps nestled in the Adirondacks.

Other proponents of nature included writers and artists. Some of James Fenimore Cooper's novels, including the most famous, *The Last of the Mohicans: A Narrative of 1757* (1826), take place in the Adirondacks. The many graphic artists who were drawn to the natural beauty of the region's lakes, waterfalls, trees, and mountains helped to popularize the wilderness.

Beginning in the 1820s, a group of artists embarked on the first of many sketching trips to the Adirondacks. Several produced enduring portraits of the region's landscapes. These include Thomas Cole's *Schroon Mountains, Adirondacks* (1838), Sanford Robinson Gifford's *A Twilight in the Adirondacks* (1864), and Nelson Augustus Moore's *Boating on Lake George* (1869).

### Wilderness Living

The philosophers and artists were followed by more affluent adventure-seekers and urban families desiring to experience nature. This wave was sparked in large part by William H. Murray's book *Adventures in the Wilderness; Or Camp-Life in the Adirondacks* (1869), which popularized and romanticized the region. Hardy, rough-hewn locals—a few of them women—hired out as guides to navigate the tourists along the streams, lakes, and rivers, into the caves, and across mile upon mile of wilderness. Locals also worked in the surging tourist trade and as servants or construction workers for rich city folk who arrived to vacation and explore the Adirondacks. Many of these urbanites, hailing from New York City and Chicago, craved hunting and fishing trips for the sheer thrill and novelty. To vacation in the Adirondacks was also a symbol of elitism and prestige. The popularity of the region gave way to permanent summer camps.

### The Great Camps

The camps, later dubbed the Great Camps, became popular destinations for the affluent. The Vanderbilts, Rockefellers, and other well-known families and their household servants traveled several hours to the Adirondacks, carrying heavy bundles and supplies for the trip. Each family owned and managed its own Great Camp, which comprised various buildings built in a rustic style. Each building within the camp served a specific function, such as dining, sleeping, or indoor recreational activities. These wealthy vacationers greatly contributed to the swift construction of hotels and railroads in the Adirondacks; this development had a reciprocal effect by helping to accelerate the number of tourists visiting the region and contributed to efforts to preserve the region.

The tourism boom in the Adirondacks took a drastic downturn following the Great Depression, an economic crisis that devastated Americans during the early 20th century. Many wealthy families, forced to cut extravagant spending, such as yearly summer trips to the Adirondacks, abandoned their Great Camps. Some of these Great Camps have been restored and are open for viewing or overnight stays to the tourists and visitors that frequent the Adirondack Park today.

### Preservation

The Adirondack State Park was made possible by conservation efforts that began almost 150 years ago with Verplanck Colvin. Colvin, who had spent several years in his young adulthood exploring the Adirondack Mountains and wilderness, surveyed the region in the 1870s. Concerned that the land and its natural resources were being neglected and exploited, particularly due to logging, he played a key role in persuading the state legislature to establish, in 1885, the Forest Preserve. This measure was one of the first of its kind in the nation.

More measures to preserve the land followed. In 1892, the Adirondack Park was officially created. The Park's boundary, consisting of both public and private land, came to be known as the Blue Line, referring to the color of the boundary line on maps. In 1894, an amendment (now known as Article XIV) was added to the New York State constitution to ensure the preservation of the Park. Further measures, such as the formation of the Adirondack Park Agency in 1971, assured that land use and development would be regulated. Public and private land use in the Park continues to be subjected to various guidelines, regulations, and restrictions despite periodic appeals to slacken rules to advance business development and economic growth. As a result, the Park maintains much of its natural beauty, a feature that has yet to grow out of style with 21st century tourists and permanent and seasonal residents.

### For Visitors

In contrast to the sparsely populated Adirondacks of previous centuries, the park now sustains a population of 130,000 and counting, and is visited by 10 million tourists annually. Tourists revel in an infinite number of activities, such as camping, hunting, hiking, exploring, and nature and wildlife watching. Other popular activities include mountain climbing, horseback riding, four-wheeling, cross-country skiing, spelunking, snowmobiling, boating, and other water sports. Tourists also visit French and Indian (1754–1763) and Revolutionary (1775–1783) war sites, and in the fall, wander the Adirondacks to see the foliage set ablaze in autumn colors. Popular museums and landmarks, such as the Wild Center in Tupper Lake, the Adirondack Museum in Blue Mountain Lake, Fort Ticonderoga, and John Brown's Farm State Historic Site (the home of famed abolitionist John Brown who led a failed raid at Harpers Ferry), provide hands-on learning about local wildlife and intimate glimpses into historic places, photographs, art work, and memorabilia of the Adirondacks. Unlike other parts of the region, remnants of Native American culture (with the notable exception of canoeing) are, for the most part, imperceptible, since those Native Americans who did come into to the Adirondacks were generally just passing through.

Many offerings in the Adirondacks attract the athletically inclined. Lake Placid, a town famous for its Olympic past, is a popular training site for winter Olympic hopefuls. For hikers, the Adirondacks provide a surfeit of trails to explore. Some mountain climbers take the challenge to climb 46 of the region's high peaks for the chance to become members of the illustrious Forty-Sixers. The first Forty-Sixers were Herbert Clark and George and Robert Marshall, who completed their climbs in 1925. The first woman to achieve this status (and ninth Forty-Sixer) was Grace Hudowalski, who made her final climb on Mount Esther in 1937. As of December 31, 2010, 7,009 individuals were listed on the Forty-Sixers membership roster. (A separate list is maintained for individuals who brave the peaks during winter. They are known as winter Forty-Sixers.) Another popular Adirondack activity is the Adirondack Canoe Classic, commonly referred to as the 90-Miler. The original course of this three-day race was a route used by early pioneers, known as the "Highway of the Adirondacks." The course ran from Old Forge, through many rivers and lakes, to the New York State Boat Launch on Lake Flower. The current course runs from Old Forge to the Village of Saranac Lake.

### Cultural Distinctions

While each year millions of tourists stream into the Adirondacks for day trips, weekend stays, and prolonged vacations, the locals, known as Adirondackers, call the region home. They drive cars, shop at grocery stores, eat at fast-food restaurants, wear jeans, T-shirts, and the same popular fashions worn in major cities, and live in modern homes—all in the seclusion of the Adirondacks. It is the Adirondackers who provide much of the cultural backdrop and folk traditions for which the region is known. The locals are far from a homogenous group. Some Adirondackers can boast that their ancestors lived in the park for several generations back; other are newly transplanted from across the nation and the world.

One major issue that divides communities concerns the continued development of the region. Adirondackers are split on the heated issue of whether to promote or resist economic development. Although development could potentially provide jobs for locals and prevent individuals and families from having to leave the region in search of employment, many Adirondackers desire to keep the park as it is. As it stands, the Adirondacks are heavily protected by New York State, and restrictions are placed on private as well as public land use.

As the arguments over whether to develop or preserve the Adirondacks rage, many of the locals remain active in popular hobbies and traditions of the region. The many nature lovers and amateur and professional artists, woodworkers, folksingers, photographers, poets, and writers find inspiration in their beloved Adirondacks. Artist William P. Wiatr lives and paints in the Adirondacks, creating natural landscapes and wildlife paintings from scenes in his own backyard. Adirondack furniture is crafted by locals and imitated by countless others here and abroad. Adirondack furniture is made from timber and ranges from the famous Adirondack chair, simple and utilitarian, to elaborately designed woodwork. Historic, locally made furniture is displayed in museums; contemporary furniture is sold online and in stores throughout the nation.

#### Grab a Chair

The Adirondack chair was first built and used in the Adirondack Mountains region, but today is found throughout the nation. The popular outdoor chair has a distinct style, comprising a rounded fan-shaped back and broad, flat armrests. The chair was first called the Westport chair, as it was built in Westport, a town near Lake Champlain, most of which is situated in the Adirondack State Park.

The chair was designed in 1903 by Thomas Lee, who was experimenting with constructing a comfortable outdoor chair for his summer home in Westport. Lee showed his chair to Harry Bunnell, a local carpenter, who secured a patent for the design in 1905 without Lee's knowledge. Bunnell's chairs were made out of hemlock, painted dark brown or green, and had his name on them.

At some point, the chairs became known as Adirondack chairs. They came in several styles, such as benches and rockers. Over the decades, the popularity of the chair for use on lawns spread across the nation. Though cushion-free, the Adirondack chair is widely regarded as very comfortable. Today, the chairs come in many different colors, and are considered to have an aesthetic appeal. Popular home improvement shows, such as *This Old House* (1979–), have featured episodes instructing audiences on how to build an Adirondack chair of their own.

Local singers and musicians add to the folksy charm of the region. Adirondack music is a patchwork of many influences and traditions. It can trace its roots from the music of England, Scotland, Ireland, New England, Canada, New York, Germany, as well as the region itself, all blended together over many generations. Such music is generally passed on from memory and delivered in an unadorned fashion with or without the accompaniment of an instrument. Common instruments used are fiddles, accordions, banjos, and harmonicas. Dancing and foot tapping accompany certain songs. Although some of the traditional songs are lost, many have been preserved by folklorists, as well as by the singers who learned them from family or community members and continue to perform them.

### Images in Popular Culture

Adirondack history and heritage have been preserved in other popular forms. In addition to photography and painting, the region has been extensively memorialized in fiction and nonfiction. Adirondack native and historical-fiction writer Jennifer Donnelly set *A Northern Light* (2003) in the Adirondacks, enmeshing the real-life notorious Gillette Murder Case of 1906 into the story. Joseph W. Brownell also wrote about the infamous case in *Adirondack Tragedy: The Gillette Murder Case of 1906* (1986). *Ski and Snowshoe Trails in the Adirondacks* (2003), by Tony Goodwin, details the natural landscape and wildlife of the region. *Contested Terrain: A New History of Nature and People in the Adirondacks* (1999), by Philip G. Terrie, focuses on contemporary challenges. *Breaking Trail: Remarkable Women of the Adirondacks* (2004) by Peggy Lynn and Sandra Weber explores the fascinating world of historic and contemporary women who have lived in the region. Several books such as Anne LaBastille's *Woodswoman I: Living Alone in the Adirondack Wilderness* (1976) and *The Wilderness World of Anne LaBastille* (1992) and Maitland C. DeSormo's *Noah John Rondeau: Adirondack Hermit* (1991) probe the lives of individuals who have chosen to live alone in the woods. In 2008, the Public Broadcasting Service (PBS) aired a documentary, *The Adirondacks.*

Through art, woodwork, literature, and other forms of expression, Adirondackers demonstrate their pride in their home and folk traditions. From wild hunting ground to well-preserved tourist destination, the Adirondacks have managed to both evolve and resist the pull of modernization and development that permeates so many American cities and towns, where highways, skyscrapers, and large shopping and business complexes dominate the landscape. The Adirondacks remain, at least for a time, a bastion of a bygone era where pioneers and settlers roamed, where the simple life of hardy folk is preserved, where one can still find wide open spaces and endless stretches of woods and sky.

***See also*** Chicago, Illinois; Harpers Ferry; New York, New York; State and National Parks; Walden Pond

### Further Reading

Kaiser, Harvey H. 2003. *Great Camps of the Adirondacks*. Jaffrey, New Hampshire: David R. Godine.

Lynn, Peggy, and Weber, Sandra. 2004. *Breaking Trail: Remarkable Women of the Adirondacks*. Fleischmanns, New York: Purple Mountain Press.

Schneider, Paul. 1997. *The Adirondacks: A History of America's First Wilderness*. New York: Henry Holt and Company.

Terrie, Philip G. 2008. *Contested Terrain: A New History of Nature and People in the Adirondacks*. Blue Mountain Lake, New York: The Adirondack Museum.

Weston, Harold. 2008. *Freedom in the Wilds: An Artist in the Adirondacks,* edited by Rebecca Foster. Syracuse, New York: Syracuse University Press.

## African Burial Ground

The African Burial Ground National Monument is located in Lower Manhattan, New York City. The site comprises a burial ground that holds the remains of more than 400 free and enslaved African descendants, a memorial, located on Duane Street and African Burial Ground Way, and a visitor center, located at 290 Broadway in the Ted Weiss Federal Building. In 1993, the monument was added to the National Register of Historic Places and designated a National Historic Landmark. In 2006, President George W. Bush dedicated the monument as a National Monument, adding the African Burial Ground National Monument to the list of the most iconic and important sites in the nation. The African Burial Ground is especially significant as it is deemed one of the most important urban archeological finds of the 20th century and is one of few landmarks that memorializes African descendants in slavery.

### Historical Perspectives

The African Burial Ground was originally known as the Negroes Burial Ground. The Negroes Burial Ground, which encompassed 6.6 acres, was established in the 1690s on the outskirts of New Amsterdam. New Amsterdam, which would later become New York City, was a settlement founded by the Dutch in 1625. Both the Dutch and the British, who seized control of the settlement and renamed it New York in 1664, used African slave labor to help develop the region.

Not all Africans or their descendants were slaves. Some blacks were free, but their freedom was severely restricted. Blacks were not regarded as equal to European descendants and often forced to live in segregated communities and use separate schools, hospitals, and other facilities. A case in point was the construction of a separate burying place, the Negroes Burial Ground, located outside New Amsterdam. Contemporary archeologists ascertained that some 15,000–20,000 men, women, and children were buried at this site. By the 19th century, slavery in New York had been abolished, and the Negroes Burial Ground was obscured by landfill and cement to make way for new buildings.

It was not until 1991 that the Negroes Burial Ground was rediscovered. During the construction of the Federal Office Building in Foley Square, remains from the burial ground were exposed. The news of this discovery was dispersed in local and national newspapers, generating a mix of emotions—as well as controversy. Scholars, historians, and archeologists were exhilarated by the discovery of the remains and the numerous artifacts that were buried with the remains. Unfortunately, no records of the deceased were found among the remains or elsewhere.

For many African Americans, the discovery was a somber reminder of slavery and many centuries of exclusion from mainstream society. Other emotions included anger and sadness over the fact that the burial ground had not been protected. The fact that the slaves' remains had been disdainfully disregarded was seen as a parallel to the way the rights and freedoms of blacks in the 20th century had been egregiously flouted. Yet many African Americans were hopeful, anticipating a profound positive outcome from the discovery. They saw an opportunity for city officials to publicly demonstrate, through a commemoration or memorialization, the importance of the burial ground, as well as a chance to educate the public on slavery in New York and the contributions of African descendants in America. Soon after the discovery of the remains, the United States General Services Administration funded the African Burial Ground project.

### Controversy

As work on the project began, criticism mounted and made its way into newspapers nationwide. One major criticism was that the African-descendant community in New York City and experts in related fields were not initially approached for consultation. Steps were eventually taken to include members of the African American community, and specialists like Mike Blakely, scientific director of the team at Howard University, were brought in to head the study of the African Burial Ground. All told, the African Burial Ground project unfolded over the course of nearly two decades.

### Artwork

Early on, artist tributes were exhibited at the Ted Weiss Federal Building, which had originally been intended to be erected on the African Burial Ground (the building was moved to a new location nearby). One of the works of art was Houston Conwill's *The New Ring Shout*, created in 1994, a ground display that includes a mixture of symbols, text, patterns, and other markings within a circular pattern. In 1998, Barbara Chase-Riboud's sculpture *Africa Rising* was installed, and in 2003, Frank Bender's *Unearthed* was added. Bender reproduced the likenesses in his bronze sculpture from the remains of an elderly woman and a young man and woman, using forensic facial identification.

### Reinterment and Dedication

Following the installation of the artist tributes in the federal building, the remains that had been removed from the site for analysis were reinterred and the African Burial Ground National Monument Memorial was established. The reinterment at the burial site took place in 2003 and included an African ceremony, the Rites of Ancestral Return. In attendance were political leaders such as New York mayor Michael Bloomberg and Jesse Jackson, the Boys Choir of Harlem, and Poet Maya Angelou. The memorial dedication in 2007 was attended by several dignitaries and popular African American celebrities as well as Artist Rodney Leon, who had won the competition to design the memorial. The memorial itself is an expansive 25-foot granite monument with many features, including the Wall of Remembrance, with a chronology of major events related to the history of the site and ancestral pillars that indicate the location where the remains are located.

### Visitor Center

In 2010, a new facility, the African Burial Ground National Monument Visitor Center, was added to the African Burial Ground National Monument. It was built inside the Ted Weiss Federal Building. This facility, which includes a theater, a shop, and classroom space, provides historical background and resources to educate the public about the African Burial Ground. It fills in many gaps in the public's knowledge and awareness of slavery in New York, the impact of slavery on African descendants, and the important contributions of slaves in America. A film, guided tour, and interactive exhibits infused with compelling facts and images weave together to form a moving narrative of human struggle, transcendence, and restoration.

The burial site, visitor center, and memorial combine to form a meaningful American landmark. Not only is the site a resting place and memorial for the centuries-forgotten African residents of New York, the monument offers an enlightening and oftentimes emotional experience for visitors. The site also represents a shift in the American view of African descendants, underscoring the fact that the monument speaks to the hearts and souls of all Americans who believe in justice, equality, and the rule of law.

***See also*** Arlington National Cemetery; Grant's Tomb; New York, New York; New York World Trade Center: Twin Towers and Ground Zero

### Further Reading

"African Burial Ground." *National Park Service*. http://www.nps.gov/afbg/index.htm.

Berlin, Ira, and Harris, Leslie. 2005. *Slavery in New York*. New York: The New Press.

## Air Force Academy

The Air Force Academy, formally known as the U.S. Air Force Academy, is a sprawling 18,000-acre institution located in Colorado Springs, Colorado. The institution is one of five U.S. military academies. These

Air Force Academy Chapel in Colorado Springs, Colorado. The design of the interfaith Cadet Chapel, initially a source of much controversy, is now considered a stunning example of modern architecture. (Laura Gangi/Dreamstime.com)

academies offer four-year degrees, as well as military, leadership, and officer training. Established in 1955, the Air Force Academy is the youngest of them all. From the start, the academy, with its sleek, novel design, has garnered media and public attention as an architectural achievement and forerunner of modern design. Its storied reputation as a military institution has placed it in the ranks of the most prestigious institutions in the nation. Prospective students, seeking ambitious military careers, clamber for admission. The institution is also a draw for the general public, as tourists want to see one of the most iconic structures in American history.

**Historical Perspectives**

The idea of establishing an Air Force Academy was talked about at the beginning of the 20th century, if not earlier. Military leaders like Lieutenant Colonel A. J. Hanlon recognized the need for an institution to service the aviation component of the military. After all, the Army and the Navy had their own academies. But from the start, America's aviation force was not autonomous. In 1907, when the Aeronautical Division, the fledgling version of the Air Force, was established, it was part of the U.S. Army Signal Corps. The Aeronautical Division would go by several different names, such as Aviation Section and Air Service, and be transferred here and there within the Army structure. It was not until some 40 years later that the National Security Act of 1947 would establish the Department of the Air Force, with which the fourth branch of the military gained its independence. This helped set in motion the creation of an Air Force Academy, where elite leaders in the Air Force would be trained.

Within a year, the elaborate process of developing the Air Force Academy had begun. A board comprising civilian and military educators began developing a curriculum. In 1949, an advisory commission got to work on choosing a site from a staggering 580 proposed locations. In 1954, President Dwight Eisenhower officially approved the establishment of the U.S. Air Force Academy, and Secretary of the Air Force Harold Talbott made the final decision on the site for the institution: Colorado Springs, Colorado. In that same year, Skidmore, Owings, and Merrill (SOM) received the contract to design and build the Academy. SOM's architectural plans for the new institution veered significantly from the long-established utilitarian designs that defined other academies, such as West Point and the U.S. Naval Academy. SOM had in mind to create a groundbreaking modern structure.

### Architecture

The Air Force Academy is well known for its innovative architecture. Whereas the structures of West Point, built in 1802, and the U.S. Naval Academy, built in 1845, were designed in standard conservative styles such as Gothic, Georgian, and English Tudor in the customary materials of brick, stone, and granite, the Air Force Academy buildings were designed along sleek, modern lines and feature glass walls, steel, and aluminum. The American media was attracted by the story of SOM's designs and kept their journalistic gaze trained on the construction efforts as they came to life in Colorado. Media critics regularly published negative articles about the construction project. Many military and civilian communities were taken aback by SOM's nontraditional choices, such as the proposed design of the Cadet Chapel. Construction on the chapel began in 1955 and ended in 1962 and cost several million dollars. Standing 150 feet tall, the chapel's most pronounced feature is a row of 17 massive spires that appear, even to contemporary eyes, futuristic. In the 1950s and 1960s, the spires were regarded as one of the structure's most radical elements.

Today, the Air Force Academy campus is universally celebrated for its modern appearance. It is now one of the most popular tourist attractions in Colorado. Millions of visitors flock to the institution each year. The Cadet Chapel, once scorned, is considered one of the most arresting features of the Academy and a breakthrough example of modern architecture. In 2004, the Cadet Area, comprising academic buildings, dormitories, a ballroom, and other facilities, was designated a National Historic Landmark.

### Popular Imagination

The Air Force Academy has enormous appeal, especially among aspiring cadets, the term used to refer to students who attend the Academy. Historically, the armed forces, whether the Army, Navy, Marines, or Air Force, have always captured the popular imagination. Classic (and often overly romanticized) war films, heroic narratives, valiant victories in real wars, and media propaganda have contributed to the popularization of the armed forces, particularly among men (historically, women played severely restricted roles in the military).

Contributing to the popularity of the armed forces are the symbols associated with it. The military has always symbolized masculinity, heroism, and patriotism, as well as opportunities for employment, distinguished careers, and benefits, such as free college education. People are drawn to specific branches, such as the Air Force, for a number of reasons, real or mythicized. For example, many individuals may join the Air Force for no other reason than an attraction to the mystique of airplanes or an abstract belief that it is the most elite branch in the military.

### Selection Process, Education, and Training

The Air Force Academy represents one of the most ambitious career tracks for individuals who want to be officers in the Air Force. The sense of prestige is accentuated by the tough selection process and rigorous education and training offered at the Academy. Aspiring cadets must demonstrate excellent potential via various means, such as passing fitness tests, scoring acceptably on admission tests, and obtaining nominations from a congressional sponsor or other competitive means. Some individuals may attend the 10-month program at the U.S. Air Force Academy Preparatory School to better their chances for admission.

Once admitted to the Academy, cadets face an intensive curriculum. The Academy offers courses in science, engineering, social sciences, humanities, and fitness, military, leadership, and combat survival training. Involvement in intramural and intercollegiate athletics is required. Optional course work for cadets includes flying, navigation, soaring and parachuting, and aviation courses (the Air Force Academy is not the only military institution to teach flying). The faculty is composed of mostly military Air Force officers. Discipline and the Cadet Honor Code are stressed throughout the four-year program. The Cadet Honor Code governs the ethical conduct of cadets. First year cadets, also referred to as fourth class cadets or, among cadets at the Academy, as *doolies,* meaning slave or servant, must make the oath that they will not lie, steal, or cheat. All cadets receive free tuition and a monthly stipend.

The Academy has a national and international reputation of excellence. Its sports teams and bands, for example, have accomplished many exemplary feats. The Academy's intercollegiate athletic teams, such as Air Force Falcons football, boxing, ice hockey, and men's and women's rugby teams show a pattern of strong and consistent wins. The Academy also has numerous bands; many of them, such as the Marching Band and the Concert Band, perform on local, national, and international stages for parades, concerts, and presidential events. Sports and musical events have helped a great deal to portray the Academy to the public in a favorable light.

### Controversy

The Air Force Academy has been beset with a number of public controversies involving honor scandals, minority enrollment, and allegations of sexual harassment and religious intolerance. At least half a dozen scandals involving cheating occurred between 1965 and 2007. These scandals created tension on campus and were followed up by investigations and actions to address the underlying problems.

After the first women were admitted to the Academy in 1976, women cadets experienced many trials and obstacles. Antagonistic attitudes toward women were, in the beginning, acute. Some women were allegedly exposed to sexual harassment. To this day, women and minorities are underrepresented at the Academy, though the Academy works to try to redress the problem.

### Milestones

Notwithstanding these challenges, notable men and women Air Force Academy graduates have made great contributions to the armed services and the country. Brigadier General Ruben A. Cubero, class of 1961, was the first Hispanic to be named Dean of the Faculty of the Academy. Charles V. Bush, class of 1963, was one of the first three African Americans to attend and graduate from the Academy. Susan Helms, class of 1980, went on to become an astronaut, and Shawna Rochelle Kimbrell, class of 1998, became the first female African American fighter pilot.

In 2005, allegations of racial intolerance to cadets who had alternative beliefs and worship practices were raised. In 2010, the Academy, whose cadets are primarily Christian based, established an outdoor worship area for cadets who practice pagan religions.

### For Visitors

Visitors to the Academy number in the hundreds of thousands, according to the institution's website. Visitors must follow certain rules and restrictions when at the Academy. They must supply a driver's license and submit to security measures before admittance.

The first stop for visitors is the Barry Goldwater Air Force Academy Visitor Center, a 31,600-square-foot building that features exhibits and a gift shop. The exhibits feature information about the history of and life at the institution. A theater inside the center shows a promotional film about the Academy. Visitors may take self-guided tours to such popular places as the Cadet Chapel, Arnold Hall, and Honor Court, which exhibits statues and memorials. Visitors may also attend concerts. Nearby attractions and activities include hiking and jaunts to popular sites showcasing local and American history. Colorado's mountainous and serene natural beauty of the archetypal and romanticized Western Frontier provides much enjoyment. Notable destinations include Cheyenne Mountain State Park, Cheyenne Mountain Zoo, Pioneers Museum, the Money Museum, and the Garden of the Gods.

***See also*** U.S. Naval Academy; West Point

### Further Reading

Nauman, Robert Allen. 2004. *On the Wings of Modernism: The United States Air Force Academy.* Urbana: University of Illinois Press.

Schading, Barbara, and Schading, Richard. 2007. *A Civilian's Guide to the U.S. Military: A Comprehensive Reference to the Customs, Language, and Structure of the Armed Forces.* Cincinnati: Writer's Digest Books.

Schemo, Diana Jean. 2010. *Skies to Conquer: A Year inside the Air Force Academy.* Hoboken, New Jersey: John Wiley & Sons.

Smallwood, William L., and Ross, Sue. 2007. *The Air Force Academy Candidate Book.* Monument, Colorado: Silver Horn Books.

Stiehm, Judith. 1981. *Bring Me Men and Women: Mandated Change at the U.S. Air Force Academy.* Berkeley: University of California Press.

*U.S. Air Force Academy.* http://www.usafa.af.mil/.

## Air Force One

Air Force One is the name given to an aircraft used for presidential transport. The most recognizable Air Force One aircrafts have included the Boeing 707 and Boeing 747. Air Force One airplanes have appeared in various designs and color schemes over the years. Today's version is a blue and white Boeing 747 with the words United States of America emblazoned in large letters on each side, with the American flag painted on the tail.

No ordinary plane, Air Force One looms large in the national and international imagination. It's not just that Air Force One is considered the most prestigious plane in America, or that it belongs to the President of the United States of America, or that only a highly select group of individuals are allowed aboard as passengers. Air Force One is a potent symbol denoting prestige and power that resounds across the world.

### Historical Perspectives

Air Force One was not the first plane ever used by an American president. Franklin D. Roosevelt was the first president to fly in a plane. He did so when he was transported in the *Dixie Clipper,* a Boeing 314 flying boat, in 1943 to the Casablanca Conference to strategize with European Allies during World

War II (1939–1945). Subsequent planes were designated specifically for presidential use but were not yet called Air Force One aircrafts. These aircrafts included a VC-54C named the *Sacred Cow,* which transported Presidents Roosevelt and Harry S. Truman. Truman also flew in the *Independence,* a Douglas VC-118. Both the *Sacred Cow* and *Independence* are displayed at the National Museum of the U.S. Air Force in Dayton, Ohio.

After President Dwight D. Eisenhower took office, following Truman, the term "Air Force One" entered into the American lexicon in order to distinguish Eisenhower's plane, *Columbine II,* also known as Air Force 610, from a plane named Eastern 610. In 1959, Eisenhower became the first president to travel in the Boeing 707—the aircraft that would serve as Air Force One for the next seven presidents, namely John F. Kennedy, Lyndon B. Johnson, Richard Nixon, Gerald Ford, Jimmy Carter, Ronald Reagan, and George H. W. Bush. There were actually two versions, aircrafts 27000 and 26000.

### Modern Air Force One

Beginning in 1990, the Boeing 747 was used as Air Force One, replacing the Boeing 707. There are two versions of this plane as well: the 28000 and 29000. The 747 is superior to the 707 in many ways: it flies faster and farther without refueling, carries a larger number of crew members and passengers, and has additional amenities (most recently, Internet connectivity) that the previous aircraft did not. The 747 can range 9,600 miles and travel at a maximum speed of 701 miles per hour. The plane also has armor-plated windows and is able to defend itself against electromagnetic pulses and heat-seeking missiles.

Elaborate security measures have been implemented to protect U.S. presidents and their planes. Security and guards constantly monitor the plane at the Andrews Air Force Base where it is stored when not in use. Although the public can tour parts of the base, tours of Air Force One are not permitted. Guards keep watch of the fuel and the refueling trucks and oversee maintenance and repair. Security is also on hand to oversee the takeoff and landing of the aircraft. In times of emergency, American presidents have additional forms of transportation at their disposal, including warships, battleships, and a special craft called the "Doomsday Plane." The Doomsday Plane is intended to be used by presidents so that they can carry on their duties in times of extreme crisis. To ensure the safety of the president during travel, clearance for takeoff is always guaranteed, and other planes are prohibited from flying within a certain range of Air Force One.

Air Force One is not all high-tech gadgetry and surveillance. Encompassing 4,000 square feet of space, Air Force One includes cabins and compartments for staff, the press, and Secret Service agents, a spacious conference room, a lavish presidential suite, a presidential office, galleys, a workroom, and half a dozen restrooms.

Augmenting the glamour of Air Force One is the fact that this aircraft is a highly exclusive environment. Air Force One is a world few know intimately, though its image appears ubiquitously on television and in newspapers and imaginatively, often melodramatically, in other forms in popular culture.

### Images in Popular Culture

The image of Air Force One is frequently seen in popular culture. Images of presidents and their planes appear in abundance in magazines, newspapers, websites, and televised reports. Media events often center around presidents going to, coming from, or appearing near Air Force One, many times alongside their spouses. A little-known fact is that the president's walk toward Air Force One is carefully crafted, as Kenneth T. Walsh explains in his book *Air Force One: A History of the Presidents and Their Planes* (2003). The walk begins from the South Lawn at the White House, leads up a staircase to the plane, and culminates on a platform at the entrance of the aircraft, where the president customarily smiles, waves, and poses for photographers and camera crews.

Television and newspapers portray numerous images of presidents with Air Force One. Historic photos include those of Lyndon B. Johnson, who was inaugurated aboard the aircraft in 1963, and Richard Nixon, who posed dramatically in front of the plane, with arms outstretched giving the V for victory sign with both hands before leaving office after a scandal in 1974. More recent photos depict George W. Bush peering at New Orleans from the window of Air Force One in the aftermath of Hurricane Katrina in 2005. In 2009, National Geographic's *Onboard Air Force One* television series captured Barack Obama, the first African American president in the nation, riding Air Force One for the first time in 2009 when he was the president-elect. Images of presidents in or near Air Force One play an important role in society, helping to underscore the president's authority, aggrandize the president's image, create an ambience of power and mystique, and generate emotional responses like patriotism and solidarity.

Images of Air Force One are also used effectively in popular fiction, whether to add tension and drama or to provide a touch of realism and authenticity. A particularly popular image in action films, the aircraft actually had a major role in *Air Force One* (1997), starring Harrison Ford. A large part of the film takes place on the plane, as Ford, portraying the president, faces off against terrorists. Director Wolfgang Petersen imaginatively infuses the aircraft with fantastical gadgets like an escape pod. A fictitious Air Force One makes an appearance in *Independence Day* (1996), the patriotic movie pitting the military against malevolent aliens. In this movie, the president and his cabinet escape an alien invasion of the White House on Air Force One. Air Force One computers are compromised by robotic aliens in the mega hit *Transformers* (2007). *Superman: The Movie* (1978) and the popular television series based on Superman, *Smallville* (2001–2011), features Superman rescuing Air Force One. Air Force One has also made appearances in *Doonesbury,* the comic strip, other comic books, wherein Air Force One sometimes comes to a catastrophic end, and television dramas, like *The West Wing* (1999–2006) and *Commander and Chief* (2005–2006).

### Cultural Distinctions

Air Force One has popped up in unexpected places such as in urban youth subcultures, the music industry, and professional sports. In 1982, Nike, Inc. created Air Force 1, an athletic shoe named after the president's famous aircraft (Nike has produced several versions of this shoe for everyday use or for athletic events). By naming the shoe after Air Force One, Nike indirectly transferred the symbols of prestige and power to their shoe. These symbols combined with the popularity of basketball and athletic shoes in youth subcultures, initially in urban African American communities, made for a successful formula.

The shoe's popularity spread to basketball stars and hip-hop celebrities. NBA stars appeared in games donning various versions of the shoe. The 2002 rap hit entitled, "Air Force Ones," by hip-hop star Nelly makes references to and sheds insight into urban youth culture. In the rap, Nelly describes the shoe's popular colors, such as those that match the color schemes of star basketball teams and popular ways to wear and maintain the cleanliness of the shoes. He also compares his shoes to his car, another significant emblem in hip-hop and youth subculture.

Nelly's viewpoint on this popular shoe is not his alone. His outlook and practices are reflective of youth and hip-hop subcultures across the nation and increasingly across the globe. Through the varied rituals and elaborate fashion trends associated with the Air Force 1 and its subsequent versions, combined with the empowering symbols imparted by the name "Air Force One," youth and hip-hop subcultures demonstrate their brand of coolness, power, and prestige.

***See also*** Camp David; New Orleans, Louisiana; White House

**Further Reading**

Cross, James U. 2008. *Around the World with LBJ: My Wild Ride as Air Force One Pilot, White House Aide, and Personal Confidant*. Austin: University of Texas Press.

Dorr, Robert F. 2002. *Air Force One*. St. Paul, Minnesota: Zenith Press.

Hardesty, Von. 2003. *Air Force One: The Aircraft That Shaped the Modern Presidency*. Chanhassen, Minnesota: North-Word Press.

Walsh, Kenneth T. 2003. *Air Force One: A History of the Presidents and Their Planes*. New York: Hyperion.

## Alamo

The Alamo is a mission compound located in San Antonio, Texas. Built in 1744, the mission functioned in various ways as a church, hospital, and military post. But its most celebrated role was as the site of a historic battle and a symbol of resistance, courage, and self-sacrifice. The Battle of the Alamo occurred in late winter of 1836 between the Texans and the Tejanos, a term referring to Texans of Mexican descent, on one side, and a Mexican Army led by Antonio Lopez de Santa Anna on the other. The battle ended catastrophically for the Texans, yielding few survivors. Legendary icons Davy Crockett, Colonel James Rezin Bowie, and Colonel William Barret Travis died, and the mission suffered near-destruction.

The Alamo, a Catholic mission in San Antonio, acted as a fortress where Texas fought for independence from Mexico. (Neonriver/Dreamstime.com)

The battle has gone down in history as a critical event leading up to Texas's independence and statehood. Inspired by the valor and defiance shown at the Alamo, Texans mobilized for war against the Mexican Army at San Jacinto in 1836, where Texan soldiers shouted out the infamous battle cry, "Remember the Alamo!" The Texans were victorious, though they did not officially gain independence until the end of the Mexican–American War (1846–1848).

Echoes of the battle cry still linger today. An enduring symbol, the Alamo has lived on in legend, literature, paintings, song, films, and television. The landmark has also endured in its restored form as one of the most popular tourist sites in Texas.

**Historical Perspectives**

The Alamo was one of several Roman Catholic missions built by the Spanish in North America, particularly in California and Texas. Five missions, including the Alamo, were built in San Antonio, Texas alone. Construction of the Alamo, originally known as the Mission San Antonio de Valero, began in 1724. The compound consisted of a church and several buildings encircled by a wall, which was constructed to provide defense against attacks by Native Americans. Spanish missionaries managed the compound, utilizing it to educate the indigenous populations they converted to Christianity. In 1792, Spain secularized the missions, which were eventually abandoned. In the early 1800s, during Mexico's war for independence from Spain, Mexican soldiers occupied the mission compound and converted the barrack into a hospital. They also changed the mission's name to the Alamo, after the town Alamo de Parras in Coahuila, where many of the soldiers lived. At the end of the Mexican War of Independence in 1821, Mexico obtained present-day Texas and other land.

Mexico's hold on Texas was precarious at best. Many Americans settled in Texas, and the population swelled rapidly. In 1834, some 30,000 American immigrants lived in Texas, legally or not. The Mexican population was under 8,000. This ratio was not the only issue that unsettled the Mexican government. Texans were, generally, rebellious toward Mexican rule, and, in fact, openly challenged their control. When Santa Anna, president and military leader, implemented an oppressive autocracy, frustrations flared among Texans and Mexican citizens. As the flames of resistance stoked hotter, tensions morphed into uprisings and outright war. More than half a dozen major battles transpired before the Battle of the Alamo.

**Napoleon of the West**

Antonio López de Santa Anna was a military leader and president of Mexico 11 times from 1833 to 1855. He is most infamously known as the formidable adversary of the Americans during the Texas War of Independence. Santa Anna was born in Mexico on February 21, 1794. At the age of 16, he joined the army. During the Mexican War of Independence, he fought initially on the Spanish side and then switched to the Mexican side and was rewarded with a promotion to General. In 1829, he garnered acclaim by contributing to the defeat of the Spanish when they attempted to retake Mexico.

In the next decade, Santa Anna rose to greater power in Mexico and in 1833 he was elected president. During his presidency, his rule over Mexican states such as Texas was harsh; he eliminated many rights that Mexicans and immigrants living in Texas enjoyed, and restricted immigration. Americans in Texas revolted in response. Though Santa Anna defeated the rebels at the Battle of Alamo, he was ultimately defeated at the Battle of San Jacinto in 1836.

Santa Anna's warring days were not yet over. Santa Anna was defeated in both the Pastry War (1838–1839), a conflict that occurred when France invaded Mexico, and the Mexican-American War (1846–1848). At the conclusion of the Mexican–American War, Mexico lost much of the land they had controlled, from Texas to California.

Santa Anna's last period as president began in 1853 but in 1854 the citizens of Mexico became embittered against him when he sold off lands to the United States, and in 1855, he was deposed. He died on June 21, 1876.

### Battle of the Alamo

General Sam Houston, a pivotal leader in the Texas Revolution, had wanted the Alamo destroyed and did not intend for a campaign to occur there. But James Bowie and William Barret Travis opposed Houston's decision, choosing to defend the Alamo, which the Texans were using as a garrison. Later, they were joined by Davy Crockett. All three men were notable swashbuckling pioneers in their time; they all played prominent roles during the period of Texan resistance to Mexico. The infamous Bowie knife took its name from Bowie. Of the three, Davy Crockett is considered the most legendary. Crockett was a nationally recognized hero, adventurer, hunter, soldier, and politician. His exploits, whether true or embellished, appeared in a contemporaneous bibliography and autobiography.

Bowie, Travis, and Crockett faced horrific odds at the Alamo. The Alamo was not built for the purpose of war, and the number of defenders at the garrison was alarmingly small (historians assert that the defenders totaled some 200, while the Mexican Army consisted of 1,800 to several thousand soldiers). Travis did his best to prepare for Santa Anna by bolstering the walls and bringing in cannons. But the response to Travis's desperate letter for more defenders came too late. Despite the odds against them, the Texans held their ground valiantly during a 13-day siege that began on February 23. On March 6, Santa Anna and his soldiers broke through the Alamo ending the battle. Few Texans survived.

#### A Texas Legend

Sam Houston (1793–1863) was a lawyer, military leader, and politician. Born on March 2, 1793, near Lexington, Virginia, Houston is regarded as an iconic frontier hero, particularly in Texas, where he played an instrumental role in the state's early development. Houston's life was shaped by the fact that his father was a Revolutionary War veteran. After his father's death, the Houston family moved to eastern Tennessee, where Sam learned the language and culture of the Cherokee. Years later, Houston fought bravely in the War of 1812 and the Creek War in 1813 and 1814.

Following these military actions, Houston pursued a path in politics in Tennessee. He studied law and was elected district attorney. In 1823 and 1825, he was elected to Congress and went on to become the governor of Tennessee in 1827.

By the 1830s, Houston found himself leading soldiers in the Texas Revolution against forces led by Mexican General Antonio López de Santa Anna. On April 21, 1836, Houston's victory at San Jacinto contributed greatly to Texas independence.

After the war, Houston continued to play a prominent role in the state that he is so closely associated with. In 1836, the city of Houston was named after him, and he was elected the first president of the Republic in 1836. Once Texas became a state in 1846, he served as a U.S. senator from 1849 to 1859.

### Images in Popular Culture

The tragedy at the Alamo not only served as a rallying call to war and the eventual independence of Texas, it prompted a pop-culture phenomenon. Paintings depicting the Alamo materialized early on. Mary Maverick produced one of the earliest drawings, a sketch of the Alamo Mission, in 1838, and Theodore Gentilz painted a depiction of the final assault in *The Fall of the Alamo* in 1844. Popular songs were composed with the aim of increasing morale in times of war. Songs like "The Ballad of Davy Crockett" topped the charts and heightened the romantic ambience of the heroes of the Alamo.

Literature was another medium in which the Alamo lived on and flourished. The Daughters of the Republic of Texas, stewards of the Alamo, maintain a large library containing books on the subject. According to Donald Langmead, author of *Icons of American Architecture: From the Alamo to the World Trade Center* (2009), the library contains more than 1,000 books, both nonfiction and fiction, for adults and children. Among the literary works written about the Alamo are memoirs by both Mexican soldiers and Texans. John Henry Brown wrote the first of many historical treatments in a pamphlet called

**King of the Wild Frontier**

Davy Crockett was a folk hero, military hero, and politician. He was born David Crockett, the fifth of nine children, in Greene County, Tennessee, on August 17, 1786. In those early days, Tennessee was not yet a state, and Crockett was raised according to frontier traditions. At only eight years old, he was taught how to use a rifle and to hunt, helping provide food for the family.

Crockett fought in the war of 1812, participating in the massacre of a Cree Indian town of Tallasahatchee, Alabama. After he was discharged from service in 1815, Crockett began a career in politics. He was elected to the Tennessee State House of Representatives and served from 1821 to 1823. He was elected to Congress in 1826, 1829, and 1833. Contributing to his popularity during these years was his reputation as a frontier hero, which was based on a combination of fact andromanticized mythology of the old frontier.

After Crockett was defeated for reelection to Congress, he joined the War for Independence in Texas. On March 6, 1836, he was killed in San Antonio, Texas, while defending the Alamo.

*The Fall of the Alamo* (1843). A number of plays were written about the Battle of the Alamo, as well as the hero Davy Crockett. Historians, however, assert that the majority of the literature is infused with more myth than fact, such as portraying Texan soldiers as larger than life, exaggerating death scenes of heroes like Davy Crockett, and depicting the Mexican army as one-dimensional villains.

Overall, movie and television accounts fared little better in presenting factual accounts of the Alamo. Since the early days of film, the Alamo has been a popular topic. Lucrative films include those that were rooted in American heroism as it was commonly displayed in the rugged Western Frontier or in battle. Early films include William F. Haddock's *The Immortal Alamo* (1911), D.W. Griffith's *Martyrs of the Alamo* (1915), and Robert N. Bradbury's *With Davy Crockett at the Fall of the Alamo* (1926). The Alamo remained a subject of choice in movies like *The Man from the Alamo* (1953) and the ever-popular Disney miniseries based on the life of Davy Crockett, dubbed the "King of the Wild Frontier." This miniseries delivered a highly imaginative and wildly popular account of Crockett and the Alamo. The most influential film, however, was John Wayne's *The Alamo* (1960). Like the films before it, *The Alamo* was heavy on mythic heroism and sensationalism. Contemporary documentaries, television miniseries, and films lend a more authentic retelling of the Alamo. Noteworthy productions include *Remember the Alamo: American Experience* (2004), a documentary produced by PBS, and the film *The Alamo* (2004). This latest version of *The Alamo* was not a success at the box office, but critics conceded that the film presented more historical accuracies than previous films.

### For Visitors

The most credible and popular presentation of the Alamo in contemporary times is the historical site itself. Rebuilt and reconfigured to accommodate modern conveniences, the Alamo receives millions of visitors each year. The most popular building is the chapel, known as the "Shrine of Texas Liberty." Its façade is one of the most recognizable and duplicated images in print, postcards, T-shirts, and other paraphernalia. The site features a multitude of historical and educational displays and activities. Visitors may view historical artifacts, weapons, maps, a battle excavation site, and an audio and light show describing the Alamo before the battle of 1836. The Wall of History chronicles Texas history. Visitors can listen to talks at the Calvary Court Yard, see exhibits and a movie in the Long Barracks, and browse the gift shop. Near the Alamo site are the historic Emily Morgan Hotel and Crockett Hotel, and an IMAX theater that plays the film *Alamo: The Price of Freedom*.

The Alamo is a heavyweight in popular culture, as well as in the pantheon of important places in American history. The idea of a small but intrepid group of soldiers fighting and dying for independence is lodged deeply in the American psyche. The Alamo embodies a reoccurring motif in American history of individuals fighting for freedom, independence, individuality, and their adopted homeland. Centuries later, the Alamo continues to resonate strongly with Americans, conjuring feelings of reverence and patriotism, deeply connecting Americans to their heritage.

***See also*** California; Texas

**Further Reading**

*Alamo*. www.thealamo.org/main.html.

Castañeda, Carlos E., ed. 1971. *The Mexican Side of the Texas Revolution*. Washington, DC: Documentary Publications.

Davis, William C. 2006. *Lone Star Rising: The Revolutionary Birth of the Texas Republic*. College Station: Texas A & M University Press.

Davis, William C. 1998. *Three Roads to the Alamo: The Lives and Fortunes of David Crockett James Bowie, and William Barret Travis*. New York: HarperCollins.

Flores, Richard R. 2002. *Remembering the Alamo: Memory, Modernity, and the Master Symbol*. Austin: University of Texas Press.

Langmead, Donald. 2009. *Icons of American Architecture: From the Alamo to the World Trade Center*. Westport, Connecticut: Greenwood Press.

Santa Anna, Antonio López de. 1988. *The Eagle: The Autobiography of Santa Ana*. Austin, Texas: State House Press.

## Alaska

Alaska is the 49th state of the United States of America. The country's largest state by landmass, it has one of the smallest populations. Alaska's population consists mostly of people born out of state, with Native Americans and Native Alaskans making up the largest minority group. Major industries in the state are fishing and oil. Defined by its breathtaking mountains, lakes, and wilderness regions, Alaska is rich in minerals and other natural resources.

Situated far from the continental United States, Alaska is thus a noncontiguous state. The state is in the uppermost northwest corner of North America, bordering Canada to the east, the Arctic Ocean to the north, and the Pacific Ocean to the west. The closest state, Washington, is separated from Alaska by Canada's large landmass and the great expanse of the Pacific Ocean. Anchorage, Alaska's largest populated city, is an incredible 2,250 miles away from Seattle, Washington, by car.

A more popular way to reach Alaska is by cruise ship, from which tourists can view the stunning glacier-rich waters and marine life, like orca and humpback whales. Once in Alaska, visitors will find sweeping wilderness regions and pristine remote living. Rugged Alaska dominates the bustling modern urbanization that exists in cities like Anchorage, Juneau, and Fairbanks. It is indeed the state's great outdoors and untamed isolation that has defined the region and what captivates the national imagination.

### Historical Perspectives

Native Alaskans, who arrived some 20,000 years ago, were the first humans to establish communities in the pristine and untamed wilds of Alaska. Some anthropologists contend they migrated across the Bering Strait land bridge; others theorize that many may have come by boat. For thousands of years, indigenous Alaskans, comprising the Athabascans, Aleuts, Inuit, Tlingits, and Haidas, lived in relative freedom, unobstructed from practicing their distinct way of life. This life was characterized by intricate customs

A full-size cruise ship looks like a toy miniature as it navigates the many icebergs in Disenchantment Bay that have broken free of mighty Hubbard Glacier in Alaska. Hubbard Glacier is the largest tidewater glacier in the world and a highly popular destination for cruise ships touring Alaska. (Lawrence Weslowski Jr./Dreamstime.com)

and religious beliefs, languages, songs, storytelling, dance, artwork, and an intimate relationship with the land.

The Europeans who came to Alaska beginning in the 18th century severely disrupted the indigenous culture. The British and the French came first but soon left. Then came the Russians. The indigenous population suffered considerably. Many died from disease; others were enslaved. Native Alaskans were often forbidden to speak their own language, practice their religion, or perform the dances and other rituals that were essential to their way of life.

In 1867, U.S. Secretary of State William H. Seward purchased the territory from Russia for $7.2 million. Though this was considered a bargain price, the acquisition was unpopular. With the purchase cast as "Seward's folly" by the press, the Secretary of State was initially ridiculed for purchasing Alaska, which was considered too wild, too impenetrable, and too far away.

However, with the emergence of the Klondike Gold Rush in the late 19th century, Alaska proved to be a lucrative purchase. The discovery of gold during the summer of 1897 in the Yukon Territory, a region in Canada that borders the Arctic Ocean, Northwest Territories, British Columbia, and Alaska, sparked a feverish gold rush. Within the first year, at least 100,000 gold-seekers, including famous writer Jack London, set out to find their fortune.

Mining for gold was no easy task; neither was the hazardous and brutal journey to reach the gold fields. Many failed and returned home, but a number of towns were established in the process. These communities were akin to those that appear in classic Western films, where frontier justice and rugged individualism reigned supreme.

Alaska experienced incremental development in the ensuing decades. During World War II, the military built the Alaska Highway (also known as the Alaska–Canada Highway and the ALCAN Highway), linking Alaska to the United States, making travel to and from the region easier, and contributing to the region's growth and development. In 1959, nearly 100 years after Seward's purchase, Alaska became a state. Several decades later, in 1974, work began on the construction of an oil pipeline from Prudhoe Bay to Valdez, Alaska. Oil production is one of the largest contributors to the state's wealth and is, generally, fully supported by the locals. In this same decade, Alaskan Natives enjoyed the passing of the Alaska Native Land Claims Settlement Act, which returned millions of acres to them. Conservation measures were established to protect large natural spaces in Alaska and to create more national parks, refuges, and preserves.

**The Great American Writer**

Jack London was a prominent 20th-century author. He was born John Griffith Chaney on January 12, 1876, in San Francisco, California. The name London was derived from his stepfather, John London; the name Jack was what London began calling himself, in his youth.

Early on, London experienced a grueling life of hard labor. His assortment of jobs included pirating oysters, shoveling coal, and working in a cannery. He also spent a great deal of time reading for personal enjoyment. In 1893, London discovered his writing talent when his mother persuaded him to submit a story to a writing contest. After he won the competition, hebegan submitting manuscripts to many publishers without success. After briefly attending the University of California at Berkeley and prospecting gold in the Yukon, London returned to California and pursued writing. Finally, in 1899, he began publishing stories in the *Overland Monthly,* and in 1903, he published his first novel *The Call of the Wild,* a novel about a sled dog in the Yukon, which was a literary success.

London's writing life flourished for many more years. He wrote prolifically, and many of his works, such as *White Fang* (1906), were extremely popular. His works covered themes such as his experiences in the Yukon, as well as sympathetic portrayals of the working class and criticism of capitalism (London was a socialist). London died on November 22, 1916.

### Contemporary Perspectives

Alaska has seen myriad changes in recent years. Major cities like Anchorage and Fairbanks have burgeoned and look similar to other modern-day U.S. metropolises, complete with Starbucks, McDonald's, business developments, and elaborate road systems. In these urban areas, wildlife sightings are less frequent and neighbors reside in close proximity to one another. Though life is dramatically different from frontier days, modern-day living is not without its challenges, according to some Alaskan Natives, whose youth, in particular, are frequently entrapped by drug and alcohol abuse and Western cultural influences. In this environment, Western culture—not native traditions and culture—often takes precedence.

### For Visitors

Alaska offers unique experiences to its visitors, as well as its residents. Known as the "Last Frontier," Alaska is associated with all things wild, rough, rugged—and remote. As most states within the continental United States become increasingly swallowed up and uniformly defined by shopping malls, industrial complexes, bountiful conveniences for daily life, ever-expanding urban development, and sweeping concrete highways, Alaska remains primarily a region of natural wild spaces and remote villages and towns, native and nonnative. Many areas are only accessible by ferry or plane. In some towns, businesses close by 5: 00 P.M. (in contrast to all-night eateries and stores in metropolitan regions), and pizza deliveries must be transported by plane.

To the outsider, Alaskan living spaces and small towns are a throwback to the early frontier days. Salmon hang from wooden racks outside log cabins, locals travel with rifles along unpaved roads, and sightings of bear, moose, eagles, and other wildlife are commonplace in many areas. Some Alaskan natives live in traditional ways in the Bush, a vast region off the road system where many communities live off the land.

Going further off-grid, Alaska provides sundry opportunities for adventure in its plentiful natural spaces. Among Alaska's popular parks and forests are the Denali National Park, Glacier Bay, and Kenai Fjords. In all, there are over 100 state parks and recreation areas and 2 national forests, Tongass and Chugach, in Alaska. Common activities in these areas include kayaking, fishing, hiking, hunting, camping, and exploring.

### Images in Popular Culture

Just over 50 years old, Alaska State remains a largely untamed wilderness that appeals to the adventurous aspect of the American psyche. Americans travel far and wide to see its natural wonders for themselves, but many more experience Alaska through television and film. One of the first film treatments of Alaska was the critically acclaimed *Eskimo* (1933), which vaulted Ray Mala, of Jewish and Eskimo heritage, to Hollywood stardom.

Not all television programs set in Alaska have been successful, but their appearance in the popular culture demonstrates the deep impact Alaska has on the national imagination. In the 1950s and 1960s, interest in frontier life manifested in televised treatments of the Klondike Gold Rush experience such as in *The Alaskans* (1959–1960) and *Klondike* (1960–1961). The television series *Kodiak* (1974) featured a stalwart Cal "Kodiak" McKay portrayed by Clint Waler and his Eskimo sidekick Abraham Lincoln Imhook, played by Abner Biberman. In the 1990s, the award-winning show *Northern Exposure* (1990–1995) explored Alaskan life through quirky comedy and an eclectic cast of characters.

Alaska continued to inspire a series of more recent films. The film *The Edge* (1997), starring Anthony Hopkins and Alec Baldwin, portrayed Alaska in all its chilling rawness, as the main characters find themselves in an impossible situation following a plane wreck. They brave injury, bitter temperatures, scabrous terrain, hunger, and interpersonal conflict while being stalked by a ferocious bear. Other notable films based on wilderness, wildlife, and survival in Alaska include *White Fang* (1991), adapted from a novel written by Jack London, *Grizzly Man* (2005), and *Into the Wild* (2007). Like *The Edge,* many movies based on Alaska underscore the precariousness of the region. In *Grizzly Man,* a documentary, Timothy Treadwell makes close contact with bears in the wild, but in the end, he and his girlfriend are killed by one. In *Into the Wild,* a film based on the biography by John Krakauer, Christopher McCandless, played by Emile Hirsch, pursues his dream of escaping society and materialism and living off-grid in nature. Alaska is at the center of his dream, but, when he arrives, he finds life brutal and harsh. Ill-prepared, McCandless dies from starvation. McCandless's life was also portrayed in the documentary *The Call of the Wild* (2007).

Alaska is also the setting for films that address other themes. The popular film *The Simpsons Movie* (2007) explores environmentalism in Alaska from a comedic point of view. Movies that deal with parts of Alaska's seasonal long days of sunlight and darkness include the thriller *Insomnia* (2002), which takes place in a fishing town called Nightmute. The vampire horror film *30 Days of Night* (2007), a film adapted from a comic book miniseries, is set in Barrow. The theme of isolation and its heightening effect on the fear of locals in the small town of Nome is illustrated in the alien abduction movie *The Fourth Kind* (2009).

Alaska has also cropped up as a setting for reality television. Popular reality programs include *Deadliest Catch* (2005–), *Ice Road Truckers* (2007–), *Tougher in Alaska* (2008), *Out of the Wild: The Alaska Experiment* (2008), *Alaska State Troopers* (2009–2011), *Gold Rush Alaska* (2010–), *Alaska Wing Men* (2011), and *Flying Wild Alaska* (2011–). Other high-profile programs include *The Toughest Race on Earth: Iditarod* (2008) and *Sarah Palin's Alaska* (2010–2011). These programs feature high-adrenalin action and individuals braving extreme situations. *The Deadliest Catch* explores the high-adventure and notoriously perilous fishing industry. *Sarah Palin's Alaska* profiles Palin's adventurous life in Alaska, fishing in bear-saturated regions, road tripping to small towns, caribou hunting above the Arctic Circle, as well as camping, rafting, logging, and gold mining at other locations. Palin, a former Alaska governor, emerged on the national political scene in 2008 as a vice presidential nominee alongside presidential hopeful John McCain. Palin, who is also a wife and mother of five, appears in popular culture as a woman who can do it all and is firmly rooted in the Alaskan way of life.

Some Alaskans express mixed emotions in regard to the way Alaska is depicted in popular culture. Some see themselves and the world that they love and experience; others see sensationalism and inaccuracies. These programs, nonetheless, have helped to popularize and perpetuate the image of Alaska as the epitome of wild and precarious living, of a place where only the tough and wilderness-savvy survive.

*See also* Cruise Ships; Hollywood; Iditarod; McDonald's; Off-Grid; Seattle, Washington; Starbucks

**Alaska's Palin**

Sarah Palin is a politician most famously known for being the vice presidential running mate in John McCain's presidential campaign of 2008. Palin was born on February 11, 1964, in Sandpoint, Idaho. She was three years old when her parents, Charles and Sally Heath, moved to Alaska to work in a school in Skagway. Palin grew up with a love of the outdoors, enjoying sports such as hunting. After graduating from Wasilla High in 1982, Palin was crowned Miss Wasilla. In 1987, she earned a bachelor's degree in journalism from the University of Idaho and then worked as a television sports reporter in Anchorage, Alaska.

In the following decade, Palin began her political career. She was elected to Wasilla City Council in 1992 and as mayor of Wasilla in 1996. From 2006 to 2009, she served as the state of Alaska's first woman governor. She was also the youngest governor in the state's history. On August 20, 2008, she was introduced as John McCain's running mate on the Republican ticket.

During this period, Palin was the focus of much media scrutiny. Reporters criticized her for what they contended was her lack of knowledge and limited experience in politics. Comedian Tina Fey, who bore a great likeness to Palin, parodied her public persona on *Saturday Night Live* (1975–). But Palin accumulated positive attention as well, as she promoted the positive image of a modern woman who could do it all as a mother, politician, and avid outdoor enthusiast.

Following the Republican loss in the presidential campaign, Palin resigned as governor, went on tour promoting her book, *Going Rogue: An American Life* (2010), and appeared on her own television reality show, *Sarah Palin's Alaska* (2010–2011)

### Further Reading

Blum, Howard. 2011. *The Floor of Heaven: A True Tale of the Last Frontier and the Yukon Gold Rush*. New York: Crown Publishers.

Campbell, James. 2004. *The Final Frontiersman: Heimo Korth and His Family, Alone in Alaska's Arctic Wilderness*. New York: Atria Books.

Grieve, Guy. 2007. *Call of the Wild: My Escape to Alaska*. London: Hodder and Stoughton.

Hansen, Sig, and Sundeen, Mark. 2010. *North by Northwestern: A Seafaring Family on Deadly Alaskan Waters*. New York: Thomas Dunne Books.

Haycox, Stephen. 2006. *Alaska: An American Colony*. Seattle: University of Washington Press.

Hensley, William L. Iggiagruk. 2009. *Fifty Miles from Tomorrow: A Memoir of Alaska and the Real People.* New York: Sarah Crichton Books.

Muir, John. 2011. *Travels in Alaska.* Boston: Houghton Mifflin.

## Alcatraz

Alcatraz, also known as The Rock, was a notorious maximum-security federal prison. Nowadays it is a popular museum operated by the National Park Service, one of several dozen must-see tourist destinations that make up the Golden Gate National Recreation Area. Popular images of Alcatraz show a towering lighthouse, the main cellhouse, and the tattered warden's house atop a steep and rocky terrain where sparse plumes of brush and grass grow. The facility is located on Alcatraz Island in San Francisco Bay, one-and-a-half miles from San Francisco, California. Alcatraz functioned first as a military prison, from the late 1850s to 1934, then as a federal prison, from 1934 to 1963. In 1969, Native Americans occupied the island in an unsuccessful attempt to reclaim the land. Although Alcatraz is situated in a natural oasis that supports a variety of interesting plants, birds, and other wildlife, the facility holds its rightful place as one of the most infamous prisons in the nation's history. The appeal of this gray, forbidding Rock, associated from its beginnings with punishment, hardship, and sinister personalities, is proof, if any is needed, that American culture is irresistibly drawn to grim stories, whether for the sheer horror of it, or as symbolic warning of what will happen to those of us who misbehave.

### Historical Perspectives

Alcatraz Island was first discovered by the Spanish, who explored the California coast in the late 1700s. Juan Manuel de Ayala named the island *La Isla de Los Alcatraces* (the Island of the Pelicans). Adapting the Spanish name, the island soon became known even to English speakers simply as Alcatraz.

Ownership of Alcatraz changed hands more than a few times. Julian Workman acquired the island in 1846 from Mexican governor Pío de Jesus Pico. In the same year, the Military Governor of California, John C. Fremont, purchased the island for the U.S. government for $5,000. In 1850, they took control over the island with some controversy, considering Fremont did not receive compensation or reimbursement. The government constructed a lighthouse and a fortress on the island to protect the San Francisco Bay area, which was then experiencing rapid population growth as a result of the Gold Rush. Construction commenced in 1853, resulting in a sturdy garrison equipped with cannons and batteries.

**Fremont: California Pioneer**

John C. Fremont was an explorer and politician who was born in Savannah, Georgia, in 1813. In the 1830s, Fremont found himself progressing as a surveyor for lands to be used by the Charleston and Cincinnati Railroad, and in 1838, he was commissioned as a second lieutenant in the U.S. Corps of Topographical Engineers. Over the next 12 years, Fremont led many expeditions in the West arriving in California in 1846. He supported American efforts to annex California, as had been done with Texas. In the same year, a revolt was waged. For a time, Fremont commanded the so-called Bear Flaggers, based on the name of the make shift flag that Americans used to symbolize their fight to make California a Republic. In the year the revolt began, California obtained its independence and obtained statehood in 1859. After serving as a senator for the state, Fremont served in the Union Army during the Civil War (1861–1865) and from 1878 to 1881, he served as Governor of Arizona Territory. He died on July 13, 1890.

### Military Prison

In the ensuing years, the government shifted its use of Alcatraz Island from military garrison to minimum-security military prison. In 1907, the prison was called the Western U.S. Military Prison, and in 1915, it was called the Pacific Branch, U.S. Disciplinary Barracks. As early as 1859, the island served as a military prison for soldiers who had committed crimes or violated regulations. The number of prisoners increased during the Civil War (1861–1865) and Spanish–American War (1898), necessitating the gradual development of additional facilities to support a growing prison population. In the 1890s, Hopi men were tragically imprisoned at Alcatraz, largely as a result of their resistance to efforts to be Americanized. The years between 1908 and 1912 saw major renovation and expansion, including the advent of electricity, a cellhouse with 600 one-man cells, a dining hall, kitchen, hospital, a recreation yard, and a new concrete tower (the original lighthouse had been damaged during the 1906 San Francisco earthquake). Reuben B. Turner designed the new facilities, and prisoners provided the labor. The military prison was closed in 1934, ushering forth Alcatraz's most infamous era.

### Federal Prison

The federal prison on Alcatraz operated for 29 years, from 1934 to 1964. During this time the complex featured numerous buildings and spaces to support prison life. Apartments, a bowling alley, and soda fountain shop for staff and their families, the warden's house, a recreation yard, and of course the main cellhouse were located within the vicinity. For supplies, such as water and sundry necessities and luxuries, inhabitants were dependent upon regularly scheduled deliveries that came to the island by barge, and upon the ferry, which would transport them to the mainland. Though contact with the outside world was severely restricted, the prison left an indelible mark on American society.

The prison itself had a formidable reputation as a hellhole. Conditions inside were grim and severely regimented. Prisoner schedules for eating, rest, and recreation were strictly regulated. Misbehaving prisoners were punished by solitary confinement in Spartan cells with little to eat or drink. The prison wardens were infamous for managing Alcatraz with a heavy hand.

Alcatraz's isolated location, grim appearance, and reputation for impenetrableness also added to the facility's chilling mystique. Concrete structures on a cheerless, rocky, and remote island surrounded by ice-cold, violent waters made an imposing, even daunting, impression on the

#### Public Enemy No. 1

Al Capone was an organized-crime boss. Born Alphonso Capone in Brooklyn, New York, on January 17, 1899, to parents who had immigrated from Italy, Capone was arguably the most infamous crime boss in the nation. He began his illicit career when he joined the James Street boys gang as a teenager after he was expelled from Catholic school. During a scuffle, he acquired the trademark scar on his left cheek that earned him the nickname Scarface.

On the eve of Prohibition, Capone moved to Chicago. By 1920, criminal organizations were making the most of the abundant opportunities for bootlegging that emerged once Prohibition began. Capone managed gang leader Johnny Torrio's Four Deuces, a speakeasy, gambling joint, and brothel. He also infiltrated government and law enforcement. After Torrio retired in 1925, Capone inherited Torrio's vast empire of nightclubs, brothels, gambling dens, and speakeasies.

Unlike other mob bosses, Capone reigned flamboyantly. His flashy dress and equally ostentatious headquarters at the Metropole Hotel captured the imagination of the public. Many believed that Capone was connected to the St. Valentine's Day Massacre, which took place in 1929 and resulted in the deaths of seven men affiliated with the mob. In 1930, the Chicago Crime Commission designated Capone Public Enemy No. 1. It was Eliot Ness, an agent with the U.S. Prohibition Bureau, and his team who managed to finally capture Capone after several unsuccessful attempts. On October 17, 1931, Capone was found guilty of several counts of tax evasion. After serving a sentence of six-and-a-half years, he was released. He died on January 25, 1947. Capone and the celebrated Ness have been depicted profusely in books, cartoons, films, and television.

public. Newspapers and radio broadcasts of the day touted the invulnerability of the prison, especially owing to the fact that state-of-the art modifications totaling $263,000 were made to heighten security. It was believed that escape from Alcatraz was nearly impossible and that, if prisoners discovered a way out, they could not prevail against the obstacle awaiting them outside: the cold and turbulent waters of the Bay. Only 14 escape attempts were ever made during this period. Only one of them yielded a measure of success: Frank Morris, John Anglin, and Clarence Anglin pulled off an elaborate escape and launched a makeshift raft into the Bay in 1962. It is alleged that they drowned, but their bodies were never recovered. This escape was included in J. Campbell Bruce's book *Escape from Alcatraz* (1963) and adapted into the 1979 film by the same name. This popular film starred Clint Eastwood, Fred Ward, and Jack Thibeau.

Alcatraz was equally infamous for its inmates. Some of the most notorious prisoners in the nation were imprisoned there, many of whom were sent from other prisons where they had posed problems or committed violations. The federal prison on Alcatraz was created, in large part, in response to the explosion of criminals and criminal organizations that flourished during the period of Prohibition and the Great Depression. Gangsters like Al "Scarface" Capone, the powerful organized-crime boss from Chicago, and the Ma Barker gang made headlines and were the subject of or inspiration for characters in comic books, radio broadcasts, and movies. Gangsters made for sensational news. Whether depicted as heinous villains or smooth-talking and fashionable mobsters, gangsters fascinated the American public.

Other noteworthy prisoners included Robert Franklin Stroud, known as the Birdman of Alcatraz, who acquired his nickname by keeping birds while at Leavenworth penitentiary. At 26 years, Alvin "Creepy Karpis" Karpowicz held the record for the most years at Alcatraz. Ellsworth Raymond "Bumpy" Johnson was an African American mob boss from Harlem, New York.

Although, the prison was closed in 1963 due, in part, to the massive costs to operate the institution, Alcatraz would not be erased from the nation's memory.

> **The Birdman of Alcatraz**
>
> Robert Franklin Stroud was a prisoner who served part of his sentence at the infamous Alcatraz Federal Penitentiary. Popularly known by his moniker, the Birdman of Alcatraz, Stroud was born on January 28, 1890, in Seattle, Washington. After running away from home, Stroud moved to Alaska, where he became a pimp. In 1909, he murdered a bartender who failed to pay one of Stroud's prostitutes. In 1911, he was sent to McNeil Island in Washington State to serve his sentence. Unmanageable and violent, Stroud was transferred to Leavenworth Federal Penitentiary in Kansas in 1912.
>
> While at Leavenworth, Stroud killed a guard after he was denied a visit with his brother. For his crime, Stroud received a life sentence without parole and was placed in a segregated unit. It was during this period that Stroud developed an interest in canaries, after finding an injured bird and was permitted to keep canaries. He raised and studied hundreds of birds and published two books, *Diseases of Canaries* (1933) and *Stroud's Digest on the Diseases of Canaries* (1943).
>
> After serving some 30 years at Leavenworth, Stroud was transferred to Alcatraz in 1942. Though he was prohibited from raising birds, he was still known as the Birdman. In 1959, Stroud was transferred to the Medical Center for Federal Prisoners in Springfield, Missouri. He died on November 21, 1963.

### Native American Occupation

Perhaps assisted by the draw of the very name, Alcatraz, the Native American occupation of Alcatraz Island was covered extensively in the news. The first two attempts by Native Americans to occupy Alcatraz Island occurred on March 9, 1964, and November 9, 1969. Both involved a small number of individuals and were short lived, lasting 4 hours in 1964 and less than 24 hours in 1969. These occupations addressed the contentious disputes between Native Americans and the federal government over land rights and claims that came to a head during the turbulent 1960s. Historical wrongs and broken treaties prompted Native Americans to challenge the U.S. government.

The occupation of Alcatraz that began on November 20, 1969, the third of its kind, made front page news. Some 100 Native Americans, mostly students from the American Indian Studies Center at the University of California at Los Angeles, landed on Alcatraz Island and claimed it as their own. They established a council to govern the island, but aspirations of further development and demonstrations of self-determination foundered due to internal turmoil and disruptions by hippies and others with clashing agendas who sought to promote their own brand of culture and lifestyle choices. On June 11, 1971, police and other law enforcement agencies ended the occupation. Nonetheless, the occupation brought Native American issues to national and international audiences and strengthened the Native American movement. A sign that reads "Indians Welcome" is a remnant of that historically significant day and is visible to the millions of tourists that have visited Alcatraz.

### Bumpy Johnson

Ellsworth Raymond Johnson was a notable African American prisoner at Alcatraz. He was born in Charleston, South Carolina, on October 31, 1905. To protect him from the racially hostile environment of the South, Johnson's parents sent him to live with family in the North. However, Johnson found trouble in the North, pimping, thieving, and burgling. He served a significant amount of time in prison before he turned to racketeering in Harlem, New York, during the 1930s, working with mob boss Stephanie St. Clair.

Johnson was wellknown by his sobriquet, Bumpy, which referred to the bump on his head, in Harlem's criminal underground and among the African American celebrities who frequented the neighborhood. He was also known for the kindness he showed children. His reputation for not kowtowing to anyone made him legendary. He earned his reputation in the violent war that unfolded between him and gangster Dutch Schultz.

In the early 1950s, Johnson was indicted for conspiracy to sell heroin. Though he insisted that he had been framed, Johnson was imprisoned from 1954 to 1963 at Alcatraz. During his imprisonment, it was alleged that he assisted in the 1962 escape attempt of Frank Morris and John and Clarence Anglin. On July 7, 1968, Johnson died from heart failure. After his death, he was popularly depicted in films such as *Shaft* (1971), *Escape from Alcatraz* (1979), *The Cotton Club* (1984), and *American Gangster* (2007).

## For Visitors

Alcatraz, long known as the one place in America people wanted to stay out of, was opened to tourists in 1973. The draw is not hard to understand: curious crowds want to see the infamous institution and get a sense of what life there must have been like for themselves. After all, Alcatraz is the most notorious prison in popular American culture, and the facility housed some of the most nefarious criminals ever known. Tourists glimpse a world that was long restricted from the view of the general public, heavily cloaked under an aura of mystery and notoriety. Tours include visits to the cellhouse, a digital audio tour, a museum store featuring authentic prison artifacts, and a film in the theater that documents Alcatraz's history. Tourists also explore the Alcatraz Gardens, which feature plants planted on the island in the 1800s.

For many visitors, the eerily vacant cellhouse with its sterile and polished floors and rows of barred cells is a space of mystery and fascination. The space conjures feelings of apprehension for some. Indeed, history records eight prison murders, five suicides, and several insanity diagnoses. One popular rumor has it that the cellhouse is haunted; this theory was investigated on the paranormal investigation television show *Ghost Hunters* (2004–). Alcatraz souvenirs are extremely popular, allowing visitors to take with them a piece of America's more infamous history.

### Images in Popular Culture

The popularity of Alcatraz extends well beyond the California tourist industry into the popular culture of the entire country. America's fascination with Alcatraz is demonstrated in songs, books, films, video games, and television shows. Alcatraz has inspired an eclectic assortment of musicians, including country singer June Carter Cash, Christian rock band Capital Lights, and rapper San Quinn. Works of both nonfiction and fiction about Alcatraz or its denizens abound. The Birdman of Alcatraz inspired the novel *Birdman of Alcatraz: The Story of Robert Stroud* (1955) by Eugene Gaddis and a 1962 film. Other notable films include *Point Blank* (1967), *Terror on Alcatraz* (1987), *The Rock* (1996), and *Half Past Dead* (2002). Alcatraz has also made guest appearances in films such as *The Enforcer* (1976), *X-Men: The Last Stand* (2006), and *The Book of Eli* (2010), and popular televisions shows such as *Charmed* (1998–2006), *Ghost Hunters*, *MythBusters* (2003–), and *The Simpsons* (1989–). In 2012, a new television series, *Alcatraz*, premiered. More than a dozen video games feature Alcatraz as a major or minor part of the game.

### In Conclusion

The pervasiveness of Alcatraz in American popular culture speaks loudly to the pronounced impression that it has made and the popular allure of both crime and punishment. Alcatraz the island is itself a warning to all: its forlorn and rocky façade perfectly mirrors the barren lives that were lived in the prison it housed. Its ongoing appearances in multiple media formats keep its striking history alive and accessible to new generations around the globe.

***See also*** California; Harlem; Hopi Reservation; San Francisco, California; Soda Fountain

### Further Reading

Babyak, Jolene. 1988. *Eyewitness on Alcatraz, Life on the Rock as Told by the Guards, Families & Prisoners.* Berkeley, California: Ariel Vamp Press.

Fortunate Eagle, Adam. 2002. *Heart of the Rock: The Indian Invasion of Alcatraz.* Norman, Oklahoma: University of Oklahoma Press.

Esslinger, Michael. 2003. *Alcatraz: A Definitive History of the Penitentiary Years.* Carmel, California: Ocean View Publishing.

Fortunate Eagle, Adam. 2002. *Heart of the Rock: The Indian Invasion of Alcatraz.* Norman: University of Oklahoma Press.

Wellman, Gregory L. 2008. *History of Alcatraz Island, 1853–2008.* Charleston, South Carolina: Arcadia Publishing.

## Algonquin Hotel

The Algonquin Hotel is located in New York City. Founded in 1902, the hotel is a historic icon in the city, one that was designated a New York City landmark in 1987 and a literary landmark in 1996. The Algonquin is best known for its association with a literary crowd that frequented the hotel during the 1920s. The group, which became known as the Algonquin Round Table, went on to establish individual careers of distinction that impacted the nation. Guests and tourists are drawn to the hotel for its elegance and to remember the many legends who made the hotel their rendezvous point in the fabled past.

### Historical Perspectives

The Algonquin Hotel, a limestone and red brick structure, opened on November 22, 1902, on 59 West 44th Street. Within the vicinity were theaters and exclusive clubhouses, including the Yale and Harvard Clubs, the Bar Association, the New York Yacht Club, and the Century Association. Before the decade was over, Frank Case took ownership of the hotel. In addition to the usual high society crowd, the hotel attracted an eclectic group of artists and writers, both men and women. The group known as the Algonquin Round Table formed in 1919 and met for lunch daily in the hotel for about a decade.

The presence of this group at the Algonquin was on the surface peculiar, because many of them could not actually afford the high-priced meals. Thanks to Case, the group was treated well, provided with their own table and free food. The Algonquin was one of few places in the area where men and women could gather together. Most clubs were at the time restricted to men of a certain financial status, or who were affiliated with a particular institution, such as an Ivy League college. Some members, who met at the Algonquin during their lunch hour, worked at the nearby *Vanity Fair,* an upscale magazine publisher.

### The Round Table

Not including the guests who sometimes joined the gathering, the Algonquin Round Table comprised some 30 members, including novelists, playwrights, actors, editors, illustrators, and directors. Robert F. Benchley was an actor and the managing editor of *Vanity Fair.* Writer Dorothy Parker worked as a drama critic for *Vanity Fair* and the *New Yorker.* Her poems and short stories appeared in the magazines of the time. Marc Connelly, a playwright, won the Pulitzer Prize for the play *The Green Pastures.* Edna Ferber's work included the novel *Show Boat* (1926), which was adapted into a massively popular musical. Husband and wife Harold Ross and Jane Grant founded the still-running and popular *New Yorker* magazine. Drama critic Alexander Woollcott, who was both the original actor and the model for the central character in the famous play *The Man Who Came to Dinner,* was a founding member. Harpo Marx, another member, would become famous as a mute clownish character in an iconic series of movies in which he appeared with his siblings as the Marx Brothers.

The members of this versatile group met primarily to socialize, play cards, plan elaborate

#### A Writer in New York

Dorothy Parker was a poet, short-story writer, critic, satirist, and screenwriter.

She was born Dorothy Rothschild on August 22, 1893 in Long Branch, New Jersey and moved to New York City to pursue a writing career.

Parker's writing career took a positive turn beginning in the second decade of the 20th century. She sold her first poem to *Vanity Fair* in 1914. In 1915, she accepted an editorial position with *Vogue* and from 1917 to 1920, she worked for *Vanity Fair.* She married her first of three husbands, Edwin P. Parker, in 1917. In 1919, she joined several other writers for lunch at the Algonquin Hotel. The luncheon became a daily gathering of literary and artistic individuals famous for their wit and intellect, known as the Algonquin Round Table.

Parker enjoyed more achievements during the 1920s and 1930s. In 1922, she published her first short story, "Such a Pretty Little Picture." During the 1920s and 1930s, Parker wrote book reviews for *The New Yorker*. Her first collection of poems, *Enough Rope*, was published in 1926 and other collections followed. In 1929, Parker received the O. Henry Award for her short story, *Big Blonde* and-her collected fiction, *Laments for the Living,* was published in 1930.

During Parker's marriage to her second husband, Alan Campbell, they embarked on a collaborative screen writing career in Hollywood. With the exception of *A Star is Born* (1937), which received an Academy Award nomination, the films they worked on did not achieve critical acclaim. During Parker's lifetime, she embraced Communism and supported civil rights activism. At her death on June 6, 1967, she bequeathed her estate to Dr. Martin Luther King Jr.

practical jokes, and, on a few occasions, produce a creative work. In 1922, the gatherings resulted in at least two productions. "An anonymous entertainment by the Vicious Circle of the Hotel Algonquin," was performed by members of the group at the 49th Street Theatre. A revue titled "The 49 ers," was written by the group but performed by others at the Punch & Judy Theatre. By the mid-1920s, the group became so popular that curious individuals visited the Algonquin for lunch merely to witness the legendary gatherings.

### Contemporary Perspectives

Since the Algonquin Hotel's illustrious past, the hotel has undergone renovations and restorations to maintain its appeal to modern-day guests. However, many traditions remain, such as the Algonquin Cat that roams the lobby and the free *New Yorker* magazine (the famous magazine was founded by some of the members of the Round Table) that is issued to overnight guests. The tradition of keeping the so-called Algonquin Cat, which began in the 1930s, was the subject of the book, *Algonquin Cat: A Story,* written in 1980 by Val Schaffner and illustrated by Hilary Knight.

### Images in Popular Culture

Frank Case, the owner of the hotel, commemorated his experiences at the Algonquin in *Tales of a Wayward Inn* (1938), a memoir, *Do Not Disturb* (1940), and *Feeding the Lions: An Algonquin Cookbook* (1942). Other tributes to the Algonquin include the Academy Award winning documentary *The Ten-Year Lunch: The Wit and Legend of the Algonquin Round Table* (1987) and the film *Mrs. Parker and the Vicious Circle* (1994).

### For Visitors

Guests of the Algonquin Hotel enjoy richly furnished spaces and three different dining facilities, including the famous Round Table room. Within the vicinity are several world famous landmarks such as Times Square, the Statue of Liberty, and Chinatown.

***See also*** Academy Awards (Oscars); Chinatown; Great Lakes; Harvard University; New York, New York; Statue of Liberty; Times Square; Yale University

### Further Reading

*Algonquin Hotel.* http://www.algonquinhotel.com.

*Algonquin Round Table.* http://algonquinroundtable.org.

Fitzpatrick, Kevin C. 2013. *A Journey into Dorothy Parker's New York.* Berkeley, California: Roaring Forties Press.

Hirsh, Jeff. 2008. *Manhattan Hotels: 1880–1920.* Charleston, South Carolina: Arcadia Publishing.

## Ambassador Hotel

The Ambassador Hotel was once a glamorous establishment frequented by the stars and dignitaries of Los Angeles, California, located across the street from another popular venue, the Brown Derby Restaurant. The hotel catered to overnight guests and permanent residents, but its claim to fame was its Coconut Grove, a nightclub that showcased both up-and-coming and legendary performers. The hotel is known also as the place where Robert F. Kennedy, who was campaigning for president at the time, was assassinated on June 5, 1968. (His brother President John F. Kennedy had been assassinated on November 23, 1963.)

In the wake of such tragedy, the Ambassador Hotel and its nightclub carried on, but it soon declined as the vicinity was ravaged by crime and drugs. In 2006, the hotel was demolished. An elementary school, middle school, and high school have since been constructed on the site. But the memory of the hotel lives on as one of the many famous and historic locales in Hollywood.

### Historical Perspectives

In 1921, when the Ambassador opened, it was immediately famous for its Mediterranean and tropical themes, elegant rooms, lavish ballrooms, swimming pool, and the nightclub known as the Coconut Grove. The nightclub was decorated with kitschy artificial palm trees that had been used in the movie *The Sheik* (1921). The biggest names and the brightest stars in Hollywood were drawn to the nightclub.

During the early years, when silent pictures had not yet been replaced by the talkies, actors such as Charlie Chaplin, Howard Hughes, Gloria Swanson, and Norma Talmadge visited often. Chaplin was an English comic actor and filmmaker whose character, the "Tramp," brought him immense fame and fortune. His toothbrush mustache, thick eyebrows, derby hat, and bamboo cane were recognizable around the world. Hughes was a rich and powerful filmmaker. Swanson's career, which began in silent films, was later defined by *Sunset Boulevard* (1950), a film about a woman who is consumed by delusions of rekindled stardom. Talmadge was a prominent star in popular melodramas.

Such was the importance of the hotel to the Hollywood elite that on January 11, 1927, three dozen individuals representing the film industry met at the Ambassador Hotel to discuss the founding of the International Academy of Motion Picture Arts and Sciences. In 1929, this organization established the first Academy Award ceremony. The glamorous event, which continues to this day, was hosted at the Ambassador Hotel at least a dozen times.

Through the decades, the Ambassador Hotel and the Coconut Grove maintained their allure. Entertainers such as Frank Sinatra, Bing Crosby, Nat King Cole, and Dizzie Gillespie performed the velvety smooth or upbeat jazz tunes of the 1930s and 1940s to audiences packed with celebrities and industry heavyweights. Howard Hughes and Gloria Swanson were among the residents who lived for extended periods at the hotel. Several presidents also stayed there.

### Robert F. Kennedy's Assassination

Born on November 20, 1925, Robert F. Kennedy was the seventh of nine children belonging to the illustrious Kennedy family of Brookline, Massachusetts. Kennedy lived a formidable life. From 1961 to 1964, he served as the Attorney General of the United States. As attorney general, Robert campaigned against organized crime and supported the civil rights movement. On November 22, 1963, his brother, then-president John F. Kennedy, was assassinated.

After serving as senator from the state of New York from 1965 to 1968, Robert announced his intention to run for the presidency. The Ambassador Hotel was still perceived as one of the hottest venues in town when Robert Kennedy visited in 1968 to give his victory speech after winning the California primary. After the speech, he walked through the hotel kitchen. Shortly after midnight on June 5, 1968, gunfire rang out. Several others were hit, but Robert alone died from the injuries. The shooter was Sirhan Sirhan, a Palestinian immigrant. Kennedy was only 42.

### Decline

For a few more years, the Ambassador Hotel was popularly used by the public for proms, weddings, and parties. But urban blight—crime and drugs—overwhelmed the area during the 1970s. In 1988, the legendary hotel was closed to the public. Then owned by real-estate mogul Donald Trump, the Ambassador was used in scenes in several popular movies. Private parties hosted by the stars or industry giants were also held there.

### Images in Popular Culture

Glimpses of the elegant and unique hotel can be viewed in movies such as *The Fabulous Baker Boys* (1989), *Pretty Woman* (1990), and *The Mask* (1994). In *The Fabulous Baker Boys,* the first performance of Susie Diamond (Michelle Pfeiffer) is in the Ambassador Hotel lounge. The hotel interior is used for the scene when hotel manager Barney Thompson (Hector Elizondo) teaches Vivian Ward (Julia Roberts), a prostitute, how to use formal table place settings in *Pretty Woman.* The exterior of the Coco Bongo nightclub in the film *The Mask* was filmed at the Coconut Grove. Other films that used the hotel are *The Thirteenth Floor* (1999), where the characters go back in time to 1937; the *Aviator* (2004), a film about Howard Hughes; and *Bobby* (2006), a film about Robert F. Kennedy. Some scenes from *Bobby* were shot right before the hotel was razed. A documentary, *After 68,* which is currently in progress, will explore the hotel's storied existence, decline, and eventual controversial demolition.

### Demolition

Despite protests from many celebrities, the historic Ambassador Hotel was demolished in 2006 to build a campus that comprised an elementary school, middle school, and high school. Some remnants of the hotel—or its memory—remain, including a wall from the Coconut Grove incorporated into the campus, a reconstructed coffee shop, and parts of the pantry where Kennedy was assassinated.

***See also*** Academy Awards (Oscars); Brown Derby Restaurant; California; Hollywood; Los Angeles, California

### Further Reading

*After 68*. http://after68.com.

Burk, Margaret Tante. 1980. *Are the Stars out Tonight?: The Story of the Famous Ambassador and Coconut Grove, "Hollywood's Hotel."* Los Angeles: Round Table West.

Clarke, Thurston. 2008. *The Last Campaign: Robert F. Kennedy and 82 Days That Inspired America.* New York: Henry Holt.

## American Diner

An American Diner is a popular type of restaurant often associated with the period of the 1950s. Straight from the archives of vintage Americana, the diner has been an intrinsic part of mainstream American life. To some, it is considered a vanishing icon. In some states, such as New Jersey, New York, Connecticut, Massachusetts, and Florida, diners are still a part of mainstream life. To others, the emergence of both new and renovated diners and their influence on other restaurants and eateries is proof that diners are once again on the upswing.

These days, American diners may take the form of drive-ins, waffle houses, roadside eateries, or local hole-in-the wall restaurants. However, their traditional form embodies the diners of the 1950s and 1960s, which were the golden years of the American diner. Classic diners are narrow, elongated, prefabricated structures, embellished with shiny stainless steel, neon signs, padded bar stools, a prominent long counter, and terrazzo floors. The exteriors of many diners are garnished with quirky signs and larger-than-life statues of mascots, like the famous doggie that stands outside the Doggie Diner. Low or nonfat foods are rarely served at traditional diners. Comfort food like greasy burgers, French fries, and an assortment of other grilled and fried foods and sugary drinks, like flavored cola beverages and ice cream shakes, are common fare. Traditional workers at diners included short-order cooks or chefs donned in white aprons, white hats, and white jackets, and the occasional bow tie; busboys; and servers. Women servers commonly wore short uniform dresses in pastel tones with wide collars, aprons, and small matching hats.

This classic image of the American diner was a fixture in everyday American life. Diners appeal to mainstream appetites, providing affordable and tasty all-American meals, and a casual space to gather with friends, dates, and family. These alcohol-free establishments were especially preferred for family dining. Social customs dictate that patrons do not have to dress as formerly as they do in more expensive restaurants. Before the advent of fast-food restaurants and other modern-day venues such as shopping malls, skateparks, and cafes, there were few other options for young Americans, in particular, to socialize. However, the American diner is much more than the stylized teen hangout; it represents a colorful mishmash of American life and culture that harkens to a simpler time of home style cooking and of one-on-one interaction with family and friends with no distractions and no rush.

Checkered countertops and red stools accentuate the 50s-era feel of Lucille's Roadhouse along the historic Route 66 in Oklahoma. (U.S. Department of Transportation)

### Historical Perspectives

The American diner was born on the East Coast. In Providence, Rhode Island, in 1872, Walter Scott converted his horse-pulled wagon into an eatery. From this wagon, Scott prepared and sold food. His clientele were primarily men—male laborers and members of men's clubs. The lunch wagon industry took off, resulting in the commercial production of lunch wagons beginning in 1887. Among the major producers of lunch wagons were Thomas Buckley, Philip Duprey, Irving Stoddard, and Jerry O'Mahony. This innovation led to railway dining cars being used as eateries. By the 1920s, the term "diner" was in common usage.

Between the Great Depression and the 1960s, the American diner grew into a ubiquitous presence on the nation's highways, main streets, and small towns. After the crash of the American stock market in 1929, many Americans plunged into miserable poverty. The diner, however, thrived despite countrywide business closures and job losses. Scholars suggest that diners remained untouched because food was low cost, and the desire for good, old-fashioned meals and the society of friends and strangers was as strong as ever. During these years, the look of the classic diner took on its familiar shape, and the number of diners increased in most regions across the nation. In the aftermath of World War II (1941–1945), diners spread into fast-growing suburbs. This growth continued for the next two decades.

After the 1960s, the popularity of diners waned. This was due in part to the advent of fast-food restaurants, like McDonald's, which served hamburgers, fries, and shakes with faster service for less money. Frozen meals, like TV dinners, also took a share of the market; they could be heated and eaten at home and were an easy-to-prepare alternative to going out for a meal. These new trends in the American food industry changed American's eating habits and culture. Family gatherings at meal times were increasingly replaced by quick meals eaten in solitude or in front of a television screen. As American life became increasingly busy, the slow-paced, sit-down, social meal came to be considered less important.

Though many diners survived the lean years, the interest of the general public was renewed with the help of popular culture. Works of art, films, and television series sparked the resurgence of American diners, awakening nostalgia for a more simple way of living and highlighting the great charm many diners had always had. Although the culture of diners has changed since their golden years, diners still occupy an important place in American life and popular culture.

### Everyday Life and Images in Popular Culture

Wherever there are diners—in cities, along highways, or nestled in the suburbs—a unique culture can be found. Diners, though similar in layout, each have their own look and appeal. The first diners, like the lunch wagons, were not considered respectable places for women or children. Diners have never had many frills, and in the early days they tended to be grungy places that, since many were open 24 hours, attracted an assortment of local characters and ne'er-do-wells.

Though the frills never came, by the 1950s, the diner had become a place for families and teens, a well-established symbol of American prosperity, innocence, and mirth. The image of an adolescent couple sipping a cherry Coke from two straws, and the young boy sitting on a stool in a diner portrayed in Norman Rockwell's idealistic painting, *The Runaway* (1958), are reflections of these halcyon days. Middle-class American teens in the film *American Graffiti* (1973) and in the iconic television series *Happy Days* (1974–1984) portray the innocuous troubles and innocent fun of teenage life in the 1950s. Critical scenes take place at local teen hangouts: Arnold's Drive-In in *Happy Days* or Mel's Drive-In in *American Graffiti.* The drive-ins in these fictional accounts underscore the fact that these such eateries were the natural habitat for American youth coming of age and seeking social interaction with friends, the opposite sex, and the occasional nemesis.

These idealized popular images conjure nostalgia for some Americans, but for others, such as African Americans, they belie the reality of American life, which was that such experiences and apparent innocence were for whites only. In many places in the North and especially in the South, discriminatory laws prohibited blacks and whites from using the same facilities well into the 20th century. There remains today a wide gap between the nostalgia that parts of white America have for the 1950s, and the rampant prejudice and economic barriers experienced by African Americans.

In modern times, diners reflect the diversity of the nation. In major cities, for example, the culture in diners often changes from block to block, according to the ethnic makeup of the neighborhood, or by region. Jewish communities, for example, serve Jewish specialties, like matzo ball soup, along with a general American menu. Greek diners offer gyros; diners in the South sell grits, and, in Maine, fresh seafood is sure to be on the menu. Banter in these establishments may be peppered with foreign languages or regional slang and accents. In the South, it is customary for waitresses to refer to patrons as "sugar" or "honey," terms that elsewhere are restricted to family and loved ones. Such regional and ethnic diners are part of the broader regional food culture differences and communities within the larger American society.

Another unique diner environment exists along the nation's highways. Roadside diners attract truckers, travelers, motorcyclists traveling in caravans, vacationers, and other denizens of the highway, offering traditional diner food on a stretch of unfamiliar highway. In places where human populations are sparse, interaction between patrons is limited. Patrons keep to themselves, except for casual conversations that occur with the servers.

Curiously, these roadside diners, though devoid of social interaction, nonetheless frequently appear in the popular media. A common plot element in films is the stereotypical brutish American, sometimes a trucker or motorcyclist, who clashes with the naïve traveler in a diner. Pee-wee in *Pee-Wee's Big Adventure* (1985) is chased by the boyfriend of a waitress he befriends at the famous Wheel Inn Restaurant in the shadow of the Cabazon Dinosaurs in Cabazon, California. After Superman relinquishes his super powers in *Superman II* (1980), he is beaten up by a truck driver in a diner. Of course he returns to the diner in a subsequent scene and beats up the same truck driver. In *Paul* (2011), two British tourists take a road drip to see American extraterrestrial sites. While at a diner in Roswell, New Mexico, they clash with two stereotypical American caricatures.

In the modern city or suburbs, patrons don't generally go to diners to listen to music on the jukebox (if there is one). Friends and family go to enjoy one another's company over a meal that is not on the list of recommended health-conscious foods. Diners are considered places where meals are savored slowly and conversations linger beyond the obligatory piece of pie or the last drop of coffee or cup of Joe.

Several American television shows have taken advantage of the diner as a convenient setting for social interactions. *Seinfeld* (1989–1998) and *Sex in the City* (1998–2004) featured recurring scenes set in the local diner. Diners are portrayed as male-bonding spheres in television series such as *Men of a Certain Age* (2009–2011) and in films like *Diner* (1982). *Alice* (1976–1985) and *Roseanne* (1988–1997), depict surly, wisecracking servers in working-class diners (in contrast to another server stereotype, the syrupy-sweet diner waitress in *Paul*). In such environments, dry humor and companionship, not the second-rate food, are the focal points for the hardworking patrons.

Diners can also be used to show the lonely side of the human experience. The Edward Hopper painting *Nighthawks* (1942) is considered a quintessential representation of the American diner in the city. The painting depicts the exterior of a diner late at night. Through the windows, artificial light illuminates three lonely patrons and an attendant. The painting symbolizes alienation, isolation, and loneliness—themes that are also used to describe American city life. In certain film and television genres, diners are depicted as gritty and bleak, as in the *Nighthawks* painting. Diners are frequently used as settings in police or detective shows and films. Such diners are frequently cast in dark lighting, and the servers appear impersonal and detached. At some unspecified hour in the middle of the night or before dawn, patrons eat and drink in sullen silence. Against this backdrop, the main characters, cops or detectives, discuss work in serious tones. This image is a realistic one for metropolises like New York City.

Another unconventional depiction of diners is presented in horror films. Horror genre directors will often play against common, generally accepted ideas and present those ideas in an entirely unexpected way. For example, in *The Blob* (1958), an alien in the form of jellylike substance terrorizes a town. The blob chases two teens into a diner. The diner—a symbol of security, fun, and comfort—becomes a place of fear and anxiety. In the horror science fiction film, *Legion* (2010), the director, Scott Stewart, turns the plot topsy-turvy when a seemingly harmless, elderly woman transforms into a demon in a diner in front of the patrons. In ensuing hours, the patrons hide out in the diner as they are attacked by malevolent forces.

## In Conclusion

The American diner has many faces in both society and popular culture; it can be bright and lively, warm and comforting, or cold and impersonal, grim or frightening. It's a purely American invention that has evolved as the times demand. At the heart of the diner is the home-style American food served in a no-frills, casual setting, and unpretentious appeal that attracts Americans from all walks of life.

*See also* Cabazon Dinosaurs; California; Main Street; McDonald's; New York, New York; Skateparks; Suburbia

**Further Reading**

*American Diner Museum*. http://www.americandinermuseum.org/site/.

Eastman, Michael, Gass, William H., and Brinkley, Douglas. 2008. *Vanishing America: The End of Main Street Diners, Drive-Ins, Donut Shops, and Other Every Day Monuments*. New York: Rizzoli.

Fieri, Guy, and Volkwein, Ann. 2008. *Diners, Drive-Ins and Dives: An All-American Road Trip . . . with Recipes!* New York: HarperCollins.

Gutman, Richard J. S. 2000. *American Diner: Then and Now*. Baltimore: The John Hopkins University Press.

Kittel, Gerd, and Snow, Richard F. 1998. *Diners: People and Places*. New York: Thames and Hudson.

McKeon, Elizabeth, and Everett, Linda. 2003. *The American Diner Cookbook*. Nashville: Cumberland House Publishing.

Witzel, Michael Karl. 1999. *The American Diner*. Osceola, Wisconsin: MBI Publishing.

## American Museum of Natural History

The American Museum of Natural History (AMNH) is one of the nation's premier museums. Located in the Upper West Side of Manhattan in New York City, the Museum looms large in size as well as in the numbers of its visitors. The Museum comprises 4 floors and 25 interconnected buildings and holds over 30 million specimens and cultural artifacts. The enormous space contains numerous halls, such as fossil halls, mammal halls, and culture halls, and other popular displays and dioramas. The Rose Center for Earth and Space features space-themed exhibits. The Museum also contains classrooms, auditoriums, working areas for scientists, and a vast natural history library. Dedicated to advancing scientific and cultural knowledge through original research and making this research accessible to the general public, the Museum of Natural History plays an important role in American society. Importance, however, is one thing; popularity is another. The Museum's popularity, at least with mainstream America, was not by any means immediate.

At nearly 150 years old, the Natural History Museum has managed to endure the passage of time, as well as win the hearts of many in the American public. Historically, this was no facile task, given the fact that institutions linked to the arts, humanities, and sciences can be considered elitist, highbrow, academic, and dull or unexciting. The Natural History Museum, however, has seen its mainstream popularity slowly climb to its current status as one of the country's most distinctive and beloved museums. For it is in one place that the Museum houses both the Darwinian story of our origins and a history of the North American continent's early inhabitants, as well as the amazing assortment of animals they share the land with. The appeal of discovering our American roots is nowhere greater.

### Historical Perspectives

The AMNH was founded and supported by individuals of influence, status, and considerable wealth. Naturalist Dr. Albert S. Bickmore spearheaded a campaign in the 19th century to establish the Museum. With the backing of powerful and wealthy individuals such as J. Pierpont Morgan, Andrew H. Green, Theodore Roosevelt Sr., and William E. Dodge Jr., Bickmore's dream became reality in 1869.

The first exhibits were displayed in the Central Park Arsenal. In 1874, U.S. president Ulysses Grant laid the cornerstone for the Museum's first building during a special ceremony. The Museum flourished in subsequent decades, leading the way in many fields by sponsoring pivotal field expeditions that filled the ever-expanding space with artifacts and treasures that expanded the existing knowledge base of insights into human and animal life, the study of rocks and minerals, and the cultural diversity on planet Earth. The Museum was soon considered an eminent institution in exclusive circles, contributing greatly to the prestige of scientists like Roy Chapman Andrews, who helped inspire the creation of Indiana Jones, the iconic fictional character in a franchise that included four movies (1981, 1984, 1989, 2008), a television series (1992–1996), video games, and a theme park attraction at Disneyland. The illustrious career of Margaret Meade, one of the most well-known anthropologists in her field, included time spent as a curator at the Museum between 1946 and 1969.

### Class and Racial Patterns in Society

When the AMNH was founded, museums like it were commonly associated with a particular sect of American society. This demographic went by many names—high society, the upper crest, and the well-to-do. These men and women, usually college educated and of European descent, comprised the regular visitors at such museums. Other highbrow activities included going to concert halls to listen to the symphony or an opera, or to theaters to watch a play or ballet. These activities symbolized economic standing and prestige and implied cultural and intellectual accomplishments.

The activities and popular venues for the rich were not, in general, the same for the working classes and other populations. There were many reasons for this—limited economic means and leisure time kept the working class away from so-called highbrow events. Plus, the working and upper classes had different entertainment preferences and exhibited different behavioral responses at public institutions and places of entertainment. The nation's predominant class—the working class—indulged in activities like going to baseball games or to the movies. Museums that were popular with this class were of the variety created by P.T. Barnum, showcasing humans with assorted physical deformities and abnormalities, or sensational and outlandish abilities—not the sciences.

Moreover, racial and ethnic groups did not tend to mingle with the wealthy for many of the same reasons as the working class. (Racial and ethnic groups historically and disproportionately comprise the working classes and poor in America.) Subcultures within the country were frequently excluded, openly or not, from mainstream activities and venues, or they established their own entertainment places and institutions to reflect their culture and traditions.

### Mass Popularization

The gulf that separated the rich and the working class, European descendants and other ethnic groups as it pertains to popular activities and forms of entertainment is not now as expansive as it was in the past. These days, the AMNH, for example, receives a staggering 4 million visitors each year. Mass appeal has been a necessary component to Museum's long success. As funding from rich families and academic resources dwindled, simple popularity and entrance fees has helped sustain the economic survival of the Museum.

Various factors helped transform the Museum into the inclusive, broadly appealing, and popular institution it is today. Many of the nation's institutions were influenced by social movements, like the civil rights movement of the 1960s, which challenged racial intolerance and discrimination and promoted integration of public facilities and transportation. Although New York City did not suffer the extreme discriminatory practices typical of the South, the civil rights movement underscored the importance of racial inclusion everywhere. Efforts, made from the 1970s through the 1990s, toward supporting multiculturalism and addressing the needs of the disadvantaged in society, also had an impact on public institutions. In the 1990s, many museums reinvented themselves by promoting education for all. Today, the Museum implements educational and outreach programs for youth and adults, emphasizing the importance of reaching broad audiences. Special programs, such as free after-school programs for high school students and the Moveable Museum program, reach students with limited access to opportunity and the Museum. The Museum shows its support for diversity in such special programs as the Museum's Global Weekends, which feature different multicultural groups. The Museum also hosts programs traditionally celebrated by other cultures. An annual Kwanzaa festival, an African American celebration that takes place between Christmas and the New Year's holiday, a Living in America series, and Black History Month programs give exposure to cultures within America that were historically overlooked. To increase its accessibility to visitors, the Museum also permits guests who come to the museum to pay less than the suggested admission price.

### For Visitors

And a visit to the Museum is worth the price of admission, for the sheer magnitude of its exhibits, from the near-complete skeleton of a *Tyrannosaurus rex* to the model of the Blue Whale (famously referenced in the renowned musical comedy, *Hello Dolly*). Visitors discover sights not to be found elsewhere in the Museum's 45 exhibition halls, the Rose Center for Earth and Space (which houses the immensely popular Hayden Planetarium), and the interactive Discovery Room. Visitors have access to a research library, classrooms, shops, a food court, and cafes.

The exhibits defy the image of the naturalist, who collects butterflies and is fascinated by turtles. The halls feature the largest collection of dinosaur fossils in the world, displayed against a to-scale timeline. The mammal halls include a wintry scene featuring a pack of running wolves, Grizzly bears, and otters—all displayed in depictions of their natural habitats, often including a recent kill. Meteorites, gems, fish, and fowl—it's all there. One of the most famous features of the Museum are its many dioramas illustrating cultures such as Northwest Coast Indians, Eastern Woodlands and Plains Indians, and peoples from Africa, Asia, Central and South America, and the Pacific. The halls include artifacts, specimens, multimedia presentations, and detailed signage.

The displays are often enormous. In addition to the *Tyrannosaurus rex* and the Blue Whale, at the entrance to the Theodore Roosevelt Rotunda, there is a skeletal mount of a towering dinosaur known as *Barosauru*. In the Scales of the Universe at the Rose Center, visitors view large models of planets. In addition to the huge displays that have made the Museum famous for a century, contemporary issues, such as environmentalism, are incorporated into the exhibits, presented using the latest modern technologies.

### In Conclusion

Throughout most of the 20th century, scholars, academics, and aristocrats defined the Museum's image. Today, the AMNH has become a popular institution that appeals to the mainstream public.

***See also*** Central Park; Disneyland; New York, New York

### Further Reading

*American Museum of Natural History*. http://www.amnh.org.

Quinn, Stephen C. 2006. *Windows on Nature: The Great Habitat Dioramas of the American Museum of Natural History*. New York: Harry N. Abrams.

Sherman, Daniel, and Irit Rogoff, eds. 1994. *Museum Culture: Histories, Discourses, Spectacles*. Minneapolis: University of Minnesota.

Stern, Robert A. M., Gilmartin, Gregory F., and Mellins, Thomas. 2009. *New York 1930: Architecture and Urbanism between the Two World Wars*. New York: Rizzoli.

Wallace, Joseph E. 2001. *A Gathering of Wonders: Behind the Scenes at the American Museum of Natural History*. New York: St. Martin's Press.

## Amish Country

Amish country refers to areas in the United States populated by a religious sect known as the Amish. The national imagination associates Amish country with taking a step back in time into a world where people dressed in bygone fashions live simple lives on well-kept farms. In modern American society, where cars, cell phones, fashion diversity, processed foods, and fast living are the norm, Amish country presents an unusual sight. Amish communities, whether in Ohio, Pennsylvania, or Indiana, where populations are highest, are characteristically rural, unhurried, and sans the day-to-day noise

Annie Miller, left, walks with her husband Aaron Miller, of Fort Plain, N.Y., as they oversee construction of an electric fence at M&K Dairy Farm in Lebanon, Conn., September 2, 2013. (AP Photo/Tim Martin, The Day)

of modern living. Tranquil farmlands studded with prosperous-looking barns and farm houses, horse-drawn buggies, men in hats and long beards, and women in caps and long dark dresses are the images conjured by Amish country. Visitors will find no musical instruments, no electricity, no fast-food restaurants, or police stations; none of the trappings common in the cities, suburbia—or even the small towns in America.

The other worldliness of the Amish and their lifestyle fascinates most Americans. But that is only one of many attributes that have made Amish country a popular tourist draw. Their handmade crafts, quilts, and furniture, farm-raised produce, and culinary specialties have garnered the esteem of the American public for decades. Another draw is that Amish country epitomizes back-to-nature simple living and renders a sense of being back in time.

### Historical Perspectives

The Amish trace their lineage back to the Anabaptists, a Protestant sect that emerged during the 16th century in Europe. Other descendants of the Anabaptists are the Mennonites, the Hutterian Brethren, and the Swiss Brethren. The Anabaptists arose in opposition to some of the doctrine promoted by Roman Catholicism, the dominant religion of the day. A major issue for the Anabaptists was that they rejected infant baptism. A common practice among this religious group was to rebaptize adults who had been baptized as infants or young children. Anabaptists and other oppositional religious groups were considered radical and were frequently oppressed, imprisoned, and persecuted. At the time, religious persecution, as well as religious wars, was rampant in Europe. But the quest for religious freedom could not be quelled. New religious sects, such as the Amish, surfaced despite widespread turmoil.

The Amish church was founded by and named after Jacob Ammann in 1693. Ammann broke away from the Swiss Mennonites over several issues. Ammann believed that the church should practice excommunication and social avoidance of individuals who violated religious ordinances. He also stressed the practice of wearing simple clothes and advocated the creation of rules for acceptable grooming styles and attire. The Amish today continue to abide by most of these directives, as well as the Schleitheim Articles, adopted by the Swiss Brethren in 1527. These articles outline guidelines endorsing adult baptism, banning offenders of their laws, establishing rules for communion, advocating separation from the world, determining church leadership, and rejecting worldly judgment, violence, and oaths.

Prompted by the desire to live and worship freely and safely, the Amish, like other Anabaptists, migrated to other countries. It was in America that the Amish endured and flourished, arriving in pronounced waves from 1727 to 1770 and from 1815 to 1860. The Amish came from parts of France, Switzerland, and Germany and established settlements across the nation. Their culture and life were easily sustained in the spacious and remote environments that America offered. Nearly 300 years later, the Amish have resisted assimilation, through rejection of and detachment from worldly affairs and materialism and adherence to religious beliefs and rules and traditional ways of living that have remained largely intact through the centuries.

### Cultural Distinctions

Amish country today appears much the same as when it was first developed; however, the number of settlements and the total population of the Amish have grown considerably. Before 1900, the Amish were established in roughly nine states. Today, the Amish reside in more than 20 states. Higher concentrations of Amish reside in the mid to northern half of the East Coast. But settlements can also be found in Canada and in the South, in such states as Tennessee, Oklahoma, Texas, Florida, North Carolina, and Virginia. Today, their total population has swelled to 150,000.

Amish country in any region has distinct features. Settlements are divided by church districts. These districts often appear as pictures from scenic postcards or paintings of rural landscapes. Sprawling pastures, rolling hills, and charming ponds and streams are dotted with simple, rustic homes, barns, carriages, and stores. An industrious people, the Amish make most of what they need, including tools, equipment, shoes, clothes, and household items. They build their own homes and schools. There is nothing elaborate about the architecture of these buildings. Glaringly absent are skyscrapers, retail stores, malls, gas stations, taverns, and other contemporary structures and buildings. This pristine environment sustains the life of the Amish people.

At the center of life and culture in Amish country are faith, family, church community, societal roles, and regulations known as the Ordnung. Individual households may include grandparents, parents, and an average of seven children. Everyone who lives in Amish country attends church. However, church membership comes only through baptism, which usually occurs between the ages of 16 and 25. The Amish place great importance on meaningful relationships within the immediate family as well as with relatives and church members—essentially the entire Amish community.

Relationships among the Amish are solidified and nurtured through informal and formal interactions and shared culture. In Amish country, interactions are characteristically unobstructed by distractions. Telephones, TV, handheld video games, the Internet, and other forms of modern technology which define modern-day human interactions have no place in Amish settlements. Families eat together for meals. Parents spend time with children, instructing them on how to live the Amish way and work productively in the home and in the community. Communities, relatives or not, gather for informal visits or formal or organized gatherings such as church worship, barn raisings, weddings, and funerals. Language also binds the Amish people, who speak a German dialect among themselves.

Within this social world, roles play heavily in Amish society. Gender roles, for example, follow traditional lines. Men perform work such as laboring in the fields and woodworking. Women, on the other hand, perform duties such as preserving and preparing food, making rugs and quilts, sewing, gardening, and caring for children. Children attend Amish schools built by the Amish. With the

**Amish Plainness**

Plainness is a concept that permeates the Amish way of life and belief system. To the Amish, plainness is a visible manifestation of their beliefs, a symbol of virtue, and a way of life that the Amish believe helps cultivate character and represents the community's cohesiveness.

The Ordnung, a series of rules that the Amish live by, reinforces the concept of plainness. For example, the Ordnung delineates rules for permissible clothing, including style and color, hairstyles, and buggy design. Such styles establish uniformity throughout the community, as well as ensure that the styles are primarily functional. To the Amish, plainness is tantamount to modesty, a virtue that is encouraged among the community. Plainness also helps prevent envy and arrogance, as well as self-expression, whichis perceived as antagonistic to the cohesion of the community.

Thus, plainness is a virtue that is evident in every part of life in the Amish community, not just clothing and hairstyles. Songs, unaccompanied by musical instruments and harmony, are simple and straight forward. Typically, the songs are sung in German during worship and in English outside of church. Architecture within the community, including church buildings, barns, and homes, exudes plainness. Furnishings within the home are plain and functional. Fabrics used in clothing or furnishing are usually dark and plain.

Some Amish communities have veered away from such stringent rules. For example, many communities permit women to make quilts. Initially, quilt making was forbidden because of its association with worldly activities. However, the first quilts that were made by Amish women only came in black, brown, or blue. In contemporary times, though still plain, Amish quilts feature more colors and incorporate decorative embellishments such as embroidery.

exception of trade schools in some Amish communities, Amish schools end at the eighth grade, so the children can assist with family work.

### Rumspringa

Amish education helps prepare children to fulfill their roles in society; however, in the adolescent years, some Amish youth experience what is referred to as *rumspringa.* Rumspringa, which spans the adolescent years leading to the decision to be baptized or to leave the community, is defined differently in Amish settlements across the nation. Generally, adults permit a lessening of the rigidity of rules and expectations for adolescents during this period. Some youth, male and female, may, for example, experiment with cigarettes, cars, and mainstream fashion or travel outside their settlement. Most adolescents choose to be baptized and adhere to the Ordnung.

### Ordnung

The Ordnung, like rumspringa, varies by settlement. Divisions among the Amish are obvious to anyone who may see an individual in one settlement using a cell phone or driving a car, while in another settlement, individuals are forbidden from using such technology and modes of transportation. Divisions in the Amish church are generally denoted by "orders." Of the estimated eight orders, the Old Order Amish are the largest, and the Swartzentruber Amish are the most conservative.

The Ordnung that the Amish follow covers a wide range of areas in everyday life. Generally, in most orders, technology is outlawed. So are electricity, automobiles, and a number of other tools of modernity. Power is generated through such means as horse power, human power, windmills, and streams. Clothing and the style in which clothes are worn are issues that vary by Amish order. Commonly, men wear dark coats, round-brimmed hats, suspenders, and trousers. Married men grow long beards without mustaches. Women and young girls wear long dresses and head caps. Married women wear dresses with matching aprons and head caps affixed with straight pins (only girls can use buttons). Young girls wear hairstyles parted in the middle and wound tightly in a bun. Clothes, accessories, and grooming styles not only denote gender and status in Amish society, they represent cultural solidarity and underscore their separateness from the world and their rejection of mainstream and popular culture symbols and objects.

### Images in Popular Culture

Despite the fact that the Amish withdraw themselves from mainstream society, they have become more and more integrated into American popular culture. *Plain & Fancy,* a musical that opened in 1955 on Broadway, was among the first public depictions of this American subculture. The Amish have appeared periodically in made-for-television movies and episodes on popular television shows, such as *Louis & Clark: The Adventures of Superman* (1993–1997), *As the World Turns* (1956–2010), *MacGyver* (1985–1992), *Murder, She Wrote* (1984–1996), *Picket Fences* (1992–1996), *Judging Amy* (1999–2005), *Cold Case* (2003–2010), and *Bones* (2005–). One of the most influential films to portray the Amish in a serious drama is *Witness* (1985). This film was followed by two film comedies: *Kingpin* (1996) and *For Richer or Poorer* (1997). Among the reality shows, films, and documentaries that cover the subject of *rumspringa* are the documentary *Devil's Playground* (2002), the film *Sex Drive* (2008), and the reality show *Amish in the City* (2004).

The Amish and their themes can also be found in music videos, on the Internet, and in literature. In 1996, "Weird Al" Yankovic released a song and video, *Amish Paradise,* which parodies the Amish. The Internet is host to many sites, academic and otherwise, about the Amish. Sites such as Lehmans.com,

Lancasterpa.com, Amishshop.com, Leerburg.com, and Amishdirectfurniture.com sell Amish-made products, usually through an intermediary, since the Ordnung bans Internet usage. YouTube videos feature Amish singing and preaching. Amish literature for adults and children has a devoted audience. Authors such as Beverly Lewis, who grew up in Pennsylvania Amish country, have made a successful career writing books about the Amish. Lewis has authored more than 70 books, including several popular series.

### Issues

Popular books, television series, films, Internet sites, and tourism have brought Amish society out of obscurity and exposed them to wide audiences—but not without consequences. Images of the Amish in films and on television are not all positive. One-dimensional characterizations and disparaging parodies are common. Uncensored YouTube videos can be controversial, as well. One video shows a family allegedly questioning their participation in Amish Life. In another video, an Amish woman invites a tourist to take a picture of her for money. These images sharply contrast with the normal pattern of Amish reticence and meekness. Divulging private thoughts for the world to see is a common practice on American television talk shows, in magazines, in Internet blogs, and on social networking sites, but not in Amish culture. Picture-taking of the Amish by strangers is generally considered impolite, and to have a picture taken by a stranger for money raises fundamental questions regarding the exploitation of the Amish culture.

Exploitation is one of many issues the Amish face. The popularity of the Amish themselves raises issues when, for example, non-Amish businesses capitalize on the Amish name to create and profit from imitation products. Tourism is sometimes perceived as undermining the sacredness of the Amish way of life, when settlements are marketed as tourist attractions. And when tourists gawk and take unwanted pictures, the Amish are made to feel like exotic specimens in a museum, spectacles for tourist entertainment.

Another issue that arises from time to time is when outsiders desire to join Amish settlements. The Amish carefully guard their settlements and do not pursue new converts from outside their world. Still, outsiders covet and, at times, excessively romanticize Amish country. It is easy for outsiders to be captivated by a world so vastly different from their own, an environment that does not swarm with clutter, noise, technology, and crime. Life is deemed better, because it is everything the contemporary world is not—simple, unhurried, wholesome, uncomplicated, safe, and rich with human relationships. It is the Amish who remind the world that Amish country is not for the faint of heart; that their religion and life require diligence, hardiness, commitment, and belief. They contend that the general concepts that they abide by can be embraced and practiced in any environment, whether in the vortex of a fast-paced city or in a new housing development in a rural town.

### For Visitors

Though the Amish do not seek outsiders or the world outside their borders, visitors tend to seek them out. To a certain extent, the Amish are accustomed to visitors. Residents of neighboring communities have long visited Amish settlements to purchase handmade goods and well-crafted items not found anywhere else, or stop at roadside markets to buy vegetables and fruit.

Today, Amish country is often marketed as a tourist destination on maps and visitors' guides, and is a popular attraction. Tourists are enticed by the charm and sense of history of the place. They go to see life as it was in the past, to visit Amish shops, to take a horse and buggy ride through the area, to see the farm houses, windmills, and horse-drawn tractors, to go to restaurants, and stay at Amish bed and breakfasts. Visitors also go to take a break from contemporary life, hoping to be invigorated by a new, out-of-doors environment. While in Amish country, tourists observe the day-to-day life of the Amish as they labor on their farms, visit Amish-operated stores, and travel down long and tranquil roads in their carriages.

***See also*** Barns; Broadway; Off-Grid; Suburbia; Texas

### Further Reading

Hostetler, John A. 1993. *Amish Society*. Baltimore: The Johns Hopkins University Press.

Igou, Bard. 1999. *The Amish in Their Own Words*. Harrisonburg, Virginia: Herald Press.

Scott, Stephen, and Pellman, Kenneth. 1999. *Living without Electricity*. Intercourse, Pennsylvania: Good Books.

Shachtman, Tom. 2006. *Rumspringa: To Be or Not to Be Amish*. New York: North Point Press.

Umble, Diane Zimmerman, and Weaver-Zercher, David L., eds. 2008. *The Amish and the Media*. Baltimore: The Johns Hopkins University Press.

## Antietam Battlefield

The Antietam Battlefield is the infamous location of the most well-known battle of the American Civil War (1861–1865), a tumultuous conflict between the Union (northern states) and the Confederates (southern states). The Battle of Antietam took place on September 17, 1862, in Antietam, Maryland, and is recognized as the bloodiest day of fighting (23,000 casualties) in the nation's history and one of the first to be recorded for posterity by the new art of photography. Five days later, thanks to the fact that the Union forces held the line, President Abraham Lincoln was able to announce the Preliminary Emancipation Proclamation, declaring that slavery in the nation was abolished. Though the vast majority of the slaves would not see freedom until the end of the war, the pronouncement marked a watershed moment in the war. Thus the name Antietam has come down through history as a symbol of both emancipation and a warning of the terrible cost of war.

Americans recognized early on that what had happened at Antietam was something that should never be forgotten. The soldiers and the cause they died for—on both sides, right and wrong—must be memorialized as a reminder of the horrors of war and the importance of freedom for all. By the 1890s, work on this project was underway. In 1933, the site became a part of the National Park Service. Today, the park, known as the Antietam Battlefield, includes 3,300 acres and offers guided tours so that visitors can trace the timeline and route of the epic battle, experiencing for themselves the horror or one day of devastation. Hundreds of thousands of visitors come to the battlefield each year, a testament to the widespread desire for people to act as witness to both the tragedy and the triumph of the Civil War.

### Historical Perspectives

Following the succession of southern states from the Union, the Civil War was launched, violently pitting the two regions of the young nation against one another. On one side were the Confederate armies, desperate to preserve the agriculture and slave-based system in the South. On the other side were the Union armies, representing the interests in the North, an industrial-based region that had long ago done away with slavery. The battles of the Civil War were notoriously brutal, resulting in the utter devastation of the land and unparalleled loss of life. Antietam was one of the first battles of the war, and it left a chilling impression upon the American people.

Legendary Confederate General Robert E. Lee initiated the battle at Antietam, Maryland (known as Sharpsburg to southerners). Emboldened by recent victories, Lee wanted to drive the war to northern soil for the first time. On the early morning of September 17, 1862, some 85,000 Union solders, led by

General George B. McClellan, mobilized in Antietam to meet Lee's Confederate troops, consisting of some 40,000 soldiers. Fighting occurred in places known as the East Woods, the West Woods, the Sunken Road, in a cornfield, and over a bridge. The tide of the battle vacillated to and fro, resulting in no definitive victory on either side. As night fell after 12 hours of bloodshed, the fighting stopped, leaving 12,410 dead on the Union side and 10,700 dead on the Confederate side. On the following day, Lee and his troops returned to Virginia. The report of the staggering number of fatalities sent a shock wave across the nation.

America's reaction to the grim statistics was augmented by photographs of the battle. For the first time during the Civil War, chilling pictures of the dead were disseminated to the American people, evoking strong emotions—anger and disgust in some, fervor in support of the war effort in others. The reality of war was thus brought home to all. Lincoln's monumental Emancipation Proclamation was signed in January 1863. The nation continued to be at war until 1865.

### Contemporary Perspectives

Such is the significance of Antietam that today visitors journey to the Battlefield from all parts of the country and indeed, from all around the world. History buffs are in their element, but the pull of the monumental battle, waged over such a basic issue of human rights, makes the Antietam Battlefield a popular mainstream site for people who want to catch for themselves an echo of the war that helped shape the modern world. During the tumultuous civil rights era of the 1960s, with the country again in turmoil due to the injustices still meted out to African Americans, Antietam served as a reminder of just how long the struggle had been going on, and the overpowering need for the inequalities to end.

The site includes a visitor center with a theater, museum store, a national military cemetery, 96 monuments, and a breathtaking array of historic attractions. Self-guided and guided tours can be up to eight-and-a-half miles long (by foot, bike, or car). Visitors who go to the battlefield are treated to an extraordinary glimpse at one of America's most well-preserved Civil War battlefields, including Dunker Church, farms, and key battle sites such as at the cornfield, Sunken Road (renamed Bloody Lane because of the carnage resulting from the war), and Burnside Bridge. Burnside Bridge was named after Union Major General Ambrose E. Burnside who led forces against the Confederates during this battle.

Among the monuments featured on the battlefield are markers where soldiers and generals died in the war and battlefield towers. One marker is in memory of an adolescent bugler, Johnny Cook, who had been awarded the Medal of Honor and died at Antietam. Visitors also tour the Antietam National Cemetery, which holds the remains of 4,776 Union soldiers and 1,836 unknowns. Confederate soldiers were buried elsewhere. Other sites include McClellan's Headquarters near the Field Hospital Museum, and Lee's Headquarters in the town of Sharpsburg.

Admission fees into the park are reasonable: $4.00 per adult, $6.00 per family, and no charge for youth 16 and under, helping to ensure that this symbol of America's past remains accessible to all.

### Images in Popular Cultures

Tri-Star Pictures released the multiaward winning film *Glory* (1989). Starring a golden cast of actors including Matthew Broderick, Denzel Washington, and Morgan Freeman, *Glory* depicted the daring and tragedy of an all-black Union regiment based on the 54th Massachusetts Volunteer Infantry. The soundtrack featured the haunting music of the Boys Choir of Harlem. In the 1990s, PBS produced a provocative television series, *The Civil War.* The television series attracted 15 million viewers each night and featured authentic photographs from the Battle of Antietam.

***See also*** Arlington National Cemetery; Bunker Hill Monument; Gettysburg Battlefield

### Further Reading

"Antietam." *National Park Service*. http://www.nps.gov/ancm/index.htm.

Shaara, Jeff. 2006. *Jeff Shaara's Civil War Battlefields: Discovering America's Hallowed Ground*. New York: Ballantine Books.

Weeks, Michael. 2009. *The Complete Civil War Road Trip Guide: More than 400 Civil War Sites, from Antietam to Zagonyi's Charge*. Woodstock, Vermont: The Countryman Press.

## Apollo Theater

The Apollo Theater is a world-famous theater located at 253 W. 125th Street in Harlem, New York. When, in 1934, the theater first began operations as a venue for African American singers, dancers, and comedians—upstarts and established celebrities alike—it was an unassuming, three-story brick building. Its fame has grown exponentially through the years, its marquee bearing such names as Gladys Knight, James Brown, and Smokey Robinson. Above the marquee, the word "Apollo" appears twice: horizontally and vertically, the latter being a 15-foot-high sign in purple neon. Following renovations in 2005, the theater's façade was modernized, but the marquee still boasts the top names in contemporary African American performers.

In 1983, in recognition of the important role played by the theater in support of black performers for half a century, the Apollo became a historic landmark. Today, theatergoers flock to the Apollo not only to be entertained by contemporary artists, but also to pay homage to the honor role of past legends who once trod its boards.

**The Godfather of Soul**

James Brown was a singer, dancer, and song writer specializing in R&B, Funk, and Soul. Brown was born James Joe Brown Jr. on May 3, 1933, in Barnwell, South Carolina. During his childhood, Brown lived in extreme poverty. At a young age, he worked an assortment of jobs such as picking cotton, washing cars, and shining shoes. On Sundays, he went to church, where he enjoyed singing in the choir.

During his adolescent years, Brown turned to crime. When he was 16 years old, he was sentenced to 3 years in prison for stealing a car. While in prison, he formed a gospel choir and befriended Bobby Byrd who would play a vital role in Brown's life in later years.

In 1953, Brown was released from prison and his new life began. He and Bobby Byrd started the singing group, the Gospel Starlighters in 1955. Later, they performed as the Famous Flames in nightclubs in Macon, Georgia. In 1956, a talent scout heard their song *Please, Please, Please* and offered the group a record contract. Though the group went on tour, opening for greats such as B. B. King, the Famous Flames were not yet themselves famous.

Throughout the 1950s and 1960s, Brown performed incessantly, putting on shows with great popular appeal. The audiences went wild for his display of popular and soulful dances and impassioned singing.

Notable songs such as *Don't Be a Dropout* and *Say It Loud: I'm Black and I'm Proud* reflected Brown's social consciousness and positioned him as an activist in his own right. Rebounding from drug addiction during the late 1980s, Brown resumed performing in the 1990s. Brown died on December 25, 2006.

### Historical Perspectives

The Apollo Theater began life as the Hurtig and Seamon's New Burlesque Theater in 1914. In 1933, New York City Mayor Fiorello La Guardia instigated the closure of many burlesque theaters, including Hurtig and Seamon's. This opened the door for the building to become an African American entertainment venue in 1934, when Sidney Cohen and Morris Sussman launched the Apollo Theater (today managed by the Apollo Theater Foundation), with the idea of showcasing African American talent. This was a welcome addition for Harlem's growing African American population. The Great Migration, a movement that saw some 2 million blacks from the South to cities in the

North, occurred between 1910 and 1930, and again after World War II (1941–1945). In search of employment, better opportunity, and relief from racial oppression, African Americans made Harlem their home.

The establishment of Apollo Theater was significant for many reasons. First and foremost, the theater catered to African American audiences during an era when African Americans often performed for white audiences while blacks were denied admission. Such was the case at the famed Cotton Club, also in Harlem. The Apollo played an enormous role in the development of African American entertainment by providing a topflight venue in which African Americans could perform. This was critical for aspiring performers, who otherwise had little chance of breaking into the mainstream entertainment industry. The Apollo Theater also welcomed edgy African American comedians such as Richard Pryor, whose humor and style did not fit the mold of the straightlaced comedy found in mainstream culture. Entertainers whose careers were launched at the Apollo would go on to influence the world.

*Showtime at the Apollo,* a weekly television show ran between 1987 and 2008 and featured a talent contest as well as professional performances. Prior to performing, each contestant touched a remnant of the iconic Tree of Hope (a tree that had once stood outside the Harlem Lafayette Theater) for good luck. *Showtime at the Apollo* was notable for its popular hosts, including comedians Sinbad, Steve Harvey, and Mo'Nique; "the Executioner," the name of the person who removed contestants from the stage; and for the Apollo chorus line dancers, who danced throughout the auditorium in the opening and closing numbers of the program.

### Contemporary Perspectives

As the years passed, the Apollo continued to add to its repertoire of events. Today it encompasses a weekly Amateur Night, special concerts, a Hall of Fame, an archive project, an oral history project, and tours. An estimated 1.3 million visitors go to the theater annually. An Apollo Theater traveling exhibition shares its famed history with the nation, as it travels from one popular mainstream venue to another.

***See also*** Cotton Club; Harlem; New York, New York

### Further Reading

*The Apollo Theater*. http://www.apollotheater.org.

Burnim, Mellonee V., and Maultsby, Portia K., eds. 2006. *African American Music: An Introduction*. New York: Routledge.

Carlin, Richard, and Holman Conwill, Kinshasha, eds. 2010. *Ain't Nothing Like the Real Thing: How the Apollo Theater Shaped American Entertainment*. Washington, DC: Smithsonian Books.

Fox, Ted. 1983. *Showtime at the Apollo*. New York: Da Capo Press.

## Appalachia

Appalachia is a mountainous region that covers parts of 13 states, stretching from Alabama to Pennsylvania. For more than two centuries, Appalachia has been identified by the unique culture of its inhabitants—and by a steady stream of wild exaggerations of that culture. The denizens of Appalachia are popularly caricatured as gun-toting, moonshining mountain folk, perennially barefoot and dressed in tattered homemade frocks and overalls. They are called as "hillbillies," "backward," and other derisive terms. Needless to say, this one-dimensional and offensive portrayal is rejected by the people born and raised in Appalachia.

Appalachian bluegrass musicians Kevin Harris (banjo), Larry McWilliams (fiddle), and Nancy Muse (guitar) pose at the one-room log cabin that once served as a stagecoach stop in Tuscumbia, Alabama. (Library of Congress)

The real Appalachia struggles with a complex set of economic and social issues. Largely an impoverished region, Appalachia has not experienced the extensive modernization and economic development found in most other areas in the nation. As a result, the region's reputation belies the potential richness of its resources.

Until recently, Appalachia was not necessarily a popular place to visit. Except for social scientists, like folklorists, who recognized the cultural significance of the regions art, music, and way of life and set out to preserve the cultural traditions of Appalachia, the oppressively negative stereotypes kept tourists at bay. But over the last several decades, Appalachia has finally garnered popular attention not only as an ethnic region that has preserved an older way of life, but as a bone fide treasure trove of folk art. Today, Appalachia is a place where tourists flock to experience all that it has to offer, such as folk festivals, the breathtaking beauty of its national parks, and historical locales.

**Historical Perspectives**

The remote mountainous region known as Appalachia (not to be confused with the much larger Appalachian Mountain zone) was not formally labeled as such until the late 19th century. Prior to this period, the region was known simply as "backcountry," a term used to describe any undeveloped wilderness area where few individuals other than brawny frontiersmen and, to a lesser degree, frontiers women dared venture. Several different Native American tribes originally resided in this region. Various circumstances resulted in the migration of nonnative populations to Appalachia, beginning in the 18th century. Some came to purchase cheap property, some to get away from the increasingly crowded cities and towns, and some to work in the mines and timber industries that developed in the area.

The distinctive cultural elements found in Appalachia were formed largely as a result of the region's isolation. The population derived mostly from Scotch-Irish, German, and English ancestral heritage. Notable cultural differences exist, particularly between Appalachians who live in the northern and southern regions. For example, Appalachians who live in southern regions speak a dialect that is similar to the well-known Southern dialect.

The folk culture of Appalachia encompasses music, dance, storytelling, and craftwork. The music of Appalachia blends old Scottish and English ballads with African American influences. Homemade instruments, including the banjo, which was transplanted by African slaves, were the norm. By the early 20th century, a distinctive style had evolved. Bluegrass and country music have their roots in the music of Appalachia.

There was, however, another side to life in Appalachia. Violence was not uncommon in the region, giving rise to clan feuds that were fueled by the remoteness of life in the mountains and the corresponding decreasing influence of local law enforcement. Revolts against outside influences, such as the Regulator Movement (1760–1771) in North Carolina and the Whiskey Rebellion (1791–1794) in western Pennsylvania, also occurred. The Regulator Movement was an armed uprising against colonials. Armed resistance also occurred in the Whiskey Rebellion in response to perceived overtaxing of whiskey.

Overtaxing was a contentious issue in Appalachia, especially considering the poverty that was so pervasive in the region. Although logging and coal mining helped boost the economy at different times in Appalachia's history, those industries were ultimately unable to provide long-term work for residents or to permanently eliminate the poverty problem. For many, migration was the answer to unemployment woes. Between 1910 and 1960, over 3 million individuals from southern Appalachia left their homes, establishing enclaves in other cities and towns.

Government assistance came in intermittent waves; the most progressive being the establishment of the Appalachian Regional Commission in 1965. This commission brought progress in such forms as paved roads, sewage systems, hospitals, and schools. Today's Appalachia is economically stronger than it was in its past, but not yet on an economic par with most other places in the nation.

### Cultural Distinctions

Life in Appalachia was rustic, threadbare, and heavily entrenched in the American tradition of rugged independence. The people and the land on which they lived were ill-regarded by lowlanders and city folk. Families were largely self-reliant, subsisting on frontier activities such as farming, fishing, and hunting. Appalachians prepared and administered medicine derived from herbs and plants. They wove their own baskets and made their own quilts. True to most agricultural societies, families were traditionally large, and kinship ties were strong. In this culture, education took a backseat to day-to-day survival. Because money was scarce and access to manufactured items was limited, most household and farm furnishings and tools were handmade. Old items were continually repaired. Homes were built from timber felled in their vicinity. Made for utilitarian purposes, structures in Appalachia were simple and plain, contrasting sharply with the massive and elaborate plantation houses of wealthy landowners in the flat lands.

Appalachia and its people differed in many other ways from southern high society. During the antebellum years, affluent landowners topped the social strata in American society. These wealthy societies

> **Front Porch Culture**
>
> Prior to the 18th century, front porches were rare indeed. As the population increased and cultural traditions developed, the front porch became common place, eventually playing a critical role in everyday life for families and the community at large. Porches were most prevalent in the South, where temperatures ran high and relief could be found in the outdoors in the cool of the evening. Some porches were large enough to accommodate one or more chairs, rocking chairs, or swings; others extended around the perimeter of the house.
>
> Like the contemporary living room or den, it was a place for socialization. The porch was where people talked, received guests, drank beverages such as lemonade and tea, played games, told folk stories, listened to the radio, and waved to pedestrians. For many Americans, the front porch had become less important by the mid-20th century. It was during this period that inventions such as the automobile, air-conditioning, and television transformed daily American life. Traffic brought fumes and noise, which made being outdoors at the front of the house less appealing. Air-conditioning cooled indoor spaces and televisions drew Americans indoors like magnets.
>
> In modern America, the front porch tends to be small and infrequently used. Notwithstanding this fact, the front porch remains an architectural feature of homes across the nation.

in the South profited heavily from black slave labor, which helped give rise to an indulgent culture that included leisure time for amusements and education, rich clothes and accessories, modern conveniences, and hunting for entertainment. Slaves did all the manual labor required on the plantations and catered to other needs and whims as well, such as caring for children, washing clothes, preparing and serving meals, and transporting the landowners and their families. In this society, anything associated with mountain people, as Appalachians were sometimes called, was deemed substandard.

As time passed, the lives of Appalachians were more often perceived as hardy and resilient. Only the durable people could endure the ruggedness of mountain living, where men killed animals for survival not sport, men and women used firearms, and families toiled by the sweat of their own labor. The women of Appalachia, in contrast to upper-class women, prepared foods and medicine, raised their children, gardened, sewed, and performed all the household chores.

### Images in Popular Culture

Appalachia and its people occupy a complicated place in the popular media. Their treatment by the music industry, in cartoons, books, photography, in film and on television over the years covers the spectrum of responses and perceptions. Most popular images of Appalachia through the years have been negative.

Cartoons and comic strips epitomized how mountain people were perceived by mainstream culture. In the 1930s, Paul Webb created three characters known as the "Mountain Boys" for *Esquire* magazine. Luke, Willy, and Jake Tolliver were identical-looking brothers with long unkempt beards and disheveled hair.

These images reoccurred in films. Early silent-film companies produced a steady stream of films set in the mountains based mostly on the stereotype of mountain people as lawless and violent. Moonshine and feuds were popular themes. Although families who lived in the mountains did produce moonshine (illicitly distilled liquor) in response to prohibition and engage in inner-community conflict, the stories were made larger than life. Later films relied on derisive characters for comedic effect. The film *Deliverance* (1972) is considered one of the most offensive films in recent history. Its antagonists are portrayed, according to Harkins, as vapid and predatory. Harkins observes that this film bred similar monstrous characterizations in subsequent films, such as *Texas Chainsaw Massacre* (1974) and *The Hills Have Eyes* (1977).

On the other side of the scale, the film *A Coal Miner's Daughter* (1980) won Sissy Spacek an Academy Award for Best Actress. The film eloquently retells the life story of Loretta Lynn, who was born and raised in Virginia, emerging from humble origins to worldwide acclaim. The film itself received several Academy Awards nominations and depicted Appalachia using dignified and realistic imagery.

In the early 1900s, music groups such as The Hill Billies and the Cumberland Ridge Runners produced what is now considered country music but was then known by assorted terms, such as "Songs from Dixie" and "Old Southern Tunes." The music proved wildly popular; however, several groups cloaked their talent in stereotypical hillbilly gimmicky—such as, oversized hats, handkerchiefs, and overalls. Less obtrusively, folklorists traveled to Appalachia to record and preserve Appalachian music. Folk music has attained popularity in the form of country and bluegrass music, and folk-inspired songs permeated mainstream radio and record stores in the 1960s and 1970s. Today, the music of Appalachia is revered as a uniquely American creation that arguably influences many of the American musical traditions that followed, and is studied for its revealing connection to the storytelling and music of 16th- and 17th-century England and Scotland.

Early photographers who ventured into the mountains captured dignified images of the people and the landscapes in which they lived, and novelists idealized the lives of Appalachian frontiersmen like David Crockett. Documentaries, as well as number of books, autobiographical and otherwise, have conjured endearing and nostalgic images.

Television has produced increasingly positive images of Appalachia. *The Beverly Hill Billies* (1962–1971) mixed positive and negative images in a long-running television series. For example, the stereotypical matriarch, Granny, is ornery and no-nonsense, a symbol of a fearlessly independent and can-do woman that echoed the values promoted in the feminist movement of 1960s and 1970s. The grandchildren, although stereotypically dim-witted, were physically attractive—not depicted as characteristically toothless, disheveled, and unclean.

In recent years, images of Appalachia have leaned toward the mostly positive. Contemporary films such as *Songcatcher* (2000) and *O Brother, Where Art Though?* (2000) launched a craze for old-timey music and pride for folk life. Contemporary society has also seen a revival for all things associated with folk life, whether or not they are genuinely related to Appalachia, such as country-and-western dance clubs, folk festivals, and other traditions, culture, and dress styles.

Modern comedians such as Jeff Foxworthy and Larry the Cable Guy perpetuate the so-called redneck (a term similar to hillbilly and associated with Appalachia) humor. Redneck jokes are published in books, printed on T-shirts and sweatshirts, and are available on the Internet and dispensed to the public via e-mail messages and YouTube videos. Some sociologists argue that this brand of humor, as told by the everyday man himself and swathed in the context of good-natured and harmless fun, has helped to popularize redneck culture and is a form of self-empowerment. Others see it as business as usual, using well-worn stereotypes to make fun of people whose only crime was being poor. Either way, the trend is an indication of the fascination of life in Appalachia.

**For Visitors**

Appalachia, notable for its history, culture, and outdoor activities, draws tourists. The region has also reaped the benefits of the ever-increasing popularity of folk culture. Appalachia hosts a number of folk festivals that are popular not only with locals and a growing number of outsiders. Numbered among the popular festivals are Hillbilly Days and the American Folk Song Festival in Kentucky, and the Folk Festival in North Carolina. Homemade crafts, baskets, and quilts; traditional foods; and authentic folk music are the hallmarks of these festivals.

No longer perceived as inferior or unsophisticated, Americans travel great distances for these experiences and pay well for relics of Americana. Other attractions in Appalachia include hikes through the famous Appalachian Trail, day trips and camping trips to the Great Smoky Mountains National Park, and drives along the Blue Ridge Parkway. Dollywood and Ghost Town in the Sky are other well-known attractions that have helped change the way the public views Appalachia.

***See also*** Academy Awards (Oscars); Beverly Hills, California; Dollywood; Folk Festival; Grand Ole Opry; Great Smoky Mountains; Highlander Folk School; Mobile Homes and Trailer Parks; Texas

### Further Reading

Biggers, Jeff. 2006. *The United States of Appalachia: How Southern Mountaineers Brought Independence, Culture, and Enlightenment to America*. Emeryville, California: Shoemaker and Hoard.

Billings, Dwight B., Gurney, Norman, and Ledford, Katherine, eds. 1999. *Back Talk from Appalachia: Confronting Stereotypes*. Lexington: University Press of Kentucky.

Hardwood, Judy. 2009. *Swimming Upriver: Coming of Age in Appalachia*. Denver: Outskirts Press.

Harkins, Anthony. 2004. *Hillbilly: A Cultural History of an American Icon*. New York: Oxford University Press.

Straw, Richard A., and Blethen, H. Tyler, eds. 2004. *High Mountains Rising: Appalachia in Time and Place*. Urbana: University of Illinois Press.

Williams, John Alexander. 2002. *Appalachia: A History*. Chapel Hill: University of North Carolina Press.

Williamson, J.W. 1995. *Hillbillyland: What the Movies Did to the Mountains & What the Mountains Did to the Movies*. Chapel Hill: University of North Carolina Press.

## Apple Inc.

Apple Inc., founded in 1976, is a successful corporation that produces computers and consumer electronics. Though its products were considered expensive (though reliable) and not very competitive during the company's infancy, Apple experienced a stunning renaissance, beginning in the 1990s, becoming world famous for its innovative products and cornering a huge part of the electronics market. Apple headquarters has become a Mecca for computer and electronics buffs, and Apple retail stores are a 21st-century phenomenon, triggering media excitement, long lines, and public fervor whenever new products are released. Apple sites in cyberspace provide places for people to buy products, discuss user issues, and to share knowledge, news, and experiences.

### Historical Perspectives

Apple Inc. had its start in the living room of a house in Santa Clara Valley (also known as Silicon Valley), California. The house belonged to the parents of Steve Jobs, one of the men who would go on to be credited with Apple Inc.'s enormous success. Steve and his friend Steve Wozniak, two techno whizzes, first built computers in the Jobs family living room, then moved into the garage. In 1976, the two Steves and Ronald Wayne founded Apple Computer Inc. (changed to Apple Inc. in 2007) and released the Apple I, a personal computer. In the following year, Apple became incorporated and released the Apple II. By today's standards, these early computers were all clunky, drab creations, but the Apple II was a critical success. The computer helped launch Apple into its small but competitive position in the market. But in the mid-1980s, Apple faced a series of challenges: unpopular new products, financial losses, and internal conflict. These problems escalated when, in 1985, Jobs left the company.

Apple hung grimly on for the next 12 years, supported by loyal users who recognized that nothing could match their computers' reliability and ease of use, but the company was generally scorned by its burgeoning competitors. The company's fate turned with the celebrated return of Jobs in 1997, who served as the corporation's CEO from then until he stepped down in 2011.

With Jobs again at the helm, Apple introduced a series of leaner, lighter, and more efficient computers featuring vibrant colors and lots of bells and whistles. Apple also launched innovative technologies

Customers wait in lines to enter the futuristic glass cube entrance to the Fifth Avenue Apple Store, hoping to play with and purchase the new iPad2 tablet, March 11, 2011. (Mircea Nicolescu/Dreamstime.com)

like flat-screen monitors, the USB keyboard and mouse, iTunes, the iPod, and the iPad. These creations helped to vault Apple into one of the foremost corporations in the industry. In 2004, there were an estimated 25 million worldwide Apple users. Significantly, although Apple may not have the most users in the world, its users are regarded as the most loyal and passionate in the computer and electronics industry. In 2008, Apple reported revenue of $9.6 billion. In 2011, Fortune 500 ranked Apple as the 35th largest corporation. Today, Apple, along with its iconic logo—an apple with a bite taken from it—is recognized throughout the world. Its retail stores dot the entire country. Its products are regularly featured in films and on television. Apple has led the way toward incorporating technology into everyday American life, to the point where, for many Americans, life without Apple technology is inconceivable.

**Everyday Life**

Technology, whether produced by Apple or its competitors, is tightly woven into modern American society, both its infrastructure as well as everyday life. Americans use technology to perform an assortment of tasks, such as managing businesses, personal projects, and school work. Technological devices are used to interact socially and to provide personal entertainment, from games to music and movies.

Smart phones are used not only to talk but to send text messages, access the Internet and popular social networking sites, watch movies, play games, listen to music, and conduct business. Laptops, even smaller personal computers that go anywhere, and hundreds of accessories help Americans to use technology in more and more creative, efficient, and appealing ways. Apple keeps the new products coming, catering to the demands of America's consumer culture for more, better, and easier-to-use technology. For some, the demand for Apple products borders on obsession.

### Cultural Distinctions

Called by an assortment of names, among them Mac Zealots, Macheads, Macolytes, or Mac Addicts (Mac stands for Apple's Macintosh line of computers), diehard Apple users have developed a subculture of their own. United by a singular love for all things Apple, hardcore fans use only Apple products, believing them to be better and easier to operate than products made by other industry giants, most famously Apple's chief rival, Microsoft. Indeed, when it comes to computers, some Mac enthusiasts hold strongly to the opinion that Microsoft is Apple's arch enemy, ever striving to unfairly conquer the world, and that Apple, representing a counterculture entity, gives the power of technology to the people, rather than hiding it. To be sure, Apple computers do not have the most users, but the passion of the Mac user is widely known and like no other in the industry.

In addition to an unquenchable passion for Apple products, Mac Zealots are identifiable in other ways. For example, Mac enthusiasts can be identified by their Apple paraphernalia, including vintage Apple computers and accessories, Apple stickers, Apple T-shirts and tattoos, and haircuts displaying the Apple logo.

#### An Apple for Apple

The Apple logo is one of the most recognizable logos in the world. Apple buffs know that the first logo created for Apple depicted not just an apple but a scene that featured scientist Isaac Newton sitting under an apple tree with an apple dangling above his head. This logo, known as the Newton crest, was designed by Rob Janoff and used briefly in 1976. In the same year, Janoff designed a new logo, the rainbow. This logo depicted an apple with a bite taken from it. The apple featured, from top to bottom, green, yellow, orange, red, purple, and blue stripes. This logo was used until the late 1990s.

It was Steve Jobs who called for a new logo after he returned to the company in 1996. The new logo symbolized the company's successful efforts in rebranding itself to more effectively compete in the computer industry. It had the same shape of the former logo but removed the rainbow stripes. The result was a more modern and sophisticated looking logo. This logo, the monochrome logo, continues to appear on assorted Apple products, while the former rainbow logo remains a treasured retro image.

### Apple Headquarters

The Apple brand has become so engrained in the culture of America that the company's headquarters has become a popular tourist destination. The Apple campus in Cupertino, California, otherwise known as Silicon Valley (because numerous world-famous computer and technology companies are located there), is the largest of the four Apple corporate campuses, with the other three in Austin, Texas, Singapore, and Ireland. Completed in 1993, the Apple campus sprawls over 32 acres with six buildings situated on a street named the Infinite Loop. Dubbed the "Mothership," the buildings are closed to the public, but visitors come anyway to see the buildings and to visit the Apple Company Store, located outside the entrance.

In 2006, Steve Jobs announced plans for a new campus in Cupertino. This new campus, a four-story circular futuristic-looking building, is projected to occupy 175 acres and include a 1,000-seat auditorium, a fitness center, underground parking, and a power plant.

### Retail Stores

Starting in 2001, Apple began to open retail stores, many inside shopping centers and malls, to demonstrate and sell products and accessories and to provide support for its products. As of 2011, there were more than 300 such stores in the United States and throughout the world. Among the most famous stores is the Apple store on Fifth Avenue in New York City, which boasts 24-hour service and a spectacular all-glass, cube-shaped building. Apple stores are staffed by knowledgeable techies known as "geniuses," who, by appointment, help users to solve their Apple-product-related problems, often without charge.

Grand openings and new product releases generate enormous crowds at Apple retail stores. Visitors, unfazed by the long wait and line, bring along Apple gear, take pictures, blog or twitter about the experience while they wait, and socialize with others. New technology is promoted months ahead through media news, advertisements, websites, and social networks, thus generating the massive interest. When the iPhone, a wireless phone featuring Internet and multimedia applications, was released in 2007, it triggered a nationwide stampede to Apple stores, with fortunate buyers walking away with the most anticipated new toy of the decade and the social status that went with it.

### Macworld Conference & Expo

Apple Campuses and retail stores can be visited any time of the year, but the Macworld Conference & Expo is a one-off extravaganza. Tickets are not easily attained. Until 2005, conferences in the United States were held twice a year, usually in San Francisco in the winter and New York or Boston in the summer (with occasional conferences abroad, e.g., in Japan and France). After 2009, however, Apple no longer participated at these events. Currently, there is only one conference a year, held in San Francisco. Conferences feature technology booths, Apple-branded gifts, and parties. Before his death in 2011, the keynote address presented by Steve Jobs was one of the most anticipated moments of each conference. The climactic moment of the presentation was when Jobs casually spoke the words "One more thing" before announcing a new and scintillating product.

### Cyberspace

No overview of popular Apple locales would be complete without mention of its most often visited sites: those that exist in cyberspace. Enormous traffic flows through www.apple.com, which is the gateway to the online store, the Apple Museum, and the support forums where Mac users congregate to look for answers and share information. In addition, there is a host of unofficial sites and social network discussions (carried out through Twitter and Facebook) that cater to Mac users and Apple products. Mac users are all familiar with www.store.apple.com, where they can, at the click of the mouse, access a wide array of Apple products and accessories, lists of new products, and access to repair information. Biographies of key players, interesting facts, a timeline that traces Apple history before 1976, and product descriptions can be found at www.theapplemuseum.com.

General Apple websites proliferate in cyberspace. Some are supported by so-called Apple Evangelistas, sometimes former Apple employees, who publish news, tips, and topics in an effort to promote the corporation and its products. Other websites feature blogs covering assorted topics, threads wherein users share solutions to technical problems, and "Macspotting." Macspotting is a popular pastime for tracking famous Apple users, like Bill Clinton and Sylvester Stallone, and Apple product placement in films and television shows.

### Images in Popular Culture

The familiar Apple logo, found on the backs of computers, iPods, iPhones, and other products that people are using, are everywhere—in cafes, like Starbucks, on airplane, buses, and trains, and in libraries and cafeterias. Although Apple products are not used by everyone, everyone knows what they are. Entering the second decade of the 21st century, when technology continues to advance by leaps and bounds, Apple stands at the pinnacle of mainstream popularity.

***See also*** Boston, Massachusetts; California; Cyberspace; Facebook; Fifth Avenue; Microsoft; MIT; New York, New York; San Francisco, California; Silicon Valley; Starbucks; Texas

### Further Reading

Isaacson, Walter. 2011. *Steve Jobs*. New York: Simon & Schuster.

Kahney, Leander. 2005. *The Cult of iPod*. San Francisco: No Starch Press.

Kahney, Leander. 2004. *The Cult of Mac*. San Francisco: No Starch Press.

O'Grady, Jason D. 2009. *Apple Inc*. Westport, Connecticut: Greenwood Press.

## Area 51

Area 51 is a military base located in Rachel, Nevada. It's one of the most famous military installations in the nation—but its fame stems from an unusual source. Shrouded in mystery and conspiracy, its existence and the activities rumored to have occurred there were obscured for many years. Then, in 1989, an alleged former Area 51 worker named Bob Lazar came forward on a television station in Las Vegas to reveal that the government was experimenting with alien technology on the top secret base. His disclosure triggered a pop-culture storm. Witnesses claim to this day that the unworldly lights and aircraft flashing and zigzagging in the night skies in the area are evidence of extraterrestrial life or out-of-this-world technology. Since then, Ufologists, UFO hunters and investigators, conspiracy theorists, sightseers, and tourists flood to Area 51 to satisfy their curiosity, to catch glimpses of alien craft, and to find clues to the two big unanswered questions: What is the American government hiding? Do extraterrestrials exist?

### About the Site

Area 51 was founded in 1955. Since then, it has been referenced in various official documents by assorted names, such as Paradise Ranch, The Ranch, Watertown Strip, and Groom Lake. The restricted airspace above the base has been referred to, interchangeably, as Dreamland, The Box, and the Container. Area 51 covers 60 square miles and is located in a remote, desert region near Groom Mountain Range in Rachel, Nevada. Although there is no fence to keep out intruders, Area 51 is heavily monitored and patrolled by an elaborate network of anonymous guards in camouflage (popularly known as "camo dudes") driving Humvees, helicopters, and sophisticated sensors, microphones, and cameras. Simple signs read "restricted area," "no trespassing," "photography is prohibited," and, more ominously, warn that "use of deadly force authorized." The base is so top secret that Area 51 workers are not privy to what departments outside their sphere do and are trained to remain tight-lipped about what they themselves do.

Area 51 is one of the best-kept secrets in the nation. The American public did not know about the base's existence for many years, and the facility is still not included on U.S. maps. Only well after the fact did the public learn that Area 51 was originally designed to test aircraft, such as the U-2 Spy Plane and the SR-71 Blackbird developed by Lockheed's Skunk Works. According to William J. Birnes, author of

*Aliens in America* (2010), it was not until the 1970s that rumors surfaced about the military installation and that the government had presumably recovered an extraterrestrial spacecraft from the conspiratorial Roswell crash and sent it for study at Area 51.

In 1989, Bob Lazar was interviewed on KLAS television. He claimed that he had worked at Area 51 (evidence of his claim was not to be found at the installation) and revealed that extraterrestrial spacecrafts were being reverse engineered at the military installation. Unsubstantiated by the government, his allegations sparked a thunderstorm of popular interest, and Area 51 entered the lore of alien conspiracies and mania, where it has remained ever since. Meanwhile, the government remained silent for a considerable time—making no official announcement verifying the installation's existence or explaining what exactly was going on at the site.

**Mulder and Scully in Dreamland**

"Dreamland" is the title of a two-part episode from the sixth season of the popular science fiction television series, *The X-Files* (1993–2002), which was a series about two FBI agents, Fox Mulder (David Duchovny) and Dana Scully (Gillian Anderson), who investigate paranormal cases.

In part one of the Dreamland episode, Mulder and Scully investigate a tip about an unidentified flying object discovered in Area 51. After both agents witness the flight of an unusual spacecraft, Mulder and one of the Men in Black appear to trade bodies. The swap is caused by the spacecraft.

In part two, Scully, who is usually highly skeptical of the paranormal, must come to terms with the fact that someone else is inhabiting her partner's body as she works to unravel the mystery of exactly what happened at Area 51.

### Folklore

Inspired by the intrigue, mystery, and abundant rumors surrounding Area 51, a distinct subculture formed, and with it a broad and intricate folklore. The subculture consists of an eclectic mix of UFO enthusiasts, researchers and scientists (professional and amateur), and curious individuals around the globe. The folklore of Area 51 comprises witness accounts of strange sightings, myriad speculations of what occurs at the installation, such as meetings with extraterrestrials and top-secret projects involving ongoing secret weapons and aircraft testing, as well as weather control, reverse engineering, and time travel. These stories are communicated through books, radio, the Internet, and documentaries.

### Alternative Explanations

Not everyone is convinced that Area 51 conspiracies are founded or that Area 51 even stands up to its reputation. For example, in a documentary entitled *Area 51: America's Most Secret Base* (2002), Glenn Campbell, who founded the Area 51 Research Center that was located in Rachel, Nevada, contends that the strange flashes of light and unearthly meteoric movements of unknown aircraft that witnesses have described are, in fact, nothing unusual: just routine flight tests and exercises of newly developed aircraft.

In the new millennium, the CIA began to declassify covert programs carried out at Area 51. What was released challenged the popular theories concerning top secret activities believed to occur at the base. The CIA, as well as individuals who worked on these top secret programs, debunked the alien connection, asserting that Area 51 was used to test and develop human-piloted technology and that the base was not at all associated with extraterrestrials. Not everyone accepts this explanation; many believe that the government is continuing to cover up conspiracies and hiding the truth. Meanwhile, popular worldwide interest in the site continues unabated and visitors, year after year, make their way to Area 51.

**MIB**

Men in Black, or MIB for short, is a term that refers to mysterious men commonly depicted in black suits and sun glasses. The term is associated with shadowy men who appear at so-called alien sites such as Area 51 and Roswell. Some have alleged that such men are government agents dedicated to keeping alien existence secret. Others think they are themselves aliens. Either way, the Men in Black theme is popular in film and television. Various Men in Black have appeared as sinister characters in the television series *The X-Files* (1993–2002).

In the titular film series that was released in 1997, 2002, and 2012, the Men in Black are heroes, protecting humans from evil aliens and interacting on a galactic level with diverse aliens. The work of the Men in Black is unknown to most humans. To keep humans oblivious to this knowledge, the Men in Black selectively erase the memories of individuals who come into contact with aliens.

### Declassified Documents

In 2013, the National Security Archive declassified more than 60 documents about the secret base. The information reveals no alien cover-up but intentions of developing stealth aircraft and studying Soviet MiG fighter jets.

### Images in Popular Culture

America's fascination with Area 51 and its attendant stories about extraterrestrials, alien spacecraft, and clandestine operations have greatly influenced mainstream media. Area 51 is the setting for an attack on aliens in the film *Independence Day* (1996), the television series *Seven Days* (1998–2001), and two video games entitled *Area 51*, released in 1995 and 2005. The *Men in Black* comic book series, film, and animated television series brings to life an Area-51-like conspiracy that the government is involved in a covert extraterrestrial program. The plot of the popular movie *Transformers* (2007) centers around a hidden top-secret facility (Section 7) holding an extraterrestrial life form (Megatron). And, finally, in the comedy *Paul* (2011), Director Greg Mottola brings Area 51 emblems and lore to the screen as two English sci-fi tourists embark on the quintessential American geek road trip, starting at a Comic-Con event in San Diegoand ending at the infamous Area 51.

Area 51 has also been featured in investigative literature and documentaries. The Discovery Channel has explored the site on its website in "Conspiracies & Myths" and on several television programs.

Area 51 has captured the popular imagination of the nation and become a modern legend. It is a symbol for both the fear of government conspiracy and the hope that we are not alone in the universe.

### For Visitors

Campbell believes that, despite worldwide interest, Area 51 is not what visitors imagine it to be. Views of the installation are severely restricted and what can be seen are the ordinary buildings that are found at any military base. But the state of Nevada, with an eye on tourist revenues, has capitalized on public interest, designating Route 375, a long, isolated stretch of highway, as Extraterrestrial Highway. This highway links many points of interest associated with Area 51.

Past Groom Lake, the main gate looms unassumingly. In the desert-brush-stubbled landscape, one may view a security vehicle. A warning sign cautions visitors from trespassing. Some visitors take photographs of themselves at the infamous sign, but they can go no further. More than one tourist has videotaped their experience at the main gate and posted the video on their website or YouTube.

"The black mail box" sounds ominous, but it is simply a landmark, a mailbox owned by a local rancher that visitors use to designate the gathering spot to view reported unusual lights and aircraft observed at night. The Little A'Le'Inn is a restaurant and inn in Rachel that not only features food and accommodations but Area 51 memorabilia and maps. Patrons are encouraged to talk about their experiences at the site and alleged encounters with extraterrestrials, including those unassociated with Area 51.

Two popular stops that are no longer available to the public are the Area 51 Research Center and Freedom Ridge. The Area 51 Research Center once held all literature and media, such as films and documentaries, concerning the site. Freedom Ridge, which offers a panorama of the base, can no longer be accessed by the public.

*See also* Comic-Con; Extraterrestrial Highway; Las Vegas, Nevada; Roswell, New Mexico

### Further Reading

Birnes, William J. 2010. *Aliens in America: A UFO Hunter's Guide to Extraterrestrial Hotspots across the U.S.* Avon, Massachusetts: Adams Media.

Jacobsen, Annie. 2011. *Area 51: An Uncensored History of America's Top Secret Military Base.* New York: Little, Brown.

Patton, Phil. 1998. *Area 51: The Dreamland Chronicles.* New York: Henry Holt.

Rich, Ben R., and Janos, Leo. 1994. *Skunk Works: A Personal Memoir of My Years at Lockheed.* Boston: Little, Brown.

## Arlington National Cemetery

Arlington National Cemetery is a military cemetery that is recognized as America's most treasured national cemetery. The site honors many thousands of deceased men and women who served their country. A significantly less number of civilians are buried there too. Arlington National Cemetery is one of many popular destinations for visitors to Washington, D.C., the nation's capital, as well as for individuals who go to pay their respects to family members, friends, and loved ones. Among the most notable sites open to the general public at the cemetery are the Tomb of the Unknowns and the John F. Kennedy Eternal Flame.

### Historical Perspectives

Situated in Arlington County, Virginia, Arlington National Cemetery was established on June 15, 1864. The land for the cemetery belonged to the family estate of Mary Anna Lee, the wife of Confederate General Robert E. Lee. The original parcel included 200 acres and Arlington House, where Lee and his family lived. More acreage was added over the years to accommodate memorials for those who lost their lives in war and other historically noteworthy events.

### Gravesites

Arlington National Cemetery has the second largest number of burial sites of any national cemetery (Calverton National Cemetery in New York has the largest). Currently, there are more than 300,000 individuals buried there. The cemetery is divided into 70 sections, including, for example, Section 60 for military personnel that died in the Iraq War (2003–2011) and Afghanistan War (2001–). Arlington National Cemetery also has an extensive columbarium that holds cremated remains. Notable gravesites include the only two presidents buried at Arlington, William Howard Taft and John F. Kennedy.

### Tomb of the Unknowns

The Tomb of the Unknowns, also known as the Tomb of the Unknown Soldier, is one of the most visited sites at the cemetery. The Tomb itself, a white marble sarcophagus embellished with three Greek figures symbolizing Peace, Victory, and Valor, sits atop a hill that overlooks Washington, D.C. The Tomb memorializes the remains of Unknown Soldiers from World War I (1917–1918), World War II (1941–1945), the Korean War (1950–1953), and the Vietnam War (1965–1975). With much ritual and ceremony, Tomb

Changing of the Guard at the Tomb of the Unknowns at Arlington National Cemetery in Arlington, Virginia. (Library of Congress)

Guard sentinels preside over the Tomb of the Unknowns 24 hours a day, every day of the year. Visitors watch, spellbound, as the sentinels perform the highly ritualized walking of the mat and changing of the guards.

**Memorials and Monuments**

In addition to the gravesites, Arlington National Cemetery has many memorials and monuments. Nearly 150 trees (red maple, willow oak, Colorado blue spruce, black maple, red oak, and other species) stand throughout the cemetery as memorials to various groups, such as the 11th Airborne Division, 174th Field Artillery Battalion, and Air force Arlington Ladies. Among the 27 memorials and monuments are the Nurses Memorial, the Space Shuttle *Challenger* Memorial, and the John F. Kennedy Eternal Flame.

The John F. Kennedy Eternal Flame draws somber and quiet crowds who watch the perpetual flickering of the flame that sits above the gravesite of one of the most celebrated presidents in American history. Adjacent to Kennedy are the gravesites of his brothers Robert F. Kennedy and Edward M. Kennedy.

Like the eternal flame, Arlington National Cemetery stands as an enduring landmark commemorating the military heroes of the nation, an important symbol of American patriotism and pride.

### For Visitors

The cemetery now covers more than 600 acres. It includes a visitor center, a memorial amphitheater, the gravesites, the Tomb of the Unknowns, and many monuments and memorials. Ceremonies and rituals take place every day. The visitor center, located at the entrance to the cemetery, offers information about the cemetery, books, maps, and guidebooks. Built in 1920 in white marble, the Arlington Memorial Amphitheater is an official site for military ceremonies, such as state funerals. Major memorial services take place there on Easter, Memorial Day, and Veterans Day.

*See also* African Burial Ground; Antietam Battlefield; Bunker Hill Monument; Dealey Plaza; Gettysburg Battlefield; Grant's Tomb; New York World Trade Center: Twin Towers and Ground Zero; Washington, D.C.

### Further Reading

"Arlington House, the Robert E. Lee Memorial." *National Park Service*. http://www.nps.gov/arho/index.htm.

*Arlington National Cemetery*. http://www.arlingtoncemetery.org.

Bigler, Philip. 2005. *In Honored Glory: Arlington National Cemetery, the Final Post*. St. Petersburg, Florida: Vandamere Press.

Parzych, Cynthia. 2009. *Arlington National Cemetery: A Guided Tour through History*. Guilford, Connecticut: Morris Book Publishing.

Peters, James E. 2008. *Arlington National Cemetery: Shrine to America's Heroes*. Bethesda, Maryland: Woodbine House.

## Atlanta, Georgia

Atlanta, the state capital of Georgia, is one of the largest and best-known cities in the South. Throughout its long and often traumatic history, Atlanta has captured the nation's attention. From the start, visionaries set out to make Atlanta an important economic center, rapidly establishing it as a haven of opportunity and big-city living. During the Civil War (1861–1865), the entire country was shocked by the news that General William Sherman had burned down Atlanta. The subsequent rebuilding of Atlanta served as a gleaming example of southern rebirth and transformation.

Today, Atlanta's blend of modern urbanization and fascinating history, along with its undercurrents of traditional southern living, appeals to businesses, tourists, as well as transplants, who flock to the city from every region in the nation and corner of the world. Atlanta has it all—an expansive and modern downtown, progressive neighborhoods, historic landmarks, and plentiful opportunities for traditional and modern entertainment—sports, the arts, music, nightclubs, and restaurants galore. Since its early history, Atlanta has been a popular place to be, not only because of its landscape or attractions (with the exception of the world's largest aquarium, the Georgia Aquarium), but for its representation as an upwardly mobile, always advancing, exhilarating city.

### Historical Perspectives

Atlanta was originally inhabited by Native Americans. Explorers made first contact with a Cherokee tribe living in a village along the Chattahoochee River in 1782. The inhabitants called it Standing Peachtree, though peaches were not native to the region. During the War of 1812, Fort Peachtree was established; not long after, whites set their sights on claiming the region for their very own, naming it

Terminus. This usurpation prompted the tragic Trail of Tears, which involved the forced removal of some 17,000 Native Americans from their ancestral lands to a territory known today as Oklahoma.

Early on, Atlanta was set apart from the rest. Preparations for Atlanta's greatness began with its name change from Terminus to Marthasville in 1843 and then to Atlanta in 1845. J. Edgar Thomson recommended the name "Atlanta" because he believed it sounded more fitting than Marthasville, which could have been the name of any inconspicuous and unremarkable small town in the United States. In most areas in the South, industry was based on slave labor and agriculture. Industry and development in the southern region tended to lag behind the industry and factory-based North. Atlanta, however, was groomed to be a central railroad intersection, making it a critical port for transporting agricultural products and people. In 1845, the first locomotive arrived, and Atlanta seemed set to fulfill its destiny. But in 1861, contentions boiling between the North and the South resulted in the succession of Georgia, 1 of 11 southern states, from the Union. The Civil War began in that same year.

### Civil War

Again and again, Atlanta has emerged as a hotspot in Southern history. During the Civil War, it was a major military post and supply and medical center for the Confederates. The importance of these services to the southern front made the city a target. Casualties on the Confederate side were alarmingly high during the battles that took place in Atlanta: the Battle of Peachtree Creek on July 20, 1864, and the Battle of Atlanta on July 22. In that same year, General William Sherman ordered Atlantans to evacuate their homes. Atlanta was burned down, and its railroad system was destroyed.

### *Atlanta Constitution*

The *Atlanta Constitution*, which is now known as the *Atlanta Journal-Constitution*, has a long and illustrious history. The newspaper was founded in 1868 during a harrowing period in the South. The South had just lost the Civil War, and many areas of the region were still badly damaged. And though African Americans celebrated their freedom from slavery, conservative southerners lamented the end of the former slave-based plantation system.

The magazine contributed greatly to the recovery of the South, particularly in the state of Georgia, where it rapidly emerged as a popular and profitable venture. During the 1880s, famed journalist and editor Henry W. Grady wrote regularly in the newspaper, infusing his articles with optimism and regional pride. Coining the phrase, the New South, Grady advocated industrialization in the formerly agricultural-based region. Many heeded his call and the city's economy flourished.

The 20th century saw many changes for the popular newspaper. Some reflected the newspapers prestige, as numerous journalists and reporters were awarded Pulitzer Prizes. In 1967, Eugene Patterson, editor of the *Atlanta Constitution*, received an award for editorial writing. In 1989, Bill Dedman received the Pulitzer Prize for investigative reporting. Other changes reflected the changing times. After merging in 1950, *the Atlanta Constitution* and the *Atlanta Journal* officially became known as *The Atlanta Journal-Constitution.*

### The New South

The end of the war in 1865 and eventual return of the Atlantans in 1867 marked the start of a new era in the region. Their arrival began the arduous process of rebuilding their lives, their homes, and their city. In 1877, Atlanta became the state's capital. In the 1880s, the editor of the popular Atlanta paper, the *Atlanta Constitution*, and massively popular orator Henry W. Grady, helmed a campaign to promote the South's renewal. His speeches and writings motivated southerners to rapidly adapt to the new world in which they lived and promoted the concept of the "New South," a term that was synonymous with advancement and progress. During this period, historically black colleges and universities were established. Among the most prominent institutions in Atlanta were Morehouse College, founded in 1867; Clark College, founded in 1869; and Spelman College, established in 1881.

The establishment of academic institutions was a substantial step toward advancing black life in Atlanta, but the celebrated "New South" did little else in terms of race relations and racial progress. Though Atlanta was more racially tolerant than other places in the South and had, in fact, a substantial community of economically thriving African Americans, Atlanta also established discriminatory laws, relegating African Americans to segregated workplaces, neighborhoods, and facilities.

Racial violence, which was rampant in many areas in the South, found its way to Atlanta in 1906. This outbreak was incited, in large part, by racial tensions and incendiary articles that alleged black attacks on white women. White mobs attacked black Atlantans, killing as many as 40 blacks. Only two whites were reported dead. In the wake of this violence, conditions for African Americans remained grim for many decades. Segregation was the law for most of the South, mandating that whites and blacks navigate in worlds separated by skin color.

### Gone with the Wind

Three decades later, antebellum and Civil War Atlanta was vaulted into the national limelight through Margaret Mitchell's Civil War saga *Gone with the Wind* (1936). The novel, adapted into an award-winning film in 1939, featured palatial plantation homes and romanticized antebellum life in Civil War Atlanta. The book portrayed the troublous status of blacks as slaves, but also seemed to affirm their second-class status. Hattie McDaniel, an African American, starred in the role of Mammy and won Best Actress in a Supporting Role at the 1939 Academy Awards. She was the first African American to receive any Academy Award. Some African Americans criticized her participation as perpetuating a negative stereotype. Others praised her for trailblazing the way for African Americans in the industry.

Two decades later, the precarious position of African Americans, particularly in the South, took center stage again.

### Civil Rights Movement

The civil rights era brought the troublous racial issues of the region to the forefront. Although the movement, led largely by African American leaders, targeted the regions in the Deep South where racial confrontations and segregation were most heinous, demonstrations did occur in Atlanta. Two notable activists, W.E.B. Du Bois and Dr. Martin Luther King Jr., resided in the city, guaranteeing Atlanta's reputation as an important and historic civil rights locale. Scholar, activist, and cofounder of the NAACP William E. B. Du Bois worked as a professor at Atlanta University. Atlanta is also celebrated for numerous sites associated with Dr. Martin Luther King Jr., such as his birth home and church, Ebenezer Baptist Church.

#### CNN

CNN is a basic cable and satellite television station that is headquartered in downtown Atlanta at the CNN Center. The station was founded in 1980 by cable magnate Ted Turner, who owns the Turner Broadcast System. CNN is notable as the first station in the nation to broadcast 24-hour television news. At the time that the station was founded, it was housed in what was then known as the Omni International Complex. The complex featured two 14-story office towers, an indoor amusement park, an ice-skating rink, a hotel, shops, and restaurants. After the complex changed its name to the CNN Center in 1986, the ice-skating rink was removed, an atrium was added, and the many restaurants and retail businesses bustled with activity.

In the 21st century, CNN occupies a prominent place in the news industry. The station is one of the most popular networks in the nation. It features a high-profile and diverse cast of journalists who are well respected in the industry and popular with audiences. Born and raised in England, Christiane Amanpour, of mixed Iranian and English descent, reports on International news. Anderson Cooper and British journalist Piers Morgan host their own talk and interview shows. Dr. Sanjay Gupta is a multiple award-winning chief medical correspondent for CNN.

## Contemporary Perspectives

In the years since the Civil Rights era, Atlanta has moved steadily toward becoming a popular city. One highlight occurred in 1996 when the city hosted the prestigious Olympic Games. Preparations for the Olympics sparked an enormous revitalization of the city that continues to this day. Atlanta committed itself to developing sports teams, venues, cultural facilities, and a popular airport. Major businesses and media companies such as Coca-Cola, Delta Air Lines, UPS, Holiday Inn, Home Depot, CNN, Superstation TBS, and TNT established headquarters in Atlanta. Important historical sites, such as the Birth Home of Martin Luther King Jr., Ebenezer Baptist Church, King Center, Civil War museums, and the Margaret Mitchell House and Museum, brought in streams of tourists.

Atlanta has become an especially popular destination for African Americans. At one time, black migrations exclusively included African Americans leaving the South, where opportunities were severely restricted and racial violence and racism were dramatically higher than in other regions across the nation. In recent years, African American migrations back to the South have underscored a shift in the long-standing trend. Atlanta, for example, appeals to African Americans because of the popularity of its African American colleges and universities, vibrant and prosperous African American communities, and opportunities to embrace their cultural and racial heritage.

### Learning and Fun with Coca-Cola

The World of Coca-Cola is located in Atlanta, Georgia, and is one of the most popular attractions in the city. The attraction is the second of its kind. The first World of Coca-Cola opened in 1991 and closed in 2007, when the present attraction opened. The new attraction is located in downtown Atlanta in a complex named after the creator of the popular soft drink. The World of Coca-Cola includes the history of Coca-Cola from its beginnings as a local treasure created by pharmacist Dr. John S. Pemberton to the company's current status as a worldwide sensation. In the lobby, large Coca-Cola bottles made with assorted materials from around the world are exhibited; Coke jingles sung in different languages play in the background. Advertising artifacts are exhibited in the Coca-Cola loft. Additional attractions and activities include the Coca-Cola polar bear, the Coca-Cola mascot, and a display of the bottling process, which uses a system that was implemented at the turn of the 20th century. Another area offers visitors the opportunity to taste test products.

The remarkable history of Coca-Cola is such that the soft drink has been one of the most profitable and popular drinks in the nation. Its popularity is reflected by its shrewd advertising through iconic images, such as the signature contoured glass bottle, memorable jingles such as *I'd Like to Buy the World a Coke* in the 1970s, and sayings such as *Coke Is It!*

Coca-Cola endures as a popular soft drink in the 21st century. Its popularity contributes to the appeal of the World of Coca-Cola, which provides an in-depth exploration of the influence of the soft drink in popular culture.

## Images in Popular Culture

Unlike the usual media representations of the South, Atlanta, often referred to in hip terms such as ATL or Hotlanta, is often represented in positive and progressive ways. Among the popular shows that presented contemporary Atlanta in a positive light were *Matlock* (1986–1995), featuring an attorney with a heart of gold played by Andy Griffith, along with African Americans in strong and positive supporting roles, and *Designing Women* (1986–1993), a show about four successful modern women.

Atlanta, for African Americans in particular, has had a pronounced role in television and film. A popular reality television show, *The Real Housewives of Atlanta* (2008–), presents African American women as glamorous and successful and economically accomplished and joins the long line of similar shows based in popular locales, like Beverly Hills and New York. Tyler Perry, a prominent African American director, produced several television series and films with predominantly African American cast members, based in Atlanta. *Meet the Browns* (2009–2011) was taped in Atlanta, and *Tyler Perry's House of Payne* (2006–) is set in Atlanta. Perry's films, such as *Daddy's Little Girls* (2007) and *The Family That Preys* (2008), are also based in Atlanta. Another film, *ATL* (2006), directed by Chris Robinson, stars Atlanta rapper T.I. and features a classic love story between people from two different economic backgrounds, with, what was for many African Americans, a realistic, familiar, down-home feel.

Since the 1990s, Atlanta has become known for southern rap. For many decades, rap was dominated by the East Coast, then, later, the West Coast. Atlanta has produced some of the biggest names and groups in the hip-hop and rap industry, such as Arrested Development, Bow Wow, T.I., Ludacris, and Outkast.

### For Visitors

Visitors to Atlanta will find a city that transcends the *Gone with the Wind* stereotype. The city offers down-home living, historic landmarks, as well as a thriving urban environment. Atlanta attracts business, offering appealing sites for business gatherings and entertainment, and tourists, featuring a mix of lively attractions, clubs, activities, and traditional southern and modern cuisine. A city of increasing diversity, Atlanta has also attracted new transplants from across the nation and the globe.

***See also*** Academy Awards (Oscars); Beverly Hills, California; Cherokee Nation; Georgia Aquarium; HBCUs

### Further Reading

Allen, Frederick. 1996. *Atlanta Rising: The Invention of an International City, 1946–1996*. Atlanta: Longstreet Press.

Brown Nagin, Tomiko. 2011. *Courage to Dissent: Atlanta and the Long History of the Civil Rights Movement*. Oxford, New York: Oxford University Press.

Cohen, Rodney T. 2000. *The Black Colleges of Atlanta*. Charleston, South Carolina: Arcadia Publishing.

Davis, Harold E. 1990. *Henry Grady's New South: Atlanta, a Brave and Beautiful City*. Tuscaloosa: University of Alabama Press.

Pyron, Darden Asbury. 2004. *Southern Daughter: The Life of Margaret Mitchell and the Making of Gone with the Wind*. Athens, Georgia: Hill Street Press.

Westhoff, Ben. 2011. *Dirty South: Outkast, Lil Wayne, Soulja Boy, and the Southern Rappers Who Reinvented Hip-Hop*. Chicago: Chicago Review Press.

## Atlantic City, New Jersey

Atlantic City is a seaside resort in New Jersey. Known as "AC" or the "Las Vegas of the East," Atlantic City has long been a fixture in American popular culture and is notable as the home of saltwater taffy and Miss America Pageant. The city has also served as the inspiration for the popular board game, Monopoly.

Since its incorporation in 1854, Atlantic City has experienced several waves of popularity. In its earliest days, Atlantic City, an island located in the Atlantic Ocean, was a premier destination for vacationers. The sea-side resort brimmed with tourists—families, couples, and individuals, from newborns to the aged—drawn by the reputed health benefits of salt air and the plethora of hotels and thrilling activities for children and adults. In the 1920s, the resort drew crowds of a different sort: those desiring increasingly popular but still forbidden, illicit activities. After experiencing a period of decline, Atlantic City rose again in the late 1970s as a prominent gaming city. Notwithstanding contemporary challenges, Atlantic City remains a modern-day marvel, a place that fills the popular demand for the great American getaway, complete with endless fun and amusements.

### The Game of Money and Chance

*Monopoly* is the name of the popular board game that was created in the early 20th century by Charles Darrow. *Monopoly* was often called *Monopoly City*, because many of the places in the game were taken from or inspired by Atlantic City. Darrow's *Monopoly* game went on the market in 1933. Players pursued wealth and land acquisition according to the roll of the dice. The game featured places and street names found in the popular East Coast destination Darrow visited during his youth.

Examples of Atlantic City streets that appear in the game include Mediterranean, Baltic, Boardwalk, Vermont Avenue, and Atlantic Avenue. As in the game, four railroads serviced the city in real life. Darrow named two of them, the Pennsylvania and Reading Railroads, after actual railroads. The game's B&O Railroad did not serve Atlantic City in real life; but the Short Line was named after the actual Shore Fast Line.

A few years after Darrow's game was first introduced to the nation, the Parker Brothers began selling their version of *Monopoly*. Their game included many of the iconic landmarks used in Darrow's version. The broad appeal of the game helped spark interest in and increase the popularity of Atlantic City, which had been, in the early 20th century, largely a regional sensation.

## Historical Perspectives

Native Americans called the island now known as Atlantic City "Absegami" or "Absecon Island" (Absegami in the Leni-Lenape language means "little sea"). The region was plagued by snakes and mosquitoes, and foliage grew wild and thick on the sandy terrain. In 1838, Jeremiah Leeds braved the island's inhospitable reputation and built a cabin. More people, though in small numbers and over several decades, eventually arrived. Dr. Jonathan Pitney and Richard Osborne saw an irresistible opportunity. With the help of others, they planned to turn the luxurious soft sandy beaches and invigorating salt air and ocean waters into a healthful getaway for hardworking Americans living in nearby cities.

The definitive event in the birth of Atlantic City came with the arrival of the first train, which made the two-and-a-half-hour journey from Camden, New Jersey, in 1854. The railroad ensured the early success of Atlantic City, transporting the curious and anxious tourists from inland parts of New Jersey and Pennsylvania. The railroad brought increasing droves of tourists, which in turn increased the need for more railroads, hotels, and amusements. For many years, Atlantic City was known as the World's Playground.

## The Early Years

The city grew and flourished, stone by stone, brick by brick, in subsequent decades, becoming a place of magic not only for the excessively rich, but for America's working class as well. The majority of African Americans employed at the resort prompted the development of a predominately African American community in North side. In 1853, the first of many hotels, the Belloe House, was constructed. The Atlantic City of this period was known for its many lavish and enormous hotels, like the United States Hotel, which occupied the astonishing length of a city block, the Marlborough-Blenheim Hotel, and the Traymore Hotel. The famous boardwalk, built in 1870, extended from an inlet to the city limits and featured shops, restaurants, and ocean views. A large number of peers were built on the Atlantic shore, the Steel Pier the most famous among them. The Steel Pier, an attraction in itself, featured endless wonders, such as diving horses, Lucy the Elephant, and concerts. Besides sundry attractions, Atlantic City tourists basked under the sun and frolicked in the ocean waves. By the end of the first decade of the 20th century, Atlantic City had bloomed to a population of 60,000. But that didn't count the seasonal tourist influx: in the summer of 1919, Atlantic City saw some 450,000 visitors.

## Prohibition Years

The prohibition era may have decimated the prosperous nightclub business in other major cities, but not in Atlantic City. The resort thrived during this period. Much of the city's illicit activities—drinking, gambling, and prostitution—were maintained by notorious political boss Enoch L. "Nucky" Johnson. This winking at the law created a scandalous and titillating culture that attracted swarms of tourist activity and infamous members of the nation's underworld. To further promote the resort, the first Miss America Pageant was held.

### Contemporary Perspectives

Following several decades of growth and popularity, Atlantic City experienced a significant downward spiral, beginning in the 1950s. Many factors contributed to the resort's decline. Airplanes made it possible for Americans to visit more exotic locales in less time. The mainstreaming of cars badly damaged Atlantic City's tourism industry, drastically shortening the duration of vacation stays at the resort, and the formerly shiny and new hotels had begun to fade. When, in 1964, the Democratic National Convention was held in Atlantic City, press coverage showed the resort's wear and tear and empty streets, underscoring just how far the resort had descended from its former glory.

But when Atlantic City residents voted to approve casino gambling in 1976, the resort experienced its third major wave of popularity. In 1978, Resorts Casino Hotel became the first legal casino on the East Coast. Atlantic City would eventually become known as "The Las Vegas of the East," taking second place in the rankings as a gaming resort. The 11th casino-hotel, the Borgata, was built with a Tuscany theme in 2003. Investors aspired to build more hotels on a par with Las Vegas's super luxurious casino-hotels in Atlantic City, but impediments arose at every turn, presenting new challenges for the resort.

### Issues

For many years, Atlantic City offered the only legalized gaming opportunities on the East Coast. The slow emergence of gaming in the surrounding states of Connecticut, Pennsylvania, New York, and Delaware presented direct competition to Atlantic City, permitting individuals in those states to gamble at home rather than travel to Atlantic City. Other challenges in the new millennium, including the national economic crisis, have frustrated plans to reinvigorate Atlantic City. Addressing the survival of Atlantic City in modern times, New Jersey governor Chris Christie, who assumed office in 2010, has provided support to the city's gaming industry, such as relaxing some of the casino regulations, permitting more gaming revenue to go toward projects benefiting them, and establishing a state-run Atlantic City Tourism District.

### Images in Popular Culture

Despite contemporary challenges, Atlantic City remains a well-known and popular destination. Its history has inspired the publication of both historical and fictional books and has served as the backdrop for a number of films, such as *The King of Marvin Gardens* (1972), *Atlantic City* (1980), *The*

#### Crime and Drama on the Boardwalk

The *Boardwalk Empire* (2010–) is a television series on HBO, an American cable television channel. Adapted from the nonfiction book *Boardwalk Empire: The Birth, High Times, and Corruption of Atlantic City* by Nelson Johnson, *Boardwalk Empire* follows the life of the book's protagonist, the corrupt politician Enoch "Nucky" Johnson. The television series covers the time of Prohibition during the 1920s and 1930s and is set in Atlantic City, New Jersey. The series' title pays tribute to the most famous landmark in the city, the Boardwalk. Many historical figures appear in the series, including infamous gangsters such as Chicago's Al Capone, New York's Charles "Lucky" Luciano, and local African American gangster Albert "Chalky" White.

The series is a departure from the popular image of Atlantic City as a place of innocent fun and amusement. It focuses instead on corrupt happenings behind the scenes, as individuals strive to maintain and compete for power and wealth. Criminality in the nation was exacerbated by Prohibition. Mostly, such crime was concentrated in major cities such as Chicago and New York, but it also appeared in other areas such as Atlantic City, which was otherwise known as a middle-class East Coast family retreat. Then as now, sensational stories of gangsters and corruption are the stuff of books, films, and television.

*Bounty Hunter* (2010), and *The Fighter* (2010) and the 1982 song "Atlantic City" by New Jersey–native Bruce Springsteen. Atlantic City is given a high profile in *Boardwalk Empire* (2010–), the award winning HBO television series adapted from Nelson Johnson's book *Boardwalk Empire: The Birth, High Times, and Corruption of Atlantic City* (2002). The series chronicles the sensational and infamous life of Enoch "Nucky" Johnson, bringing to life the colorful and fascinating history of a city whose allure has proved impossible to extinguish.

***See also*** Cabin; Casino; Las Vegas, Nevada

**Further Reading**

D'Amato, Grace Anselmo. 2001. *Chance of a Lifetime: Nucky Johnson, Skinny D'Amato, and How Atlantic City Became the Naughty Queen of Resorts*. Harvey Cedars, New Jersey: Down the Shore.

Liebowitz, Steve. 2009. *Steel Pier, Atlantic City: Showplace of the Nation*. West Creek, New Jersey: Down the Shore.

Nelson, Johnson. 2002. *Boardwalk Empire: The Birth, High Times, and Corruption of Atlantic City*. Medford, New Jersey: Plexus Publishing.

Nelson, Johnson. 2010. *The Northside: African Americans and the Creation of Atlantic City*. Medford, New Jersey: Plexus Publishing.

Sokolic, William H., and Ruffolo, Robert E. 2006. *Atlantic City Revisited*. Charleston, South Carolina: Arcadia.

## Attica

Attica, otherwise known as Attica State Penitentiary, is a maximum security prison in Attica, New York. A popular site for school field trips and obligatory visits for wayward youth in special deterrent programs, Attica is mostly known for another reason. The prison is most infamous for the four-day riot that occurred there in 1971. The riot was triggered by inmates who had been subjected to overcrowding, abject conditions, and bouts of ill-treatment. Racial tensions also played a significant role. Following the riot and failed negotiations between inmates and prison officials, 39 inmates were shot and killed by police and many more were beaten and tortured. The riot brought forth a media storm, prompted nationwide prison reform, and turned the iconic phrase "Attica, Attica" into a rallying cry and political statement. In broad terms, Attica's prominence in American popular culture is not only based on its symbol of resistance to injustice. To be sure, Attica represents one of the most forbidding institutions for some of the most hard-edged criminals in the nation, conjuring, in the national imagination, a sense of foreboding awe.

### Historical Perspectives

The construction of the grim monolith that is Attica was completed in 1931. Its most pronounced feature is a vast encircling wall, which begins on either side of the front entrance, firmly hemming in the 55 acres of the prison. The wall is 30 feet high and plunges 12 feet below the ground. At the time, the newly built prison was touted as one of the most secure prisons in the nation, though it also promised to provide more humane features, such as comfortable beds, recreation rooms, and sunlight for every cell. In fact, the prison was more than adequately secure, but it featured few amenities for prisoners.

By the 1970s, conditions in Attica were worse than ever. Overcrowding had long been a problem in many prisons in the nation. In Attica, overcrowding was one of several mounting problems. African Americans and Puerto Ricans comprised the majority of the prison's population. Many felt that racism was at the root of the reason why whites got the better prison jobs and why they were often treated poorly by the white prison guards. Other contributing factors to the impending riot were low wages, stringent rules and restrictions, and lack of adequate medical care. Endeavors to seek improvements in their situation went unheeded.

America, at the time of the Attica riot, was in a state of flux and social unrest. A decade had not yet passed since the passing of the Civil Rights Act of 1964 and the nation was still struggling to adjust to life after the dismantlement of the discriminatory laws. The Civil Rights Act was a key outcome of the civil rights activism which had taken place, largely in the South. Coming at the heels of the civil rights movement, the black power movement grew out of the predominately impoverished African American neighborhoods of the inner cities in the North. This movement rallied around a doctrine of racial pride and solidarity and was, in general, opposed to the former movement's nonviolent methods and commitment to passive resistance. Among the prisoners at Attica were men who were affiliated with or influenced in some way by the black power movement. Other protest groups formed around the nation, comprising ethnic groups and college youths, many of whom had protested the Vietnam War (1965–1975). In the prisons, protests in the form of strikes and riots were, by the 1970s, not a new phenomenon.

Rifle-toting National Guardsmen exit Attica prison after putting down an inmate revolt, September 13, 1971. (Time & Life Pictures/Getty Images)

### The Riot

The Attica riot that ignited on September 9, 1971, was not formally organized. It started with an argument between prisoners and a guard. Prisoners attacked the guard and forced their way through the prison, leaving havoc in their wake. One guard was murdered. Prisoners opened cell blocks and took hostages among the population. Prisoners and officials attempted to negotiate in the midst of a maelstrom of news cameras, media curiosity, and tension.

On September 12, Governor Nelson Rockefeller—who never did comply with prisoners' appeals to make an appearance—ordered Commissioner Russell Oswald to take Attica back by force, resulting in several killings and beatings of prisoners.

In 1972, the New York State Special Commission on Attica published a report on the riot. According to some critics, progressive change, resulting from the report, came slowly to Attica (a 2005 prison-monitoring report details Attica's strengths, as well as several lingering challenges). In regard to the devastating killings and beatings, an inmate class action civil suit was not settled until 2001.

### Images in Popular Culture

In the immediate aftermath of the riot, Attica generated a media blitz. If the general public had not known of Attica before, it did as a result of television coverage and other media forms. Documentaries, television movies, and songs about the riot were produced from a sympathetic perspective. Tom Wicker, a journalist, authored his famous novel, *A Time to Die: The Attica Prison Revolt* (1975), from the vantage point of an observer witnessing the tumultuous events. Whether in seriousness or parody, the phrase "Attica, Attica" reverberated in countless pop-culture references, beginning notably with the film *Dog Day Afternoon* (1975). In this film, Al Pacino's character, Sonny, a man who has just attempted to rob a bank, repeatedly shouts the phrase in a fit of frustration when negotiations reach an impasse. A crowd of onlookers cheers him on.

The film's reference to Attica is indicative of the powerful influence of place when it is entwined with an extraordinary and historical event. In this example, invoking the name "Attica" calls to mind the public's shared knowledge of the 1971 riot and the themes of human resistance, struggle, and plight associated with that event. It also challenges the public to rally in support of human struggle. In this way, Attica irrevocably intertwines a physical place with a message of protest.

***See also*** Folsom State Prison

### Further Reading

Chermak, Steven, and Bailey, Frankie Y., eds. 2007. *Crimes and Trials of the Century*. Westport, Connecticut: Greenwood Press.

Domino, John Michael. 2006. *Attica: A Survivors Story*. Grand Rapids, Michigan: Xulon Press.

Wicker, Tom. 1994. *A Time to Die: The Attica Prison Revolt*. Lincoln: University of Nebraska Press.

## Augusta National Golf Club

Augusta National Golf Club is an eminent golf club in Augusta, Georgia, the host of the legendary Masters Tournament, also known as The Masters or The U.S. Masters. The fame of Augusta National Golf Club is broad and sweeping. Not only is it a prestigious and exclusive club, its architecture is widely acclaimed, and top golfers from around the world vie for the opportunity to win the covetous green jacket given to the winner by the previous year's winner at the conclusion of each tournament. For many years, golf was thought to be an exclusive game for the elite, but thanks to extensive television coverage and inspired marketing by the Professional Golf Association that made the players of the game into stars, its popularity in mainstream America has soared. Augusta National, as it is called, is one of the must-see courses in the world.

### Historical Perspectives

John Reid, a Scotland native, is credited with bringing golf to America last in the 19th century. After the founding of the first U.S. golf club, St. Andrews Golf Club in New York, in 1888, golf proliferated. With each passing decade, the number of golf clubs and courses increased by leaps and bounds. By 1900, there were 1000 golf clubs in the nation; three decades later, there were more than 5,700. The Great Depression in the 1930s and 1940s was a serious impediment to the rapidly rising American golf industry.

The economic challenges permeating the nation did not deter Bobby Jones and Clifford Roberts. They established Augusta National Golf Club in 1933. The first Masters Tournament kicked off the following year. British architect Alister Mackenzie, who wrote *Golf Architecture* (1920) and designed several prominent courses, such as those at the Century Country Club in New York and the Crystal Downs Country Club in Michigan, was chosen to design Augusta. The design of the course has undergone more than a dozen changes since then, and its length has increased to more than 7,000 yards. Still, the golf course is considered small compared to other major courses.

### Controversy

Since its inception, members—all men—have been admitted to the club by invitation only. For most of the club's history, this rule applied to white men. Not until 1975 did the first African American golfer, Lee Elders, play in the Masters Tournament. Nearly two decades later, in 1990, the first African American member was finally invited to join the club. Finally, in 2012, women, have been accepted as club members. The first two women to be admitted to the club were Condoleezza Rice, former U.S. Secretary State, and Darla Moore, a highly successful business owner of a private investment firm named Rainwater.

> **The First Women of Augusta**
>
> Condoleezza Rice and Darla Moore made history when they simultaneously became the first women to become members of the Augusta National Golf Club in Augusta, Georgia. Both women are primarily known for their career achievements.
>
> Rice was born on November 14, 1954, in Birmingham, Alabama. After receiving a PhD from the University of Denver's Graduate School of International Studies, Rice joined the faculty at Stanford University as a political science professor. In 1993, Rice became the first woman and African American to serve as provost of Stanford University. Through the 1980s and 1990s, she worked in various government positions thatled to her trailblazing appointment as National Security Adviser in 2001 and then U.S. Secretary of State in 2004 under President George W. Bush.
>
> Though lesser known than Rice, Moore has blazed trails of her own. Born on August 1, 1954, in Lake City, South Carolina, Moore obtained a political science degree from the University of South Carolina and an MBA in International Business at George Washington University. Her career flourished while she worked on Wall Street specializing in bankruptcy work. In 1991, she married Richard Rainwater and in 1994 became the CEO of his private investment company, Rainwater Inc. Moore has served on corporate boards such as Martha Stewart Living, the National Advisory Board of JP Morgan, and the University of South Carolina. In 1998, she was ranked as one of the top most powerful women in business. In 2002, she founded the Palmetto Institute, a research and educational organization in South Carolina.

### The Course

The relatively small size of the golf course in no way diminishes Augusta National's appeal to everyday hackers and the golf elite alike. Notable features include a challenging course embellished with a magnolia-lined driveway, several stone bridges, fountains, Ike's Pond, Rae's Creek, a memorial to honor the founders at Founders Circle, and the famous Eisenhower Cabin, which was built for former president Dwight D. Eisenhower. Each of the 18 holes is named for assorted trees and shrubs that stand on the property.

### Highlights

Augusta National Golf Club is special for other reasons than the uniqueness and beauty of the course. Unlike the other major golf tournaments, The Masters takes place at Augusta National Golf Club every year, and is the first tournament of golf season. Since 1956, the tournament has been broadcast on television. This year-after-year exposure has helped to fuel the allure that envelopes Augusta National, an allure that is made all the more glamorous by its exclusivity.

The extraordinary champions who have appeared at the tournament are another draw. Talented golfers like Tiger Woods, who, at age 21, was the youngest and first African American and Asian to win a Masters, lend their star quality to Augusta National. Golfers play not only for the title, but for the media attention, prize money, trophy, honorary membership at the club, invitations to compete in other high-status tournaments, and above all the legendary green jacket. Worn exclusively by club members while visiting the club, the green jacket is the ultimate golf status symbol. Master's winners can only wear their jacket at the club and must return it at the end of the year. The Masters at Augusta National is one of the most widely anticipated and watched sporting events in the nation.

*See also* Madison Square Garden; Super Bowl; Wrigley Field

### Further Reading

*Augusta National Golf Club*. http://www.augusta.com/.

Hudson, David L. 2008. *Women in Golf: The Players, the History, and the Future of the Sport*. Westport, Connecticut: Praeger Publishers.

McDaniel, Pete. 2000. *Uneven Lies: The Heroic Story of African-Americans in Golf*. Greenwich, Connecticut: American Golfer.

Owen, David. 2003. *The Making of the Masters: Clifford Roberts, Augusta National, and Golf's Most Prestigious Tournament*. New York: Simon & Schuster.

## Austin City Limits

Austin City Limits is both a long-running, live music television series and a three-day music festival located in Austin, Texas. The one-hour television program, broadcast throughout the nation on PBS, debuted in 1976. The festival was first held in 2002. Both have attained national and international popularity and are considered fixtures in America's mainstream music culture. Gathering to share an outdoor musical experience is an indelible aspect of American culture. Being a part of an informal social gathering, especially with the sounds of live music rocking the crowd, is a uniquely American version of excitement and fun.

### Historical Perspectives

The program's loyal fandom is evidence of America's obsession with Austin City Limits. Bill Arhos, former program manager of PBS affiliate KLRN-TV (now KLRU), created Austin City Limits, which aired for the first time in 1976. Arhos's inspiration for the program was that he wanted a platform for Austin's long history of eclectic tradition of live music. Austin, the capitol of Texas, had fostered a distinctive musical culture, with iconic clubs featuring country–and-western music, blues, Mexican music, folk music, and rock. The bevy of homespun singers in and around the college town insured a constant flow of talent. Austin, it seemed (if only to locals and entertainers), was a major music hub. In the early years, the show highlighted the region's country-and-western roots. The program eventually moved from featuring locals to hosting the most popular mainstream performers in assorted musical genres.

### About the Site: The Television Series

According to John T. Davis, the author of *Austin City Limits: 25 Years of American Music* (2000), many viewers mistakenly believe the television program is an outdoor event. As seen on television, performers appear on an outdoor stage. Behind them, subtle green plants separate them from a stunning nighttime vista, glittering city buildings, the luminous glow of the Austin Capitol Dome, and a vast sky. But this view is not real. For most of its existence, Austin City Limits has broadcast from the sixth floor of Studio 6A in the Communications Building on the University of Texas campus. (In 2011, the television program moved off-campus to Moody Theater in downtown Austin.) The audience included only 300 individuals at most, though the studio had a capacity limit of 800. To the live audience, Austin City Limits is as real as it gets; it's a Mecca for music enthusiasts as well as one of the longest running and most popular programs on PBS. Audiences are charmed by the set's intimate and down-to-earth feel and by good music performed in its purest form: live and bereft of the glitz and elaborate effects that characterize crowded concert venues in contemporary times.

### About the Site: The Music Festival

The television program's immense popularity spawned the creation of the eponymous three-day music festival in Austin's Zilker Park, which comprises over 350 acres. America loves outdoor festivals. Along with road trips and going to the beach, festivals have become an essential part of American summer fun, and Austin City Limits is among the favorite outdoor events in the nation. Most music festivals take place in the hot months of summer, but Austin City Limits usually occurs in September or October, months that can be less hot and humid. A lively affair, Austin's music festival attracts some 70,000 enthusiasts sporting shorts, jeans, tank tops, tattoos, purple hair, Mohawks, and cowboy boots. The event features food and art vendors, and temporary henna tattooing in addition to music performed by the most crowd-pleasing and provocative groups in rock, country, indie, folk, and other musical genres.

There are eight total stages. Spontaneous dancing frequently occurs near the stages. The focal point of the festival, like its progenitor television show, is popular music, simple and unembellished, and the good-time ambience of everyday American people in all their diversity.

***See also*** Texas

### Further Reading

*Austin, Texas*. http://www.austintexas.gov/.

*Austin City Limits Music Festival*. http://www.aclfestival.com.

Davis, John T. 2000. *Austin City Limits: 25 Years of American Music*. New York: Billboard Books.

Lickona, Terry, and Newton, Scott, eds. 2010. *Austin City Limits: 35 Years in Photographs*. Austin: University of Texas Press.

# B

## Bar Mitzvah/Bat Mitzvah

B'nai mitzvah has been celebrated with increasing vigor through the years. Within the various branches of the Jewish religion, the parties, in particular, have grown spectacularly in scale and in popularity. On the one hand, parents hold parties to observe their heritage, pay homage to religious traditions, and mark and celebrate an important milestone, a coming of age in the life of their children. On the other hand, b'nai mitzvah has become a cherished tradition, an event of colossal importance, especially for the celebrants. These ceremonies, like lavish birthday parties and coming-out parties of the 19th century, give cause for fun with peers, loads of gifts, and entertainment.

### Historical Perspectives

The bar mitzvah and bat mitzvah developed at different times. Unlike many Jewish observations, rituals and feasts, neither ceremony is ordained by any sacred or religious Jewish text. The bar mitzvah was established sometime in medieval times. The first known recording of a designated feast for boys occurred among German Jews and was written about by Rabbi Shlomo been Yehiel Luria in the 1500s.

The bat mitzvah took more time to develop. Because males have traditionally played the dominant roles in the Jewish religion, girls did not originally have their own ceremony. Rabbi Mordecai Kaplan was credited with starting the bat mitzvah in the United States. After observing a celebration in Italy, he gave his daughter, Judith Kaplan, the first known bat mitzvah in America (specifically, New York City) in 1922. Since the mid-20th century, observations of b'nai mitzvah have spread throughout the country, appearing normally as modest-sized affairs with emphasis placed on the religious element. In time, observations of b'nai mitzvah, although constant in some ways, have morphed and expanded, soaring to new heights.

### Cultural Distinctions

The bar mitzvah and bat mitzvah are celebrated in multiple ways in Jewish communities; however, the ceremonies customarily include a religious service led by the celebrant, a meal, gift giving, and a party. Guests, not limited to the Jewish religion, include family members, adults, and children. Preparation for the b'nai mitzvah begins early. Some youth begin learning Hebrew and the history and rituals of the religion in the first grade, so that by the time they reach 12 or 13, they are well prepared to lead services. They conduct a blessing, reading from one or more sacred texts in Hebrew and singing or chanting in Hebrew at their b'nai mitzvah. Conservative denominations may only allow girls to lead religious services before an all-female audience, if at all. Liberal denominations will permit girls and boys to perform this duty. Youth in Humanist or other secular-based denominations will read a report about family or cultural history in lieu of reading from the Torah or Haftorah. (In recent years, nontraditional celebrations of or inspired by b'nai mitzvah have been celebrated by secular Jews and non-Jews). This portion of the ceremony is, by far, the most religious and subdued element of the celebration. That which follows—the feast, gift-giving, and the party—is celebrated with an exuberance that has been compared to a wedding reception.

Not everyone who observes b'nai mitzvah goes to the lengths to which the festivities have come to be popularly known. Not everyone is on agreement that large, extravagant parties, inundated with nontraditional pop-cultural themes, are in good taste or in keeping with the religious and cultural importance of the occasion. But the trend of putting on colossal parties continues to increase. The plans may include limousine rentals, catering, and deejays playing popular tunes (pop, hip-hop, as well as traditional Jewish songs) or live entertainment. T-shirts and other mementos are given to the attendees. Gift-giving can include trips to Europe, money, jewelry, and religious items.

### Images in Popular Culture

In addition to the growing body of documentaries and literature about b'nai mitzvah, film, television, and other media have treated the subject—sometimes seriously, often comically. Primary and secondary characters become bar mitzvahs in such popular sitcoms as *The Wonder Years* (1988–1993), *The Simpsons* (1989–), and *Seinfeld* (1989–1998). Bat mitzvahs are covered in the HBO sitcoms *Curb Your Enthusiasm* (2000–) and *Sex in the City* (1998–2004). In the film *Starsky and Hutch* (2004), a comedic remake of a popular 1970s television series, the detective duo crash a bat mitzvah disguised as performing mimes in an attempt to capture the film's wealthy Jewish antagonist. *Keeping up with the Steins* (2006) is a bar mitzvah comedy featuring the Fiedlers, who want to compete with a rival family, the Steins, for the most grandiose bar mitzvah. The Steins's bar mitzvah, appearing at the start of the film, parodies the materialistic aspects of some modern celebrations. By movie's end, the Fielders have a change of heart and host a modest, warm-hearted bar mitzvah for their son.

The public has only to turn to the Internet to learn more about b'nai mitzvah or to read about or share experiences of the ceremony. The Internet has a large body of information about the Jewish religion in general, and b'nai mitzvah in particular. Sites proffer bar and bat mitzvah ideas, gifts, and vacation packages; tutors can be found online to help youth prepare for their big day. Families publish YouTube videos of their children's celebrations, and Facebook has provided a gathering place for youth to talk about their b'nai mitzvah experiences and post pictures from the event.

### In Conclusion

The b'nai mitzvah has become a modern phenomenon. What started out as a small, folksy, and exclusive affair, little known to the public, practiced by a handful of Jewish communities throughout the world, has become etched into the American Jewish tradition as well as in the national popular imagination.

***See also*** Facebook; New York, New York; Quinceañera

### Further Reading

Bennett, Roger, Shell, Jules, and Kroll, Nick. 2005. *Bar Mitzvah Disco*. New York: Brown Publishers.

Mitchell, Claudia A., and Reid-Walsh, Jacqueline, eds. 2007. *Girl Culture: An Encyclopedia*. Westport, Connecticut: Greenwood Press.

Oppenheimer, Mark. 2005. *Thirteen and a Day: The Bar and Bat Mitzvah across America*. New York: Farrar, Straus & Giroux.

Rappaport, Jill, and Solomon, Linda. 2007. *Mazel Tov: Celebrities Bar and Bat Mitzvah Memories*. New York: Simon & Schuster.

## Barbershops

Barbershops are places where men receive shaves, beard trims, and haircuts. Whether in small towns, metropolitan cities, or the far reaches of the perilous Western Frontier of olden days, barbershops have been routinely visited by men, sometimes daily or weekly. Cleanliness, neatness, and smart cuts and trims were outward indicators of attractiveness, refinement, and good citizenry. But men were drawn to more than the desire to look good or presentable. Barbershops provided experiences that reinforced male identity, reaffirmed male bonding and conversations, provided a rite of passage for boys entering adulthood or the military, and in some circumstances, provided an outlet for uncensored talk and a forum for political work.

### Historical Perspectives

Barbering is an ancient practice found in many countries. Barbers not only groomed their patients but also performed medical procedures on them. Medical treatments included extracting teeth and bloodletting. Bloodletting, an obsolete procedure that involved drawing blood from a patient, was believed to

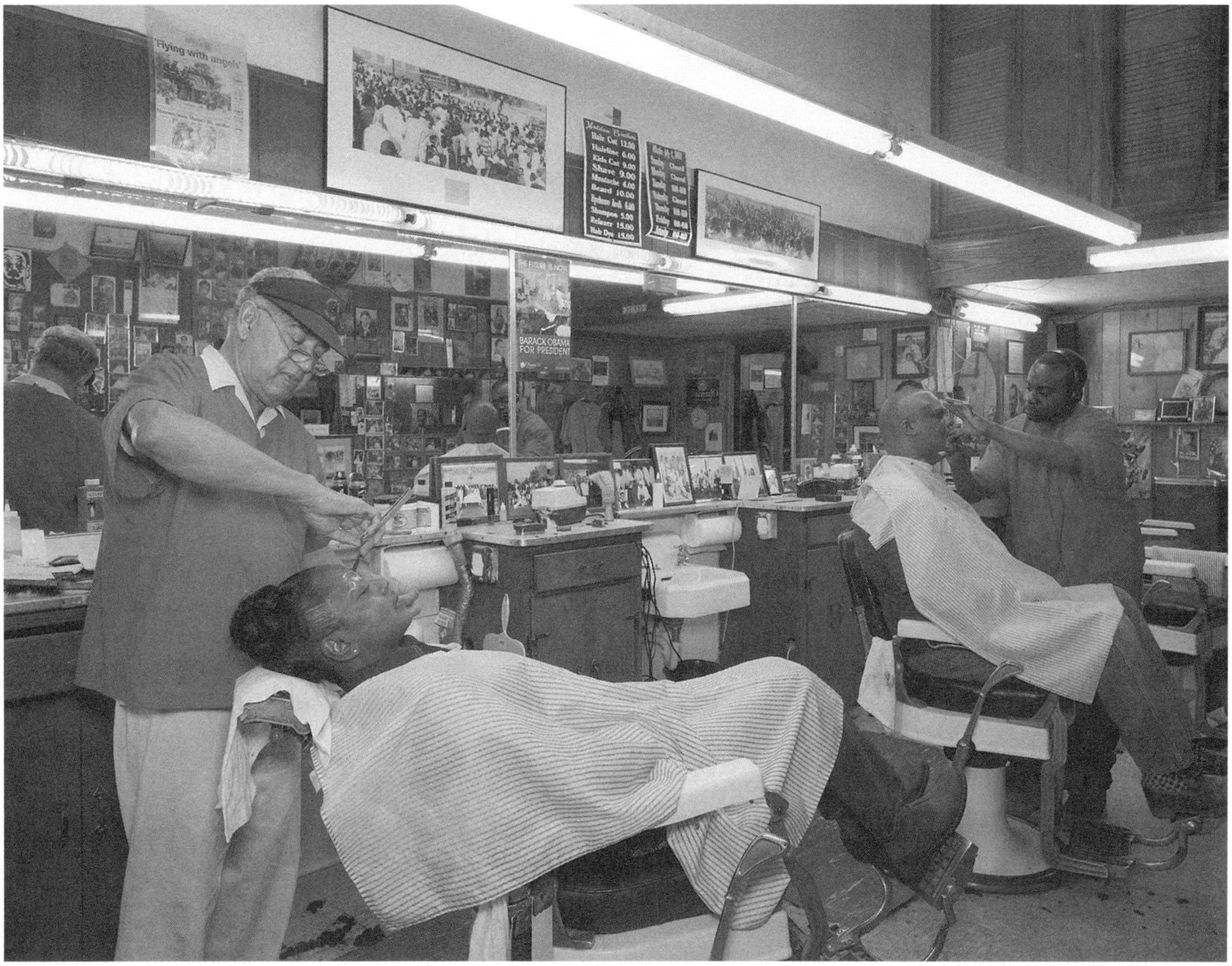


The Malden Brothers Barbershop in Montgomery, Alabama, ca. 2010. Martin Luther King Jr. and other civil rights figures, as well as generations of Montgomery residents, have come to the Maldens for hair care and community, since the late 1950s. (Library of Congress)

be highly beneficial for every malady imaginable. Barbershops arrived in the New World with the first settlers. Early on, they were simple places. On the frontier, barbershops were as roughly hewn as the cowboys, homesteaders, and occasional desperados that frequented them. As time passed, American barbershops expanded and prospered, becoming fixtures, like the town square and the village church, in most every town and city.

The heyday of the barbershop occurred between 1880 and 1940. According to barber scholar, Christian R. Jones, a number of inventions and breakthrough developments in American industry and business, along with a growing interest in fashion, were the cause for this, prompting the glamorous transformation of the barbershop. New tools and mail-order opportunities aided the barber; the Transcontinental Railroad helped augment the expansion of barbershops and barber schools across the nation, and barbershops reaped the benefits of America's booming economy and demand for a professional look. Jones also describes England's influence on America during Queen Victoria's monarchy (1837–1901), which not only resulted in a fierce affection for opulent designs and architecture but also inspired formal couture and hairstyles. Premier barbershops were decorated extravagantly with marble, expensive woods, and luxuriously comfortable chairs. They offered baths, perfumes, boot blacking, and cigars to their clientele, in addition to fashionable cuts and other grooming procedures.

### Cultural Distinctions

All barbershops, fancy or not, eventually became known for certain distinguishing features. The shop's trademark barber pole, affixed outside the barbershop, signaled to the world that this was a place of business reserved exclusively for male grooming. Barber chairs that reclined and swiveled, with headrests and footstools adjusted according to the client's height, were equally recognizable. The ritual haircut was performed with clippers instead of modern scissors, and the shave, an unhurried and pleasant process performed with a straight razor, involved heat, sundry pretreatments, and a rich lather applied to the face. Following the shave, the client might receive a massage and additional ointments.

The barbershop experience offers a glimpse into American male identity and culture. Barbershops supported a concept of manhood in opposition to the tough and coarse-looking cowboy. Moreover, they sustained a culture of exclusive male relationships, first between the barber and the client and second among the clients themselves. Historically, preoccupation with personal appearance and grooming was associated with aristocracy and women. The iconic image of the unshaved and unkempt frontiersman underscored the opinion that men need not be concerned about grooming, and that male grooming had a civilizing (or softening) effect on men.

Barbering did have a civilizing effect on men, but softening had nothing to do with it. Barbershops promoted the belief that to be civilized was to be refined and well-groomed and that male grooming was socially acceptable, if not socially mandatory. As the popularity of barbershops spread across the nation regardless of economic status, the image of the groomed man increasingly became a widely accepted symbol of manliness. Thus, going to the barber, particularly during the barbershop's golden years, was a thing that the everyday man did on a regular basis, a habit that he passed on to his sons. First haircuts at the barbershop initiated young boys into the exclusive world of adult males; first shaves signaled a rite of passage into manhood.

A distinct male culture was sustained and nurtured within the environment of the barbershop. Based on the historical tradition of segregating men and women in work, play, and other social realms, barbershops were considered sacred spaces for men. In this environment, men nurtured friendships through sharing space and experience and engaging in conversations, gossip, jokes, and other talk.

In African American communities, barbershop culture contrasted in significant ways from that of mainstream white America. Along with the African American church, the community barbershop was a cornerstone of the community. Before the landmark deathblow of discriminatory laws in the 1960s, African Americans were, generally, prohibited from going to "white" barbershops. Nonetheless, African American barbershops provided safe spaces for African American to vent their frustrations concerning white privilege and dominance in society, racism and discrimination, and struggles and problems in their communities. Barbershops were also one of the places where participants in the civil rights movement were recruited and information about the movement was disseminated. Joking and amiable debates also took place in African American barbershops.

**Singing in Four-Part Harmony**

Barbershop quartets are harmonious *a capella* singing groups traditionally composed exclusively of men. *A capella* refers to singing that is unaccompanied by musical instruments. Barbershop quartets were originally created by African American men during the late 19th century. The singing was performed exclusively within barbershops, hence the name of the style of singing. The style included four-part harmony with the lead singer singing the melody in the range of second tenor. Harmony is provided by a tenor, bass, and baritone. The songs included well-known spirituals as well as improvised creations.

Not long after African Americans began performing barbershop music, whites adopted the style. By the beginning of the 20th century, barbershop quartets were mostly associated with whites, not blacks. In 1938, Owen C. Cash established the Society for the Preservation and Encouragement of Barber Shop Quartet Singing in America, also known as the Barbershop Harmony Society. Sweet Adelines International was founded in 1945 for women, who had begun to establish their own all-women barbershop quartets. Both organizations operate to this day. Today's barbershop music includes genre classics as well as popular songs in myriad genres. Barbershop quartets may popularly appear at public events such as festivals, farmer markets, and special celebrations.

### Contemporary Perspectives

Unlike African American barbershops, mainstream barbershops experienced a decline after 1940. Among the contributing reasons for the vanishing appeal of the American barbershop were the invention of razors for convenient and quick use at home, economic woes causing barbershops to scale down or close, the fashion for long hair beginning in the 1960s, and the advent of gender-neutral salons.

In recent years, barbershops have made a comeback. Nostalgia, curiosity, fad-consciousness, and the increasing importance placed on male grooming and male-only spaces in some subcultures are at the heart of contemporary popular interest in barbershops. New barbershops, particularly in metropolitan areas, are constructed as replicas or swanky modernized versions of old-time shops. Many modern barber shops offer services such as manicures and pedicures. The more lavish barbershops charge exorbitant prices for in-demand accessories and services.

Within the African American community, the role of the barbershop in popular culture has maintained its continuity. Barbershops did not disappear in large numbers in predominately African American neighborhoods and sections in cities and towns. Some barbershops cater to older men; others cater to younger men who desire modern styles and treatments. Some shops maintain a dated, spare, and bland appearance with a folksy ambience. Others are markedly modernized with upscale furnishings, décor, and lighting.

### Images in Popular Culture

The barbershop's leap from real life to film and television dramatizes its importance and popularity across the years and in many subcultures in America. In Western films, the barber and barbershop are like the bartender and saloon, a fixture in old Western towns. Audiences are offered glimpses into the barbershop in classics like *High Noon* (1952), *High Plains Drifter* (1973), and *Unforgiven* (1992). Generally, the good guys are clean-shaven, while the bad guys sport grubby beards and unkempt mustaches. A classic portrayal of the barbershop appears in the wholesome *The Andy Griffith Show* (1960–1968). In the mob film *The Untouchables* (1987), infamous Chicago mob leader Al Capone gets a shave. In the HBO television series *The Sopranos* (1999–2007), which plays on the real-life gangsters of the 1920s, the characters' personas were built not only on lawlessness but on fashionable suits and meticulous grooming habits. The military film *Full Metal Jacket* (1987) starts off, in rapid sequences, with close-ups of young men getting buzz cuts in a barbershop. The buzz cut symbolizes not only their coming into manhood but their initiation into army boot camp and foreshadows the dramatic life to follow.

The African American barbershop is vaulted into the spotlight in other films. Popular comedic films like *Coming to America* (1988) and the *Barbershop* series (2002, 2004) portray African American barbershops from a comedic point of view but still touch upon serious, if not controversial issues. The popularity of the barbershop films resulted in a television spin-off, adding to other barbershop-themed programs on television. *Sharp Talk with Al Sharpton* (2005–2008) featured host Al Sharpton, a civil rights activist and political commentator, interviewing African American leaders in politics, business, and the entertainment industry in Levels Barbershop in New York City. *Cuttin' Up* (2004) featured host hip-hop entrepreneur and rapper Jermaine Dupri interviewing African American celebrities in barbershops in Atlanta, Georgia; Miami, Florida; and New York City. After the first African American president, Barrack Obama, took office in 2009, President Obama's long-standing barber, Zariff, received a lot of attention when it was announced that he would continue cutting the president's hair.

### In Conclusion

From Westerns to mobster films, small-town life to contemporary ethnic communities and chic urban environments, the barbershop's presence in fiction and reality is telling. Long after the illustrious days of barbershop's popularity had dimmed, barbershops remain an indisputable American institution.

***See also*** Atlanta, Georgia; Beauty Shops; Chicago, Illinois; Man Cave; Miami, Florida; New York, New York; Old West; Saloons, Bars, and Taverns

### Further Reading

Abecassis, Tally, and Sauve, Claudine. 2005. *Barbershops*. London: Black Dog Publishing.

Briston, Doug. 2010. "Barbers and Barbershops." In *The American Beauty Industry Encyclopedia*, edited by Julie Willett, 36–40. Santa Barbara, California: Greenwood Press.

Harris-Lace well, Melissa Victoria. 2004. *Barbershops, Bibles, and BET: Everyday Talk and Black Political Thought*. Princeton, New Jersey: Princeton University Press.

Hunter, Mic. 1996. *The American Barbershops: A Closer Look at a Disappearing Place*. Mount Horeb, Wisconsin: Face to FaceBooks.

Jones, Christian R. 1998. *Barbershop: History & Antiques*. Atglen, Pennsylvania: Schiffer Publishing.

## Barns

Barns are buildings traditionally used on farms to shelter animals, to store crops, and to store equipment. Barns are not exclusive to America. Indeed, the custom of building and using barns were brought with the early settlers, such as the English, Dutch, and Swiss, from their native countries. In America, barns were designed according to cultural influences, available resources, specific needs, and the environment itself. During the so-called golden era of barn building, which lasted from the 1700s to the mid-1900s, barns were a fixture in the rural environs of the country and an essential part of the working farm life and culture.

Since the end of the golden era, traditional barns have suffered a marked decline. Through the efforts of organizations and individuals, including farmers themselves, many barns have undergone conversion into myriad nontraditional uses. Thus, the barn, regarded as a symbol of an American heritage, has been preserved, as well as transitioned from a space that was exclusive to farming, to an adaptable space that has been used to create many popular attractions for the American public.

### Historical Perspectives

Upon the arrival of the settlers into the New World in the 17th and 18th centuries, agriculture was the dominant industry. Naturally, the settlers, coming from disparate countries such as England, Germany, Switzerland, and the Netherlands, built structures that were familiar to them in their settlements. Before the 19th century, barns were built primarily out of logs. They were one of several buildings that were required to run a typical farm. From the start, barns came in myriad shapes and sizes.

### Types of Barns

Barns were constructed in rural areas throughout North America. Specific types of barns, with sundry variations, were often found in particular regions. In addition to those discussed in the following, many other barn types were found throughout the nation. The most common material used for barns was wood, but other materials, such as stone and brick, were also frequently used. Barns were commonly painted red, a color that may have originally been used because it was easier and inexpensive to create. Later, the color was preferred because of custom.

The Dutch barn was prominent in the state of New York, where a large Dutch community settled before the British claimed the area. The Dutch barn had an appearance similar to a traditional church with an A-frame roof. Inside, the barn featured a threshing floor and cattle stalls. Before the 19th century, families lived in one area of the barn. After the 19th century, families lived in separate homes.

Germans made popular the Philadelphia barns, which took the name of the city where they were built. The English barns were popular with the English settlers. This style, which was popular in such states as Vermont, evolved over time; however, the general appearance included a gable roof and a pair of hinged doors on the eaves-side wall. When more space was required, the barns were extended horizontally rather than vertically.

Circular and polygonal barns were traditionally associated with Shakers and Quakers. The bank barn, which was usually built on the side of a hill, comprised a lower level for animals and an upper level for the threshing floor and storage. Found popularly in the South and the Southeast, especially in Appalachia and the Ozarks, crib barns are usually one story and may comprise up to six cribs or storage areas. The most recognizable style of barn was the prairie barn or Western barn. Due to the need for storage space for the sizable farms and herds in the American West and Southwest, the prairie barn is much larger than early barns. Another distinction of the prairie barn is its gambrel roof.

### Cultural Distinctions

In the extremely physical world of the farm, the individual's connection to the earth was strong; the passage of time was monitored by the cycle of planting and harvesting; and the barn was an essential structure. The women controlled the domestic realm in the home: cooking, cleaning, taking care of the children, and making clothes. The barn was associated with adult and older adolescent males, who fed and cared for the livestock and stored away the harvest, equipment, and fodder, such as hay and grain.

The children also played important roles, carrying out chores such as feeding the pigs and chickens, collecting eggs, gathering wood, and fetching water.

The barn also served as a shelter for social functions. To offset the days of hard labor, communities departed from their farms and traveled to a barn designated for special events, such as the popular square dancing. In this way, the barn functioned, like the general store and church, as a space where the community gathered and potential courters mingled. Barn raising provided another opportunity for social interactions in the community, as neighboring farmers from the community gathered to pool their strength and building skills while the farm wives provided the victuals.

### Contemporary Perspectives

In the mid-20th century, a dramatic transformation occurred on the nation's farms. Technological advances and big corporate farming were on the rise; the traditional family-owned farms waned. Though not wholly obsolete, the traditional farm increasingly relied on new technologies for storage, labor, and animal husbandry. In this climate, old barns—ramshackle and faded—stood neglected; others collapsed under the strains of age, weather, and disuse. Many barns were torn down when farms were closed or replaced by modern structures made out of metal.

Despite the dwindling numbers of barns in the nation, their solid structures and rugged designs were still loved, and individuals found creative ways to use and preserve them rather than dismantle them. With increasing traffic on the open highways, farmers located along the interstates sold advertising space on the roofs of their barns; such ads were easily visible to travelers on the road. Barns were rented out for weddings, converted to living spaces and used as vacation lodgings, restaurants, and permanent homes. Barns were also converted into retail spaces, museums, and churches.

### Images in Popular Culture

The barn's place in America has changed significantly over the years. During its golden era, the barn, sturdy and utilitarian, was a symbol of labor, livelihood, and simple living. In modern times, the barn plays a less life-defining role in society. Rather, the barn has emerged as an object of education, play, and entertainment. Children in the developmental stage of the English language learn the names of farm animals and the sounds that farm animals make. Barns serve as an educational tool for youth who visit farms during school field trips. Barns are used as a source of child's play, incorporated into various toy items and decorative design in classrooms or bedrooms. Youth and adults go to state and country farms to explore barns filled with animals for petting or viewing.

The barn has also been depicted in a romantic way, particularly through the paintings of such artists as William Sydney Mount, Grandma Moses, Andrew Wyeth, and Warren Kimble.

### For Visitors

In most any rural environment in the nation, travelers may discover barns, in use or not, in open fields along the highways. Some barns operate as tourist attractions, where visitors immerse themselves in learning about and participating in hands-on events related to farm life.

In Arcadia, Oklahoma, the renovated round barn, built in 1898, now operates as a museum filled with U.S. Route 66 memorabilia. In Millersburg, Ohio, Yoder's Amish Home, which has been open to the public since 1983, features activities such as tours through a unique Amish barn. The Billings Farm & Museum in Woodstock, Vermont, manages several barns such as a chicken barn, horse barn, and cow barn. During Harvest Weekend in the month of October, barn dances are scheduled.

***See also*** Amish Country; Appalachia; Billings Farm & Museum; Highways; Philadelphia, Pennsylvania; U.S. Route 66

**Further Reading**

Danbom, David B. 2006. *Born in the Country: A History of Rural America*. Baltimore: Johns Hopkins University Press.

Endersby, Elric, Greenwood, Alexander, and Larkin, David. 2003. *Barn: Preservation & Adaptation: The Evolution of a Vernacular Icon*. New York: Universe Publishing.

Leffingwell, Randy. 1997. *The American Barn*. Osceola, Wisconsin: Motorbooks International.

Radojkovic, Jon. 2007. *Barn Building: The Golden Age of Barn Construction*. Erin, Ontario: Boston Mills Press.

## Barnes and Noble

Barnes and Noble (B&N), touted as the nation's largest book retailer, also sells magazines, newspapers, music, video games, and assorted items such as journals, stationery, and bookmarks. Originally established as a printing business in 1873, the company has since generated over 700 retail stores and over 600 college bookstores. In recent years, Barnes and Noble established an online bookstore and released the popular electronic reader (e-reader) known as the Nook.

Well established as a popular institution in everyday American life, the retailer has thrived despite competition from other major retailers, and, more recently, the nationwide trend toward online book sites

With over 700 stores nationwide, Barnes&Noble is the largest book retailer in the United States. (Sean Pavone/Dreamstime.com)

and digital books read on electronic devices. Virtual bookstores and e-books have threatened to eradicate the traditional bricks and mortar stores and their paper books bound in illustrated hard or soft covers. Americans, albeit in decreasing numbers, still go to B&N stores throughout the nation.

The appeal of B&N harkens back to America's past, where quaint bookstores were commonly found on most any Main Street in America. The bookstores played an important part in everyday American life to the point that they were sometimes taken for granted and not seen as a vital part of popular culture. B&N, though larger than its archetypes, still draws individuals in search of an experience.

A typical retail store includes tables and comfortable chairs, food and drink, and opportunities to scour through books and magazines, and interact, face-to-face, with other individuals. B&N is a place where friends meet over coffee; book clubs meet to discuss the latest read; adults and youth get lost in bestselling novels; and everyone buys books as gifts or to add to the bookshelf of keepers at home.

### Historical Perspectives

Barnes and Noble started out in 1873 as a book printing business founded in Wheaton, Illinois by Charles M. Barnes. Barnes' son, William Barnes, and G. Clifford Noble opened the first bookstore in 1917. The headquarters were eventually moved to 122, 5th Avenue in New York City, and in 1965, Barnes and Noble College Booksellers became a subsidiary of B&N. In 1971, Leonard Riggio purchased the company, which, at the time, was performing miserably.

Riggio implemented a number of ameliorative actions, such as producing television advertisements and offering discounts on books listed on *The New York Times* bestselling books. This helped steer B&N toward success and broaden the company's popularity. B&N built an increasing number of retail stores across the nation, began publishing its own books, and reissued out-of-print titles and classics. B&N also acquired businesses such as B. Dalton Booksellers (most often found in malls) and Game Stop stores; however, these acquisitions would not be permanent (B&N no longer owns these stores). In recent years, B&N has benefited from massive public demand for books launched by high-profile moguls like Oprah Winfrey, star of a popular talk show, who started a book club and regularly made book recommendations, and J. K. Rowling, author of the massively read *Harry Potter* series.

### Contemporary Issues

To local booksellers, B&N's success was a singular threat. Independent bookstores, usually housed in smaller buildings with a limited number of titles, could hardly compete with the giant retailer. Backed by mega profits, greater resources, and deeper discounts, B&N easily bested the local independent bookstores. B&N also built stores in neighborhoods where there were no local bookstores. The era of local bookstores seemed doomed to end. Independent bookstores closed in record numbers.

B&N was not without its competitors. Borders, similar in look and organization to B&N, presented a formidable competition in the market for many years. That is, until it folded in 2011. Costco and Walmart, super retailers that dabble in a wide assortment of products, sometimes offered its customers deeper discounts than B&N.

A more formidable challenge came from Amazon.com and other online retailers, which became all the rage and indeed altered the book industry in substantial ways. Instead of going to bookstores, many Americans turned to their Internet to buy books (in traditional format or digital versions), music, and video games. These products tended to be more competitively priced and fit the growing tech lifestyle of everyday Americans.

Online book purchases contributed to the demise of yet more local bookstores, as they made it less appealing for the public to buy books the traditional way at all bricks and mortar stores, whether folksy independent stores or corporate giants like B&N. The Internet permits users to buy books online from the comfort of their homes or from anywhere in the world, delivered to the door at comparable prices. For retailers, the Internet drastically lowered the cost of running a bookselling business. The invention of e-books and e-readers streamlines the reading experience, is environmentally friendly (saves trees), and falls in line with the American public's ongoing pursuit for the greatest and newest in technology.

Farsighted B&N has ensured its place in the future of the industry by adapting to popular trends. B&N launched its own online website in 1997, catering to children and adults, book lovers, and music lovers. It released its own e-reader, the Nook, in 2009, attempting to get a share of the digital market opened up by Amazon.com's Kindle. The Nook allows readers to purchase and read books and other media, as well as to utilize the Read In Store feature. Although B&N's online business and Nook are flourishing, the retail stores maintain their supremacy—at least for now—among the decreasing number of bricks and mortar bookstores.

### Cultural Distinctions: The Bookstore Experience

There was a time in the not-too-distant past when the public primarily went to bookstores to purchase books. Bookstores were among the common retailers found in the nation's malls and plazas and along its major thoroughfares. Going to the bookstore, then and now, was something that Americans indulged in as a leisure activity. Sometimes construed an elitist activity, over time, Barnes and Noble attracted customers from all economic and educational backgrounds.

Today, most B&N retail stores feature cafes that sell Starbucks coffee, sweets, and an assortment of snacks. Comfy chairs, tables, and an array of books sectioned by assorted themes provide a home-like experience. B&N stores promote conversation, study, and quiet reflection and exploration that can go on for hours. Events such as book signings and lectures provide opportunities for readers to interact with their favorite writers. When individuals are asked on Internet sites to share their feelings about books and bookstores, actual or electronic, many assert that they prefer bricks and mortar bookstores. Many agree that online sites and e-books are more efficient, but they do not conjure the meaningful experiences that come with real books and bookstores.

For many, the earliest experiences with books begin in childhood. Children's books, with their assorted sizes and vibrantly illustrated pages, stir collective memories of childhood and popular bedtime stories. Other memories are even more sensory—the smell and the sound and feel of pages made from paper add to the nostalgic value of book reading. Readers share an undeniably pleasant experience to browse through book stacks or linger over a cup of coffee and a book.

### In Conclusion

To this day, B&N continues to attract book lovers unwilling to abandon a long-standing American tradition. There is no denying, however, that the survival of the stores depends upon maintaining a balance between the old and new.

***See also*** Costco; Cyberspace; Library of Congress; Main Street; The Mall; National Archives; New York, New York; New York Public Library; Starbucks; Walmart

### Further Reading

Garten, Jeffrey E. 2001. *The Mind of the CEO*. New York: Basic Books.

Striphas, Ted. 2009. *The Late Age of Print: Everyday Book Culture from Consumerism and Control*. New York: Columbia University Press.

Thompson, John B. 2010. *Merchants of Culture: The Publishing Business in the Twenty-First Century*. Cambridge, United Kingdom; Malden, Massachusetts: Polity.

# Baseball Hall of Fame

The Baseball Hall of Fame, known formally as the National Baseball Hall of Fame and Museum, located in Cooperstown, New York, showcases prominent stars of baseball, and is a repository of all things baseball, past and present. Baseball, the nation's beloved sport, has deep roots in American popular culture. For most of the late 19th and early 20th centuries, the sport consumed the national imagination, with baseball legends ranking along side Hollywood movie stars and military heroes.

Baseball mania made inevitable the building of the Baseball Hall of Fame and Museum, which opened in 1939. Even today, when the game lags behind football as the most popular sport in the nation, the Baseball Hall of Fame attracts hundreds of thousands of visitors each year. Visitors include passionate baseball fans, collectors of baseball memorabilia, baseball players, and tourists, all sharing the desire to explore the history and traditions of this most beloved of American sports.

### A Baseball Icon

Babe Ruth is a legendary professional baseball player who played for the Boston Red Sox, the New York Yankees, and the Boston Braves in the early days of the 20th century. He accumulated numerous records, such as most home runs (714), a record he held until Hank Aaron of the Atlanta Braves broke the record in 1974.

Born George Herman Ruth Jr. on February 6, 1895, in Baltimore, Maryland, young Ruth was a handful for his parents. Ruth's parents, who owned a tavern, could not easily manage their son, who enjoyed wandering the streets and getting into mischief like skipping school and chewing tobacco. When Ruth was seven years old, his parents sent him to St. Mary's Industrial School for Boys. While there, the monks taught the boy how to play baseball. Ruth had developed extraordinary skills by the time he reached mid-adolescence. Jack Dunn, a baseball owner, became 19-year-old Ruth's parental guardian so that he could play on his minor league team, the Baltimore Orioles. While playing for Dunn, Ruth was called "Dunn's new babe," and then "Babe" Ruth.

Ruth rapidly transitioned from the minor leagues into the majors. Ruth initially played for the Boston Red Sox, beginning in 1914, contributing to three of the team's championships. In 1919, he signed with the Yankees. Throughout Ruth's spectacular career, the American public adored him.

In 1935, Ruth played for a short period for the Boston Braves. Though he hit three home runs in a single game, he retired the following week. In the following year, he was inducted into the Baseball Hall of Fame. He died on August 16, 1948, but is still remembered as one of the greatest players the game has ever seen.

## Historical Perspectives

Baseball, an offshoot of a game called "rounder," has been played in America since the second half of the 18th century, but its specific origins are unclear. A.G. Spalding, a sporting goods owner and baseball player, established the Spalding Commission in order to uncover the mystery of who invented the game and when and where it happened. In 1907, the commission alleged that a Union officer in the Civil War (1861–1865) named Abner Doubleday was responsible for originating the game in Cooperstown in 1839. Though it was later determined that he was not the inventor, the tradition held for many years, and Doubleday and Cooperstown were heralded as the inventor and birthplace of baseball, respectively.

Stephen C. Clark capitalized on the distinction awarded to his hometown and spearheaded the efforts to establish a hall of fame in Cooperstown. On June 12, 1939, the Baseball Hall of Fame opened with spectacular fanfare. Some 15,000 individuals descended upon the small town. Representatives from major league teams were present, and the first five inductees—Tyrus Cobb, George Ruth (Babe Ruth), Walter Johnson, Honus Wagner, and Christy Mathewson—were honored.

## Baseball Experiences and National Memory

Generations of Americans shared baseball memories. American boys collected baseball cards, which pictured uniformed players in striking poses above baseball statistics. Baseball was synonymous with vendors selling hotdogs and popcorn, rousing renditions of the sport's anthem "Take Me Out to the Ball Game," and the indelible sound of the crack of the bat against the ball. Family outings to baseball's distinctive stadiums were the norm, and the game was called, "the national pastime." Since 1939, the Baseball Hall of Fame has been an indelible part of the baseball experience.

### For Visitors

The Baseball Hall of Fame has grown, transformed, and expanded since its opening. These days, the Museum looms large on Main Street, the town's shop-lined arterial. John Thorn, the author of *Treasures of the Baseball Hall of Fame* (1998) describes the Hall of Fame and Museum experience as magical and breathtaking. There is much to see, and many nostalgic exhibits, video presentations, and artifacts to explore. The Museum holds some 35,000 artifacts, and its library holdings are in the millions. For individuals who cannot visit the Museum in person, many books and the official website offer images, but neither can compare to standing in the Museum in person. It could take many hours, if not days, to experience the Museum's offerings in their entirety.

Highlights on the first floor include the Hall of Fame Gallery, which contains famous plaques, each engraved with the picture of a Hall of Famer and a brief profile; the Baseball at the Movies exhibit, consisting memorabilia and brief films; the Perez-Steele Art Gallery; and the Sandlot Kids Clubhouse. The second floor features the Grandstand Theater, built to resemble old Comiskey Park. This floor also features artifacts including uniforms, baseball hats, and bats. The Pride and Passion exhibit features the Negro Leagues, the predominately African American baseball teams that were prohibited from playing in integrated teams until 1947. Diamond Dreams covers women in baseball. African Americans were not inducted into the Hall of Fame until 1971, though they had participated in the game since baseball's earliest days. The first woman inducted into the Hall of Fame was an African American woman, Effa Manley, who co-owned the Newark Eagles with her husband during the era of the Negroes Leagues. She was inducted in 2006.

On the third floor, visitors can see replicas of World Series rings, view an exhibit on Hank Aaron,

#### Baseball Trailblazer

Born Jack Roosevelt Robinson on January 31, 1919, in Cairo, Georgia, Robinson was one of five children raised by a single mother. After graduating from John Muir High School and Pasadena Junior College, Robinson attended the University of California, Los Angeles, but did not graduate due to financial hardship. However, by this time, Robinson had had many years of experience playing football, basketball, track, and baseball. After leaving California, Robinson played semiprofessional football in Honolulu, Hawaii, and then joined the U.S. Army. While in the Army, he served as a second lieutenant from 1942 to 1944. His military career ended in an honorable discharge after he refused to sit in the back of a segregated bus during boot camp.

After his stint in the army, Robinson was selected by Branch Rickey, president of the Brooklyn Dodgers, to integrate the major leagues. In 1944, Robinson began his trailblazing career, wearing the uniform number 42. Robinson bravely with stood the barrage of verbal taunts from the crowds. Throughout such trying experiences, some individuals with in the league showed their support for Robinson and the goal of integrated baseball. In time, Robinson became increasingly embraced by the fans. Following a long career with the Dodgers, Robinson was traded to the New York Giants in 1956 and retired in 1957.

After baseball, Robinson was an executive for the Chock Full O' Nuts coffee company and restaurant chain, helped establish the Freedom National Bank, and served on the board of the National Association for the Advancement of Colored People. In 1962, he became the first African American to be inducted into the Baseball Hall of Fame. In 1972, his number was retired. Robinson died on October 24, 1972. Following his death, his widow founded the Jackie Robinson Foundation to provide scholarships and mentoring programs for students.

**The History of Women in Baseball**

Women in baseball occupy a significantly different place in the national imagination compared to men. Whereas men in baseball garnered positive public attention from the start, women attracted controversy. When women began playing baseball in the 1860s, the prevalent thought was that strenuous exercise for women was dangerous and unhealthy, as well as indecent and unlady like. Indeed, in this period, the concept of women attending colleges and universities was seen as slightly radical.

But a small percentage of women did attend institutions of higher learning, and it was at women's colleges such as Vassar College in New York that women's baseball teams first formed. In 1866, baseball became a popular club activity. The women's baseball clubs faded in the 1870s due to the public's vociferous objection to the activity.

Other women in baseball phenomenon, the Bloomer Girls, fared much better, enjoying popularity beginning in the 1890s. The Bloomer Girls were clubs comprising mostly women and one to three men. The various clubs formed baseball teams that played against teams of men.

During the 1920s, Lizzie Murphy emerged as a female baseball star, playing in exhibitions with professional players such as Babe Ruth.

During World War II, Chicago Cubs owner Phillip Wrigley founded the All-American Girls Professional Ball League. From 1943 to 1954, the league filled a need created bya dwindling reserve of male players as a result of the war and was thus well received by its audiences. It was in this glittering era that the movie *A League of Their Own* (1992) was set.

In more recent history, women's baseball has continued through the promotion and support by various organizations such as the International Baseball Federation, which was founded in 2004, and organizes the biannual Women's Baseball World Cup.

and listen to presentations about artifacts in the Museum. The Records Room features statistics, awards, World Series rings, an inductee database, and movies showing great moments from various World Series. In the Sacred Ground section, visitors explore information about ballparks, such as the South End Grounds in Boston, Comiskey Park in Chicago, and Ebbets Field in Brooklyn. Other exhibits feature information on Minor League players and items from baseball popular culture, such as baseball cards.

### In Conclusion

Above all else, the Baseball Hall of Fame houses a collection of true sports Americana. For many, it brings back memories of childhood, of a shared passion for a thrilling game, of heroes in baseball caps, and of distinctive uniforms sliding into home plate. Thanks to the Museum, the historic moments and memories of a legendary all-American sport are preserved and immortalized.

***See also*** Boston, Massachusetts; Chicago, Illinois; Country Music Hall of Fame; Fenway Park; Football Hall of Fame; Hollywood; Main Street; Rock and Roll Hall of Fame; Wrigley Field

### Further Reading

Berlage, Gai Ingham. 1994. *Women in Baseball: The Forgotten History*. Westport, Connecticut: Praeger Publications.

The National Baseball Hall of Fame and Museum, National Geographic, and Mulroy, Kevin. 2005. *Baseball as America: Seeing Ourselves through Our National Game*. Washington, DC: National Geographic.

*National Baseball Hall of Fame and Museum*. www.baseballhall.org.

Sugar, Bert. 2009. *Bert Sugar's Baseball Hall of Fame: A Living History of America's Greatest Game*. Philadelphia: Running Press.

Withers, Ernest C. 2004. *Negro League Baseball*. New York: Harry N. Abrams.

## Beale Street

Beale Street is a historic street located in Memphis, Tennessee. Known in its heyday during the early 20th century as "the Main Street of Negro America," Beale Street was once the heart of local African American life and is world renowned for the blues and jazz music that was developed there. The artists that

View down Beale Street in Memphis, Tennessee. The revitalized tourist district bears little resemblance to the street that bore witness to the trials of the civil rights movement and served as the home of the Memphis Blues sound, but honors the location's heritage with musical venues and festivals. (Natalia Bratslavsky/Dreamstime.com)

played there, the vibrant crowds it attracted, as well as the nonstop bustle imparted legendary status to the street. Sadly, by the 1960s, the street had deteriorated drastically, but it was not forgotten. In 1966, parts of the street were declared a national historic landmark, and in 1977, an act of Congress proclaimed Beale Street Home of the Blues. The ensuing decade brought forth the renewal of Tennessee's beloved icon.

Renovation greatly altered the street's look and ambience. Not only had most of the original buildings vanished, the Beale Street crowd who traversed the area day and night was not the same. The newly developed street had been refashioned for a new crowd of racially diverse tourists. More than a place to acquire trinkets, T-shirts, mugs, and keepsakes bearing Beale Street's name, today's Beale Street offers many amusements, including a medley of modern and retro-style restaurants, clubs, and shops, and an opportunity for visitors to be where history was made.

### Historical Perspectives

Beale Street started out in 1819 as Beale Avenue, a reasonably important thoroughfare not quite two miles long, running from east to west, from the Mississippi River to Pigeon Roost Road. The area was inhabited by merchants, aristocrats, and a sparse population of black slaves. Greater numbers of blacks began to migrate to Memphis during the Civil War (1861–1865). By the end of the war, the black population had leapt to nearly 40 percent, and the locals had grown accustomed to being entertained by a number of traveling artists and musicians, like the Young Men's Brass Band.

In subsequent years, the evolution of Beale Avenue was influenced by two major events: demographic changes in the area and the legalized racial stratification of southern society. The population in Memphis was deeply hit by a series of infectious disease outbreaks in the 1860s and 1870s. The outbreaks resulted in a large exodus of whites and a disproportionate number of deaths among whites. With the emergence of legalized segregation in the South, the blacks that were left behind were forced to live within the color line, fashioning a distinctly different world, largely managed and operated by the blacks themselves.

Robert Church, a wealthy African American who played a prominent role in the development of Beale Avenue, purchased property in the area and contributed profoundly to the locale. He financed one of the premier street attractions, Church Park, which drew blues artists and illustrious speakers. Celebrated blues artist W.C. Handy eventually transplanted to the area, helping to craft the so-called Memphis Blues sound and creating several popular tunes, many of them about the popular street. One of the songs, "Beale Street Blues," is credited for changing the name of Beale Avenue to Beale Street.

### Father of the Blues

W. C. Handy, known as the "Father of the Blues," was a song writer, composer, and musician. Born on November 16, 1873, in Florence, Alabama, Handy is best known for his role in popularizing blues music. His was a long, hard road to a career in music. As a child, his father, an Episcopalian clergyman, only allowed Christian music to be played in the house. When the chance came, young Handy joined a minstrel show, though he was only a teenager. Minstrel troupes were common in the late 19th century. Indeed, many African American singers and performers enjoyed such careers. Typically, the African American troupes, which featured singers, actors, and performers, traveled within African American communities in the South.

During his pursuit of a musical career, Handy traveled widely and had many different experiences. He played with and led bands in the Midwest and the South. While in Mississippi in the early 20th century, Handy discovered the blues when he heard an African American playing a guitar and singing at a train station. This discovery profoundly influenced Handy's career. In 1909, he penned the blues song "Mr. Crump," renaming it "The Memphis Blues." Because he did not have the rights to the song, Handy was not able to profit greatly from its subsequent popularity. This experience prompted him to partner with Harry Pace to establish the Pace and Handy Music Company.

Handy would go on to create 60 music compositions. In 1941, he published his autobiography, *Father of the Blues,* a name he was known by because of his pioneering work in commercializing the genre. He died on March 29, 1958, the year that a movie based on his life, *St. Louis Blues,* was released. Legendary singer Nat King Cole was cast to play Handy.

## Cultural Distinctions

The music of W.C. Handy was one of multiple factors contributing to the special ambience of Beale Street. The culture of the area was influenced by its many unique establishments, as well as by the colorful local denizens and visitors who thronged the street. Businesses, both African American and white-owned, were prolific and eclectic. There were shops, music clubs, restaurants, places to gamble and loiter, and even a church, called the Beale Street Baptist Church. The street attracted a wild array of activity, such as men and women going about their daily mundane routine, voodoo doctors selling their charms, men preaching on street corners, and performers singing and playing music. Famous entertainers included the likes of Cab Calloway, Louis Armstrong, Bessie Smith, and B.B. King. The clubs vibrated with the sound of music, laughter, and high-spirited voices. Beale Street was a fundamental center for African American music and entertainment and of bustling African American community.

### Contemporary Perspectives

By the 1960s, Beale Street's golden era had dimmed. The declining popularity of blues music, an economic downturn in local African American communities, and events associated with the civil rights movement contributed to the end of the street's greatest era. When Dr. Martin Luther King Jr., a major leader in the civil rights movement, arrived in Memphis in 1968 to support the city's sanitation workers strike, most of the establishments on Beale Street had closed. Bond and Sherman assert that broiling racial tensions and turmoil caused by violent backlash against marchers and the assassination of Dr. King at the nearby Lorraine Motel led to the ultimate demise of Beale Street.

> **Empress of the Blues**
>
> Bessie Smith is a name synonymous with the blues, though later in life, she sang jazz songs, adapting to the new trends in music. Smith was born Elizabeth Smith in Chattanooga, Tennessee, on April 15, 1894. She was one of seven children. By 1906, her parents and several of her siblings had died. After the loss of her last surviving parent, Smith and her siblings were raised by their aunt. To help support the family, she and another brother performed on the street. Smith sang while her brother played the guitar. In 1912, Smith joined a traveling minstrel show. Minstrel shows were one of only a few outlets for African American musicians and actors. While performing with a different troupe, the Rabbit Foot Minstrels, she met and was mentored by Ma Rainey, one of the most successful African American blues singers of the time.
>
> Smith would join the ranks of popular blues singers when she began singing under contract with Columbia Records in 1923. In that same year, she married Jack Gee. Her career, which included hits such as "Downhearted Blues," flourished throughout the decade.
>
> The 1930s proved a challenging decade for Smith. Her marriage ended in 1929, and the coming of the Great Depression severely challenged her career. The decade was also difficult for the blues genre in general, as jazz had become the new musical fashion. Smith adapted to the changing times and sang jazz songs, as well. Her life was tragically cut short when she died as a result of a car accident on September 26, 1937.

### For Visitors

Efforts to revitalize the street began in earnest in the 1980s. Bond and Sherman point out that among the goals guiding this project were the hope of generating commercial success and honoring a legacy. The project, however, included the decimation of all but two of the original establishments: A. Schwab's and Hudkins Hardware. Only A. Schwab's remains to this day. Today's Beale Street features new establishments such as the Pig barbecue restaurant, the Hard Rock Café, Mr. Handy's Blues Halls, and B. B. King's Blues Club. At King's Palace, tourists can order a bowl of gumbo and listen to live music. The former Daisy Theater is now the Beale Street Blues Museum. A basketball arena, the FedEx Forum, now resides on Beale Street. Visitors can buy voodoo charms at Tater Red's. Along the sidewalk, the names of notable artists who helped augment the Beale Street name are emblazoned on the Beale Street Brass Note Walk of Fame.

### In Conclusion

Popular entertainers, both nationally and locally known, continue to be drawn to this place more than a century after entertainers were first swept in the vortex that was Beale Street. Though dramatically transformed, the memory of Beale Street endures, and its appeal remains untarnished.

*See also* Bourbon Street; Broadway; Congo Square; Lorraine Motel; Main Street; Mississippi River

### Further Reading

Bond, Beverly G., and Sherman, Janann. 2006. *Beale Street*. Charleston, South Carolina: Arcadia.

King, B. B., and Ritz, David. 2011. *Blues All around Me: The Autobiography of B.B. King*. New York: HarperCollins.

Lewis, Selma S., and Kremer, Marjean G. 1996. *The Angel of Beale Street: A Biography of Julia Ann Hooks*. Memphis: St. Luke's Press.

McKee, Margaret, and Chisenhall, Fred. 1981. *Beale Black and Blue: Life and Music on Black America's Main Street*. Baton Rouge: Louisiana State University Press.

## Beauty Shops

Beauty shops are places where women go to receive hair treatments, such as washing and conditioning, styling, and cuts. Beauty shops go by many other names: hair salons, beauty salons, hair spas, and so on. Differences in the services provided vary. For example, beauty salons may provide hair treatments only or additional services such as manicures, pedicures, and facials. Beauty shop, in this instance, refers primarily to shops that treat women's hair.

The beauty shop has played a vital and unique role in American life. Though its role and appearance in the daily lives of women have changed considerably over the years, the beauty shop endures in the 21st century as a place where women go to establish their looks; a place that reflects trends in American fashion and style and stands as an emblem of women's timeless quest to be beautiful. The beauty-shop culture also continues to retain some of its former relevance in women's social lives. Trips to the beauty shop still mark some milestones in American life.

### Historical Perspectives

In the 18th and 19th centuries, barbershops met the hairdressing needs of men, but women beautified themselves at home. Mothers brushed, braided, cut, and styled their daughters' hair. Sisters and friends helped each other concoct elaborate styles. In the South, privileged women tended to have their hair styled and other personal needs administered by slaves or paid laborers. Only a scant number of women ventured into barbershops to have their hair styled.

Beauty shops began to surface during the early 20th century. The bob craze of the 1920s helped spark the emergence of beauty shops that catered strictly to women. Many men scoffed at the concept of sharing their males-only domain with women. Indeed, during this time in history, much of society was delineated by gender, including social clubs, schools, household chores, and employment.

The number of beauty shops increased in ensuing years. Technology advancements, the advent of beauty schools and specialized products, America's growing obsession with fashion, and the influence of glamorous celebrities were among the contributing factors that increased the demand for more beauty shops. The 1950s and 1960s saw a boom of beauty shops, particularly as hairstyles, such as bouffant and beehive, grew higher and more complex, involving intricate techniques and hair pieces. Promises to look like your favorite celebrity made the beauty shop trend irresistible to many women.

The advent of unisex chain salons in the 1970s changed the Americans' way of thinking about hair shops. Unisex salons marketed to men and women and provided quick, impersonal experiences at low costs and high convenience to clientele. In the 21st century, America enjoys a hodgepodge of beauty shops, barbershops, and unisex salons, found in small towns, big cities, and local neighborhoods.

### Cultural Distinctions

Beauty-shop culture varies by region, neighborhood, and ethnic enclave. Many of the most distinct differences in beauty shops are those that can be divided by race. For many decades, mainstream beauty shops excluded African American women, just as African Americans, in general, were excluded from most of mainstream American life. The fact that black hair is different than white hair also contributed to the unique development of the African American beauty shop. Madame C.J. Walker was an African American trailblazer who launched a successful black hair business in the early 20th century. In time, black women created beauty schools and beauty shops of their own.

Hairdressers were commonly women, and the women clientele and hairdressers, generally, came from the same community. The fact that these women knew each other, shared similar experiences and histories, worshiped at the same churches, and shopped at the same stores imparted a strong sense of solidarity and friendship. Women talked about their families, their problems, gossip, local and national news and shared recipes and housekeeping tips. Their reasons for going to the beauty shop were often the same.

Meticulous, fashion-conscious, or affluent women wore self-styled fashions or went to beauty shop more frequently than other women. But for most women, everyday life was denoted by mundane and unspectacular coiffures. For these women, going to the beauty shop preceded a personal milestone or special event. Special occasions, such as birthdays, weddings, Sunday worship services, and social gatherings prompted trips to the beauty shop. A first visit to the beauty shop was a rite of passage for American girls, no matter her race.

Beauty shops, for African Americans, functioned in one other way that distinguished them from mainstream beauty shops. Black beauty shops, like black barbershops, played an important role during the activism of the 1960s and 1970s. There information was dispensed by word of mouth, brochure, or flyer.

By the late 20th century, the role of beauty shops in the lives of women had changed. Women's relationships tend to be restricted between client and hairdresser in today's beauty shop. The clientele is now larger and more diverse. In many situations, clients do not know one another. The increasing number of male hairdressers has also added a new element to beauty-shop culture, though women do form close relationships with their male hairdressers. Though beauty shops do not practice overt discrimination, beauty shops tend to continue to be separated, by

**The History of the Mani**

Little is commonly known about the history of nail salons, where the manicure, also known popularly as the "mani," is performed. The care and beautification of the nails is an ancient practice associated with such countries as China and Egypt, when the practice was mostly associated with, but not limited to, royalty. Typically, royalty wore dark shades of polish; red was particularly popular among the ruling classes. In the 19th and 20th centuries, nail hygiene and beautification was practiced more widely. During the 1920s, France made popular a glossy lacquer that predated today's nail polish. Many American women imitated this practice, though the practice had not yet gone mainstream.

In subsequent decades, companies such as Revlon contributed greatly to the commercialization of nail products. In the 1930s, they created nail enamel in assorted colors and sold them in drug stores and department stores at prices the public could afford. In the 1940s, glamorous film stars, appearing in the innovative color technology of the era, popularized red-painted nails. In this same period, the nation's burgeoning middleclass enjoyed new luxuries. For women, going to the beauty parlor emerged as a popular activity. Many such parlors began providing manicure and pedicuretreatments, which were taught in cosmetology schools.

In the 1970s, Jeff Pink was at a Paris runway when he was inspired to create the so-called French manicure. This nail treatment, which exaggerates the natural look of nails by painting the nail bed with a translucent pink color and the tip of the nail with a white color, became massively popular and continues to be so to this day. By the late 20th century, artificial nails became immensely popular. Though manicures and pedicures are typically enjoyed by adult women, the trend has also been embraced by adolescent girls and men (men usually experience the hand and feet treatments excluding the applications of nail color).

client preference, by race and ethnicity. Visits to the beauty shop have increasingly become a common occurrence, as well as an event that precedes special occasions, such as weddings and school dances.

**Hair Care Tycoon**

Madame C. J. Walker is celebrated for her trailblazing role as an African American woman entrepreneur and for the contributions she made to the black hair care industry. She is also credited with becoming the first self-made woman millionaire (using today's money equivalent).

Walker was born Sarah Breedlove on December 23, 1867, near Delta, Louisiana, to parents who had been slaves. After the death of her husband, Sarah and her daughter moved to St. Louis, Missouri. There, she worked in a laundry and attended night school.

Sarah's career path changed in the 1890s. Precipitating this change was a scalp infection she developed that caused considerable hair loss. She concocted a hair product to address her issues, which helped restore her hair. This product proved beneficial to others.

In 1906, Sarah married Charles J. Walker, who worked in newspaper advertising. In 1910, Walker, who promoted herself as "Madame C. J. Walker," founded her Madame C. J. Walker Manufacturing Company, whose headquarters was based in Indianapolis, Indiana. Through her company, Walker amassed considerable wealth, while revolutionizing the black hair-care industry with innovative products and processes such as a hair straightening process that utilized a hot comb. Walker also utilized the so-called Walker Agents, who went door-to-door to sell her products in African American communities.

She expanded her influence in Latin America and the Caribbean. She was dedicated to philanthropic work, supporting educational opportunities, elderly care, antilynching activism, and the National Association for the Advancement of Colored People. After she died on May 24, 1919, at the young age of 51, her daughter became the new owner of the company. To this day, Madame C. J. Walker's products are purchased online through the company website.

## Images in Popular Culture

Film, more than television, has featured beauty shops as integral parts of the narrative. *Steel Magnolias* (1989) is a memorable comedy-drama involving the women who work at and patronize Truvy's Beauty Parlor. An early scene features one of the protagonists in the parlor preparing for her wedding day. Laughter mingles with tears as they cope with the vicissitudes of life, providing a stirring and heart-warming glimpse into the private and intimate lives of women. *Beauty Shop* (2005) depicts the everyday happenings and crises of an urban African American beauty shop. Things get interesting when a white woman is hired on as a hairdresser. *You Don't Mess with Zohan* (2008) is a coarse comedy featuring popular comedian Adam Sandler cast as an unlikely hairstylist, a former Israeli counterterrorist, who wins the hearts of elderly clientele in New York City. The reality television show *Chicagolicious* (2012–) provides a glimpse into a modern salon in Chicago.

## In Conclusion

Real beauty shops may not provide adventurous experiences as colorful as those rendered in modern film, but they remain an intrinsic part of American life.

***See also*** Barbershops; Chicago, Illinois; High School; New York, New York; Weddings

## Further Reading


Banner, Louis. 1983. *American Beauty*. New York: Knopf.

Furman, Frida Kerner. 1997. *Facing the Mirror: Older Women and Beauty Shop Culture*. New York: Routledge.

Gill, Tiffany M. 2010. *Beauty Shop Politics: African American Women's Activism in the Beauty Industry*. Urbana; Chicago: University of Illinois Press.

Rooks, Noliwe. 1996. *Hair Raising: Beauty, Culture, and African American Women*. New Brunswick, New Jersey: Rutgers University Press.

Willett, Julie, ed. 2010. *The American Beauty Industry Encyclopedia*. Santa Barbara, California: ABC-CLIO.

Willett, Julie. 2000. *Permanent Waves: The Making of the American Beauty Shop*. New York: New York University.

## Beverly Hills, California

Beverly Hills is a city in Los Angeles County, California. Historically linked to nearby Hollywood, Beverly Hills conjures images of posh lifestyles, flashy cars, and luxurious homes. Other popular images include palm-tree-lined streets and archetypal socialites in designer clothes and sunglasses, toting a chic bag. This is no Main Street icon; rather, Beverly Hills is believed to attract individuals who have either attained or aspire to a glamorous life. In actuality, the wealthy comprise a small percentage of the population. But this in no way mars Beverly Hill's mystique in the national imagination. Beverly Hills to this day exudes the aura of old Hollywood and living there is an emblem of social status.

### Historical Perspectives

The region known today as Beverly Hills was once the home of the Tongva, a Native American group that inhabited California. The Tongva called this region the Gathering of the Waters because of the water that collected in the area, directed there by three canyons: Franklin, Coldwater, and Benedict. The resulting streams fed a lush oasis that swarmed with living things, such as fowl, antelope, and (after the arrival of the Spanish) horses. Following the arrival of the Spanish in 1769, a smallpox epidemic and conflict with Europeans decimated the native population. Subsequent decades brought forth occupation by ranchers, cowboys, and oil speculators. Burton Green and the Rodeo Land and Water Company were the first to develop the area for residential homes in 1906 (after finding no oil in the region). Architect Wilbur D. Cook laid out a plan for the town, planted trees of many varieties, and carved out sizeable plots for future homes. In 1911, Beverly Gardens Park opened, and the Beverly Hills Hotel, a multipurpose facility where locals wed, convened for church, and stayed one or more nights while traveling through, was established in 1912. In 1914, Beverly Hills was incorporated.

### Growth and Development

The Beverly Hills of Hollywood legend began in the 1920s, growing simultaneously with America's nascent film industry. Hollywood interest in Beverly Hills began as early as 1917 with property and business investments. In 1919, Douglas Fairbanks and Mary Pick ford, the silent-movie power couple who built the mansion Pick fair in Beverly Hills, helped prompt the mass influx of Hollywood elite: directors, producers, and actors. The Beverly Hills Hotel and the city's many mansions served as a magnet for the ultra rich, the glamorous, and other celebrities. They came for a luxurious getaway, a taste of the indulgent life, entertainment, celebrity parties, and physical activities like golfing, tennis, and swimming. The ephemeral Beverly Hills Speedway, which lasted from 1920 to 1924, was another draw to visitors and residents.

### Contemporary Perspectives

The development of Beverly Hills continued in ensuing decades, fashioning itself into a Mecca of glamour, exclusivity, and haute shopping. The area was also known for popular nightclubs, thrilling nightlife, and spectacular landmarks. The Electronic Fountain, considered a modern wonder at the time, was erected in 1931 in the Beverly Gardens. It features a statue of a Tongva man and an illuminated water fountain with changing colors. During the 1950s, a decade that saw the quickening of the middle class and the rise of suburbia, Beverly Hills made room for even more lavish living. Spacious homes no middle-of-the-road wage-earner could possibly afford were constructed in the hills. Indeed the hills provided a physical barrier between the affluent celebrities and professionals and the rest of the locals, many of them renters. Streets in Beverly Hills became world famous for their haute shops. Rodeo Drive, for example, comprises three blocks of shoppers' paradise, featuring by the 1970s the biggest names in retail, like Tiffany &

Company, Chanel, Coach, Prada, and Gucci. In an environment where physical appearance, name, income, and social status play figurative roles, anything less would be unimaginable.

**A Hollywood Star**

Mary Pickford was an actress, producer, and screenwriter. One of the most influential women in Hollywood, Pickford was born Gladys Mary Smith on April 8, 1892, in Toronto, Ontario, Canada. She began her career on the stage at the age of five. Some 10 years later, Pickford moved to New York, seeking a career on Broadway. In 1907, she took her stage name at the suggestion of David Belasco, a theatrical producer. In the same year, she made her Broadway debut at the Belasco Theatre in William de Mille's play, *The Warrens of Virginia.* In 1909, she had a minor role in *Her First Biscuits,* directed by D. W. Griffith, the first of 40 short films she would appear in.

Pickford's film career took off immediately and grew by leaps and bounds. During the age of the silent film, her prolific acting career included her first feature-length film, *A Good Little Devil* (1914). She was loved by the public around the world and known as America's Sweet heart.

Pickford's growing status in Hollywood put her in a unique position and allowed her to exert control over the direction of her own career. In 1919, she along with Douglas Fairbanks, Charlie Chaplin, D. W. Griffith, and William S. Hart founded United Artists. Pickford then formed the Mary Pickford Company to produce films for United Artists. The following year, Pickford and Fairbanks married in Glendale, California, and moved into a mansion they called Pickfair. Pickford increased her influence even further with the creation of Pickford-Fairbanks Studio in 1922 and by cofounding the Academy of Motion Picture Arts and Sciences in 1927. Though she ended her film career with *Secrets* (1933), she continued to produce films.

### Images in Popular Culture

Beverly Hills's popularity has inspired a long string of films and television series. Since the 1950s, Hollywood has played on and in some cases exaggerated the Beverly Hills mystique. One recurring theme is to position ordinary people in the elitist environment of Beverly Hills or to exaggerate their differences against privileged Beverly Hill personalities. In the television program *The Beverly Hillbillies* (1962–1971), a stereotypical backward hillbilly family gets rich, packs all their belongings on their 1921 Oldsmobile, and moves to Beverly Hills. In the popular movie series *Beverly Hills Cop* (1984, 1987, 1994), a street-wise African American cop from Detroit, played by Eddie Murphy, encounters the privileged world of a Beverly Hills precinct. Television programs, such as *Beverly Hills, 90210* (1990–2000) and films like *Clueless* (1995) and *Beverly Hills Chihuahua* (2008, 2011) parody the Beverly Hills materialistic and shallow stereotype.

### For Visitors

While some consider the Beverly Hills culture excessive and materialistic, none deny that the city remains a popular destination for nearly 100 years after its birth. No longer the exclusive playground of Hollywood socialites, Beverly Hills provides high society living for modern-day celebrities, as well as professionals and anyone else who can afford it. Fine dining, luxurious hotels and homes, and shopping are among the trademarks of Beverly Hills. Out-of-town shoppers pay exorbitantly for designer labels and tourists spend enjoyable vacations touring the celebrity homes and mansions and exploring the legendary shopping districts and famous streets.

***See also*** Appalachia; California; Detroit, Michigan; Hollywood; Los Angeles, California; Main Street; Suburbia; Tiffany & Company

### Further Reading

Artunian, Judy, and Oldham, Mike. 2004. *Movie Star Homes: The Famous to the Forgotten*. Santa Monica, California: Santa Monica Press.

Wanamaker, Marc. 2006. *Beverly Hills: 1930–2005*. Charleston, South Carolina: Arcadia.

Wanamaker, Marc. 2005. *Early Beverly Hills*. Charleston, South Carolina, Arcadia.

## Billings Farm & Museum

The Billings Farm & Museum is located in Woodstock, Vermont. Established in 1871 by Frederick Billings, the facility, at nearly 150 years old, still functions as a working farm. In the late 20th century, the farm added a museum to promote public education about farms and farming, a heritage that runs deep in American life and history but is increasingly fading into distant memory. Through exhibits, interactive activities, and tours, Billings Farm & Museum keeps alive the experiences that were once a predominant part of American life. The fact that the farm is one of the most popular attractions in the region is a testament to the appeal of farms even in modern times.

### Historical Perspectives

Frederick Billings (1823–1890) never intended to become a farmer. Born in Royalton, Vermont, he graduated from the University of Vermont in 1844, then moved to San Francisco, California, and in 1848 where he practiced law as a land claims attorney. His success resulted in a partnership in the firm, Halleck, Peachy, and Billings.

A dairy farmer pats one of his cows as he prepares to feed them oats on Billings Farm in Woodstock, Vermont, in August 2011. (Edward Fielding/Dreamstime.com)

Billings shifted course from lawyer to farmer after acquiring 250 acres in Vermont from Charles Marsh in 1869. Over the course of 10 years, his farm grew and flourished, so much so that he hired George Aitken to assist him as the farm manager in 1884. The farm featured a house, the farm manager's office, and structures for livestock, which included Jersey cows, sheep, horses, oxen, and chickens.

The prized Jersey cows, acquired in 1871, formed the basis of a commercial dairy. Draft horses (large breeds of horses suitable for pulling wagons and machinery rather than for riding) were used along with the ox to carry out the heavy labor on the farm. Such animals were fixtures on farms prior to the invention of the tractor. Billings sold the meat and the wool of his Southdown sheep, which he imported from Britain. At their peak, there were several hundred sheep on the farm.

The success of Billings Farm was evident as the farm neared its 20th year. Its size had grown to 1,000 acres and the dairy was producing some 5,000 pounds of butter each year. Though Billings died in 1890, the farm achieved national notoriety in 1893, at the Columbian Exposition in Chicago, Illinois. The farm's Jersey cows amazed the crowds. The cow, Lily Garfield was declared the "Champion Heifer of the World."

### Contemporary Perspectives

Today, the dairy continues to produce commercial products, and farming is carried out the old-fashioned way. Currently, three teams of draft horses are kept on the farm: Jim and Joe, Percheron geldings, Lynne and Sue, black Percheron mares, and Tom and Jerry, Belgian geldings. Teams of oxen are trained on the farm and used in demonstrations to educate the public on the historical uses of such animals. Presently, the Billings Farm maintains a much smaller herd of sheep than during Frederick Billings's time. The farm also maintains a number of chicken breeds.

In addition to the working farm, Billings Farm manages educational exhibits and programs. Many of the exhibits are displayed in barns. The exhibits include artifacts as well as information on farm life and history, including events specific to the Billings Farm. Visitors view farming techniques, the dairy farm and its animals, and farm-related activities such as butter making and afternoon milking. Visitors learn about 19th century farm activities in the Vermont Farm Year in 1890 Exhibit and explore the 1890 farm house.

### For Visitors

Opportunities abound for guests on the farm. Farm programs are geared toward school groups and adults. For individuals seeking an immersion experience, a 12-week internship program is available from May to August. Eligible applicants must be undergraduate or graduate students enrolled in national academic institutions. Living quarters for the interns are located in the historic farm house. Billings Farm also hosts several popular events, such as its annual quilt exhibition. Craft events such as rug braiding, natural dyeing, and tinsmithing draw crowds. Wagon rides are offered periodically throughout the year.

### In Conclusion

The creation of Billings Farm & Museum as a popular attraction demonstrates how far removed our modern nation is from its agricultural heritage. In the increasingly urban society, farms hearken to a time and place that has been romanticized and sentimentalized. In the absence of firsthand knowledge and experience of farm life, the modern world marvels at the seemingly arcane world of farming the land, making butter, milking cows, and tending livestock. It is this knowledge and work that are maintained and preserved on Billings Farm. The educational aspect of the farm serves to educate and captivate a contemporary audience.

***See also*** Barns; Chicago, Illinois

**Further Reading**

*Billings Farm & Museum*. http://www.billingsfarm.org/.

Danbom, David B. 2006. *Born in the Country: A History of Rural America*. Baltimore: Johns Hopkins University Press.

Winks, Robin W. 1998. *Frederick Billings: A Life*. Berkeley: University of California Press.

## Billy Bob's Texas

Billy Bob's Texas is a country-and-western nightclub. Touted as the "World's Largest Honky-Tonk," Billy Bob's is a super sized version of one of the South's most iconic places of entertainment. Billy Bob's Texas offers its patrons an array of popular and regional entertainment, such as live performances, country-and-western dancing, bull riding events, food and drink, billiard tables, and arcade games.

Since 1981, Billy Bob's Texas has received 15 million visitors. Locals and tourists go to the popular nightclub for fun; some go for an experience that is deeply rooted in southern culture. Beyond the lure of the earthy twang of acoustic guitars and the collective stomp of cowboy boots against a hardwood dance floor, visitors are drawn to Billy Bob's Texas's world-renowned fame. Few other nightclubs of this type can boast multiple triumphs as The Country Music Club of the year, Country Music Association Club of the Year, and Academy of Country Music Club of the Year. Moreover, Billy Bob's Texas is where stars are born and where the brightest stars in country perform every Friday and Saturday night.

### Historical Perspectives

The building where Billy Bob's Texas now resides, in the Fort Worth Stockyards, has served many different purposes. It was originally built in 1910 as a cattle barn. In 1936, it was enlarged and redesigned to hold over 1,000 animal stalls and an auction ring. Later, it served as an airplane manufacturing plant and then Clark's Department Store.

In 1981, Billy Bob Barnett and Spencer Taylor launched Billy Bob's Texas, riding the wave of success created by the mainstreaming of country-and-western music and dance. After going bankrupt in the winter of 1988, Holt Hickman, Steve Murrin, and Donald K. Jury reopened the nightclub late in the fall of the same year. Billy Bob's Texas has enjoyed ongoing success ever since.

Famous Billy Bob's Texas bar is a Fort Worth, Texas, landmark and a big tourist destination in the Cowtown section of the city. (Anthony Aneese Totah Jr./Dreamstime.com)

### About The Site

Billy Bob's Texas is no ordinary honky-tonk. Traditionally, honky-tonks, which emerged at the turn of the 19th century, were commonly spartan one-room establishments, with little or no frills, where working-class locals went to unwind and be entertained, have a smoke and drink beer, listen to local singers and musicians, and dance. Patrons at the local honky-tonk tended to be part of the same community. Most everyone knew the popular country-and-western dance forms and was partial to the now universally identifiable attire: Western shirts, cowboy boots and hats, sizable belt buckles, jeans for the men, and long skirts for the women.

Unlike the old-time honky-tonk, Billy Bob's Texas is above all else enormous and offers assorted activities. The building itself is a prodigious 127,000 square feet, accommodating more than 6,000 people. It features concrete plaques bearing the handprints and autographs of countless country-and-western legends and an array of attractions more lively and colorful than the traditional honky-tonk. Amid the electric lights and state-of-the art sound system are a concert stage, a dance floor, a honky-tonk stage, a casino, arcade, and bars. Patrons can buy traditional country-and-western wear, souvenirs, and mementos at the gift shop. Billy Bob's Roadhouse café serves up a variety of foods; its main fare consisting of southern cuisine, like barbecue, catfish, and potato salad. The indoor bull-riding arena features real cowboys and live bulls. Visitors can take pictures with an artificial bull, reserve space for meetings, weddings, and parties, and dance or watch dancing in the dance hall. Visitors may also buy tickets to see some of the biggest names in the country-and-western industry and other popular music genres, as well as local entertainers.

**Boot Scootin' Boogie**

Line dancing is a form of dance that takes place with a group of people. Participants line up in rows and execute the same movements in a synchronized manner. In country-and-western dancing, the tradition is often compared to the folk dances that were transplanted from European countries to America during the nation's early history. Rural dances in the southern region of the nation are the direct descendants of European folk dances. However, unlike traditional folk dances, line dancing typically does not incorporate couples dancing or contact between dancers.

Line dancing is most directly descended from the 1970s disco era, when America saw a variety of new dances emerge. The "Electric Side," a popular song and accompanying dance, was all the rage. In this same era, country-and-western line dancing emerged, reflecting the far-reaching influence of disco music. Dances such as "Walkin' Wazi" and "Cowboy Boogie" were among the line dances that were introduced in the 1970s.

Into the 1980s and beyond, the increasing popularity of the country-and-western genre with mainstream audiences coincided with the fusion of pop and rock-androll. At the same time, more line dances, varying in complexity and incorporating some traditional country-and-western steps, were introduced to the public. Specific line dances were associated with hits such as Ray Cyrus's "Achy Breaky Heart," which was released in 1992. Some songs have several versions of line dancing.

Today, country-and-western line dancing is popularly performed at clubs. Typically, instructors schedule sessions where they teach the steps. Line dancing may be performed casually or competitively.

### Dress Attire

Billy Bob's Texas's take on the modern-day honky-tonk mixes the old with the new. To be sure, Billy Bob's Texas continues the legacy of country-and-western song and dance. Western attire remains the popular mode of dress for patrons, and cowboy boots remain the preferred footwear, especially for dancing, providing for easy sliding across the hardwood floor. Patrons perform traditional dances like the two-step and line-dancing, which incorporates modern dance steps.

### Patrons

The crowds that fill Billy Bob's Texas differ from the traditional honky-tonk. The many honky-tonk still in operation in Texas and other states maintain a stark appearance that seems likely to attract only diehard country-and-western fans. But tourist-friendly Billy Bob's Texas attracts many curious individuals and casual fans from across the nation and around the world. This is thanks in part to the mainstreaming of country-and-western music and dance, as well to the mass appeal of the nightclub itself. Billy Bob's Texas is akin to other large roadside attractions or tourist destinations, in that it offers assorted activities, wrapped up in modern lighting and an attractive ambience that appeals to broad audiences. The nightclub also encourages patrons new to country and western to immerse themselves into the culture, whether through trying on Western attire from the gift shops or participating in dance lessons.

### Images in Popular Culture

Billy Bob's Texas has made a deep impact on popular culture, not only as a form of entertainment but as a recognizable dancehall and nightclub in popular television shows, films, and music videos. The popular nightclub has appeared in television programs, such as *Dallas* (1978–1991) and *Walker Texas Ranger* (1993–2001) and in films, such as *Over the Top* (1987), *Baja Oklahoma* (1988), and *Pure Country* (1992).

***See also*** Barns; Casino; Texas; Video Arcade

### Further Reading

*Billy Bob's Texas*. http://billybobstexas.com/.

"Billy Bob's Texas." *Texas State Historical Association*. http://www.tshaonline.org/handbook/online/articles/xdb02.

Folkins, Gail Louise. 2007. *Texas Dance Halls: A Two-Step Circuit*. Lubbock: Texas Tech University Press.

Giordano, Ralph G. 2010. *Country & Western Dance*. Santa Barbara, California: Greenwood.

Lane, Jack, and Allen, Tommy. 2003. *The Texas Honky-Tonk Trail*. Bloomington, Indiana: Author House.

Malone, Bill C., and Neal, Jocelyn R. 2010. *Country Music, U.S.A.* Austin: University of Texas.

## Biltmore Estate

The Biltmore Estate is located in Asheville, North Carolina. This magnificent estate, a remnant from the Gilded Age, which includes as its centerpiece a four-story mansion, was owned by George Vanderbilt (1862–1914), scion of the famous East Coast Vanderbilt family. The Vanderbilt's fame and wealth arose in the 19th century and continued for many generations. The name was prominently associated with philanthropy, the arts, and their spectacular mansions. Many individual family members owned and maintained one or more mansions. Their permanent and seasonal dwellings were primarily located in the states of New York and Rhode Island, though other homes were built in Massachusetts, New Jersey, Vermont, and Florida. Such was the beauty and historical significance of these lavish estates that many were declared national historic landmarks.

George Vanderbilt's Biltmore Estate, touted as the largest privately owned home in the nation, is now a national historic landmark. Since the 1930s, it has operated as a popular tourist destination. During the war, art from the national gallery was stored there. Visitors flock to such estates to view the private residences of the exceedingly rich and to view the astounding architecture that they left behind.

### Historical Perspectives

Though names such as Vanderbilt and Rockefeller are widely recognized, the means by which such families attained their wealth and their complicated familial connections are less well known. The lineage of the Vanderbilt family in America begins with the arrival of Jan Aertsen van der Bilt in America in the mid-17th century. Born in Holland, van der Bilt settled in Brooklyn, New York. For several

> **Glamour and Adversity in the Gilded Age**
>
> The Gilded Age is the term that refers to the 1880s and 1890s in America. The term originates from the novel *The Gilded Age: A Tale of Today* (1873) by Mark Twain and Charles Dudley Warner. The term has both positive and negative connotations.
>
> On the positive side, it refers to a time of wealth and unimagined advances in the nation. The era saw developments such as the production of steel, iron, and oil; the construction of sky scrapers; the invention of electric street cars; and the completion of the first transcontinental railroad. The titans of these industries emerged as the nation's elite.
>
> On the other hand, the Gilded Age was a time of crisis, turmoil, and corruption. Child labor, unsafe working conditions, extreme poverty, and over crowded ethnic slums cast shadows over America's golden image. Immigrants, who arrived during this period in massive waves, industrial workers, and farmers, did not share in the prosperity. Corruption and greed in business, politics, and government propelled Twain and Warner to write their satirical novel, *The Gilded Age.* America's glittering success was portrayed in this novel as a gilded object, that is to say, covered only superficially in a layer of gold.
>
> Efforts to address America's failings resulted in real progress and reform, which in turn resulted inhumane laws for workers, resources for immigrants, and laws to control corruption in government.

generations he and his family worked as farmers. From this lineage was born Cornelius Vanderbilt (1794–1877), who was van der Bilt's great-great grandson. Known as "The Commodore," Vanderbilt began his wage-earning career after he purchased a boat at the age of 16 and began ferrying passengers from New York to Staten Island. By the age of 18, he owned two boats and was captain of a third boat. In later years, he amassed great wealth in the shipping and railroad industries. It was this Vanderbilt who began the familial legacy of opulence, philanthropy, and influence. He and his wife Sophia (1795–1868) had 13 children.

William Henry Vanderbilt (1821–1885), the fourth child of the Commodore and Sophia, amassed even greater wealth than his father. Starting as manager of one of the family farms on Staten Island, he went on to become the president of the New York Central Railroad company in 1877. He and his wife, Maria Louisa (1821–1896), had eight children. Their youngest child was George.

## Construction

George Vanderbilt enjoyed traveling, journeying regularly both within the nation and abroad. During a trip to the mountains in North Carolina, Vanderbilt became enamored with the wild beauty, particularly the spot where he would build his future home. This dwelling later became a place he and his wife, Edith Stuyvesant Dresser (1873–1958), and daughter Cornelia (1900–1976) could use as a retreat.

After acquiring 125,000 acres of land, construction began in 1889 (*Biltmore*). Vanderbilt invited his family and friends to his home on Christmas Eve in 1895. (Vanderbilt was not yet married. He and Edith married in 1898). They were the first to see the home that everyone was talking about. Indeed, the Biltmore Estate was the largest construction effort for a private home in the nation. The name Biltmore comprises two meanings: "bilt," which refers to the Dutch region where the Vanderbilt ancestors had lived, and "more," an old English term which means hilly countryside.

The home itself was designed by architect Richard Morris Hunt, who patterned the house on 16th century French architecture. The home included 250 rooms, 35 bedrooms, and 65 fireplaces (*Biltmore*). The grounds, some 125,000 acres, were designed by Frederick Law Olmsted, who was one of the two landscape designers who planned Central Park. The basement level featured a swimming pool, gymnasium, and bowling alley. The estate was also a working farm, where herds of sheep, pigs, poultry, and cattle were kept. Woodlands, gardens, nurseries, and a dairy farm with some 200 cows were managed on the estate (*Biltmore*).

Next to the estate, Vanderbilt constructed Biltmore Village, originally a company town to house the individuals who worked on his estate. Homes, a hospital, shops, a school, and a church were built for the residents. In the 20th century, Biltmore Village was incorporated into Asheville.

### Contemporary Perspectives

In 1956, Biltmore was inherited by William Amherst Vanderbilt Cecil (1928–) following his mother's death and converted into a tourist attraction. Cecil's parents were John Francis Amherst Cecil (1890–1954) and Cornelia Stuyvesant Vanderbilt. His brother George Henry Vanderbilt Cecil (1925–) inherited Biltmore Farms, which had operated as a dairy farm during George Vanderbilt's lifetime. The estate underwent restoration from the 1970s to the 1990s. To this day, the attraction is a local treasure and an enduring national icon.

### Images in Popular Culture

The movie *Richie Rich* (1994) was filmed at the Biltmore Estate. The posh mansion and its grounds appear in numerous scenes in the film that was adapted from the titular comic book character, who's touted as the world's wealthiest kid.

### For Visitors

Biltmore's appeal has not faded. Indeed the estate attracts numerous visitors, including high-profile guests such as President Barack Obama, Bill Gates, the cofounder of Microsoft, and Gates's wife, Melinda Gates. Visitors can explore most of the mansion, as well as its gardens and winery. Lodging at the Inn at Biltmore Estate is available on the grounds. Excursions to the old Biltmore Village take in historic structures such as the All Souls Cathedral, an Episcopal cathedral and original cottages. The village also features locally owned shops and restaurants such as Chelsea's, the Village Tea Room, and the Tea and Vine, a gourmet tasting shop.

*See also* Central Park; New York, New York; Microsoft

### Further Reading

*Biltmore*. http://www.biltmore.com.

Covington Jr., Howard E. 2006. *Lady on the Hill: How Biltmore Estate Became an American Icon*. Hoboken, New Jersey: John Wiley.

Patterson, Jerry E. 1989. *The Vanderbilts*. New York: H.N. Abrams.

## Birmingham, Alabama

Birmingham, a city in Alabama, is well known for the historic and revolutionary events that occurred there during the civil rights movement of the 1960s. Like many cities in the South, Birmingham's history is rooted in traditions of racial intolerance, racial violence, and discriminatory laws that relegated African Americans to the lowest stratum in southern society. For these reasons, Birmingham was, at one time, a destination for civil rights leaders and activists looking for strategic sites from which to challenge and dismantle segregation. Decades later, Birmingham has become an important symbol of the civil rights movement, bearing witness to the immense struggle and many lives lost during the nonviolent civil rights struggle. Today, Birmingham not only serves as a memorial of a pivotal chapter in America's history but is an example of American transformative power, having transitioned into a thriving city with modern appeal, shopping, fine dining, art venues, distinguished institutions of higher learning, and other major attractions.

### Historical Perspectives

The Elyton Land Company gave life to Birmingham in 1871 in the wake of the turbulent Civil War (1861–1865). While many southern cities, devastated by the war, struggled to rebuild themselves, Birmingham was established with great promise. Named after a booming industrial city in the United Kingdom, Birmingham, Alabama benefited richly from abundant deposits of iron ore, coal, and limestone, railroad development, and inexpensive labor provided by immigrants and newly freed black slaves. Birmingham flourished, particularly from the 1880s to the 1920s and following World War II (1939–1945). Its rapid growth helped earn the bustling town the nicknames "The Magic City" and "The Pittsburgh of the South" (Pittsburgh was then a major industrial town in the North).

### The African American Experience

Birmingham's success belied the growing tensions percolating within its borders. African American communities increasingly became the target of racial violence. Profuse bombings occurring between 1945 and 1962 earned Birmingham a sinister moniker—"Bombingham," and an African American neighborhood that was frequently assailed with bombs became known as "Dynamite Hill."

Racial violence was not the only concern for local African Americans. Disparities in every aspect of life in Birmingham were pervasive. African Americans were forced to submit to Jim Crow Laws, edicts that maintained the color line via facilities separated by color. African American facilities were usually inferior to white facilities. Discriminatory practices in regard to housing, employment, and the court system were also rampant. Underscoring this antiblack environment was the banning, in 1956, of the National Association for the Advancement of Colored People, a civil rights organization that formed in 1909 to challenge segregation, in Alabama.

### Alabama Christian Movement for Human Rights

The fact that the NAACP was outlawed in Alabama did not deter civil rights activists. Reverend Fred Shuttles worth formed the Alabama Christian Movement for Human Rights (ACMHR) in the same year that the NAACP was banned. He and other activists participated in several nonviolent demonstrations, such as sit-ins and marches in Birmingham.

In 1961, Shuttles worth aided the Freedom Rides, a demonstration coordinated by the Southern Christian Leadership Conference (SCLC) and the Congress for Racial Equality (CORE). The freedom riders comprised mostly African American and white college students, who challenged the law that forbade discriminatory practices on interstate public transportation and facilities. Their goal was to travel to the Deep South through cities such as Birmingham where overt racism and racist practices were commonly known to be more heinous than anywhere else. News reporters indeed reported that activists endured harsh beatings in Birmingham, as well as in Anniston, Georgia.

The violence against activists in Birmingham brought forth critical attention to the movement. Resistance, as many activist leaders saw it, played favorably to the struggle. Crises, brought on by negative resistance and multiple arrests of demonstrators challenging the laws, helped to generate attention and worldwide empathy that often prompted intervention and change. In 1962, Shuttles worth invited Dr. Martin Luther King, who emerged as a nationally known leader of the civil rights movement during his involvement in the Montgomery, Alabama, Bus Boycott to stage a demonstration campaign in Birmingham. Birmingham was well known by the activists as being one of the most segregated and resistant cities in the region.

### Birmingham Campaign

King launched the Birmingham campaign in 1963. Following a mass meeting, one of several that took place at the 16th Street Baptist Church, activists took to the streets of Birmingham for a nonviolent march. Some 50 activists, including King, were arrested on April 12, 1963. However, King's arrest, as well as the historic letter he penned while incarcerated (*Letter from Birmingham Jail* [1963]), brought enormous attention to the movement. King was not only released with the help of President John F. Kennedy, but he and the Birmingham campaign became an object of media frenzy.

A subsequent demonstration, called the Children's Crusade, began on May 2. The Children's Crusade was one of the most controversial demonstrations of the movement. Marching children, holding hands and signing protest songs, plunged through the streets of Birmingham. To the shock and utter amazement of the world, following via newspapers and television footage, children and other activists present were subjected to Eugene "Bull" Connor's fury. Connor, commissioner of public safety, ordered that fire hoses and police dogs to be turned on the marchers. The images of marchers being assailed by police brought forth embarrassment to America and garnered sympathy from the nation and abroad, forcing government action. The subsequent desegregation of Birmingham came ploddingly; violence, however, was swift.

The violence continued unabated in the aftermath of the world-famous civil rights demonstrations. On May 11, the Gaston Motel, where Dr. King stayed during the campaign, and the home of King's brother, A. D. King, were bombed. Several months later, on September 15, the news that the 16th Street Baptist Church had been bombed, killing several young girls and injuring many, stunned the world, bringing home the viciousness of the anti–civil rights movement violence and prompting recognition of the need for social change in America.

**SCLC for Civil Rights**

The Southern Christian Leadership Conference (SCLC) is a civil rights organization that was founded in 1957 in Atlanta, Georgia, by a group of ministers. The organization was established in the wake of the Montgomery Bus Boycott, a 13-month campaign (1955–1956) that desegregated buses in Montgomery, Alabama.

The leader of that boycott, Dr. Martin Luther King Jr. was the SCLC's first president. Initially, the organization focused on supporting efforts to desegregate buses in the nation. It eventually expanded its scope to include the work of combating poverty and segregation in all its forms. The organization implemented nonviolent tactics such as marches, demonstrations, boycotts, and sit-ins. Members of the organization were frequently subjected to arrests and violence.

The organization was most active and visible during the 1960s. It was in this period that the SCLC launched many campaigns, typically joining forces with other civil rights organizations.

The 1963 campaign in Birmingham, Alabama, combined the forces of the SCLC and the local Alabama Christian Movement for Human Rights. The campaign made headlines as a result of multiple arrests of activists and the use of extreme police tactics, such as police dogs and fire hoses, against protestors.

The SCLC participated in other high-profile campaigns such as the March on Washington for Jobs and Freedom and the Selma Voting Rights Campaign. In the 21st century, the SCLC remains vigilant in the struggle against racism, racial profiling, and discrimination.

### Contemporary Perspectives

Racial progress eventually came to the city of Birmingham. Though no city has completely eradicated social disparities, Birmingham has made substantial strides. Today, Birmingham is a bustling city that caters not only to its growing modernity and diversity but to its historic importance to the nation and world. Within the context of its urban appeal, it boasts a sophisticated downtown dotted with handsome lofts and condos, fashionable retail stores and chic restaurants, some boasting menus fused with southern cuisine, and the nationally recognized University of Birmingham. Although Birmingham does not currently have a professional major sports team, university sports command extreme loyalty from locals. Birmingham also offers an esteemed Museum of Art and other arts-based attractions, a strong corporation base in its downtown area, a zoo, a theme park, and a lively nightlife in an area known as "Five Points South," along with a number of annual festivals and events.

Despite Birmingham's modernity, the city is still known for the landmarks in civil rights history that occurred there. Birmingham draws a steady population of tourists to its nationally recognized Civil Rights District. The district includes notable landmarks such as the 16th Street Baptist Church and the Birmingham Civil Rights Institute. The institute, established in 1992, features a popular museum and research center. Birmingham's memorial to its climactic history and visible urbanization are proof of the city's commitment toward recognizing its past—both its struggles and triumphs—as it marches onward toward progress.

***See also*** 16th Street Baptist Church

### Further Reading

Arrington, Richard. 2008. *There's Hope for the World: The Memoir of Birmingham, Alabama's First African American Mayor*. Tuscaloosa: University of Alabama Press.

*Birmingham Civil Rights Institute*. http://bcri.org/index.html.

Connerly, Charles E. 2005. *The Most Segregated City in America: City Planning and Civil Rights in Birmingham, 1920–1980*. Charlottesville: University of Virginia Press.

Eskew, Glenn T. 1997. *But for Birmingham: The Local and National Movements in the Civil Rights Struggle*. Chapel Hill: The University of North Carolina Press.

Fazio, Michael W. 2010. *Landscape of Transformations: Architecture and Birmingham, Alabama*. Knoxville: University of Tennessee Press.

Huntley, Horace, and McKerley, John W. 2009. *Foot Soldiers for Democracy: The Men, Women, and Children of the Birmingham Civil Rights Movement*. Urbana: University of Illinois Press.

McKiven, Henry M. 1995. *Iron and Steel: Class, Race, and Community in Birmingham, Alabama, 1875–1920*. Chapel Hill: The University of North Carolina Press.

## Bloomingdale's

Bloomingdale's is a high-end retailer that was established in New York City in 1860. Among the top-10 oldest retailers in the country, Bloomingdale's has always been associated with luxury shopping. Over the years, the retailer's fame has spread to include the mainstream public, not just the excessively rich and famous and the fashion world. The retailer is famous for its European imports, iconic "Brown Bag," and designer labels, as well as its historical, cultural, and legendary importance to the nation and the world.

### Historical Perspectives

Bloomingdale's grew out of Bloomingdale's Hoopskirt and Ladies' Notions Shop. This shop was founded in 1861 in New York's Lower East Side by Benjamin Bloomingdale and his son, Lyman. This store, and its later manifestations, played a profound role in the development of New York, as well as the nation. Not yet 100 years old, America was still perceived by parts of the world as a backward frontier, bereft of fashion sense and vision. Europe, especially France, was considered one of the most important fashion

View of the iconic Bloomingdale's store at the intersection of 59th St. and Third Avenue in Manhattan in January 2009. (Alexandre Fagundes De Fagundes/Dreamstime.com)

Meccas of the world. Fashion, to some, was a significant indicator of a nation's power and influence. The Ladies Notions Shop helped keep America in the loop in regard to women's fashion consciousness, providing upscale clothing to women nationwide—at least to individuals who could afford their retail.

When the famous hoopskirt grew out of fashion, the innovative Bloomingdale brothers, Lyman and Joseph, opened a new store in 1872. The first Bloomingdale's Brothers Great East Side Bazaar debuted at 56th and Third Avenue in Manhattan (in 1886, the store moved to its current location, 59th and Lexington Avenue, which is now considered its flagship location). Despite potentially disastrous circumstances—the store was situated in a working-class neighborhood and far from its competition in the main shopping district—the store thrived. Unlike other retailers, the Bazaar featured a variety of retail items rather than specializing in one product. The brothers also opened an office in Paris, France, one of the fashion capitals of the world, a move that made it easier to stay abreast of fashion trends and to import fashion back to America. Eventually, local development in the neighborhood, the establishment of the Metropolitan Museum of Art, the New York subway system, and Central Park, helped to ensure that "Bloomie's" was at the center of one of the most chic areas of New York City.

### Evolution

In 1929, the physical Bloomingdale's building was redesigned and expanded to encompass the entire city block. In 1949, the brothers launched their first branch store in Queens. In 1961, the first of their popular designer shopping bags went on sale, and the famous "Brown Bag" appeared in 1973. Bloomingdale's fame may have been solidified long ago, but the store reached its pinnacle in the 1970s. More than half of Bloomingdale's customers lived nearby, but the retailer also attracted celebrities: famous fashion designers like Ralph Lauren, Calvin Klein, and Pierre Cardin, and an impressive cast of the international elite, such as Queen Elizabeth II. The historic Bloomingdale's on Lexington Avenue became a must-see destination for visitors to New York who bought up souvenirs marked with the famous "Bloomie's" moniker. In 1978, Bloomingdale's increased its mass appeal and accessibility when its By Mail Catalog was launched. In the 1980s, another prosperous decade, Bloomingdale's added more stores across the nation.

### Contemporary Perspectives

Today, Bloomingdale's has adapted to the 21st century, remaining as relevant to the American public and the world as ever. Any product purchased at Bloomingdale's denotes prestige. Its signature items, the brown bags, come in various sizes, such as the "Little Brown Bag" and "Medium Brown Bag," and "Little Brown Cosmetic Bag." To date, there are 36 Bloomingdale's stores in 12 states, offering a wide range of products, among them clothing, footwear, handbags, bedding, furniture, jewelry, beauty products, and household items. An online website caters to contemporary audiences in an era wherein the Internet and virtual technology loom large.

### Images in Popular Culture

Whether in real life, radio, television, or film, the name Bloomingdale's has been used throughout the years to denote prestige, wealth, and high fashion sense. Woody Allen, a New York native and director who is famous for his films set in the most famous of American cities, has the protagonists of his film *Manhattan* (1979) meet at a Bloomingdale's cosmetics counter. In the popular television series, *Friends* (1994–2004), Rachel, one of the protagonists, works and shops at the famous retailer. In *Serendipity* (2001), the protagonists find love at Bloomingdale's.

### In Summary

More than 100 years on, Bloomingdale's is still relevant in American society. Today, the retailer reaches more mainstream customers than could have been imagined when it first opened its doors. Its name continues to influence fashion and retail shopping around the world.

***See also*** Central Park; Fifth Avenue; Metropolitan Museum of Art; New York, New York; Subways; Tiffany & Company

### Further Reading

Brady, Mazine. 1980. *Bloomingdale's*. New York: Harcourt Brace Jovanovich.

Brockmann, Jorg, and Harris, Bill. 2005. *One Thousand New York Buildings*. New York: Black Dog & Leventhal.

Pease, Steven L. 2009. *The Golden Age of Jewish Achievement: The Compendium of a Culture, a People, and Their Stunning Performance*. Sonoma, California: Deucalion.

Traub, Marvin. 1994. *Like No Other: The Bloomingdale's Legend and the Revolution in American Marketing*. New York: Times Books.

## Bodie, California

Bodie, California, formerly a prosperous and notorious gold town in the West, is today a popular ghost town. Bodie lies in a desolate region in the Sierra Nevada Mountains. In winter, the town is pummeled with heavy snows and frigid temperatures; the summers are arid and warm. Little grows there except sagebrush, a classic backdrop for a Hollywood Western. During its heyday in the second half of the 19th century, miners, proprietors, families, and a lively criminal element complete with outlaws and prostitutes, made Bodie one of the "wickedest towns in the West."

Today, Bodie is a skeleton of its former self. The remaining structures have been maintained but not restored. Though in former days, adventurous men and women braved the dangers of the legendary town to seek gold and a life in the West, the town now attracts only tourists, enchanted by its history. Bodie is one of the last remaining authentic emblems of America's pioneer heritage, the mythical, legendary, and infamous Wild West.

### Historical Perspectives

Bodie was founded in 1876, some 17 years after gold was first discovered in the area by William S. Bodey. Bodey was one of five prospectors who made their way through precarious terrain to the area now

View of the once-thriving city of Bodie, California, now a ghost town. (Larry Gevert/Dreamstime.com)

known as Bodie. After finding gold, Bodey and one other prospector stayed in the area over the winter. But winters in the Sierra Nevada Mountains could be treacherous. When a blizzard stormed through, Bodey died.

As was often the way in the West, the discovery of gold brought more gold seekers and the eventual establishment of a mining camp. The area where Bodey and the other prospectors found gold became known as Bodie, in honor of the fallen prospector. The misspelling of the town name was started by Robert W. Howland, a sign painter, who liked his spelling better than the original. The town folks agreed.

### Everyday Life

As Bodie grew and prospered, the population of the town swelled. At its peak, some 10,000 people lived there, and gold and silver mining produced a staggering $100 million in today's figures. The treeless town itself expanded to include nearly 200 homes and several restaurants, saloons, and flat-faced stores. The town featured the Bodie Cemetery, a school, a jail, a barbershop, the Miner's Union Hall, the DeChambeau Hotel, a railroad depot, and several brothels. Within these structures, families and outlaws mingled and went about their daily work and social activities. Organized sports, such as baseball, wrestling, and footrace, were popular pastimes among Bodieites. For a brief period, Bodie also had a suburban neighborhood, built in 1878, where workers and their families lived near their work. Today, there is no trace or explanation of the disappearance of this Bodie suburb.

### The Criminal Element

Mining was not the only activity going on in Bodie. Bodie was a notorious site of lawlessness. Saloon gunfights, prostitution, and ruffians gave the gold town a sensationalized reputation. Its most infamous rogues helped perpetuate the concept of the "Bad Man from Bodie." These men, including the likes of Rattlesnake Dick, James Blair, Harry Dugan, and Billy Deegan, routinely made the papers. Popular fiction about such men was written by authors such as E. H. Clough. Clough's story, entitled "The Bad Man of Bodie," was published in the *Argonaut*, a newspaper in San Francisco, in 1878 at the onset of the wave of intense crime that persisted through 1882.

### Preservation

Bodie was not destined to last long. By the late 1880s, the economic structure of the town had begun to unravel. Many Bodieites sold their homes and moved away. In the early decades of the 20th century, James Stuart Cain attempted to save the town by purchasing property and structures in the town, believing that one day Bodie would rise up again. But Bodie continued to experience setbacks. A fire in 1932, started by a toddler nicknamed "Bodie Bill," destroyed a great many of the structures, leaving 175 buildings intact. World War II (1941–1945) brought on mining restrictions that further crippled the town.

When in the 1960s the state of California stepped in to save Bodie by purchasing it, there was but one resident, a lone caretaker, left in the town. In 1962, Bodie was established as a state park. It was also designated a State Historical Landmark and a National Historic Site. This acquisition, as well as protests from individuals concerned about the environment, has helped protect Bodie from mining operations that could potentially damage the environment and the town.

### Images in Popular Culture

Bodie does not appear much in contemporary media these days, due mainly to the decline of the Western as a genre in movies and on television. In 1929, Universal Studios arrived in Bodie to produce a film,

*Hell's Heroes* (1930), about three outlaws in the West. Bodie was featured in a History Channel series on *Gold Rush Ghost Towns* (released on DVD in 2005). In addition to the thrillers written during the town's lawless days, several contemporary books have been written about the town and its checkered history.

### For Visitors

Today, some 200,000 visitors come to Bodie each year. Visitors explore the parts of the town that survived the 1932 fire and, by special tour, see prohibited sections. In addition to the 175 buildings, tourists can visit the museum that once served as the Miners Union Hall, a center of social activity, and where, in 1881, a mob lynched a murderer in front of the building.

Fascination with the West, including remnants from that world such as ghost towns like Bodie, is as strong as ever. Indeed, Bodie is assured a long life as a popular travel destination and treasured landmark of American history for generations to come.

***See also*** Barbershops; California; Hollywood; Old West; Saloons, Bars, and Taverns; San Francisco, California; Suburbia

### Further Reading

McGrath, Roger D. 1984. *Gunfighters, Highwaymen, and Vigilantes: Violence on the Frontier*. Berkeley: University of California Press.

Piatt, Michael H. 2003. *Bodie: "The Mines Are Looking Well . .": The History of the Bodie Mining District*. El Sobrante, California: North Bay Books.

Sprague, Marguerite. 2003. *Bodie's Gold: Tall Tales and True History from a California Mining Town*. Reno: University of Nevada Press.

Till, Tom, and Jordan, Teresa. 2001. *Great Ghost Towns of the West*. Portland, Oregon: Graphic Arts Center.

Watson, James, and Brodie, Doug. 2002. *Big Bad Bodie: High Sierra Ghost Town*. San Francisco: Robert D. Reed Publishers.

## Bok Kai Temple

Bok Kai Temple is a sacred place of worship for Taoists. It has also been used as a meeting place and a court of law. Located in Chinatown in Marysville, California, Bok Kai was a central part of religious life for Chinese settlers in America and is today regarded as one of the oldest structures of its kind in Chinese American history. Bok Kai stands as an enduring symbol of the religious and cultural roots of the Chinese in America, linking Chinese descendants to their heritage, as well as providing all people the opportunity to explore and experience a culture different from their own. To many, the temple is also valued for its Old World architecture.

### Historical Perspectives

The Chinese, mainly from the Canton province, were among the wave of people that poured into California during the Gold Rush era in the middle of the 19th century. Areas within American cities and towns where the majority of Chinese lived and created their own ethnic communities were known as Chinatowns. Founded in 1850, Marysville's Chinatown flourished during its first 50 years. The popular Chinatown provided Chinese laborers and gold seekers with places to live, shop, dine on authentic cuisine, and indulge in entertainment and artistic pursuits. Indeed, the Marysville Chinatown featured two opera houses, the Gee Kong Tong Opera House and Low Yee Opera House. One of the earliest

(1854) and most important structures built in this area was a temple known as Bok Kai Mui, situated near the Yoruba River. The temple, which means Temple (Mui) of the North (Bok) side of the stream (Kai), contained sacred tablets and images of deities or gods worshipped by the Chinese.

After the original Bok Kai Mui Temple fell into disrepair, a new one, the Bok Kai Temple, was built along the Yuba River where a bathhouse was once located. Bok Kai Temple, generally translated as God of the Dark North, was dedicated in 1880. Although several gods are recognized in the temple, Bok Eye, a water deity, occupies a prominent place. Bok Eye is believed to provide protection from flooding and evil. This deity was critical to Marysville's Chinatown, owing to the fact that the residences were situated so close to a river. In the beginning, Bok Kai Temple was primarily a place of worship; the temple is still an important place of worship for Taoists everywhere but is also considered a historically important and endangered landmark, as well as a popular destination for tourists, Chinese and non-Chinese alike.

### Bok Kai Festival

One of the most popular times of the year to visit the temple is during Bok Kai Festival, also known as Bomb Day. A lavishly celebrated event, the Bok Kai festival marks the birthday of the deity Bok Eye and occurs annually, on the second day of February or March, and usually lasts two days. In 2010, the festival celebrated its 130th year. During the festival, large fireworks and good luck rings explode in the air. Spectators scramble to retrieve the rings as they fall to the ground. The festival also includes a lively parade featuring martial art performers, floats, lion dancers, and marching bands. Individuals participating in the parade usually wear traditional Chinese clothing. But the parade and other festivities also feature modern attractions, such as modern vehicles incorporated into the parade, a Bomb Day Queen, multicultural performances, and tours of the Chinese American History Museum of Northern California.

Absent from contemporary festivals is the Golden Dragon, known as Gum Lung in Chinese. Its appearance was believed to scare evil away. When it first arrived in Marysville from China, in the 1890s, it was over 150 feet long. Decked in silk and jewels, Gum Lung was the first parade dragon in America and, until World War II (1941–1945), was regarded as the most popular. Chinese communities throughout the nation would borrow it for parades, and it was exhibited at the 1939 World's Fair in New York. Eventually, Gum Lung was replaced by two parade dragons and stored away in the temple.

### In Conclusion

More than 150 years after its founding, Bok Kai Temple still stands, displaying the treasured ancient murals depicting scenes from Chinese culture. For many years, as a result of wear and tear, the temple was placed on a list of most endangered structures in the nation. Through the efforts of the Chinese community, the National Trust for Historic Preservation, and other supporters, the temple has been restored, enabling it to remain the cornerstone of Marysville's Chinatown, an emblem of America's diverse religious and cultural heritage.

*See also* California; Chinatown

### Further Reading

*Bok Kai Temple*. http://www.bokkaitemple.org/.

Lee, Jonathan H.X., and Nadeau, Kathleen M., eds. 2011. *Encyclopedia of Asian American Folklore and Folk life*. Santa Barbara, California: ABC-CLIO.

Tom, Brian, Tom, Lawrence, and the Chinese American Museum of Northern California. 2008. *Marysville's Chinatown*. Charleston, South Carolina: Arcadia Publishing.

## Boston Marathon

The Boston Marathon is the oldest marathon in the United States and one of the most popular marathons in the world. At 26 miles, 385 yards, the marathon challenges runners over a diverse terrain. The Boston Marathon, like any other marathon in the world, is a test of physical and mental endurance; for many runners, just crossing the finish line, regardless of time, is the goal. Starting from Main Street, runners course through various towns, up notorious hills, and past thick crowds of animated spectators. The annual marathon, which takes place on the third Monday in April, entices marathoners from across the globe, elite runners, first-timers, and celebrities. Marathons symbolize prestige, accomplishment, and exclusivity. The Boston Marathon has a special reputation because of the level of difficulty of the course, as well as the fact that only participants who meet stringent qualification standards can participate. As the oldest U.S. marathon, it stands out as a history-making event in a city made famous by its integral role in American history, a relationship that is supported by the fact that the Boston Marathon is run on Patriot's Day, a civic holiday in Massachusetts.

### Historical Perspectives

The Boston Marathon may have been the first organized marathon in the nation, but it was not the first in the world. The first organized marathon occurred in Athens, Greece, at the Olympics in 1896. The term "marathon" harkens back to 490 BC when, it is believed, Pheidippides, an Athenian soldier, was sent to request help from Sparta. He had to run 150 miles in two days to carry out this task. After the Greeks triumphed over the Persians in the Battle of Marathon, Pheidippides ran 26 miles from Marathon to Athens to report the Greeks's victory. After uttering this message, he died.

America's first marathon was held in Boston on April 19, 1897, the year following the marathon at the Olympics. John Graham is credited for having organized the first Boston Marathon, a small race from today's perspective. The first race included only 15 marathoners who ran 24.5 miles. But no women were allowed. John J. McDermott won in a time of 2: 55: 10.

### Evolution

As time passed, the Boston marathon grew and developed. In 1924, more than a decade and a half after the first modern Olympics, the length of the race was extended to 26 miles, 385 yards. The first woman, Roberta Gibb, did not participate in the Boston Marathon until 1966, and such was the sentiment that women's lives would be endangered by such a strenuous race, that she had to do so illegally. So Gibb secretly joined the race after it had started. Later in the next year, Katherine Switzer signed up using a man's name. Women were finally allowed to enter the Boston Marathon in 1972, and in 1975, participants in wheelchairs were allowed.

The marathon has grown into a sporting phenomenon in contemporary times. More than 20,000 participants, men and women, participate in the Boston Marathon, a far cry from its original 15 participants. Marathons now take place in all 50 states in the nation, including Washington, D.C. For the super-avid marathoner, membership to the 50 States Marathon Club is a badge of achievement. Boston, however, ranks at the top of the best races in the world. This is due to its prestige factor (racers have to qualify and it was the first U.S. marathon), the scenic and historic neighborhoods runners bound through, and the local attractions (marathoners frequently stay for several nights or more in the town in which they race).

### Cultural Distinctions

The marathon community is a subculture in itself. At the top of the chain are the elite runners who enjoy celebrity status (professional marathoners not only garner prestige but large sums of money at the finish line.) Running may consume the lives of the elite runners, particularly during training season. But running has gone mainstream, too, becoming a way of life for many nonprofessional aficionados.

The American running culture includes running magazines, books about marathons and training, and marathon sites on the Internet. Amateur runners form local organizations or train with members for various charity foundations. Runners are seen at any time of day, jogging, alone or in groups, through neighborhoods in suburbia, city parks, esplanades, and on school tracks. Training often occurs in gyms and fitness clubs and on treadmills at home. Sports stores, in response to the growing appeal of marathons, have expanded their lines of clothing, gear, and running shoes for this ever-growing community. Mainstream and health food stores alike sell popular energy drinks, meal bars, and other accessories marketed to runners to enhance the running experience.

### Horror at the Boston Marathon

The Boston Bombing was an unprecedented domestic terrorist attack that occurred at the Boston Marathon on the afternoon of April 15, 2013, a date known as Patriot's Day in Boston. The bombing resulted in 3 deaths and over 260 injuries when two pressure-cooker bombs went off near the finish line on Boylston Street.

The Federal Bureau of Investigation and local police began a massive manhunt. Photographs and surveillance video of two suspects were released on April 18. An MIT police officer was allegedly killed by the suspects, an SUV was carjacked, and gunfire was exchanged between the suspects and police in Watertown, Massachusetts. Tamerlan Tsarnaev, one of the suspects, was killed during the exchange. Dzhokhar Tsarnaev, the other suspect and Tamerlan's brother, escaped. During the search that ensued, residents within the vicinity were asked to stay indoors; businesses and public transportation were closed. Finally, on the evening of April 19, Dzhokhar was discovered hiding in a boat in a residential backyard.

The victims, many of whom lost limbs, set about the business of recovering from the horrific event. In a show of love and caring by the city and the country, they have been honored in many ways since the bombing. There were on going tributes to the victims during Red Sox's games at Boston's famed Fenway Park.

Since the bombing, the world has learned a great deal about the suspects. Tamerlan, who left behind a wife and child, was alleged to be the most radical of the two brothers. Reports suggest that the brothers planned the bombing as retribution for unspecified deaths caused by American operations in the Muslim world. Both brothers were born in republics of the former Soviet Union. The brothers and their family moved to America in 2002 as refugees.

## Race Day

The Boston Marathon is a media event. Televised worldwide, from start to finish, news coverage sends the thrilling events of the race into the living rooms of running fans and casual viewers alike. Newspapers, television, and the Internet are filled with stories and compelling interviews about participating marathoners. Media coverage also includes sensational stories about cancer survivors and octogenarians, costumes worn by some of the marathoners, and race results for winners and high-profile professional runners. Some 500,000 spectators hold parties, cheer on the marathoners, and raise homemade signs for relatives and friends in the race. The event is an extraordinary and often emotional experience, as racers, young and old, staggering or limping, walking or sprinting, push through to the finish line.

## Tragedy

On October 15, 2013, two bombs exploded at the Boston Marathon near the course. Three victims died that day; many others, including bystanders and racers, adults and children, suffered injuries. Many lost arms and legs as a result. One suspect, Tamerlan Tsarnaev, was killed during an encounter with the police. Dzhokhar Tsarnaev, another suspect and Tamerlan's brother, is currently in custody.

*See also* Boston, Massachusetts; Gyms and Fitness Clubs; Main Street; Suburbia; Washington, D.C.

**Further Reading**

*Boston Athletic Association*. http://www.baa.org/.

Cooper, Pamela. 1998. *The American Marathon*. Syracuse, New York: Syracuse University Press.

Derderian, Tom. 1994. *Boston Marathon: The History of the World's Premier Running Event*. Champaign, Illinois: Human Kinetics Publishers.

## Boston, Massachusetts

Boston is the capital of Massachusetts and one of the oldest cities in the nation. The city has been known by many names such as Athens of America, Cradle of Liberty, Bean Town, and City on a Hill. Located in the northeast corner of the United States, along the harbor that shares its name, Boston epitomizes the quintessential New England city. With bright, colorful autumns, snowy winters, blossoming flowers in springtime, and warm, pleasant summers, Boston offers its visitors four appealing seasons and a treasure

The distinction between past and present in Boston is frequently blurred, as seen here in Faneuil Hall, a popular tourist destination and shopping center that has functioned continuously as a marketplace and meeting space since 1742. (Tupungato/Dreamstime.com)

trove of early American history as well as modern attractions and amusements. The city, which includes more than 600,000 residents, is notable for being the home of the legendary Boston Tea Party, the famous Kennedy family, Harvard University, the Boston Marathon, seafood cuisine, and major sports teams including the Boston Celtics, Boston Red Sox, and New England Patriots.

### Historical Perspectives

The original inhabitants of the area that is now eastern Massachusetts were a small tribe of Algonquian-speaking Native Americans. The first European settlement in the area was founded in 1628, only two decades after the first permanent English settlement in America, Jamestown, was established by Puritans who came in droves to escape religious oppression. They soon named their settlement "Boston," after the town in England they had come from. The settlement flourished, quickly establishing viable shipbuilding and fishing industries, and becoming the capital of the Massachusetts Bay Colony in 1632.

During the French and Indian War (1754–1763), the colonists aided the British in their violent struggle for control over territories in North America.

#### Boston Tea Party: Then and Now

The Boston Tea Party has two associations. The original association refers to an event in history that occurred on December 16, 1773, when a group of Massachusetts patriots seized 342 chests of tea in a nighttime raid on three tea ships. Disguised as Mohawk Indians, the group boarded the ships and threw the tea into the water. This action was a part of a series of protests staged by the colonials in protest to the perceived excessive demands of the British.

The Boston Tea Party was a direct protest against the Tea Act, which gave the East India Company a monopoly on the sale of tea and levied a tax on the tea, which colonists did not have an opportunity to vote for or against. For many colonialists who were already intent upon breaking away from British rule, the Tea Act was just one more issue that added to their frustrations with England. Historians single out the Boston Tea Party as one of the most significant events to have occurred in the lead-up to the American Revolution. Indeed, the event is celebrated as a symbol of the defiance of the colonialists.

Two centuries later, the term "Tea Party" was used to describe a movement that emerged in the 21st century. The name of this movement reflects the group's intent to align themselves, in a symbolic way, with the celebrated patriots of the pre–American Revolution era. It is also an acronym for "taxed enough already." In 2006, a conservative political party calling itself the Tea Party was founded. In the 2010 mid-term elections, many members of the Tea Party were elected on the Republican ticket. This eventually resulted in a split in the Republican Party, as differences arose between more moderate Republicans and the increasingly radicalized Tea Party.

### American Revolution

The English celebrated their victory in the French and Indian War by imposing oppressive and restrictive taxes on the colonists. Taxation was the means by which the British hoped to recover the enormous costs of the war. The colonists, however, bristled under the excessive demands and plotted ways to resist. A secret organization called the Sons of Liberty was formed throughout the colonies; public demonstrations were staged; and riots erupted in the streets.

One of the most pivotal moments in American history occurred when, in 1773, colonists in Boston dumped crates of tea from three British ships into the sea in protest of the high tax on this commodity. This event became known as the Boston Tea Party. Tensions soon erupted and full-blown skirmishes occurred. The colonists rebelling against British rule were known as patriots.

On April 18, 1775, Boston locals William Dawes and Paul Revere set out on their legendary "midnight ride" to warn colonists that British troops were on their way to Lexington and Concord. The Battles of Lexington and Concord followed the next day, with the minutemen and the local militias winning the day. More tense moments in Massachusetts followed, including the British victory in the Battle of Bunker Hill in Charlestown.

In March of the following year, the British left Boston, and on July 4, 1776, the Declaration of Independence was signed by the leaders of the forthcoming nation. The American Revolution had begun and would not end until 1783.

### Civil War

In 1822, Boston, by then known for its many thriving industries as well as its academic institutions and literary figures, became a city. Immigrant migrations, primarily Irish in the early days, swelled the cities numbers. Famous authors who called Boston their home included Ralph Waldo Emerson, Nathaniel Hawthorne, Louisa May Alcott, and Henry David Thoreau.

Boston, which had played an instrumental role in the birth of the United States as an independent nation, free from British rule, was also poised to play a historic role in the American Civil War (1861–1865). The Civil War pitted North against South, free states against slave states. At the time the Civil War erupted in 1861, African Americans in Boston had enjoyed freedom and considerable liberties for nearly 80 years (Massachusetts ended slavery in the state in 1783). The state teemed with abolitionists, men and women who openly denounced slavery, supported the Underground Railroad, and plowed through the nation to mobilize supporters. In 1863, Massachusetts governor John A. Andrew authorized one of the first African American infantry regiments, the historic 54th Massachusetts Volunteer Infantry, commanded by Robert Gould Shaw.

**Revolutionary Hero**

Paul Revere was a major figure during the American Revolution. Born on January 1, 1735, in Boston, Massachusetts, Revere was the eldest of seven children. He apprenticed with his father, Apollos Rivoire, a French immigrant who Americanized his name. In 1757, Revere married his first wife, Sarah Orne. They had eight children. After Sarah's death, Revere married Rachel Walker, with whom he had another eight children.

Industrious, Revere expanded his income with additional work as an engraver and dentist. Although he did well, he was conscious of the increasingly domineering ways of the colony's British overlords. Constanttax increases, for example, roiled many in the Massachusetts colony and elsewhere.

When colonialists decided to take action to protest taxation without representation by the British, Revere became an ardent leader of the cause. He spied on British soldiers and participated in the famous Boston Tea Party in 1773. In 1774 and 1775, Revere worked for the Boston Committee of Correspondence and the Massachusetts Committee for Safety as an express rider. He carried news, messages, and documents to distant locations such as New York and Philadelphia.

On April 18, 1775, Revere went on his famed ride, now popularly known as the Ride of Paul Revere, to Lexington, Massachusetts, to warn Samuel Adams and John Hancock that the British troops were marching to arrest them. During the ride, Revere stopped at each house along the way to alert the residents. The Battle of Lexington followed, launching the American Revolution.

Contemporary visitors to Boston can visit Paul Revere's home, one of many landmarks run by the Paul Revere Heritage Project in Boston.

### Boston Brahmins

In many cities in the nation, particularly during the early years of their history, the wealthy classes exerted extraordinary influence. In some cities, the aristocratic classes were classified by such terms as "old money" and "new money." In 1861, writer Oliver Wendell Holmes coined the term "Boston Brahmins" to describe the ruling class of his city. The term "Brahmin" originates from the Hindu term that is used to describe a member of the highest class among Hindus. In Boston, the term described a particular set of aristocrats whose ancestral line could be traced to the settlers of the Plymouth and Massachusetts Bay colonies. Of English descent, Protestant, and wealthy and powerful, these families dominated the politics of the city and delineated the rules and social culture of high society. Their children attended exclusive private schools or boarding schools and then went on to prestigious institutions of higher learning, primarily Harvard. Marriage was restricted to other individuals within this society. Neighborhoods, such as Beacon Hill, were historically restricted to these families. The Boston Brahmins looked down upon outsiders, an attitude that only intensified as Boston experienced mounting immigration.

### Immigration

Beginning in the 19th century, immigrants arrived in Boston in diverse groups, such as the Italians, Chinese, Jewish, and African Americans. The largest group to settle in Boston was the Irish, as the potato famine in Ireland, which occurred between 1845 and 1849, triggered massive migration. The Brahmins were unwilling to share their wealth and power with the newcomers. But their discriminatory practices against the immigrant populations sparked resistance in the form of political mobilization that challenged the status quo of Boston society.

### The Fitzgeralds and Kennedys

The Fitzgeralds and Kennedys were two prominent Catholic families of Irish descent that challenged the rule of the Boston Brahmins. John Francis Fitzgerald, who was also known as "Hony Fitz," was born on February 11, 1863, in the North End, which was then a predominately Irish enclave in Boston. Joseph P. Kennedy, whose ancestors had also emigrated from Ireland, was born in Boston on September 6, 1888. Kennedy was the father of America's 35th president, John F. Kennedy. Both men rose to prominence and popularity in their respective fields. Fitzgerald served from 1892 to 1894 in the Massachusetts State Senate and from 1895 to 1901 and in 1919 in the U.S. House of Representatives representing the Democratic Party. He also served as the mayor of Boston. During Fitzgerald's time in office, he garnered a positive reputation among the poor, working classes, and immigrant population, thanks to his support of their causes and his willingness to fight against the oppressive treatment of Boston's immigrant communities. Kennedy was a leader in the steel industry, invested in various Hollywood studios, and served as an ambassador to the United Kingdom from 1938 to 1940.

The legacy of Kennedy and Fitzgerald continued on for many generations. The two families were launched into national and international fame when Joseph P. Kennedy and Rose Fitzgerald married in 1914. Their union produced nine children, one of whom, John Kennedy, became the president of the United States in 1961 and was tragically assassinated in 1963. To this day the Kennedy family, including extended family members, occupies a prominent place in American politics and in the public eye.

### Contemporary Perspectives

Boston, like many metropolitan cities in the nation, has moved along with the currents of change and modernization, though it has also managed to maintain its many historic places. Today Boston's sundry history-rich attractions support a heavy tourism industry, drawing each year many thousands of tourists to swell its resident population of 600,000.

A modern face-lift has reinvigorated the city by adding a new highway, a convention center, hotels, and a revitalized downtown and Boston Harbor. Visitors seek out ethnic enclaves, historic neighborhoods and homes, popular institutions of higher learning, monuments galore, museums, historic trails, bars and taverns, and yearly festivals and celebrations. Sports fever runs high for professional sports such as the Red Sox who play baseball in the historic Fen way Park in Boston, and the New England Patriots who play football at the Gillette Stadium in Fox borough, a suburb of Boston. Fen way Park is especially packed during the most anticipated games of the season when the Red Sox play against the New York Yankees. This rivalry is more than a century old.

### Images in Popular Culture

Boston has often been represented in the media, particularly in contemporary films and television. The award-winning film *Glory* (1989) showed the heroism of the 54th Volunteer Regiment and its Captain, Robert Gould Shaw. Many contemporary films and television series, utilizing Boston as a backdrop, perpetuate popular perceptions of the city: Boston accents, gritty, working-class neighborhoods, and dreary urban landscapes appear in popular films such as *Good Will Hunting* (1997) and *Mystic River* (2003). Urban life and modern drama are highlighted in television series like *Spencer: For Hire* (1985–1988) and *Boston Legal* (2004–2008). The television series *Boston Public* (2000–2004) grappled with the tough issues and challenges common in contemporary urban high schools. *Cheers* (1982–1993), one of America's most iconic television shows, featuring a local bar and zany characters was set in Boston. Boston—whether perceived as a place of historical import or an urban metropolis—remains a major center of diverse American life.

### For Visitors

One of the city's most popular historical attractions is the Freedom Trail, which covers two and a half miles and features 16 historic sites. One such site is the Boston Common, which was designated "common land" in 1640 and is used today for assorted public activities. The Freedom Trail features the Granary Burying Ground (burying place for famous patriots such as Samuel Adams and Paul Adams), the first public school in the nation, Paul Revere's House, and the Bunker Hill Monument.

Other points of interest are the city's immigrant and ethnic neighborhoods. Among the earliest ethnic groups to arrive in Boston were African Americans, the Irish, Italians, Portuguese, and European Jews. Boston pays homage to local African American history with its famous Black Heritage Trail, featuring sites and monuments such as the Museum of African American History, the African Meeting House, the first African American church in the nation, and the Robert Gould Shaw Memorial. The Irish influence in Boston is honored by the Irish Cultural Centre, an annual film festival, many pubs and restaurants, and an Irish Heritage Trail including 20 sites such as the Rose Kennedy Garden, the Boston Irish Famine Memorial, and Fen way Park. Homage is paid to one of the most famous Irish descendants, former president John F. Kennedy, at the John F. Kennedy National Historic Site, which features his birth home and the John F. Kennedy Presidential Library and Museum. A Kennedy walking tour features seven historic stops, including the Bellevue Hotel and an apartment, two residences of John F. Kennedy. The Omni Parker House Hotel was a site of importance for Kennedy as well as his grandfather Fitzgerald. The Old City Hall, where Fitzgerald served as mayor, the Irish Famine Memorial, JFK's Senate Headquarters, and Faneuil Hall are other stops on the walking tour. Other popular ethnic sites include the North End, a historic Italian neighborhood, and Chinatown.

Boston is not only a city of rich heritage and diversity, it is also a popular college town. Most American college towns are thought of as small and sleepy places. Metropolitan Boston, however, has over 50 colleges, universities, and specialized institutions. Prominent Boston institutions of higher learning are its prestigious Harvard University and the Massachusetts Institute of Technology.

***See also*** Boston Marathon; Chinatown; Fen way Park; MIT; Plymouth Colony

### Further Reading

Duncan, Russell. 1999. *Where Death and Glory Meet: Colonel Robert Gould Shaw and the 54th Massachusetts Regiment.* Athens: University of Georgia Press.

Dunwell, Steve, and Linden, Blanche M.G. 1996. *Boston Freedom Trail.* Boston: Back Bay Press.

Emilio, Luis F. 1995. *A Brave Black Regiment: The History of the 54th Regiment of Massachusetts Volunteer Infantry, 1863–1865.* New York: Da Capo Press.

O'Connor, Thomas H. 2000. *Boston A to Z.* Cambridge, Massachusetts: Harvard University Press.

O'Connor, Thomas H. 2002. *Eminent Bostonians.* Cambridge, Massachusetts: Harvard University Press.

## Boulder, Colorado

Boulder is a city in northern Colorado. From its origins as a gold-rush town in the fabled West, Boulder has grown to a population of 103,000, which makes it one of the largest cities in the state, though the city is much smaller than major metropolitan U.S. cities such as Boston, Los Angeles, and New York. Nonetheless, Boulder consistently tops the list of best places to live in the nation. Dominated by sunny, blue skies, a pleasant, dry climate, and abundant open recreational spaces, Boulder is a favorite among lovers of nature and the outdoors. Its small-town ambience and large college population (nearly 30,000) make Boulder family-friendly and thus a magnet for young adults.

### Historical Perspectives

The region now known as Boulder, situated at the base of the Rocky Mountains, was originally inhabited and visited by various Native American tribes, including the Arapahoe, Ute, Cheyenne, Comanche, and Sioux. Zebulon Pike and John Fremont, American explorers, were among the first whites to map out the region. Upon discovering gold in 1849, the mad dash to Colorado began. In 1858, the first European settlement was established in the area, and the development of Colorado's cultural identity took root. That identity has long centered on a commitment to the preservation of the environment.

In 1877, the state's largest university, the University of Colorado, opened its doors.

### Cultural Distinctions

As a popular college town, Boulder has attracted hippies, particularly during the 1960s, and a continual stream of liberal-minded youth. Love of the land and the outdoors is a statewide preoccupation, one that reinforces health, fitness, and eco-consciousness among students and residents alike. Today, Boulder boasts more than 54,000 acres of preserved land used for public parks and open recreational space. Hiking, biking, rock climbing, walking, and skiing are among the popular activities on top in Boulder. Museums, shops, and local festivals help the residents of Boulder share their local culture and lifestyle with the world. Boulder is the archetypical laid-back American town, one that promotes a love of outdoor activities and a healthy lifestyle—what many call the best of American living.

***See also*** Boston, Massachusetts; Los Angeles, California; New York, New York; Old West

### Further Reading

Pettem, Silvia. 2006. *Boulder: Evolution of a City*. Boulder: University Press of Colorado.

Ubbelohde, Carl, Benson, Maxine, and Smith, Duane A. 2006. *A Colorado History*. Boulder, Colorado: Pruett Publishing.

## Bourbon Street

Bourbon Street is a legendary street, extending 13 blocks from Canal Street to Esplanade Avenue, in New Orleans, Louisiana. During New Orleans's biggest annual festival, Mardi Gras, Bourbon Street is filled to overflowing with revelers. On every other evening of the year, tourists and locals flock to the hundreds of popular venues along the famous thoroughfare. Bourbon Street offers an array of amusements, such as local cuisine and drink, music and dance, shopping and exploring, and adult entertainment. The local flavor of these venues, the historical roots of the area, and the unique architecture that distinguishes this street above all others make it one of the most popular places in the country.

### Historical Perspectives

Bourbon Street is a very old street, and the culture that flourishes there is influenced by diverse peoples—Native Americans, French, Spanish, American, and African descendents—that inhabited the region that is known today as Louisiana. The original inhabitants included the Atakapa Indians, Caddo Indians, Chitimacha Indians, Choctaw Indians, Houma Indians, Natchez Indians, and Tunica Indians. New Orleans, a city in Louisiana, was founded in 1718 by Jean-Baptiste Le Moyne de Bienville. Bienville, a colonizer from Montreal, Quebec, known as the Father of New Orleans, played an instrumental role in the development of the city, not only as a colonizer but as governor of French Louisiana for four terms. Adrian de Pauger and Le Blonde de la Tour created most of the original design of the city, including the laying out of the French Quarter and the city streets, many of which were named after the royal houses of France and Catholic saints. Bourbon Street, then known as Rue Bourbon, for example, was named after a French royal family, the House of Bourbon.

Spain purchased Louisiana in 1763, and, in 1803, the United States acquired the land via the historic Louisiana Purchase.

### Evolution

Bourbon Street's identity has evolved over the years, uniquely blending its mixed cultural roots and gaining a world-famous reputation as a hub for myriad amusements, many of which are considered bawdy and risqué. The names of the streets and other locales, as well as much of the architecture that remains today, can be traced back to their French and Spanish roots. The popular local cuisine that is served up in Bourbon Street restaurants is an amalgamation of cultural influences, such as French, Spanish, and African. The descendants of the African population, largely brought in to the region as slaves, were major contributors to the creation of jazz in the early 20th century. Performed on the streets or in the many disreputable establishments that rapidly sprouted along Bourbon Street, jazz, with its lively beats and intricate, improvisational melodies, became the signature sound of the region, a sound that quickly spread throughout the nation.

The 20th century saw the development of Bourbon Street as a major center for adult entertainment. Bourbon Street became a mainstay for scandalous amusements, drinking, prostitution, burlesque, and exotic dance shows. Individuals, such as itinerant servicemen, seeking a good time went to places such as the Casino Royale and the 400 Club. As the century progressed, more strip clubs and nightclubs opened, tantalizing individuals with their bright lights and modern features.

### Highlights

Risqué entertainment is not all that Bourbon Street offers. Other points of interest include renowned bars, restaurants, hotels, music clubs, festivals, and other attractions. Established in 1806, The Old Absin the House, formerly an importing firm, became a saloon that featured the legendary Absin the House Frappe. Because absin the is illegal, it is now made with Herbsaint. One of the most popular alcoholic drinks in New Orleans, "The Hurricane," is imbibed at Pat O'Briens, a bar established in 1933. One of the most celebrated Bourbon Street eateries is Galatoire's Restaurant. This restaurant was founded in 1905 and specializes in French Creole cuisine.

Popular music clubs feature jazz, blues, and rock and roll, and among the world-renowned festivals that occur on Bourbon Street are Mardi Gras, the Food and Wine Festival, a music festival, and a gay festival known as the Southern Decadence Parade. Bourbon Street is also known for its gay community. A section of the street hosts many venues, such as nightclubs and bars. Café Lafitte In Exile, founded in the 1950s, is the oldest gay bar in the nation. Other popular tourist attractions include boutiques and souvenir shops, museums, and spectacular hotels.

### Images in Popular Culture

Bourbon Street's greatest influence in the popular media has been in blues music and fiction. To this day, jazz musicians pay tribute to the legendary sound, and tourists from across the world migrate to Bourbon Street to hear the music that made the city famous. Many popular books are set against the lavish and decadent backdrop of this famous arterial. Interest in Bourbon Street abounds, bearing witness to the lasting appeal of one of America's most famous streets.

***See also*** French Quarter; Mardi Gras; New Orleans, Louisiana; Saloons, Bars, and Taverns

### Further Reading

Buerkle, Jack Vincent, and Baker, Danny. 1973. *Bourbon Street Black: The New Orleans Black Jazzman*. New York: Oxford University Press.

Davis, Francis. 2003. *The History of the Blues: The Roots, the Music, the People*. Cambridge, Massachusetts: Da Capo Press.

McKinney, Louise. 2006. *New Orleans: A Cultural History*. Oxford, New York: Oxford University Press.

Swenson, John. 2011. *New Atlantis: Musicians Battle for the Survival of New Orleans*. New York: Oxford University Press.

## Bourbon Trail

The Kentucky Bourbon Trail is a world-famous destination known primarily for its many bourbon distilleries. The trail also comprises several other attractions, such as a museum, heritage center, and a facility that makes the barrels that impart the signature flavor to the bourbon. Although bourbon has been a Kentucky tradition since the 1700s, the Bourbon Trail was not established until 1999. These days, the trail draws massive crowds, reaching near the 2 million mark each year. The Bourbon Trail is not only famous for its unique whiskey, a craft that is taken seriously in the region, but it's a nationally recognized travel destination steeped in bucolic charm, history, and pride.

### Historical Perspectives

Kentucky's earliest settlers arrived in the region during the 1700s. Mostly farmers, these settlers made distilled whiskey from their surplus grain. This process prevented waste and provided a diversion from their hard work and labor. The whiskey also was used, like money, to barter for necessities and wants. In the late 1700s, bourbon got its name from a county in the region named "Bourbon County," which was stamped on the barrels used to transport the whiskey down the waterways to various locations. It was eventually discovered that this transportation process imparted a distinct taste and amber color to the whiskey (the barrels used for this purpose had been charred to sterilize them, causing the sugars in the whiskey to caramelize. During transport, the combination of heat and cool temperatures along the Ohio and Mississippi rivers also favorably affected the bourbon).

According to Bernie Lubbers, author of *Bourbon Whiskey: Our Native Spirit* (2011), the first of two golden ages of bourbon began in the 1850s. In 1857, Ben Parley noted that it appeared that every adult in Kentucky drank bourbon whiskey. By that time, there were many distilleries in the area. American soldiers received partial payment in weekly rations of whiskey.

The Jim Beam Stillhouse and bourbon distillery at Clermont, Kentucky, a bucolic stop along the Bourbon Trail. (Dreamstime.com)

By the early 1900s, the prominence of whiskey in American life had diminished considerably. One of the main factors that reduced the popularity of bourbon was prohibition, which lasted between 1920 and 1933. During this time, whisky was predominately marketed legally as a medicine. The late 1940s saw the rise of the notorious moonshine drivers in Kentucky, as well as North Carolina and other states. Mostly men, these drivers drove fiercely and fast through the night under the light of the moon to transport illicitly distilled liquor. These nightly rides frequently necessitated the skill to out drive and outmaneuver local law enforcement and, eventually, in 1947, gave rise to NASCAR racing. Nearly two decades later, Congress declared Bourbon a distinctive product of the United States.

**For Visitors**

Kentucky Bourbon was ushered into its second golden age by the establishment of the Kentucky Bourbon Trail, which was founded by the Kentucky Distillers' Association in 1999. The Bourbon Trail features tours and whiskey-tasting at six distilleries (visitors must be 21 or older), among them the Maker's Mark Distillery, the Buffalo Trace Distillery, and the Wild Turkey Distillery.

It is recommended that visitors take two days to explore the Bourbon Trail, at the end of which, visitors who collect stamps at each distillery receive free Kentucky Bourbon Trail T-shirts. Bardstown, a major stop along the trail, features historic buildings, Jailer's Inn, a popular bed and breakfast and former jail, and the Oscar Getz Museum of Whiskey History. Bardstown is also where the annual Bourbon Festival has been held since 1992. Other points of interest include Churchill Downs, Thunder over Louisville, and the Kentucky Derby Festival.

Bourbon's second golden age is maintained not only through the popularity of the Kentucky Bourbon Trail. Magazines, such as *Malt Advocate* and *Bourbon Review,* help to encourage and maintain public interest, and, in 2007, the United States Senate declared the month of September "National Bourbon Heritage Month."

***See also*** Churchill Downs; Mississippi River; Napa Valley; Saloons, Bars, and Taverns

### Further Reading

Cecil, Sam K. 2010. *Bourbon: The Evolution of Kentucky Whiskey.* Nashville: Turner Publishing.

Cowdery, Charles K. 2004. *Bourbon, Strait: The Uncut and Unfiltered Story of American Whiskey.* Chicago: Made and Bottled in Kentucky.

*Kentucky Bourbon Trail.* http://kybourbontrail.com/.

Lubbers, Bernie. 2011. *Bourbon Whiskey: Our Native Spirit: Sour Mash & Sweet Adventures.* Indianapolis: Blue River Press.

## Broadway

Broadway, a street in New York City, is world renowned as the home of theater in the city and indeed the nation. To locals and tourists alike, it is difficult to imagine that this spectacularly lit area was once ensconced in brush and forest. Today the street and sidewalks are chock-full of human activity: taxis, street vendors, and theatergoers from around the world. The extravagant marquee lights, giant theatrical posters, and the countless theaters proclaim that this is the place to see the most popular musicals, plays, and operas in the nation, performed by the most illustrious names in show business.

### Historical Perspectives

The street today known as Broadway has a history many centuries old, stretching back to the days when Manhattan Island was inhabited by Native Americans, such as the Lenape. In those days it was called the Wickquasgeck Trail and was then, as now, a major thoroughfare.

The Wickquasgeck Trail continued to play an important role as control of the island changed hands over the years. After the Dutch settled on Manhattan in 1624, the trail became known as *Heere Straat*, the first of many name changes during that period. One of those names, *Breedeweg,* was favored by the British, who took over the Dutch colony in the latter half of the 17th century. They changed the name of the road to its English translation, "broad way."

Broadway's development as a hub of theater activity began under British control. The first venue, The Beggar's Opera, a popular British ballad opera, debuted in 1750. Famous actors, such as the English actor Junius Brutus Booth, patriarch of the famous Booth family of actors, helped to popularize theater in the New World.

### American Musicals

More theaters were soon constructed, particularly after America's birth as a nation in 1776. Forerunners of what would come to be known as the American musical began in the 1790s, but their popularity would not rise until the late 1800s when productions such as *The Elves* (1857) and *The Seven Sisters* (1860) would make headlines. Most scholars credit the musical *The Black Crook* (1866) as ushering forth America's enduring musical tradition.

Broadway's popularity increased over the decades. In the 1900s, attendance at Broadway theaters was driven upward by the construction of New York's subway system and Longacre Square, now known as Times Square. The blaze of white lights along Broadway inspired the street's nickname, "the Great White Way," in 1902. Broadway's golden years are considered to have occurred between the 1940s and 1960s, though today, the popular musicals of yesteryear mingle with modern productions. Classic revivals include *42nd Street, Showboat, West Side Story, Grease,* and *Phantom of the Opera.* Among the contemporary musicals are *Beauty and the Beast, Titanic, The Lion King, Mamma Mia,* and *Shrek.*

#### The History of the Musical

The musical seems to have always been a part of America. Indeed the genre has its roots in revolutionary times, though it took another century to establish itself. Common musical performances in America's early history were operas, burlettas, and pantomimes. In the 1800s, French and Viennese operettas became popular in America. Later influences were the massively popular but rough-hewn variety and minstrel shows, as well as vaudeville and burlesque shows. Many music scholars credit *The Black Crook,* which was first performed on September 12, 1866, at Niblo's Garden, a theater on New York's Broadway, with being the first American musical.

Many writers and composers etched their names in history by penning the timeless songs featured in musicals. During the 1900s, such hits included Florenz Ziegfeld's *Follies.* In the 1920s, Broadway burst with productions created by such individuals as Cole Porter, Rodgers and Hart, and the Gershwin brothers. *Showboat* (1927) by Oscar Hammerstein II, was both a massive popular hit and a critical success. In the 1930s, the golden age of the American musical, musicals such as Cole Porter's *Anything Goes* (1934) took the nation by storm. Rodgers and Hammerstein's *Oklahoma* (1943) and Jerry Brock's *Fiddler on the Roof* (1964) continue to be performed to this day.

Though the golden age of the musical has passed, New York's Broadway is still regarded as synonymous with the American musical.

### Legacy

The appeal of Broadway and its inseparable association with the American musical has secured its place in American popular culture. Composers such as George and Ira Gershwin, Cole Porter, and Oscar Hammerstein, for example, are familiar names throughout the country. The pinnacle of success for actors is to perform in a theater on the legendary street, and it is a given that America's premier productions take place there. Audiences clamor for tickets year round.

Broadway hosts some 39 theaters, many of them located in the general vicinity, on streets that are considered a part of the Broadway Theater District. Theaters are designated by size. "Broadway theaters" hold 500 or more theatergoers. "Off Broadway theaters" have between 100 and 499 seats, and "Off-Off Broadway theaters" have less than 100 seats. At Off Broadway and Off-Off Broadway theaters, audiences will more likely find non mainstream, experimental productions featuring lesser-known actors.

Other cities in other states have theater districts, but Broadway remains the foremost location for the American musical in the country.

***See also*** New York, New York; Subways

**Further Reading**

Greenfield, Thomas Allen. 2009. *Broadway: An Encyclopedia of Theater and American Culture*. Westport, Connecticut: Greenwood.

Grumet, Robert Steven. 2011. *First Manhattans: A History of the Indians of Greater New York*. Norman: University of Oklahoma Press.

Long, Robert Emmet. 2001. *Broadway, the Golden Years: Jerome Robbins and the Great Choreographer-Directors: 1940 to Present*. New York: Continuum International Publishing Group.

Stempel, Larry. 2010. *Showtime: A History of the Broadway Musical Theater*. New York: W.W. Norton and Company.

## Brooklyn Bridge

The Brooklyn Bridge is a structure in New York City that spans the East River, linking Brooklyn and Manhattan. Before the building of the bridge, travel to and from the island of Manhattan was restricted to boats and ferries. Commerce and rapid population growth necessitated the construction of the bridge. More than an economic necessity, the Brooklyn Bridge was considered an extraordinary achievement, nothing short of a modern-day miracle in the early years of American industrial growth. Construction

Brooklyn Bridge at dusk in September 2013. (Mihai Andritoiu/Dreamstime.com)

began in 1869 and was not completed until 13 years later in 1883. For many years, the bridge was the largest suspension bridge in the world.

Long after other bridges and the famous New York skyline reared up around it, the Brooklyn Bridge endures as a New York icon. It is celebrated for its architectural beauty and as a symbol of American ingenuity and achievement.

## Historical Perspectives

Having no structural link between Brooklyn and Manhattan made for a difficult life for residents. For nearly 200 years, residents relied on the ferry service to cross the 500 yards of the river. The journey was long and fraught with challenges, particularly in winter, when the river froze. In 1866, the New York State Legislature selected John Roebling, an engineer, to undertake the enormous task of building a bridge. Many thought it could not be done. But Roebling, who had emigrated from Germany in 1831, believed the contrary. He had extensive experience, having successfully built several aqueducts and the Niagara Suspension Bridge that connected New York Central and Canada's Great Western Railway. At the time, Roebling's Cincinnati–Covington (now John A. Roebling) bridge was the longest bridge in the world.

The construction of the bridge was a gargantuan task, one that Roebling did not live to see completed. Not long after work began in 1869, Roebling's foot was crushed by a ferry. He died from gangrene sustained as a result of the accident. His 32-year-old son, Washington Roebling, took over. When, the bridge was completed, the length of the main span was 1,562 feet, the width 85 feet, and the height towered to 273 feet.

The construction costs were high. The bridge cost New York $15.2 million, which equates to $2.2 billion in today's money. Other costs not measured in dollars and cents included the 27 deaths that occurred during the construction process, and the 13 years of exhausting physical and mental labor that it took to see the Brooklyn Bridge to completion.

In the wake of the many sacrifices and struggles that went into the building of the bridge, New York celebrated big. The opening ceremony took place on May 24, 1883, with the Brooklyn Bridge standing in its full glory, new steel glistening. National and local leaders, such as U.S. president Chester Arthur and New York governor Grover Cleveland were present, as were more than 14,000 invitees and gatherers. The ceremony featured a marching band and speeches. The day included fireworks and the crossing of some 150,000 people over the bridge.

## Images in Popular Culture and Everyday Life

The Brooklyn Bridge has long been an archetypal symbol of New York. Imprinted on postcards, prints, and photographs, the bridge is a widely recognizable structure. It's an unmistakable backdrop in films and television, even as it is an essential part of everyday New York life. Each year, thousands upon thousands of residents, and travelers depend upon the bridge, crossing it by vehicle, truck, foot, or bicycle. A popular tourist destination, the Brooklyn Bridge draws visitors from around the world. For many Americans, the bridge conjures a sense of pride and links them to a remarkable past.

*See also* New York, New York

## Further Reading

Haw, Richard. 2005. *The Brooklyn Bridge: A Cultural History*. New Brunswick, New Jersey: Rutgers University Press.

Langmead, Donald. 2009. *Icons of American Architecture: From the Alamo to the World Trade Center*. Westport, Connecticut: Greenwood Press.

McCullough, David G. 2001. *The Great Bridge: The Epic Story of the Building of the Brooklyn Bridge.* New York: Simon & Schuster.

Reier, Sharon. 2000. *The Bridges of New York.* Mineolla, New York: Dover Publications.

## Brown Derby Restaurant

The Brown Derby was the name of four restaurants that operated in California. The first Brown Derby—the only one constructed in the shape of a derby hat—opened in 1926 on Wilshire Boulevard across from the famous Ambassador Hotel. In 1936 it was moved to the corner of Wilshire and Alexandria. The Hollywood Brown Derby opened in 1929. The third Brown Derby, located in Beverly Hills, opened in 1931, and the fourth opened in 1941 in the Los Feliz neighborhood. Of the four restaurants, the Hollywood Brown Derby was the most famous, due to its massive popularity with the stars and movers and shakers in the movie industry. By the 1970s, the shifting interests of a new generation of stars led to a fading of the restaurant's glory. In 1994, the original Brown Derby was demolished.

### Historical Perspectives

The idea of the Brown Derby was conceived one day in 1925 at the legendary Ambassador Hotel, a Hollywood hotspot where stars gathered to be entertained with music, dance, and fine food. At this time in Hollywood history, the influential film town was still young; the films in production were neither in color nor audible. Still, the region was immersed in glamour and power and was the object of the public's fascination.

On that evening, three men sat together and discussed the idea for a new venue to cater to industry elites and celebrities. The men, Herb K. Somborn, a movie producer, Wilson Mizner, a playwright, and Sid Grauman, whose claim-to-fame included Grauman's Chinese Theatre, were themselves a part of the Hollywood mystique. At this gathering over dinner, details began to take shape in regard to the restaurant's theme. Mizner's commented that if food and service were good, "people would probably come to eat it out of a hat." The hat theme stuck (Cobb and Willems 1996). The men decided upon the name the Brown Derby and the shape of a hat for the building's construction.

In the following year, the Brown Derby became a reality. As planned, the restaurant was built across the street from the Ambassador in the shape of a hat. Also as intended, the servers and wait staff were meticulous in every way, their uniforms immaculate. The restaurant was an immediate hit. Indeed, its popularity led to the building of the Hollywood Brown Derby in 1929.

The year 1929 was an important one in Hollywood. In that year the so-called golden age of Hollywood was launched—a time of youthful vigor, beauty, sensational fame, and an abundance of films, produced with sound, which impacted the world. Within the district of Hollywood, studios and theaters proliferated. Residences for the rich and famous sprouted along legendary streets. The Hollywood Brown Derby proved to be an essential space for the burgeoning stars and workers in the film industry. The restaurant thrived in the center of the boomtown that was Hollywood.

The restaurant's success was influenced by several factors. The Brown Derby was a place where guests could relax and enjoy good meals with friends, peers, spouses, and romantic interests. But the Brown Derby was not a place where guests dined in anonymity: the restaurant was itself a stage. The low, brown booths made it possible for guests to "see and be seen" (Cobb and Willems 1996). For privacy, Hollywood's elite were allowed to use the American Room, which was opened in 1938 and featured private entrances.

Robert H. Cobb was another contributing factor to the popularity of the Hollywood Brown Derby. Cobb became president of the restaurant following the death of Somborn in 1934. Cobb carried on the tradition of the restaurant's exceptional service and flawless management. He was also genial to his guests. Many of the celebrity guests were his friends; he spent time with them, hunting, talking, and dancing. Even the world would come to know him indirectly through the popularity of the Cobb Salad, which he invented one night. The recipe includes chicken breast, lettuce, romaine, avocado, bacon, hard-boiled eggs, Roquefort cheese, and old-fashioned French dressing and has become an American classic.

**America's Salad**

Today, the Cobb salad is deemed a standard item on any American menu. The salad is offered at fine dining restaurants, mom and pop diners, fast-food restaurants, lunchroom cafeterias, and vending machines. But few know the history of this ubiquitous meal. The salad was created at the Brown Derby in Hollywood, California, by Bob Cobb, who owned the restaurant.

In 1937, Cobb searched his kitchen for a late night snack to prepare for himself and Sid Grauman (founder of Grauman's Chinese Theatre). By combining the ingredients lettuce, an avocado, romaine lettuce, watercress, tomatoes, a cold breast of chicken, a hard-boiled egg, chives, cheese, bacon, and French dressing, Cobb made history. According to the story, Sid Grauman enjoyed Cobb's creation so much that he ordered the so-named Cobb Salad the next day.

The salad became one of the most popular dishes at the Brown Derby. Its fame quickly spread throughout the city and the nation. Though the original Brown Derby is no longer in operation, Disney opened a reproduction of the original Brown Derby in Orlando, Florida, in 1989. The restaurant features Cobb's famous salad on its menu.

### Highlights

The specialness of the Hollywood Brown Derby was a result of management, the time, the place, as well as the people that frequented the restaurant. Even during the 1930s, in the midst of the Great Depression, the Brown Derby remained a cherished icon. During this same period, Cobb welcomed a Polish artist who wanted to draw caricatures of the famous patrons in exchange for meals. Eddie Vitch's caricatures grew famous themselves as they began to cover the walls of the restaurant. Hundreds of black and white caricatures were displayed, receiving enormous attention from the public, including the Hollywood elite who competed for top placement of their caricatures. Cobb ensured that the placements were always apropos to the changing tides of power and relationships. The caricatures depicted such stars as Jean Harlow, Marlene Dietrich, Errol Flynn, Cary Grant, and Charlie Chaplin.

### End of an Era

In 1970, Cobb passed away, leaving his wife Sally Cobb to take over the business. In 1975, the Brown Derby chains were acquired by Walter Scharfe and Elisabeth Khittl-Scharfe. The restaurant stayed in business but it was a different era. Though some occasionally returned to their favorite dining retreat, the majority of the stars had aged, moved, or passed away. The new generation found many other amusements. The golden age had faded. In 1985, the Hollywood restaurant closed for repairs of damage sustained after an earthquake. In 1994, after another earthquake, the restaurant was demolished.

### Images in Popular Culture

The Brown Derby restaurant has been immortalized in television and books. In a 1955 episode of the comedic sitcom, *I Love Lucy* (1951–1957), Lucy Ricardo (Lucille Ball) visits the famous restaurant while visiting Hollywood. In the episode, Lucy's zany antics play out against the backdrop of the restaurant where she has a star struck encounter with real-life movie star William Holden. The Brown Derby is commemorated in the book *The Brown Derby Restaurant: A Hollywood Legend* (1996), written by Sally Wright Cobb and Mark Willems and in several cookbooks, published in 1962, 1976, and 2009.

### Contemporary Perspectives

Today, all four Brown Derby restaurants have closed. The original location across from the Ambassador closed in 1980. In 1982, the Beverly Hills operation ceased. The Feliz site, which operated as Michael's Los Feliz Restaurant from the 1960s to the 1990s and then as Louise's Trattoria, was sold in 2012. Replicas of the restaurants stand at Disney's Hollywood Studios in Florida and at the MGM Grand Hotel in Las Vegas, Nevada.

***See also*** Ambassador Hotel; California; Disney World; Grauman's Chinese Theatre; Hollywood; Las Vegas, Nevada; Los Angeles, California

### Further Reading

Cobb, Sally Wright, and Willems, Mark. 1996. *The Brown Derby Restaurant: A Hollywood Legend*. New York: Rizzoli.

Jewell, Richard B. 2007. *The Golden Age of Cinema: Hollywood, 1929–1945*. Malden, Massachusetts: Blackwell Publishing.

## Bunker Hill Monument

The Bunker Hill Monument is a 221-foot granite obelisk that was erected in Charleston, Massachusetts, in 1842 to commemorate the eponymous Revolutionary War (1775–1783) battle fought in 1775. This monument has great import in that it was one of the first monuments built by Americans, and it commemorated one of the first major battles between the colonists, also known as the patriots, and the British. A popular destination to this day, the Bunker Hill Monument, located along Boston's Freedom Trail, is an iconic reminder of America's struggle to nationhood, a significant memorial that speaks to American patriotism and the desire to never forget the country's heritage.

The Bunker Hill Monument in Charlestown, Massachusetts, as seen from the harbor. The memorial, one of the earliest built in the United States, commemorates the Battle of Bunker Hill during the American Revolution and is part of the Freedom Trail. (Americanspirit/Dreamstime.com)

### Historical Perspectives

Ironically, the monument commemorates not a triumph for Americans but a demonstration of steely defiance and bravery. The Battle of Bunker Hill, which occurred on June 17, 1775, which was one of the first engagements in the American Revolution, ended in defeat for the colonists. The Patriots were vastly outnumbered and, compared to the British, sorely inexperienced, despite the presence of commanders who were veterans of the French and Indian War (1754–1763), such as Colonel William Prescott, Colonel John Stark, and General Israel Putnam. Some 2,400 British troops fought against 1,500 Americans, who fought hard and valiantly. At the end of three assaults, the British sustained deep casualties, numbering some 1,034 individuals. American casualties numbered between 400 and 600. The colonist's defeat did not portend the ultimate outcome of the war, for as history shows, the patriots won the American Revolution and America became an independent nation in 1776.

The first monument at the site of the battle was not the granite obelisk that stands today. Members of King Solomon's Lodge of Masons erected the first monument in 1794, an 18-foot wooden pillar commemorating fellow mason Major General Dr. Joseph Warren, who died during the third assault of the Battle of Bunker Hill.

### About the Site

Three decades after the erection of the Joseph Warren monument, efforts to build a monument to commemorate the battle began. The Bunker Hill Monument Association played a pivotal role in raising funds for the monument. Solomon Willard, a prominent architect in Massachusetts, designed and oversaw the construction. The structure, consisting of 6,700 tons of granite, with 295 stone steps within the obelisk leading to an observatory overlooking the city, was built in 1842 and dedicated in the following year. A statue of Col. William Prescott, built by William Wetmore Story and dedicated in 1881, stands near the obelisk. An exhibit lodge features a statue of Warren and a diorama of the battle. In 2007, a museum was built across the street.

### In Conclusion

Nearly 200 years after it was built, the Bunker Hill Monument continues to draw crowds. The site is the last of several Revolutionary War sites along Boston's Freedom Trail. New Millennium visitors are invited to picnic on the vast green spaces surrounding the monument. Also popular are the monument's winding stairs and the view of nearby Boston from the obelisk.

*See also* Boston, Massachusetts

### Further Reading

"Bunker Hill Monument." *National Park Service*. http://www.nps.gov/bost/historyculture/bhm.htm.

Nelson, James L. 2011. *With Fire and Sword: The Battle of Bunker Hill and the Beginning of the American Revolution*. New York: Thomas Dunne Books.

Wheildon, William Willder, and Bunker Hill Monument Association. 1865. *Memoir of Solomon Willard: Architect and Superintendent of the Bunker Hill Monument*. Charleston, South Carolina: Monument Association.

## Burning Man

Burning Man is an annual one-week event that has taken place in the Black Rock Desert in Nevada since the 1990s. The number of participants at a recent event passed 48,000, the size of a small city. Burning Man is known for going beyond the ordinary festival; it is an experience that promotes freedom of expression, creativity, and community. To detractors, the event may appear chaotic and strange. But it is its unconventional elements that attract newcomers and bring back returning participants year after year.

### Historical Perspectives

Credit for founding Burning Man goes to Larry Harvey and his friend Jerry James. As the story goes, Harvey and James burned an effigy of an eight-foot man on the summer solstice, June 21, 1986, on the Baker Beach in San Francisco, California. Rumors abound as to what the effigy symbolized, and why the structure was burned but what is known is that, at the heart of the ritual, is a popular term used by Harvey: radical self-expression. The burning of this effigy was an instant sensation, and Harvey and James were joined by others in subsequent years.

### About the Event

Over time, Harvey and others developed one of the most popular and unusual events in America. The organizational aspects of the event are basic. Each year with the event has a theme. Tickets may be acquired by anyone (children 12 and under are free) but participants must provide their own food, water, and shelter. The event promotes radical thinking, community, and creativity.

As participation in the event grew over the years, so did the size of the main attraction—the wooden man—and development of the Burning Man culture. By 1988, the wooden man stood 40 feet tall. In 1991, neon lighting was added to the structure. These days the wooden man is customarily burned on the Saturday proceeding Labor Day.

### Cultural Distinctions

Burning Man looks little like a garden-variety event. Vendors, professional performers and artists, and passive spectators have no place in this environment. Instead, the event is participant focused; freedom of expression is encouraged. Costumes, from the ordinary to the bizarre, and nudity are common. There is a Woodstock-like quality to the place, wherein participants frolic, dance to music, play music, and build temporary dwellings.

The temporary dwellings are set up in an area referred to as "Black Rock City." Participants set up individual camps or camps within so-called villages and theme camps. Theme camps are spaces created to elicit community involvement around the theme at the discretion of its creators. Transportation to and from the various camps and activities is customarily by foot or bike.

Art, fire, and transformation are at the foundation of Burning Man. Individuals and groups transport art of assorted sizes and kinds to the event, or they create art on-site. Art may include sound, fire, interaction, or any other form. While art is generally uninhibited, participants must still follow guidelines and register their creations.

Fire is a pivotal part of the event. In addition to "the Burn," a term that refers to the burning of the Burning Man statue, the event is inundated with fires; participants burn their artwork or other symbolic effigies that they create. At night, the desert is ablaze with campfires and multiple activities involving fire, such as artwork burning, effigy burning, fire walking, fire dancing, fire jumping, and fire breathing.

Perhaps the most important aspect of Burning Man is its effect on the participants. A number of participants contend that the event is life changing: transformational, a way to open the mind to self-discovery and new thought patterns and to the exploration of new modes of creativity. For some, this results in a change of career and lifestyle.

### In Conclusion

Burning Man is off the beaten path in terms of location—127 miles away from the nearest airport in Reno, Nevada—but its growing popularity makes it one of the most exciting events of the year.

***See also*** Folk Festival; San Francisco, California; Woodstock

### Further Reading

*Burning Man*. http://www.burningman.com/.

Doherty, Brian. 2004. *This Is Burning Man: The Rise of a New American Underground*. New York: Little, Brown and company.

Jones, Steven T. 2011. *The Tribes of Burning Man: How an Experimental City in the Desert Is Shaping the New American Counterculture*. San Francisco: CCC Publishing.

Traub, Barbara. 2011. *Desert to Dream: A Dozen Years of Burning Man Photography*. San Francisco: Immedium.

# C

## Cabazon Dinosaurs

The Cabazon Dinosaurs are two immense dinosaur statues in Cabazon, California. The enormously popular roadside attraction, touted as the world's largest dinosaurs, can't be missed while traveling along Interstate 10, the fourth longest highway in the nation. Like most roadside attractions found along remote stretches of highway, the dinosaurs were designed to draw in tourists who may be seeking amusement to break up the monotony of road. Such attractions typically mark the location of a place to purchase food, water, and gas and to stretch one's legs. The Cabazon Dinosaurs, also known as Claude Bell's Dinosaurs, were meant to increase business at Claude Bell's Wheel Inn Cafe. The Dinosaurs comprise two giant structures, a 45-foot tall and 150-foot long Apatosaurus named Dinny the Dinosaur and Mr. Rex, a three-story high Tyrannosaurus Rex.

According to the Cabazon Dinosaurs website, the attraction is viewed by some 12 million passersby annually, as they traverse Interstate 10. In contemporary times, the dinosaurs have lost some of their shiny newness, and, according to today's standards, they may be considered a little garish and unsophisticated. However, their faded, nostalgic campiness has itself become a draw, providing modern tourists with a glimpse into simpler times.

### Historical Perspectives

Years after the Wheel Inn Café opened its doors in 1958, Claude Bell, the owner of the café and well-known Knott's Berry Farm sculptor, set out to create a giant attraction to entice customers. The first dinosaur, Dinny, took 11 years to complete. Dinny, a 150-ton structure, is made from material salvaged from the construction of Interstate 10. Dinny houses a gift shop and museum. Stairs inside Dinny lead up to the dinosaur's gaping saw-toothed mouth. The second dinosaur, Mr. Rex, was built in 1981 and originally featured a giant slide in his tail. The slide was filled in, but stairs inside Mr. Rex lead to the dinosaur's mouth, where visitors can view their surroundings from between the snarling teeth. In the mid-1990s, the Bell family members sold the property.

### Images in Popular Culture

The Cabazon Dinosaurs played a significant part in the popular film *Pee-Wee's Big Adventure* (1985), an American cult classic. The film transports Pee-Wee, a rosy-cheeked man played by Paul Reubens, dressed in a gray suit and a red bow tie, into various screwball situations as he travels to iconic places

Mr. Rex, a 100-ton concrete model of Tyrannosaurus rex, was of one of several massive dinosaur sculptures built to attract travelers to a roadside diner in the town of Cabazon, west of Palm Springs, California. (Library of Congress)

in the nation. In Cabazon, he befriends a waitress and is then chased by her jealous trucker boyfriend, while the Cabazon Dinosaurs loom in the background.

The scene described previously reaffirms that the roadside attraction is alive and well in American culture, even in the midst of an increasingly sophisticated and technologically advanced modern society. In this world, kitsch is a work of art and amusement requires no elaborate graphics or spectacular mechanics.

### For Visitors

Today, the Cabazon Dinosaurs are a favorite attraction in Cabazon, having a population 2,500. A Christian-based attraction, the museum promotes creationism rather than evolutionism. There are self-guided tours, toy dinosaurs, gemstones, and fossils to buy, and a dino dig (a sandpit laid out like a paleontological site where children can dig for prizes). The Wheel Inn Café is still open for business.

*See also* California; Knott's Berry Farm

### Further Reading

Butko, Brian, and Butko, Sarah. 2007. *Roadside Attractions: Cool Cafés, Souvenir Stands, Route 66 Relics and Other Road Trip Fun*. Mechanicsburg, Pennsylvania: Stackpole Books.

*Cabazon Dinosaurs*. http://www.cabazondinosaurs.com//.

Lovett, Anthony, and Maranian, Matt. 2009. *L.A. Bizarro: The All-New Insider's Guide to the Obscure, the Absurd, and the Perverse in Los Angeles*. San Francisco: Chronicle Books.

## Cabin

A cabin is a simple one- or two-room dwelling built with logs or other rough materials. Cabins are commonly associated with American frontier life, conjuring images of the solitary trapper or mountain man, as well as the archetypal hardy frontier family. Emerging concurrently with the frontier cabin were the cabins lived in by the poor, particularly in rural areas, and by the severely oppressed such as the black slaves. Cabins were thus an integral part of early American life. Over time, cabins came to be used in other ways, such as vacation homes or rentals on the ocean, at the lake, or in the woods, and as summer dwellings at camp for youth. Some cabins were furnished as luxurious permanent homes, belying the very name, "cabin." In modern times, the cabin symbolizes American values such as independence and rugged individualism, as well as curiously contradictory economic stations in life (both poverty and wealth). For yet another segment of the population, the cabin symbolizes the ultimate getaway and off-grid refuge.

### Colonials and Frontiersmen

Cabin-making was common in the densely wooded regions of European countries such as Scandinavia. The skill was brought to America by the early immigrant settlers. When European settlers, such as the Finnish, Swedish, the Swiss, and the Germans, arrived in America in the early 18th century, they found the log cabin to be an ideal dwelling for the woodsy region of the eastern seaboard. Early settlements were located in densely forested areas; cabins did not take long to build. Settlers from other countries learned the skill and adopted the custom. Though some used their cabins as permanent dwellings, others, such as farmers, built them for temporary use while they built their permanent homes. By the 19th century, the cabin had become inextricably linked to unpretentiousness, humbleness, and industriousness. Thus, a politician who claimed to be born in a cabin was seen as an individual who could commiserate with the common person, someone who projected the modest, can-do, and independent spirit that was so admired. By contrast, the wealthy were regarded suspiciously. Thus Abraham Lincoln used the tale of his birth in a log cabin to endear himself to the American public.

Poor frontier families headed into the wilderness with little more than a wagon full of supplies and an ox. They grew their own crops, hunted with rifles for food, made their own clothing, fished in the rivers and lakes, and built simple cabins. They made their own furniture, tables, benches, and beds of corn husks or leaves. Sometimes, cabin building was a communal affair that lasted about a week. When the cabin was completed, owner and neighbors celebrated with music, dance, and strong drink.

Sometimes life in a log cabin on the frontier was highly romanticized by the press and writers of the times. Men of the frontier, such as Daniel Boone, Davy Crockett, Christopher Houston, and Kit Carson, were written about in compelling ways as celebrated hunters, trappers, explorers, fighters, and leaders. Their skills and intimate knowledge of the frontier and Native American culture made them folk heroes in the eyes of their contemporaries. Symbols such as raccoon caps, rifles, and the iconic cabin embodied their courage and strength.

### Fur Traders, Trappers, and Loggers

From the 17th century to the late 19th century, the mountain men, many of them fur traders and trappers, roamed the untamed wilderness areas of North America. Countries such as France, England, and America invested heavily in the fur industry. Major trade routes emerged in the Great Lakes region and the Rocky Mountains. The men in the field often learned to speak multiple languages, a skill that was needed as they traded with various Native American groups and buyers from abroad. They endured extreme weather conditions, the hazards of dangerous and unknown terrain, and hostile encounters with wild animals as well as other humans. Often traveling alone, they lived and worked in the heart of the wilderness, building temporary dwellings as needed. Their homes varied, depending on their needs, the environment, and the weather. Common dwellings included lean-tos, lodges, dugouts, sod houses, and cabins.

Cabins were, not surprisingly, common abodes for loggers. The American logging industry thrived from colonial times to the early 20th century. During the heyday of the industry, temporary logging camps and permanent towns were built. Log cabins were thus built in boom towns across such states as Washington, Oregon, California, Minnesota, and Michigan.

### Slaves

Slaves in America lived in a variety of dwellings. Those who worked in a trade or in the slave owner's home were often accommodated with basic housing. Slaves who worked in the fields lived in inferior quarters, often cabin structures, though not necessarily made of logs. Particularly in the early years of slavery, huts were not uncommon. Some were shacks made of inferior products; some were made to match the plantation owner's home. All of the dwellings were small and vastly inferior to the plantation owner's spacious and elegant home.

The slave quarters were bereft of comfort, drafty, and without flooring. Care was rarely taken to maintain and prevent cracks, holes, and wear. But this did not take away the beauty of the plantation home, as the slave quarters were deliberately built in an area that could not be easily seen, either by means of distance or some natural barrier like trees. The slave quarters were thus invisible to the plantation family and their guests. Little thought was given to the poor conditions in which the slaves lived, reflecting the low value that the slave held in society.

Conditions inside the quarters were also squalid. The dwellings were often bereft of furnishings, meaning no chairs, no beds, and no decoration. Some slaves, particularly the women, worked through the night quilting and sewing. Storytelling, by men and women, often took place in the evening. Cooking took place either indoors or outdoors. Some slaves kept small gardens and animals near their quarters. Because of the village aspect of the quarters and the community-minded traditions brought from Africa, slaves often formed a tightly knit community.

### The Rich, the Artists, and the Intellectuals

By the beginning of the 19th century, individuals of higher economic and social standing began making trips to the wilderness for recreational hunting and fishing and vacation getaways. These individuals could afford the expense and had the leisure time to go off to the woods for adventure. Cabins made the perfect wilderness destination. Thus began a new era wherein men hunted for sport rather than survival and spent time in the wilderness for recreation and fashion rather than as a way to make a living. Their cabins were anything but sparse and functional; often such dwellings were handsomely decorated.

For family vacations, the wealthy built larger and more lavish cabins. Rustic architecture was the rage in getaways in the forests of the East Coast. The famed Adirondack cabins, which were built by prominent families such as the Vanderbilts and Rockefellers, were the talk of the society pages. Cabins were also popular with the intellectuals, philosophers, poets, and artists who ventured into the woods and mountains. Henry David Thoreau, for example, was famous for his two-year stint living on the shores of Walden Pond in a small cabin, where he wrote and spent time in deep thought. The so-called writer's cabin would emerge as a symbol of an idealized space for inspiration and creativity.

### Summer Campers, Vacationers, and Homeowners

The latter half of the 19th century saw the birth of the summer youth camp. The first organized camp, the Gunnery, was founded in Washington, Connecticut, in 1861. More camps ensued, among them were those maintained by Boy Scout groups and the YMCA. The yearly summer retreat became a fixture in American youth culture. For several decades, only boys were allowed to enjoy this pleasure. As the 20th century dawned, summer camps expanded to include girls as well as specialized camps for the disabled, churches, and colleges. Summer camps featured wooden cabins, often fitted with bunk beds. Restrooms and dining areas were located in separate facilities. These camps might have lakes for swimming and trails for hiking. Camp leaders taught wilderness skills and other outdoor activities, such as archery, and led the campers in activities such as singing and storytelling around a campfire. Often located in a state or national park, the summer camps were designed to instill an appreciation for nature and the outdoors.

After the mainstreaming of the automobile, interest in cabin living surged for vacationers and homeowners. During the vacation boom of the 1950s and 1960s, cabin rentals were a popular option for American tourists. Cabins provided a sense of adventure, nostalgia, and "make believe," as Americans looked for excitement outside their comfortable lives in the suburbs. The trips to the cabin also provided a break from the so-called hustle and bustle of modern life. Suburbanites and city dwellers appreciated the natural scenery, the fresh air, and the quiet.

As the automobile increased traffic to the nation's state and national parks, increased wages allowed a larger percentage of Americans to acquire second homes for weekend and extended getaways. For those homeowners already living in pristine settings, the emergence of the prefabricated cabin became an option.

Whether used as a vacation home or a permanent home, many modern-day cabins have undergone dramatic transformations. They feature electricity, multiple rooms or lofts, lavish open spaces, running water, indoor plumbing, designer furniture, and luxuries such as skylights and Jacuzzis. The fanciest cabin homes are constructed with multiple stories using assorted contemporary designs.

### Images in Popular Culture

Cabins from both frontier days and slavery times have been restored and preserved for posterity, and are on display in museums and national parks. Popular destinations such as the Abraham Lincoln Birthplace and the Davy Crockett Birthplace feature frontier-style cabins. The Great Smoky Mountains National Park features several historic landmarks, including preserved cabins from the 1800s to the 1900s.

One of the earliest popular references to slave cabins was in the book *Uncle Tom's Cabin* (1852) by Harriet Beecher Stowe. Stowe's work of fiction, which portrayed the hardships of slavery, played a seminal role in girding the abolitionist movement. The Evergreen Plantation in Wallace, Louisiana, features 22 original slave cabins that are open to the public for tours. These cabins appeared in Quentin Tarantino's film *Django Unchained* (2012). In 2013, it was announced that a South Carolina slave cabin would be restored and exhibited at the National Museum of African American History and Culture.

In the movies, the lone cabin in the remote location has emerged as a setting for films in the horror genre. These films commonly depict gruesome, nightmarish, and darkly distorted events. In the *Secret Window* (2004), Mort Rainey (Johnny Depp) is an author who retreats to the archetypal writer's cabin; strangeness ensues, disrupting his idyllic environment. In films such as *Friday the 13th* (1980), *Evil Dead I* and *II* (1981 and 1987), *Cabin Fever* (2002), *The Woods* (2006), and *Cabin in the Woods* (2012), the tranquil cabin setting has been transmuted into a place of utter fear and horror.

### In Conclusion

Since the days of the Mayflower, cabins have been a fixture in American society. Their continued presence in contemporary life, whether as preserved relics from bygone eras or as modern retreats, reflects just how integral these structures are to American society.

***See also*** Adirondacks; Appalachia; California; Great Lakes; Great Smoky Mountains; Lincoln Log Cabin; Minnesota; Suburbia; Summer Camp; Walden Pond; YMCA

**Further Reading**

Kaiser, Harvey. 1982. *Great Camps of the Adirondacks*. Boston: D.R. Godine.

Lohmann, Roger A. 1990. "Four Perspectives on Appalachian Culture and Poverty." *Journal of the Appalachian Studies Association* 2, 76–91.

Mulfinger, Dale. 2001. *The Cabin: Inspiration for the Classic American Getaway*. Newton, Connecticut: Taunton Press.

Tunis, Edwin. 2000. *Frontier Living: An Illustrated Guide to Pioneer Life in America*. New York: Lyons Press.

Vlach, John Michael. 1993. *Back of the Big House: The Architecture of Plantation Slavery*. Chapel Hill: University of North Carolina Press.

Wright, Gwendolyn. 1983. *Building the Dream: A Social History of Housing in America*. Cambridge, Massachusetts: MIT Press.


## Cabrini-Green Housing Project

Cabrini-Green is a public-housing development in Chicago, Illinois. Due in large part to the heavily publicized instances of crime and violence that have occurred there, Cabrini-Green is among the most notorious housing developments in the nation. Cabrini-Green long embodied the crisis and chaos of urban city life for America's poor and its historically oppressed ethnic groups (in particular, its predominately African American residents). Its 3,607 red-brick and white units, housing at its peak some 15,000 people, covered 70 acres. For many residents of Chicago, the towering housing development marred Chicago's stunning city skyline, which otherwise evoked a sense of promise and progress. In March 2011, the last Cabrini-Green building was demolished, the result of an ambitious effort to transform and elevate the nation's living spaces for poor and low-income families.

### Historical Perspectives

Cabrini-Green was a project funded by the federal government to provide housing for impoverished communities. Named after St. Francis Xavier Cabrini, a Roman Catholic patron, Cabrini-Green was one of numerous housing developments built around the nation between 1942 and 1962. In the post–World War II (1941–1945) era, most of the residents were of Italian extraction, with some Irish, Puerto Rican, and African American. Beginning in the 1960s, African Americans, many of them descendants of the African Americans who had migrated from the South in the 1940s, dominated Cabrini-Green. Many of those who migrated expected to find solace against the brutal culture of racial violence and discrimination in the North. Instead, they were frequently met with despair, alienation, unemployment, poverty, and racial discrimination, all of which contributed greatly to the rise of criminal activity, gang involvement, and drug use. These issues, combined with the dismally poor, unkempt, and poorly maintained conditions of the units—where boarded-up houses, graffiti, rat and cockroach infestations, tattered rooms, and substandard amenities were commonplace—added to a vortex of despair and violence.

### Controversy

Headline news reports of the institutionalized violence rampant in Cabrini-Green shocked the world. In 1970, two policemen were killed by snipers. In 1981, gangs killed 11 individuals. In 1992, a seven-year-old was killed by a stray bullet, and in 1997, a nine-year-old girl was raped and poisoned, leaving her mute, blind, and paralyzed.

A moving truck arrives to load the possessions of Annie Ricks and her family after she was forced to leave the Cabrini-Green public housing complex on December 9, 2010, in Chicago, Illinois. Ricks and her family were the last remaining residents in the last remaining high-rise building in the complex. The setting for the 1970s TV show *Good Times*, the complex once housed 15,000 residents, and was notorious for its crime, gangs, and drugs. (Tim Boyle/Getty Images)

### Issues

The federal government's solution to the endemic problems at Cabrini-Green and similar projects was to demolish the developments and fund new housing opportunities. The response from the tenants of Cabrini-Green was mixed. Some feared that they would be displaced. Long-time residents could not imagine home anywhere else. But some tenants were overjoyed, realizing that the destruction of Cabrini-Green meant an opportunity for a new and better life. Some tenants mobilized to ensure that their community would be protected during the process: not displaced, not rendered homeless, and not, as they had been for so long, neglected and taken advantage of. The development was demolished between 1996 and 2011, the process intentionally gradual to help manage the stressful removal of the tenants.

But for many former Cabrini-Green tenants, the transition to a new location was not smooth. At one such location, North Town Village, a new, mixed-income residence that provided well-maintained town homes for affluent professionals and middle- and low-income families, 79 units were made available for the ex-residents of Cabrini-Green. But the tenants had to pass a screening process, including a criminal background check and mandatory drug tests. Tenants who successfully moved into

North Town Village had positive experiences with their new neighbors and their new homes, but many reported that the gang activity had followed them to their new homes. Cabrini-Green tenants who were moved to the Wentworth Gardens development were met with territorial violence and hostility.

As former Cabrini-Green tenants settle into their new lives, Chicago is hopeful that, despite ongoing challenges, the horizon will be brighter for a segment of community long neglected by a system that contributed to the perpetuation of the poverty, crime, and other social ills.

### Images in Popular Culture

The image of Cabrini-Green appeared at the beginning and at the end of the 1970s hit, *Good Times* (1974–1979), a television series about a struggling African American family who survive good times and bad with laughter, love, pride, and an indomitable spirit. The images of Cabrini-Green suggested that this was the setting in which the Evans family lived. Cabrini-Green was also the setting for the horror film *Candyman* (1992) and was used in a television episode of *The Chicago Code* (2011).

### In Conclusion

For years, Cabrini-Green has appeared in popular media and in real life as a symbol of American blight and tragedy, representing an unglamorous and disturbingly vivid real side of the nation's underbelly. Its passing marked a new beginning for its former residents, but also served as a painful reminder of the ultimate failure of the government projects.

*See also* Chicago, Illinois; Ghetto

### Further Reading

*Cabrini-Green*. http://www.cabrini-green.com/.

Pattillo, Mary. 2007. *Black on the Block: The Politics of Race and Class in the City*. Chicago: University of Chicago Press.

Popkin, Susan J., Gwiasda, Victoria E., Olson, Lynn M., Rosenbaum, Dennis P., and Buron, Larry. 2000. *The Hidden War: Crime and the Tragedy of Public Housing in Chicago*. Piscataway, New Jersey: Rutgers University Press.

Venkatesh, Sudhir Alladi. 2002. *American Project: The Rise and Fall of a Modern Ghetto*. Cambridge, Massachusetts: Harvard University Press.

Whitaker, David T., and Jensen, Blair. 2000. *Cabrini-Green in Words and Pictures*. Chicago: LPC Group.

## Cadillac Ranch

The Cadillac Ranch, located in Amarillo, Texas, is a site that features public art sculptures. Just off Interstate 40, near US Route 66, the Ranch consists of 10 Cadillac cars, partly buried, nose down in the earth, slanted at an angle matching the Great Pyramids of Egypt. Unlike many roadside attractions, this one encourages participation and interaction.

Since their installment in 1974, the Cadillacs have been spray-painted, marked, signed, and photographed, and parts have been pulled off and taken away as souvenirs. Every so often, the cars are repainted so that the ritual of graffiti can begin anew. This site is irresistible to artists and anyone else drawn to the idea of leaving their mark on a piece of Americana. But not everyone participates;

many visitors simply go to watch others paint or to simply view the famous Cadillac Ranch. Like any landmark or roadside art exhibit, the Cadillac Ranch beckons to human curiosity and pays tribute to an important icon in popular culture.

### Historical Perspectives

The idea for Cadillac Ranch is credited to Stanley Marsh III, a wealthy Texan, and a group of architects known collectively as the Ant Farm, based out of California. In 1973, Marsh funded the installation, providing the land on which the art would stand and the money to purchase 10 decrepit Cadillacs. The project was completed in 1974. Cadillac Ranch originally rested in a wheat field and then was moved to a cow pasture. Both properties are privately owned, but visitors are free to visit the sculptures at no cost.

### Meaning and Symbols

A common activity at Cadillac Ranch is to speculate on the meaning and symbolism of the sculpture. One of the purposes of Cadillac Ranch is to exhibit the evolution of the Cadillac's signature tail fin from 1949 to 1963.

The first Cadillac tail fin was introduced in 1948. The flashy fins decreased in size over the years until, by 1965, they disappeared altogether. This timeline coincides with America's so-called golden years, a time of poodle skirts, American diners, classic cars, optimism, and innocence that descended, in the 1960s, into protest, war, and general unrest and uncertainty.

Viewed in this light, the sculptures pay homage to a popular American classic, as well as track an idyllic era in American history. But the decrepit, half-buried cars of Cadillac Ranch can also symbolize decay, materialism, and destruction. In the end, visitors must draw their own conclusions as to what the exhibit means, and to many, the sculpture celebrates freedom of expression.

#### Cadillac Craze

The Cadillac, also known popularly as the Caddie, is one of America's most enduring classic cars. Many individuals had a hand in its development in 1902, but Henry Martyn Leland, who also built the Lincoln, played a particularly critical role. It was Leland, a precision machinist, who managed to retain the support of the Detroit Automobile Company to pursue his automotive designs. In 1902, he founded the Cadillac Automobile Company, naming the company after the French explorer who founded Detroit, Antoine de la Mothe, Sieur de Cadillac. In the same year, Leland released America's first Cadillac. The car's maximum speed was 25 miles per hour and cost $750 dollars, which is equivalent to more than $20,000 in today's money.

General Motors, founded in the decade that saw the debut of the Cadillac, created its Cadillac Division in 1909. Under General Motors, the Cadillac underwent decades of development, stylistic changes, and upgrades, including a switch from wood to all-metal frames. The Cadillac quickly became synonymous with power, thanks to its new and improved engine and fine and elegant design.

Cadillac's reputation as a luxury car is reflected in the fact that the car has been the choice of many celebrities. During the 1950s, Elvis Presley drove a Caddie. Pink Caddies have been associated with many pop culture stars. In 1968, Mary Kay Ash, who founded the extremely lucrative direct sales company that bears her name, acquired a pink Cadillac. "Pink Cadillac" is the name of a song by Bruce Springsteen that was released in 1982. In 1985, Aretha Franklin released the Grammy award winning song, *Freeway of Love*, whose lyrics make reference to a pink Cadillac. The Cadillac has also been associated with grandparents, West Coast rappers, and urban hip-hop subculture.

### Images in Popular Culture

Images of Cadillac Ranch crop up often in songs, films, and television shows. Numerous performers, such as rock-star Bruce Springsteen, the Nitty Gritty Dirt Band, and John Stewart, have sung songs about or made references to Cadillac Ranch. Music videos have been filmed on location at the site. Images of the roadside attraction have appeared in television shows, such as *King of the Hill* (1997–2010), and the popular animation film *Cars* (2006).

### In Conclusion

Today, Cadillac Ranch remains a uniquely American modern attraction that has captured the national imagination.

***See also*** California; U.S. Route 66

### Further Reading

"Cadillac Ranch." *Roadside America*. http://www.roadsideamerica.com/story/2220.

Hinckley, Jim, and Robinson, Jon G. 2005. *The Big Book of Car Culture: The Armchair Guide to Automotive Americana*. St. Paul, Minnesota: Motorbooks.

Lewallen, Constance M., Seid, Steve, Lord, Chip, Maniaque, Caroline, Sorkin, Michael, and Ant Farm. 2004. *Ant Farm, 1968–1978*. Berkeley: University of California Press.

Pohlen, Jerome. 2006. *Oddball Texas: A Guide to Some Really Strange Places*. Chicago: Chicago Review Press.

## Caesars Palace

Caesars Palace is a famous hotel and casino. Gaming, however, makes up only a minor part of the glittering array of attractions offered by the modern-day hotel casinos. Counted among the top hotels in the nation, Caesars Palace is massive, glamorous, and extravagant. Like many hotels in the area, Caesars Palace has a theme—the Roman Empire—which is reflected in its exterior and interior architecture. The Caesars Palace theme served as inspiration for the names of the five towers, Augustus, Centurion, Roman, Palace, and Forum, which contain more than 3,000 rooms. The hotel also features luxurious accommodations, an array of high-end restaurants and shops, and big-name performances and other popular events.

### Historical Perspectives

Jay Sarno was the first owner of Caesars Palace (today Caesars is owned by Caesars Entertainment Corp.). He was the mastermind who named the hotel "Caesar," meaning ruler, in the plural form, because he wanted to signify that everyone who visited his hotel was a Caesar. The glamorous world of Las Vegas hotels surely makes its visitors feel as if they have entered upon some fantastical world in which they themselves are center stage. Work on the hotel began in 1962, and Sarno opened its doors on August 5, 1966. In the trying decade of the 1960s, rocked by protests, riots, the Vietnam War (1955–1975), and uncertainty, hotel casinos, like Caesars, provided an escape from reality. Hotel demographics comprised individuals of means—some with notorious mob connections—and individuals who simply wanted a break from mundane life in suburbia.

### Contemporary Perspectives

Today, Caesars continues to appeal to a wide range of visitors. Discounted offers make the trip affordable, and popular entertainment attracts groups from across all demographics. Since its construction,

Caesars has undergone continuous renovation, such as the addition of the Colosseum, an entertainment venue built with a seating capacity of 4,296. Newly renovated hotel casinos, constructed ever bigger and better, and with more extraordinary attractions and things to do, have become the Disneyland for adults.

**Casino Pioneer**

Las Vegas, Nevada, was created by a group of daring visionaries, though by the time Jay Sarno appeared on the scene, Las Vegas had already gone through the difficult period of establishment. Few believed that the desert could be transformed into a glittering resort that would attract people from across the globe and become a symbol of glamour and entertainment.

Born in St. Joseph, Missouri, in 1922, Sarno started out in the tile business with Stanley Mallin before moving into hotel construction. A loan from the Teamsters' Central States Pension Fund financed Sarno's first casino project, which became known as Caesar's Palace. This casino emerged as one of the most popular fixtures in the increasingly crowded gambling oasis. Caesar's Palace is regarded as the forerunner of the themed resorts in the area.

Sarno's success inspired him to construct another major casino, Circus Circus, completed in 1968. Though grand, this hotel was scaled down, owing to budgetary restrictions. Many more hotels, enormous, multi-entertainment structures, would follow in the 1980s. With plans to build another new casino which was to be called the Grandissimo, Sarno died on July 21, 1984.

### Highlights

Over the years, Caesars has featured sensational talent on its stages. Evel Knievel, a celebrated motorcycle daredevil, was one of the first major acts. On December 31, 1967, he famously attempted to jump 141 feet over the hotel's water fountain. The stunt, heavily promoted and staged with fanfare, was a failure. In 1989, Knievel's son, Robbie Knievel, made the fountain jump. Caesars Palace has also staged several star-power boxing matches, featuring such greats as Muhammad Ali, Sugar Ray Leonard, and Oscar De La Hoya. Performers at Caesars have included Magician David Copperfield, Céline Dion, Elton John, Bette Midler, and Gloria Estefan. For Dion's show, *A New Day*, a new structure, the Colosseum, was built. Other notable attractions at Caesars Palace include the Festival Fountain, a nightclub, restaurants, and the chic Forum Shops.

### Images in Popular Culture

Caesars Palace is one of the more popular Las Vegas hotels, and as such it has often appeared in film and on television. In the year after Caesars Palace opened, the hotel appeared in *Hells Angels on Wheels* (1967). Other popular films in which the hotel featured include *Rocky III* (1982), *Rain Man* (1988), *The Strip* (1999), *Ocean's Eleven* (2001), *Dreamgirls* (2006), *Iron Man* (2008), and *The Hangover* (2009). Caesars Palace appeared in television programs, such as *The Partridge Family* (1970–1974), *The Simpsons* (1999–), *The Sopranos* (1999–2007), *Friends* (1994–2004), and the reality show *Keeping Up with the Kardashians* (2007–).

### In Conclusion

Caesars Palace has made a name for itself in American society. It's where Americans and globetrotting tourists alike go for a spot of decadence, where both the rich and the working class are pampered and entertained.

***See also*** Casino; Disneyland; Las Vegas, Nevada; Suburbia

### Further Reading

*Caesar's Palace*. http://www.caesarspalace.com/.

Fischer, Steve. 2005. *When the Mob Ran Vegas: Stories of Money, Mayhem, and Murder*. Omaha, Nebraska: Berkline Press.

Holtorf, Cornelius. 2005. *From Stonehenge to Las Vegas: Archeology as Popular Culture*. Walnut Creek, California: Alta Mira Press.

Montville, Leigh. 2011. *Evel: The High-Flying Life of Evel Knievel: An American Showman, Daredevil, and Legend*. New York: Doubleday.

## Cajun Country

Cajun Country is the nickname of a region in southern Louisiana, dominated by an ethnic group known as Cajuns, descendants of Acadian exiles. "Cajun," an Anglicized version of the French word Acadien (masculine form) or Acadienne (female form), is a term that has come to distinguish a uniquely American cultural group. Migrating from France to colonies in Canada and part of what is now known as Maine, the group that became known as the Cajuns eventually settled in Louisiana during the late 18th century. Their narrative is one of harrowing turmoil, resistance, and adaptation.

Though the region and its people have been transformed and modernized following decades of acculturation, certain aspects of Cajun life have survived intact and are known the world over. Cajun culinary favorites like gumbo, Cajun music and language, as well as certain rich cultural traditions, have endured. This living glimpse into the past, along with the region's famous bayous and dense forests, have made Cajun Country one of the most well-known and oft-visited regions in the nation.

### Historical Perspectives

The predecessors of the Cajun people came from the coastal regions of France, inhabiting the French provinces Aunis, Angoumois, and Poitou. Religious wars erupted between the Catholics (including the Cajuns) and the Protestants in France. The famine and plague that followed the wars devastated the population, and, in the mid-17th century, spurred their migration to North America. Founded by Samuel Chaplain in 1604, their new home, called Acadia, originally encompassed the region now known as Nova Scotia, New Brunswick, Prince Edward Island, and part of Maine.

Hardships continued to follow the French settlers. Mostly peasants, they eventually took on the name of the region (Acadia) but were cast in this new land as second-class citizens, forced to work as indentured servants for the wealthy French. Enduring economic oppression as well as the vacillating tides of French and British conflicts, the Acadians endured constant assaults on their cultural survival. The situation reached a climax in 1713, when the British took control over much of the region and attempted to enforce the cultural assimilation of the Acadians. They did this through various means, such as transplanting Protestant colonists into Acadia and, in 1745, demanding that the Acadians pledge allegiance to the King of England. Stalwart Acadians refused to assimilate or pledge allegiance to the British Crown. Truth be told, they held no allegiance to their own native country, which they had fled in the previous century. The Acadians were punished for their defiance with mass deportation known as Le Grand Dérangement.

The deportation was a catastrophic process. Of a population of 15,000 Acadians, nearly half died from the extreme cold and diseases contracted during the brutal journey by ship. Surviving Acadians were dispersed to various locations such as France, the West Indies, New England, the Carolinas, and Georgia. Some displaced Acadians went back to Acadia, though their lands and possessions had been burned or sold. More than 2,000 migrated to Louisiana between 1763 and 1776. Acadians were attracted to Louisiana because the area was controlled by France, making it a somewhat familiar environment. Indeed, Louisiana also was a land of opportunity, where Acadians might, at last, realize the freedom that had eluded them for so long—in their ancestral home in France and, later, in Acadia.

**Louisiana**

When the displaced Acadians arrived, Louisiana was in a state of flux. The region had been settled by the French in 1714, and had operated under France's control since then. Before that, several Native American tribes had lived there, classified under three major linguistic groups, Tunican, Caddoan, and Muskhoen. The first black slaves were brought into Louisiana in 1719. In 1762, King Louis XV gave Charles II of Spain the land west of the Mississippi, including Louisiana. Native Americans, the French, African descendants, the Spanish, and other ethnic groups such as Creoles would each play a significant role in the development of Cajun Country.

Spain encouraged and assisted the mass migration of Acadians into Louisiana. Recognizing the benefit of increasing the population of the territory, Spain helped pay the transportation costs of the Acadians and provided them with equipment and land. Further migrations were prompted by Acadians from other locales seeking to reunite with their family and community. This increasing migration helped to ensure the survival of the Acadian culture for the group's descendants.

In 1800, Spain ceded Louisiana back to France. In 1803, the United States purchased the territory. In 1812, Louisiana became a state. In America, the Acadians became known as Cajuns, one of the dominant subcultures in the region.

**Cultural Distinctions**

The term "Cajun" is not just an Anglicized word; it signifies the emergence of a distinct cultural identity. Though first identified as French, then Acadian, the Cajuns adapted to their surroundings—the rivers, the prairies, and the wetlands—and made them a part of who they were. In time, the region and its people became inseparable, with Cajun Country becoming synonymous with Cajun culture and, conversely, the people becoming synonymous with the land. Cajuns became closely identified with both the way they eked out an existence on marginal lands and the folk traditions that they practiced.

By and large, Cajuns were farmers, though some made a living fishing, hunting, trapping, and ranching. Borrowing from what they learned from Native Americans, Cajuns learned how to use local plants for medicine and herbs. They combined the knowledge they brought from France and Acadia with techniques learned from Native Americans to find medicine and hunt for food in the forests. Temporary camps were built in the forests for hunting, providing food for survival and to sell for income. Boat and canoe building was an essential practice, again combining Native American and preexisting knowledge. Different boats were used for different purposes, whether traversing the swamps or the Gulf of Mexico; whether picking moss or shrimping. Some Cajuns built homes in the swamps and used boats for daily transportation.

Life in Cajun Country was not all work. Cajuns found enjoyment in a wide range of cultural activities and traditions—not necessarily their own. For example, Cajun food incorporates aspects from France, the American South, Spain, as well as Native American, and African American cuisine. Native Americans taught Cajuns how to cultivate food, such as potatoes and corn. Local seafood and meats, such as crawfish and alligator, became Cajun staples. Gumbo, one of the region's signature dishes, originated in Africa. It comprises a savory broth with rice and a meat or seafood, such as chicken or shrimp, or a Cajun sausage called *andouille.* From the Spanish and Afro-Caribbean cultures, the Cajuns borrowed spices with a bite, such as cayenne pepper and hot chili peppers. Other traditional meals, such as cornbread

**Music and Dance Cajun Style**

Zydeco refers to a unique music and dance form that originated with the Creoles in Louisiana. Zydeco music is often confused with Cajun music. Creole is a distinct culture that comprises mixed French and African American heritage. Though cultures often influence one another, the Creoles developed a distinct music and dance.

Zydeco music usually features a rubboard and has no fiddle. It features syncopated rhythms and is influenced by jazz and rhythm and blues. Unlike Cajun dancing, Zydeco dancing does not involve circling a floor. Dancing with a partner is usually performed in a tight space. In contemporary times, Zydeco music reflects the influence of modern music and dance.

Zydeco has its beginnings in the early 20th century. Rich folk music and dance were incorporated into events such as the bouchere, the community gathering that surrounded the butchering of a hog. After the work was done, the community enjoyed a "La La," a house dance. The scrub board, spoons, triangles, and accordion were instruments that were played during such dances. La La gatherings served food and charged an admission fee to raise funds for various charities and projects. The music and dancing that were performed during these parties evolved into Zydeco during the 1940s.

In time, Zydeco performers found some commercial success among the genre's fans. Celebrities, such as Clifton Chenier (1925–1987), Buckwheat Zydeco (1947–), and Geno Delafose (1971–) are remembered for their contributions to Zydeco. Zydeco dances continue to be performed at social gatherings and well-known music festivals such as the Southwest Louisiana Zydeco Music Festival. The Zydeco Music Festival in Plaisance, which debuted in 1982, is billed as the original festival of its kind.

and beans and rice, were prevalent throughout the South. Eating and the process of food preparation were relished among Cajuns.

Diversions such as music making, dancing, and other merriments were also greatly enjoyed. In Louisiana, Cajuns learned to play and make instruments, such as fiddles and accordions. Some instruments were nothing more than washboards and spoons. They played music to accompany numerous popular dances. The *Bals de Maison,* for example, is a dance party, usually by invitation only, that occurs in a host's home. Singing, often in French, as well as eating deserts and listening to lively storytelling were common features at the *veillées* which occurred in the winter months during the evening. Storytellers retold old tales, some comedic, others reflecting cultural superstitions and folk beliefs in the supernatural. In rural communities, Cajuns celebrate their own version of Mardi Gras, one of several Cajun festivities. Cajun Mardi Gras generally involves revelers, some on horseback, in colorful costumes and cone-shaped hats, performing from house to house in exchange for a chicken; songs are sung; jokes are told; and skits are staged in a festive atmosphere.

Mardi Gras is not the only Louisiana tradition that differs in Cajun Country. Cajun French developed due to the isolation of the region. Among its influences are Parisian French, Acadian French, English, Spanish, and other languages and regional dialects spoken in Louisiana. It is distinct from the French spoken in France, Canada, and elsewhere in Louisiana.

## Americanization

The decreasing number of French-speaking Cajuns in present-day Cajun Country underscores the process of acculturation that began in the region during the early 20th century. Myriad reasons contributed to the Americanization of the Cajuns. The discovery of oil in the region in 1901 brought modern employment opportunities that replaced traditional forms of work and exposed Cajuns to the outside world. The Education Act of 1922 required Cajun children to speak English in the classroom. Movies, television, and radio bombarded Cajuns with sounds and images that promoted socially acceptable mainstream behavior and culture. Music from the outside world was integrated into Cajun music and the result was extraordinarily positive and enjoyed by Cajuns and non-Cajuns. Societal pressures also made an impact, especially for younger generations of Cajuns who aspired to fit in with mainstream images and to distance themselves from what some perceived to be a backward culture.

Despite this formidable acculturation, there have been periods, such as in the 1970s and 1980s, when Cajuns experienced periods of renewed cultural pride. Such times assure that the gifts of Cajun culture will not be completely lost to the world.

### Contemporary Perspectives

Cajuns in the 21st century are strong in number; over 400,000 live in Cajun Country (a robust population of some 50,000 live in Texas; smaller populations live elsewhere). Though Cajuns have been more or less modernized, some still speak Cajun French, either in part or exclusively, as well as fish, trap, hunt, and farm for a living, dance in the traditional ways, and make that music that is so distinctly their own.

### Images in Popular Culture

Cajun music was first recorded in the early 20th century and, slowly but surely, reached mainstream popularity in the 1960s. Notable Chef Justin Wilson helped popularize authentic Cajun food on his television show in the 1980s, combining succulent recipes with his animated personality. Today, Cajun-style dishes and seasonings can be found in the aisles of any American grocery store, and popular contemporary cooking shows regularly include Cajun recipes.

Reality shows have recently showcased Cajun outdoor traditions. In *Man vs. Wild* (2006–), Bear Grylls goes to the swamps in Louisiana. He kills an alligator and catches a catfish with his bare hands, a practice referred to as hand fishing. In *Swamp People* (2010–), American audiences get an unprecedented glimpse into modern-day Cajuns engaging in their long-held tradition of alligator hunting in the Atchafalaya swamp.

Although modern life has dramatically encroached upon the region, Cajun Country still harbors remnants of the old traditions. Some have appeared in new forms, like modern Cajun music. Others, such as outdoor life and the Cajun language, resist extinction—at least for now. These remnants, even if only preserved in museums and in the backwoods of Cajun Country, are what keep alive the land, its history, its culture, and its people.

### For Visitors

Much of old-style Cajun Country has been encapsulated into museums and purposed for recreational use. The Crystal Rice Heritage farm was known for growing rice in 1890, but since the 1960s, it has been a popular tourist attraction. The Acadian Village exhibits authentic homes and antiques, providing a glimpse into 19th-century life in southwest Louisiana. Artifacts are exhibited at the Imperial Calcasieu Museum, and craftspeople and living historians share with guests' age-old traditions and cultural memories at Vermilionville, a museum and folklife park. Numerous tours venture into Louisiana's famed swamps and Houseboat Adventures offers outdoor activities, like bird watching, hunting, and fishing. The camps that were once used to hunt for survival are now used by Cajuns for recreational and vacation use. The Creole Nature Trail National Scenic Byway courses through 180 miles of preserved natural landscape, wetlands, bayous, and beaches. Some restaurants cater to certain tourist appetites for gimmicky cultural stereotypes that exaggerate folklore and old traditions.

Cajun Country is justly famous for its homespun music and myriad festivals, such as the Frog Festival, Festivals Acadiens et Créoles, and Festival de Musique, the fanciful display of horse-riding skills left over from the old ranching days. The authentic flavor of Cajun cuisine savored in the place of its birth brings countless tourists to the region. The essence of Cajun Country is evident in the easy warmth and mirth of the people and the solidarity of relatives and friends at social gatherings. It is also found in the forests and swamps that teem with life far from the urban centers.

***See also*** Mardi Gras; Texas

**Further Reading**

Ancelet, Barry Jean, Edwards, Jay, and Pitre, Glen. 1991. *Cajun Country*. Jackson: University Press of Mississippi.

Bernard, Shane K. 2003. *The Cajuns: Americanization of a People*. Jackson: University Press of Mississippi.

Brasseaux, Carl A. 2011. *Acadiana: Louisiana's Historic Cajun Country*. Baton Rouge: Louisiana State University Press.

Brasseaux, Ryan. 2009. *Cajun Breakdown: The Emergence of an American-Made Music*. New York: Oxford University Press.

Coen, Cheré D. 2011. *Exploring Cajun Country: A Tour of Historic Acadiana*. Charleston, South Carolina: The History Press.

Kilpatrick, Blair. 2009. *Accordion Dreams: A Journey into Cajun and Creole Music*. Jackson: University Press of Mississippi.

McKnulty, Ian. 2011. *Louisiana Rambles: Exploring America's Cajun and Creole Heartland*. Jackson: University Press of Mississippi.

## California

California, the third largest state by land mass in the nation, runs along the southern half of the western coast of North America. California, the Golden State, is replete with physical and cultural diversity. The state is also a place that looms large in the national imagination. Within its borders lie mountains

California's Pacific Coast Highway offers dramatic views of the coastline, such as this vista overlooking the famous Bixby Bridge in Big Sur. (Robertplotz/Dreamstime.com)

outlined against clear blue skies, the soaring trees of the Redwood National Park, desolate desert terrain, and world-famous beaches. California is home to famous American wineries, such as those located in Napa Valley, rural towns, ghost towns, ethnic enclaves, posh neighborhoods, and Los Angeles, the city with the largest population in the nation, swarming with traffic and smog. The state also contains some of the most famous tourist destinations in the world, such as Hollywood, Disneyland, and oldest Chinatown in the nation.

Fortune-seekers once made the long journey to California in the hopes of striking it rich in the gold fields, or, in the early years of Hollywood, out of a desire for stardom. Others were spellbound by perceptions of year-round sunshine, youthfulness, gaiety, and material success. At the heart of the allure of this multifaceted and population-dense state these days is its reputation as the home of the beautiful people: sun-bleached blondes, hard-bodied surfers, celebrities and socialites, and sophisticated urbanites. All this contributes to the world's fascination with California and its ranking as one of the top destinations in America.

### Historical Perspectives

The first inhabitants of the Golden State were Native Americans. When the Spanish first anchored their ship along the California shores in 1542, they estimated the population to be somewhere between 100,000 and 275,000 indigenous residents, among them such tribes as the Tcholovoni, Kule Loklo, Tolowa, Modoc, Miwok, Paiute, Chumash, and Cahuilla. Colonization of the area began in the 18th century, bringing with it Catholic missions that were established to convert Indians to Christianity and to provide protection. The Spanish put down roots everywhere in the southwestern corner of the North American continent, and their influence is still visible in the names of places, streets, and cities, as well as in the architectural style. The name of the state also has Spanish origins, as it was named after an island in a Spanish novel.

### Gold Rush

Following independence in 1821, Mexico controlled California until, in 1848, it ceded California to the United States. In that same year, gold was found in Sacramento Valley, and a feverish gold rush ensued. Turnover in gold mining towns was swift, with towns filling and vacating with meteoric speed. Some towns, known as ghost towns, remain today as vestiges of the fabled Old West. Gold, and later silver, lured people from disparate demographics: whites, European

#### Spanish Missions in America

A mission is a type of church, usually associated with Catholicism. Many missions were constructed in the American South and Southwest during the period of Spanish exploration that began in the 16th century. Missions were founded in the present day states of Florida, Texas, New Mexico, Arizona, and California. These missions were built as a result of the expeditions of such explorers as Francisco Vásquez de Coronado and Juan de Oñate. The Spanish set about converting the native population to Catholicism and to utilize their labor.

Constructed in assorted architectural styles, such as Gothic, Moorish, and Romanesque, the Spanish missions were aesthetically appealing. Thriving missions owned livestock, such as sheep and cattle, planted orchards, and farmed large areas. In order to protect themselves from hostile attack, many missions also doubled as forts or garrisons.

The missions discouraged cultural traditions, exploited Native Americans as a labor source, and, in many cases, caused large number of deaths in the Native American population, which had not been previously exposed to European diseases and so had no immunity.

Surviving missions include the San José and San Miguel de Aguaya missions in San Antonio, Texas, and 21 missions throughout California, including the San Juan Capistrano Mission. One of the most famous missions, the Alamo, was the scene of the eponymously named battle. Though the Americans lost this battle, the event motivated them to victory in the Texas Revolution of 1836.

immigrants, blacks, and Chinese. The Chinese played a prominent role in gold mining as well as in the construction of the railroad that followed. Their presence gave birth to Chinatowns throughout the Old West; the first was established in San Francisco, California, in 1850. Racial conflict festered throughout California's early history.

### Hollywood Era

Within five years of the destructive earthquake that hit San Francisco in 1906, claiming 3,000 lives, Hollywood made its first film, *The Law of the Range* (1911). This was the beginning of a film industry destined to enjoy 100 spectacular years. During the early years, Hollywood defined American glamour, creating a pantheon of movie stars, such as Clark Gable, Greta Garbo, and Grace Kelly, and the coveted lifestyle of the ultrarich and famous. And wherever those famous stars lived, shopped, or ate, the prestige and popularity of the neighborhood, shop, or restaurant grew. Locales that became synonymous with stardom were Grauman's Chinese Theater and Beverly Hills.

Today, only Paramount remains of the once powerful studios that dominated the celluloid industry—but Hollywood's mystique has yet to fade.

#### West Coast Rap

Rap, a subgenre of hip-hop, originated in New York City in the late 1970s. In its early days, rap was enjoyed predominately by African American audiences. But by the 1990s, rap artists had established national recognition.

Like their East Coast counterparts, the West Coast rappers, many of whom hailed from California, rapped about life, issues, and themes related to black communities. West Coast rappers, however, often wrote lyrics that were grittier and more aggressive and therefore controversial. Their lyrics were greatly influenced by gang and prison culture. Though not all West Coast rap music was like this, some lyrics glamorized drug use and killing, objectified women, and were laden with expletives.

Despite considerable public outrage and efforts to censor the most controversial rappers and rap groups, the music thrived, establishing the careers of notable West Coast rappers such as the Notorious B.I.G., Tupac Shakur, N.W.A., Dr. Dre, and Snoop Dog. The popular Sir Mix-a-lot is one of only a few rappers representing the state of Washington, also on the West Coast.

While West Coast rappers enjoyed considerable success, a feud fomented between some rappers from the West and East Coasts. The public became increasingly aware of this feud as a result of lyrics denigrating certain rivals. Some of the lyrics singled out record companies that produced rap music, notably Death Row Records, for various offenses. The culmination of the feud resulted in the mysterious and still unsolved murders of Tupac Shakur on September 13, 1996, and The Notorious B.I.G. on March 9, 1997. Since the murders, the West Coast–East Coast feud has faded into obscurity.

### Evolution

From the 1930s onward, California experienced rapid growth as well as growing pains. Los Angeles was selected to host the 1932 Olympic Games; Alcatraz Island opened as a penitentiary; and the Hoover Dam began providing electricity to California's growing population. In 1937, the famous Golden Gate Bridge opened, and in 1940, Los Angeles received its first of many freeways.

In 1955, the world welcomed Disneyland, one of the most iconic and popular theme parks in the world, with open arms. And during the 1950s and 1960s, almost every person on earth pined for the surf and sun of Malibu Beach. Surfing became all the rage in the 1960s. Into the new millennium, California maintains its role as a leader in fashion, in environmentalism, in popular culture, as well as in the technology that streams out of famed Silicon Valley.

### Controversy

Like any great state, California has had its share of troubles. After the Japanese attack on Pearl Harbor, many Japanese were stripped of their possessions and sent to internment camps, like Manzanar. World War II ended in 1945, but the state's large Japanese population was greatly traumatized by the experience.

In the 1960s, students at UC Berkeley rose in protests against the Vietnam War (1955–1975). Other student protests demanded the establishment of programs that acknowledged the ethnic experience, such as African American and Native American studies. Riots broke out in urban black communities, such as Watts, California, fueled by frustrations with accumulating social problems, racial conflicts, and a disaffection with law enforcement. In 1966, one high-profile activist, Huey P. Newton, cofounded an organization called the Black Panther Party in response to the pervasive poverty in black communities and the many incidents of police harassment.

The 1980s were another difficult time for many African Americans. Conservative politics implemented by then-president and former Hollywood actor Ronald Reagan dissolved much of the social progress made in disadvantaged communities. Riots erupted in response to continuing incidents of police brutality. An infamous riot occurred in Los Angeles in 1992 in response to a videotaped beating of African American Rodney King. South Central, Oakland, and Compton were notorious for their epidemic gang activity, drugs, and violence. Many of these problems have been linked, in part, to social inequalities, as well as to by-products of racism. Out of the harshness of this life emerged an extraordinary new musical genre, the West Coast rap phenomenon. Rappers like Ice Cube, Ice-T, and Snoop Doggy Dog became household names as they lived the California dream by making it big.

Other communities in California have also experienced calamity. For example, the gay community was ravaged by the AIDS epidemic. In 1991, more San Francisco men died from AIDS than from any other ailment (since then, AIDS deaths have reduced dramatically). In the new millennium, illegal immigration has emerged as an enormously controversial issue. Protests against America's attack on illegal immigrants were loudest in California, where the Mexican population is among the highest in the nation.

**Illegal Immigration**

Illegal immigration is a contentious issue. America has made efforts to regulate immigration into the country since the late 18th century. Citizenship, which is related to the immigrant issue, has historically been the dividing line between those who are welcome on a permanent basis in America and those who are not. The first major rules, written in 1790, permitted free white persons to apply for citizenship after two years of residency.

African Americans, free or enslaved, were not deemed citizens until 1868 with the passage of the Fourteenth Amendment, and Native Americans did not obtain citizen status until 1924. The Chinese Exclusion Act in 1882 suspended Chinese immigration for 10 years and barred Chinese people from obtaining citizenship.

America was much more generous to European countries during the late 19th and early 20th centuries, at least for a while. In the 1920s, America established quotas limiting the incoming migrations, favoring Western and northern Europeans.

Still, millions of undocumented immigrants have entered America, prompting a national debate on how to handle the issue. The nation is largely divided on the issue believing that illegal immigration is either beneficial or harmful. Twenty-first century protesters have pointed out the problematic nature of harsh deportation laws that separate families and cause hardships for family members who remain in America.

### Highlights and Everyday Culture by Region

California, blessed with a size, a population, and an economy larger than many small countries, is in reality made up of various regions, each with its own unique identity.

In northern California, wilderness lands and mountains dominate the environment. Home to many national parks, such as the Redwood National Park and the Lassen Volcanic National park, and scenic small and rural towns, northern Californians live close to the earth and often eco-consciously.

Coastal central California is home to Wine Country, including Napa Valley and Sonoma Valley, which feature lavish natural scenery and fashionable bed and breakfasts, galleries, wine-tastings, and tours. Santa Cruz is one of many California cities known for its bohemian way of life.

Ghost towns and the wooded mountains of the High Sierras can be found in west-central California. The High Sierras are home to the Sequoia and Kings Canyon National Parks, Yosemite National Park, and Lake Tahoe.

To the south, the posh lifestyle of Los Angeles dominates. Money and an obsession with physical beauty seem to drive the denizens of southern California. Coiffed hairstyles, trendy fashion, and new cars are rampant. Celebrity sightings, a common occurrence in Los Angeles and surrounding neighborhoods, add to the mystique of the region.

Along the coast reside the carefree and athletically inclined denizens of California's famous beaches. The most popular attractions of the notoriously hilly San Francisco and the Bay Area in northern California are the downtown center, Golden Gate Bridge, Attica, and Chinatown. The Mojave Desert in the southeast features wind-carved sand dunes and colorful deserts. And right across the border to the west is Las Vegas, America's favorite site for gaming and resort vacations.

**An Era of Surfin' and Music**

The Beach Boys debuted their music in the 1960s with a sunny and wholesome image. The five original members of the group were Brian Wilson (1942–), Carl Wilson (1946–1998), Dennis Wilson (1944–1983), Al Jardine (1942–), and Mike love (1941–). Three members of the group were brothers, one was a cousin, and the other was a school friend. They began singing in Hawthorne, California. Earlier group names had been Carl and the Passions, the Pendletones, and Kenny and the Cadets. The group relied heavily on harmony and themes that focused on love and the California beach life. The formula was an instant sensation, beginning with their first release "Surfin'." The song was released in 1961 under the name that they are best known, the Beach Boys.

Over the course of their long career, which continues to this day, the group has been challenged in many ways. Their first manager, Murry Wilson, the father of the brothers, pushed the group excessively hard. Personal challenges, such as drug abuse and inner conflict, put the group to the test. New members were added, two of the original members died. Still, the group produced hit after hit, attained worldwide fame, and never failed to attract large audiences to their concerts. Currently the group performs with the following members, Brian Wilson, Mike Love, Al Jardine, David Marks, and Bruce Johnson.

### Images in Popular Culture

Images of California are everywhere in popular culture—in books, music, television programs, and films. Books set in California reflect the state's diversity and multiculturalism. Acclaimed writer John Steinbeck wrote many California-based books, such as *Of Mice and Men* (1937), *The Grapes of Wrath* (1939), and *East of Eden* (1952). Amy Tan authored a bestselling book, *The Joy Luck Club* (1989), about the lives of contemporary Chinese Americans in San Francisco (adapted to a film in 1993). Prolific African American writer Walter Mosley's *Devil in a Blue Dress* (1990), a popular mystery novel featuring an African American protagonist, appealed to mainstream audiences and was adapted into a 1995 film.

Countless television shows and movies are set in California (for the obvious reason). For much of the 1950s and 1960s, a wholesome, all-American California image dominated. The Disneyland-inspired television series *The Mickey Mouse Club* (1955–1959) and surfing films such as *Gidget* (1959) and *Surf Party* (1964) set the tone. One of the most popular American surf bands, the Beach Boys, came out of California.

Television and film portrayed California in more diverse ways in subsequent decades. Tough city streets and gang-ridden urban neighborhoods were portrayed in movies such as the *Dirty Harry* films (1971, 1973, 1976, 1983, 1988), *Colors* (1988), and *Boyz N the Hood* (1991). Backwoods bumpkins meshed comically with California high life in the popular television series *The Beverly Hillbillies* (1962–1971). Another comical clash occurred when hip-hop culture met California bourgeoisie in *Fresh Price of Bel-Air* (1990–1996). Fit bodies and beauty went hand-in-hand with California lifeguards in the massively popular *Baywatch* TV series (1989–2001). A series of movies and television shows with vapid blonde beauty stereotypes garnered high ratings in the movies *Clueless* (1995) and *Legally Blonde* (2001, 2003). However, one attractive blonde shattered the stereotype in the action-packed *Buffy the Vampire Slayer* movie (1992) and long-running television series (1997–2003). Magic and the supernatural continued in the television series *Charmed* (1998–2006), featuring views of San Francisco, and *Angel* (1994–1996), set in Los Angeles. In 2008, the lives of privileged young adults were put under the microscope in *90210,* a spin-off of the original television series, *Beverly Hills, 90210* (1990–2000).

***See also*** Alcatraz; Attica; Beverly Hills, California; Chinatown; Disneyland; Grauman's Chinese Theatre; Golden Gate Bridge; Hollywood; Hoover Dam; Lake Tahoe; Las Vegas, Nevada; Los Angeles, California; Malibu, California; Manzanar; Mojave Desert; Napa Valley; Old West; Pearl Harbor; Redwood National and State Parks; San Francisco, California; Silicon Valley; State and National Parks; University of California, Berkeley; Yosemite National Park

### Further Reading

"California Tribes and Organizations." *500 Nations.* http://500nations.com/California_Tribes.asp.

May, Kirse Granat. 2002. *Golden State, Golden Youth: The California Image in Popular Culture, 1955–1966.* Chapel Hill: University of North Carolina Press.

Rawls, James J. 1986. *Indians of California: The Changing Image.* Norman: University of Oklahoma Press.

Starr, Kevin. 1986. *Americans and the California Dream, 1850–1915.* Santa Barbara, California: P. Smith.

Starr, Kevin. 2005. *California: A History.* New York: Modern Library.

Starr, Kevin. 2006. *Coast of Dreams: California on the Edge: 1990–2003.* New York: First Vintage Books.

Starr, Kevin, and Orsi, Richard J., eds. 2000. *Rooted in Barbarous Soil: People, Culture, and Community in Gold Rush California.* Berkeley: University of California Press.

## Camp David

Camp David is a highly secure presidential retreat in the Catoctin Mountains in Maryland. A mere 70 miles away from the White House in Washington, D.C., Camp David offers a tranquil getaway for the president and a private place to meet with national and world leaders. Media coverage often provides glimpses of presidents at the camp, and reports on their comings and goings. For the general public, this is the closest they will ever get to Camp David. Except for staff and security workers (primarily pulled from the best of the U.S. Navy and U.S. Marine Corps), secret service workers, and invited guests, the retreat is closed to the public. Nonetheless, Camp David holds a prominent place in American popular culture. Like anything associated with the president, the retreat is an emblem of political power, a place above the ordinary, whose name is held in awe.

### Historical Perspectives

Camp David, nestled in the Catoctin Mountain Park, was originally a part of a heavily wooded region that was used for logging and mountain farming. In 1935, the Works Progress Administration intended to convert much of this land into recreational areas. One area, which would become Camp David, was opened in 1938 as Hi-Catoctin, a camp designated for federal government agents and their families. Motivated to find a place to rejuvenate from illness and to contend with the pressures of work and summer heat, President Franklin D. Roosevelt transformed the camp into a private retreat and, in 1942, named it

Shangri-La. Later, President Dwight D. Eisenhower renamed the camp after his grandson David. Since Roosevelt, all U.S. presidents have utilized the retreat in some form or fashion. Officially, the camp is a military base known as Naval Support Facility Thurmont.

### About the Site

Camp David bears little resemblance to the typical sterile and institutionalized military bases. Situated on a densely wooded hill, Camp David is richly inhabited by assorted tree varieties, such as poplar, hickory, oak, and maple, and wild animals and birds, such as deer, raccoon, and blue jays. The 143 acres contain more than a dozen buildings, such as resident cabins for the president and guests, cottages, and a conference center. Among the recreational facilities are a pool, a skeet range, and tennis courts. Camp David is a popular spot to get away from the scrutiny of the public and media, as well as the high-pressure life in Washington, D.C. and the constant noise of the modern world. Camp David offers isolation and the opportunity to pursue recreational activities, such as swimming, walking the trails, horseback riding, and snowmobiling.

Presidents also use the retreat for high-profile meetings. The Camp David Accords were agreed to at a meeting that occurred in 1978 between Egyptian president Anwar al-Sadat and Israeli prime minister Menachem Begin. In 1992, George H.W. Bush's daughter, Dorothy Bush Koch, held the first wedding ever at the site. Among the notable dignitaries who have visited Camp David are former prime minister of the United Kingdom Margaret Thatcher and former Russian president Vladimir Putin.

### For Visitors

Though visitors to Camp David are by invitation only, the general public may visit the Camp David Museum. Located in Thurmont, Maryland, the museum exhibits pictures and memorabilia and has a souvenir and gift shop. With the exception of the Museum, mainstream America's only glimpse into Camp David is the intermittent photograph and passing references in the news media, adding to the intrigue and heightening the sensationalism that shrouds the president's popular retreat.

***See also*** Washington, D.C.; White House

### Further Reading

Nelson, W. Dale. 2000. *The President Is at Camp David.* Syracuse, New York: Syracuse University Press.

Swisher, Clayton E. 2004. *The Truth about Camp David: The Untold Story about the Collapse of the Middle East Process.* New York: Nation Books.

## Cape Cod, Nantucket, and Martha's Vineyard

Cape Cod and the islands Nantucket and Martha's Vineyard are frequently referenced together. All three areas are located within the same vicinity. Nantucket and Martha's Vineyard are located to the south of Cape Cod. Nantucket is 30 miles and Martha's Vineyard is 6 miles away from the cape. Twelve miles separate Martha's Vineyard and Nantucket (to the east of Martha's Vineyard). From the mid-18th century to the mid-19th century, the three areas were leaders in the whaling industry. Once whaling diminished, the areas emerged as popular tourist destinations, particularly with artists, the rich, and the famous. The attraction of Cape Cod, Nantucket, and Martha's Vineyard is not the usual bright lights, bustling arterials, spectacular sky scrapers, or endless possibilities for fun and enjoyment. Indeed, the cape and the nearby islands lack most of the visual markers of modern-day society and offer a relatively small number of attractions.

The appeal of these areas is the laid-back ambience and quietude. Scenic vistas of uncluttered skies, boats gently riding the open waters, beaches, and tranquil hills, valleys, and small towns create mystique. Little change occurs on this isolated swathe of land, which insures the slow pace and rejuvenation that vacationers seek.

### Cape Cod

In 1602, present-day Cape Cod was visited by the area's first recorded explorer, Bartholomew Gosnold, who traveled from Falmouth, England, looking for trade opportunities. Gosnold named the cape for the abundant amount of cod his crew discovered. Finding no opportunities, he and his crew stayed only for a few weeks. French explorer Samuel de Champlain visited the area in 1605 and 1606. In 1620, the cape was visited again, but this time by 101 passengers aboard the *Mayflower.* They stayed aboard the ship at Provincetown Harbor, off the coast of Cape Cod, as they drew up the Mayflower Compact, an agreement to establish and adhere by laws to govern the settlement. The group ended up establishing Plymouth Colony in Massachusetts. But, over a few decades, settlers migrated to Cape Cod, establishing Sandwich Barnstable, and Yarmouth.

Originally, the industry in Cape Cod was in farming and fishing. By the middle of the 18th century, residents wholeheartedly embraced whaling. The Wampanoag who lived in the area had instructed them on how to whale. Sperm whaling caused the cape to prosper exceedingly. But this prosperity did not last. The declining population of the whales was one factor. The discovery of oil found in other parts of the nation proved easier to acquire than the oil that was obtained from whaling. As a result of these factors, Cape Cod turned to tourism in the 19th century. During the first half of the 20th century, the region spawned a thriving artistic community. The Cape Cod School of Art, the Provincetown Players, the Barnstable Comedy Club, and the University Players Guild (now known as Falmouth Playhouse) were among the popular organizations that were established. Cape Playhouse drew notable actors such as Henry Fonda and Humphrey Bogart.

Tourism in Cape Cod received a boom during the second half of the 20th century. In the 1950s, the Mid Cape Highway was constructed. In 1961, President John F. Kennedy established the Cape Cod National Seashore. In the same decade, Kennedy summered in the so-named Kennedy Compound, a house that was built in Hyannis by his father during the early 20th century.

### Nantucket

English explorer Bartholomew Gosnold discovered Nantucket as well as Cape Cod in 1602. In 1641, Thomas Mayhew and his son, Thomas, were deeded the land. It was not until 1659 that Nantucket, which was then known as Sherburne, saw its first English settlers who had moved from Salisbury. In addition to farming and sheep herding, the growing number of residents began whaling as early as the late 17th century. From the 1700s to the 1840s, Nantucket's whaling industry was one of the most profitable in the world. In 1795, the town's name was changed to Nantucket, which translated from *Wampanoag* means "faraway land."

Alas, Nantucket's golden era diminished over the course of the 19th century. Other sources for oil replaced the whale industry. For example, oil was more easily extracted from the petroleum fields in Pennsylvania than from whales. A fire in 1846 devastated the area, and much of the male population went off to war during the Civil War (1861–1865). Many of the men did not return.

Facing such challenges, the residents of Nantucket turned to tourism. Beginning in the 1840s, rooming houses and inns welcomed summer guests. During the late 19th century, hotels were constructed. Quaint shops and eateries offering fresh local cuisine, as well as the Nantucket Historical Association's Whaling Museum are visited by seasonal visitors.

### Martha's Vineyard

Before the island was settled by Europeans, it was the home of the Wampanoag. This Native American community thrived on the land and waters of what is now eastern Massachusetts. They called their home *Noepe,* translated as "the land amid the streams." When the first European settlers arrived in 1602, the Wampanoag shared their knowledge and skill, as well as their island.

The first European arrivals to the area were Reverend John Brereton and Gabriel Archer. Both had come from England aboard the ship captained by Bartholomew Gosnold. They found an island that teemed with animal and marine life, berry bushes, and grapevines. The popularly accepted belief is that the island was named after both those prolific grapevines that grew there and the Captain's daughter, Martha.

The development of the island began many decades later. In 1641, Thomas Mayhew, who hailed from Massachusetts, purchased several islands, including Martha's Vineyard. In the following year, his son, Thomas, helped start the island's first settlement. Over the years, the indigenous population waned, and the land on which they had lived was gradually sold off to newcomers. In time, the six towns of the Island emerged: Tisbury, Edgartown, Oak Bluffs, West Tisbury, Chilmark, and Aquinnah (formerly Gay Head).

Each town has its own identity; each town thrived during the early 19th century by developing its own special trade and industry. Generally, the island's primary activities during the early years were farming and fishing. Notable distinctions include Edgartown, where whaling was the common industry. Oak Bluffs was the home of a Methodist camp meeting and, later, the first town to become a summer resort. In Tisbury, Vineyard Haven was the main vortex of the island's commercial life and residential homes. Agriculture was vital to the economies in West Tisbury and Chilmark. Aquinnah was home to many of the descendants of the Wampanoag people. The island supported not only European descendants but a small, distinct African American community. The island has also been inhabited by a large deaf community. Such was the influence of this community that a distinctive form of sign language, the Martha's Vineyard Sign Language, eventually developed and was used by the deaf and nondeaf. The community is traced back to a genetic variation that was found in the population of English descendants that settled in the area.

When Americans turned to other sources of transportation, such as trains and trucks, Martha's Vineyard, which had depended on its rich heritage of shipping and boat, was forced to adapt. The people of the island reinvented themselves and their island into a tourist destination.

### Cultural Distinctions

The identity of Martha's Vineyard is not unlike any other small town in America. The population of permanent residents is small; thus mostly everyone within a given community knows everyone else. Crime is low, the pace is slow, and friendliness is a prominent trait. Shaping the unique identity of the island is the area's maritime heritage, the community's love of the land, and the efforts to preserve that land and their way of life. More remote than a typical American town due to the fact that the island is surrounded by the Vineyard Sound, the Nantucket Sound, and the Atlantic Ocean, Martha's Vineyard exudes a feeling of being transported into another place in another time. Thus, vacationers and the people who live there are far removed from the cares, anxieties, congestion, and the technology-saturated world that often characterizes cities on the mainland.

### Tourism and Famous Visitors and Residents

Martha's Vineyard features many attractions and activities. The area's most pronounced landmarks are the beaches such as Menemsha Beach, which offers views of fishing boats, docks, and striking sunsets.

Jungle Beach is a popular nude beach. The main attraction of Lighthouse Beach is the Edgartown Lighthouse, which was built in 1828. Other attractions include the gingerbread cottages, which were built by the Methodist in the 1800s; Alley's General Store, which was built in 1858; and the Flying Horses Carousel. The gingerbread cottages are lit with Chinese and Japanese lanterns during the summer event known as the Grand Illumination, which takes place in Oak Bluffs. The general store is the oldest store on Martha's Vineyard. Constructed in 1876, the Flying Horses Carousel was originally located on Coney Island. Today, the carousel is regarded as the oldest platform carousel in the nation and is designated a national landmark. Martha's Vineyard AVA, which was established in the 1980s, is a popular attraction for wine enthusiasts.

Typical travelers to Martha's Vineyard, from the 19th century to the present, have been families of abundant means, celebrities, and an assortment of national leaders and officials. The summer, when some 100,000 visitors come to the island, is the peak tourist season. Notable seasonal migrants to the area have included the famous Kennedy family, which owned property on the island. Many wealthy African American families vacationed in Oak Bluffs. Presidents Ulysses S. Grant, William Clinton, and Barack Obama frequently vacationed on the island. Like many famous people, Jacqueline Kennedy Onassis, the wife of President John F. Kennedy, owned a home in Aquinnah to which she retreated. Her son, John F. Kennedy Jr., his wife Carolyn, and sister-in-law Lauren Bessette were killed when the plane he was flying crashed into the Atlantic Ocean near Martha's Vineyard in 1999. These legendary visitors and residents, including pop culture entertainers and writers, add to the specialness and exclusivity for which the island is known.

### Images in Popular Culture

Herman Melville is one of the first and most notable individuals to draw inspiration from the area. Captivated by the spectacular whaling industry in Nantucket, he wrote a classic American novel, *Moby Dick* (1851). Nantucket serves as an important part of the background of Melville's gripping saga about a captain who becomes obsessed with the capture of an elusive whale. In Chapter 14, which is titled "Nantucket," Melville pays homage to the area and to the heroism of the whalers. Some of the characters in the book hail from Nantucket, Martha's Vineyard, or Cape Cod. For example, Stubb, the second mate, is from Cape Cod. Tashtego, the harpooner, is from Martha's Vineyard.

Nantucket is not the only area that has received attention in popular culture. Martha's Vineyard appeared in popular magazines and televised tourism programs, as well as in films such as *Jaws* (1975) and *The Inkwell* (1994). Martha's Vineyard has also served as a setting for popular novels. The name "Martha's Vineyard" is often heard in televised news stories covering high-profile individuals living or vacationing on the island. To this day, the name "Martha's Vineyard" is associated with elegance and the refined culture of the rich and famous.

### In Conclusion

On Martha's Vineyard, fishing boats, gingerbread houses, the storied homes of bygone whaling captains, and farm houses mingle with the tourist-style shops, hotels, inns, and restaurants. The Vineyard is an example of how certain American communities have sustained themselves through the preservation of their environment and celebration of a slow-paced way of life. While other towns and cities have developed and modernized, places like Martha's Vineyard maintain and preserve their ties with their heritage. In doing so, the residents have created living memorials that continue to generate public interest, while, at the same time, ensure the community's survival.

*See also* Coney Island; Plymouth Colony

### Further Reading

Beston, Henry. 1949. *The Outermost House: A Year of Life on the Great Beach of Cape Cod*. New York: Rinehart.

Dresser, Thomas. 2010. *African Americans on Martha's Vineyard: From Enslavement to Presidential Visit*. Charleston, South Carolina: The History Press.

Dresser, Thomas. 2011. *The Wampanoag Tribe of Martha's Vineyard: Colonization to Recognition*. Charleston, South Carolina: The History Press.

Hannaford, Peter. 2012. *Presidential Retreats: Where the Presidents Went and Why They Went There*. New York: Threshold Books.

Linsley, Leslie. 2008. *Nantucket: Island Living*. New York: Stewart Tabori & Chang.

Railton, Arthur R. 2006. *The History of Martha's Vineyard: How We Got to Where We Are*. Beverly, Massachusetts: Commonwealth Editions published in association with Martha's Vineyard Historical Society.

Schneider, Paul. 2000. *The Enduring Shore: A History of Cape Cod, Martha's Vineyard, and Nantucket*. New York: Henry Holt.

Taylor, Matt. 2011. *Jaws: Memories from Martha's Vineyard*. Martha's Vineyard, Massachusetts: Moonrise Media.

## Capitol Hill

Capitol Hill is an area in Washington, D.C. that comprises major federal government buildings and several residential neighborhoods. But the area is most famous as the home of U.S. Capitol Building, where Congress meets to debate issues of importance to the nation and vote on bills that become law. Other major structures, such as the Senate and House office buildings, the Supreme Court building, and the Library of Congress, are also located there. Near the Capitol Building, and regarded as part of the Capitol Hill district, are several historic neighborhoods where government workers and ordinary citizens live and go about their daily lives. The term "Capitol Hill," however, is used in most cases to refer to the political section of the neighborhood, and, by association, it has also come to refer to the political happenings, events, hot topics, news, and legislative swirl that goes on there.

### Historical Perspectives

In 1791, President George Washington established the District of Colombia along the Potomac River to be the nation's capital. Pierre Charles L'Enfant, who Washington selected to design the capital, envisioned an elegant capital with avenues lined with trees and neat lawns on what was then rolling farmland. He designated where government buildings and monuments should go, as well as the location of residences located within the capital. Though others carried on the majority of L'Enfant's design (he was dismissed in 1792), and for a while his plans were even abandoned, his vision was eventually realized.

The U.S. Capitol Building, built in 1793 on an elevated part of the site originally known as Jenkins Hill, is one of the oldest buildings in the area. In the early years, it not only housed the Congress but also the Library of Congress, the Supreme Court, and miscellaneous government workers. The Library of Congress received its own building, the Thomas Jefferson Building, in 1897. In the early 20th century, the House Office Building (now known as the Cannon House Office Building) and the Senate Office Building (Russell Senate Office Building) were built. The U.S. Supreme Court Building would not be constructed until 1935.

Residential areas sprang up within the larger Capitol Hill neighborhood during the 19th century. Neighborhoods developed: Barracks Row, Massachusetts Avenue, NE Corridor, Eastern Market, Southwest Waterfront, and H Street. Each neighborhood developed its own unique ambience and features.

The members of Congress were the first residents of Capitol Hill. They lived in boarding houses that were located a short distance away from the capitol. Individuals who helped build the capital and Navy Yard craftsmen also resided in the area in those early days. (The Navy Yard, established in the area in 1799, provided defense to the capitol in case of attack or invasion.) Homes, in assorted architectural styles such as manor houses and Federal style townhouses, materialized along the broad avenues. These homes catered to the middle classes, which included politicians and government workers; less grandiose homes were built for the working classes. Churches, shops, and other facilities emerged. Residents patronized the Eastern Market, which opened in 1871, to buy fresh produce.

As the activity within Capitol Hill increased, the area attracted a diverse population. Immigrants, such as Germans, Irish, Southern Europeans, and African Americans from nearby states arrived in the area in search of work. They worked as laborers on the construction of the capitol and the Navy Yard. Blacks were also incorporated into the government workforce. For many decades, Capitol Hill's residential neighborhoods were segregated by race and economic status.

## Contemporary Perspectives

In many neighborhoods, the historic homes still grace the streets in the modern era, while some neighborhoods have undergone significant change. The historic Southwest neighborhood experienced urban renewal beginning in 1954. The change for many old-timers, who were displaced from their homes, was traumatic. Most of the neighborhood, home to blacks and whites, was demolished and replaced with L'Enfant Plaza, office buildings, a hotel, and an underground shopping mall.

The most prominent image of Capitol Hill remains the façade of the U.S. Capitol, where the leaders of the country, lobbyists, government workers, and journalists assemble. Behind the scenes, these same people engage in a vibrant social culture, which is fed by the nearby shops, restaurants, nightclubs, and theaters. The energy of the historic environment and the diverse residential neighborhoods is unmatched in the country.

## For Visitors

The government buildings are a popular destination for tourists. But visits to Capitol Hill should include the historic neighborhoods, rich with history and architectural beauty, the bustling streets, such as Pennsylvania Avenue, and the Eastern Market. The African American Heritage Trail includes several points of interest, such as the Bell School Site, Ebenezer United Methodist Church, and the John H. Paynter Residence. The Bell School Site is the first school designated for African Americans in the neighborhood. The Ebenezer United Methodist Church was founded in 1827 by African Americans. Capitol Hill resident John H. Paynter is notable for his seminal work, *Fugitives of the Pearl* (1930), about a large slave escape attempt that took place in Washington in 1848.

Nearby Capitol Hill there are many famous landmarks, such as the White House, the Lincoln Memorial, and the Smithsonian Institution.

***See also*** Lincoln Memorial; Smithsonian Institution; U.S. Capitol Building; Washington, D.C.; White House

## Further Reading

Campbell, Colton C., and Herrnson, Paul S., eds. 2004. *War Stories from Capitol Hill*. Upper Saddle River, New Jersey: Pearson Prentice Hall.

Gray, Mary Z. 2012. *301 East Capitol: Tales from the Heart of the Hill*. Washington, DC: Overbeck History Press.

Smith, Kathryn Schneider, ed. 2010. *Washington at Home: An Illustrated History of Neighborhoods in the Nation's Capital*. Baltimore: Johns Hopkins University Press.

## Carhenge

Carhenge is a roadside attraction situated on the golden prairie grass near Alliance, Nebraska. A replica of England's Stonehenge, which consists of large gray stones arranged in a circular pattern, Carhenge is made from gray spray-painted vintage American cars. The structure was originally constructed as a tribute to the deceased father of artist Jim Reinders. Since then, the site has emerged as one of the most popular roadside attractions in the nation. Currently, the site features other car structures and a visitor center, but the primary draw remains Carhenge, a uniquely American creation that's zany—and interesting—enough to appeal to the iconoclastic American sense of humor.

### Historical Perspectives

Carhenge was not intended to be a tourist attraction. Reinders and his family created it as a memorial to Reinders's father. The site was originally the farm where Reinders's father had lived. The design for the structure was inspired by Reinders's time in England, where he saw and studied the prehistoric circle

Alliance, Nebraska is home to the unique Carhenge, an artistic automotive homage to Stonehenge in England. (UIG via Getty Images)

of standing stones known as Stonehenge, one of the most iconic ancient monuments on the planet. The visitor center opened in 2006.

### About the Site

In terms of size and design, Carhenge is a near replica of Stonehenge. But that is where the similarity ends. Whereas Stonehenge is composed of stones, Carhenge is made from American cars. Stonehenge features immense monoliths weighing as much as 25 tons each standing upright in a circle, linked together by other stones (lintels) resting horizontally on top of them. Carhenge is made of 38 cars (each representing one of the 38 major stones of Stonehenge) spray-painted rock gray. Those cars representing standing stones are partially buried. Other cars, representing the lintels, rest on top of the standing cars.

The site includes other oddities. A car that is used as a gravestone reads: "Here lie three bones of foreign cars. They served our purpose while Detroit slept. Now Detroit is awake and America's great!" Other car sculptures, such as the *Spawning Salmon*, the *Fourd Seasons*, and the *Carnastoga*, which were designed by various artists, are collectively known as the Car Art Reserve.

The visitor center, gift shop, picnic tables, and an educational display board allow visitors to spend as much time as they like at Carhenge. The site is maintained by a group that calls itself Friends of Carhenge. The website proclaims that Carhenge is known as the second wackiest site in America.

### For Visitors

Carhenge is open year round and is free to the public.

*See also* Detroit, Michigan

### Further Reading

Butko, Brian, and Butko, Sarah. 2007. *Roadside Attractions: Cool Cafes, Souvenir Stands, Route 66 Relics & Other Road Trip Fun*. Mechanicsburg, Pennsylvania: Stackpole Books.

*Carhenge*. http://carhenge.com/.

Grzymkowski, Eric. 2012. *United States of Strange: 1,001 Frightening, Bizarre, Outrageous Facts about the Land of the Free and the Home of the Frog People, the Cockroach Hall of Fame, and Carhenge*. Avon, Massachusetts: Adams Media.

## Carlsbad Caverns

Carlsbad Caverns is an extraordinary natural wonder found in the Guadalupe Mountains in New Mexico. Some 100 years ago, the caverns were discovered by a local cowboy named Jim White. Initially exploited for guano, a natural fertilizer made from bat droppings, Carlsbad Caverns eventually became known for its treasures: some 117 chambers containing an array of unimaginably beautiful natural limestone formations. Encompassing over 46,000 acres, the caverns are among the world's largest underground chambers. In 1923, Carlsbad Caverns National Park was designated a National Monument. In 1930, it was redesignated a National Park, and in 1995, it was designated a World Heritage Site. Its beauty—unusual and extraordinary—and massiveness makes the site one of America's favorite natural wonders.

### Historical Perspectives

Carlsbad Caverns has a very, very long history. Over 250 million years ago, an inland sea occupied the place where the site is now located. As the eons passed, the remains of sea creatures, combined with

The Big Room at Carlsbad Caverns. (Marcos Casiano/Dreamstime.com)

erosion, acid rain, and other processes resulted in the formation of a massive complex of caves. These underground chambers are best known for their famous stalactites, mineral formations hanging from the cave ceiling, and stalagmites, mineral formations rising from the cave floor.

The caverns remained in total darkness and, as far as it is known, hidden from humanity until 1898, when Jim White thought he saw smoke billowing into the sky from the ground. The smoke turned out to be a black cloud of bats erupting from the ground-level opening of what would become known as Carlsbad Caverns. Over the ensuing years, White mined for guano and explored the caverns, discovering many new chambers in the process.

### About the Site

Carlsbad Caverns holds many marvels in its numerous chambers, most of them named, some the size of a town. It is also the natural habitat of the Mexican free-tailed bats. One room, known as the Bat Cave, is where the majority of the bat population lives. The Hall of the Giants is the largest room, constituting 357,469 square feet of floor space.

### For Visitors

The park is open 24 hours every day of the year except for Christmas Day. Rangers facilitate tours of the caves. The caverns can be accessed by elevator or by hiking. Unlike in White's day, Carlsbad Caverns is well lighted, so that visitors can fully appreciate and enjoy the experience. Other park activities include back-country camping and hiking in the surrounding desert and watching the spectacular display of Mexican free-tailed bats exiting from Carlsbad Caverns before sunset.

Carlsbad Caverns is justly known as one of the great natural wonders of the American landscape, a claim supported by the fact that an astounding half million visitors make the pilgrimage there each year.

*See also* Adirondacks; Bok Kai Temple; Cleveland-Lloyd Dinosaur Quarry; Crater Lake; Grand Canyon; Meteor Crater; Monument Valley

### Further Reading

"Carlsbad Caverns." *National Park Service*. www.nps.gov/cave/index.htm.

Greene, Edward J., and Conner, Maryellen. 2006. *Carlsbad Caverns: The Story behind the Scenery*. Las Vegas: KC Publications.

Jones, Ray. 2004. *USA to Z: A Celebration of American Popular Culture*. Nashville: Cumberland House.

## Carnegie Hall

Carnegie Hall is a concert venue in Manhattan, New York. Though other venues across the nation bear the prestigious name, none can compare with the original, an unmistakable rectangular, six-story Italian Renaissance–style building located at 881 Seventh Avenue in New York City. Founded in 1890 by wealthy industrialist Andrew Carnegie, the concert hall, which opened in 1891, is known as one of America's premier venues for music and the arts. Revered by concert enthusiasts, performing artists, and conductors the world over, it is on the U.S. National Register of Historic Places and is a U.S. National Historic Landmark. Its legendary appeal harkens back to its distinguished beginnings and to the brilliant array of artists who have performed within its walls. The history of Carnegie Hall is a legacy of extraordinary music, both classical and popular, in America and abroad.

### Historical Perspectives

Carnegie Hall traces its lineage back to a fortuitous encounter that occurred in 1887. Walter Damrosch, then conductor and musical director of the Symphony Society of New York and the Oratorio Society of New York, developed an amiable relationship with Andrew Carnegie and his new wife, Louise Whitefield, while aboard a ship headed to Europe. The Carnegies invited Damrosch to their estate in Scotland, where Damrosch detailed his dream of creating a concert venue where his Symphony Society and Oratorio Society could perform. Damrosch explained that the number of venues in the area was at that time limited and too small.

Enthused by the concept, Carnegie pushed forward, sparing no expense in the construction of Carnegie Hall. He hired architect and music aficionado William Burnett Tuthill and secured property near Central Park. Much pomp surrounded the building's construction. The ceremonial laying of the cornerstone was accompanied by words spoken by Carnegie himself, while Louise Carnegie used a silver trowel from Tiffany & Company to secure the cornerstone.

The opening of Carnegie Hall was celebrated with a five-day festival attended by a commanding list of who's who in prestigious New York City families, such as the Rockefellers. Opening night was May 5, 1891, and the hall was filled to capacity to listen to music by Tchaikovsky and Damrosch. Reviewers gave glowing reports, waxing eloquent about the beauty and luxuriousness of Carnegie Hall.

### About the Site

Carnegie Hall remains largely the same since its inception, though renovations have by necessity been carried over the 120 years of its existence. The venue still contains three stages, the famous Main Hall, a recital hall, and a chamber music hall. The Main Hall, now named the Isaac Stein Auditorium/ Ronald O. Perelmen Stage, seats 2,800. It is famed for its enormously high ceiling, which produces its fine acoustics and a hike of over 100 steps for concert goers with top balcony seats. The recital hall, located beneath the Main Hall, once boasted 1,200 seats. But that number was cut in half when renovations were carried out in 2003, when the hall was renamed the Judy and Arthur Zankel Hall. The chamber music hall (today known as the Joan and Sanford I. Weill Recital Hall) sits 250. The original structure also had numerous rooms for lectures, readings, and meetings, as well as practice studios for performing artists.

In 1986, the Carnegie Hall Archives was added to the complex. In 1991, the Rose Museum, which contains an exhibition about the history of the hall, was added.

### Cultural Distinctions

Though Carnegie Hall is often associated with the classics and high-brow entertainment, the performances there have always reflected the diversity and development of American popular music. Carnegie Hall has showcased jazz greats, folk music, rock and roll, and other popular music genres. In the 1960s, the Beatles—who, with their long hair, frenzied audiences, and radical sound were virtually the antithesis of conservative classical music—performed there as well. As the sounds of the times changed over the decades, Carnegie Hall opened its doors to the changing landscape of popular music.

Performing at Carnegie Hall has long been synonymous with "making it" in show business. This goes for stand-up comics as well as musicians. Groucho Marx, George Carlin, Lenny Bruce, Ray Romano, Lily Tomlin, and a host of others have graced the famous main stage.

### Contemporary Perspectives

In 1925, the family after whom Carnegie Hall was named ceased to have an ownership stake in the site. For many decades, the facility was owned by a real estate developer Robert E. Simon and his son. In order to save the building from demolition in 1960, New York City purchased the building, and a nonprofit organization, the Carnegie Hall Corporation, was created to manage the venue.

### Images in Popular Culture

Among the notable television programs that featured Carnegie Hall were Leonard Bernstein's *Young People's Concerts,* a weekly broadcast by the New York Philharmonic that ran from 1958 to 1972; *AT&T Presents Carnegie Hall Tonight,* a show broadcast on both radio and television over a 10-year period in the 1970s and 1980s; and an assortment of live performances by popular stars that continue to this day.

***See also*** Central Park; New York, New York; Tiffany & Company

### Further Reading

*Carnegie Hall.* http://www.carnegiehall.org/.

Page, Tim, and Hall, Carnegie. 2011. *Carnegie Hall Treasures.* New York: Harper Design.

Schickel, Richard, and Walsh, Michael. 1987. *Carnegie Hall: The First One Hundred Years.* New York: Abrams.

# Casino

Casinos are establishments that offer opportunities for gambling via games of chance such as cards, dice, and slot machines. Gambling in a variety of forms has been a part of American society since colonial times, whether or not the activity was considered socially acceptable or even legal. During the early 19th century, the southern city of New Orleans was a major center for adult forms of entertainment such as gambling. Later in that century, gambling establishments, known primarily as gambling halls, sprouted up in the mining camps and towns of the American West. Eventually, as most states in the nation prohibited gambling, Nevada, where it was still legal, became the center for this activity. Over the years, Las Vegas became the casino capital of the world, with Atlantic City on the East Coast in second place. In the 1980s, mega casino resorts emerged, revolutionizing the gambling industry. In the wake of gambling's growing popularity, casinos appeared elsewhere in the nation: on reservations, in select cities and towns, and on board cruise ships and riverboats. In modern times, casinos have become a fixture and widely accepted part of mainstream American life and culture.

### Historical Perspectives

In colonial America, gambling mostly involved card and dice games. Lotteries, another form of gambling, were occasionally used to raise money for public projects, such as the construction of schools. Harvard and Yale, for example, were institutions that benefited from lotteries. America has nonetheless had a love-hate relationship with the pastime. Throughout American history, gambling has been alternately legalized and prohibited.

Public acceptance and attitudes toward gambling fluctuated in accordance with societal trends. During the early colonial years, the Puritans were against gambling and did not allow members of the various New England settlements to participate in the activity. Cards, dice, as well as dancing, singing, and even squandering one's time with leisure activities were regarded as immoral. Other colonials, not bound by such regulations and expectations, freely gambled. In fact, certain games were associated with polite and high society. Others, such as cockfighting, were not, and were consequently relegated to the poor, working classes.

### New Orleans in the 19th Century

In the spirited atmosphere of New Orleans, a city that was fortuitously located at the mouth of the Mississippi River, gambling took root early and grew wildly. Thanks to the river, the city bustled with activity, becoming a major financial center and port for trade early in the century. Products of every kind were moved in and out of the port on steamboats and other vessels, headed to and from various towns and cities up river. A lively cosmopolitan community developed—as did a rather disreputable subculture. Prostitutes and ne'er-do-wells lived side by side rich merchants and plantation owners.

The rich city was infamous for its tolerance of adult forms of entertainment. Gambling took place on the riverboats and in lavish onshore establishments, where the rich in their fashionable attire played games of chance. Professional gamblers preyed on unsophisticated players. Occasionally, gamblers accused of cheating were lynched by vigilante groups.

### American West

Beginning in the 1840s, gold seekers, homesteaders, and opportunists contributed to the development of the West. The region was home to a prolific number of gambling houses and saloons that featured gambling. Although it was not considered respectable for genteel women to go into these establishments, women, as well as ethnic groups such as African Americans and the Chinese, were not actually prohibited from entering.

### Paris in Vegas

Paris Las Vegas is a uniquely American spectacle that pays tribute to one of the world's most glamorous cities. Some may call the casino garish or gimmicky; most are dazzled by the myriad entertainment opportunities.

Opening in 1999, Paris Las Vegas generated attention not because of its size (it is not particularly large), but for its French-themed furnishings and recreations. Notable features include replicas of famous French landmarks such as the Arc de Triomphe, the Paris Opera House, the Hôtel de Ville, and the Louvre. Dining options feature French cuisine from several famous regions (standard American fare is also available.)

The casino offers two Parisian-inspired retail locations: the Paris-Bally's Promenade and the shops at Le Boulevard. Shops include upscale jewelry stores, boutiques, and Le Journal and Les Enfants, where children's toys can be purchased. La Cave features French wines and imported items such as cheese and sweets.

### The Grand Casino

The MGM Grand is a casino, one of the first mega resorts to be built in Las Vegas. The first MGM Grand, built by Kirk Kerkorian, opened in 1973, paving the way for the era of the megacasinos and rekindled tourism to the area. The hotel incorporated 2,200 guest rooms and suites, five restaurants, two showrooms, a movie theater, and of course, gaming areas. The casino had a movie theme, as the name of the casino paid tribute to the famed Metro-Goldwyn-Mayer film studio (Kerkorian was the major stock holder in the studio).

In 1980, tragedy struck when a fire erupted in the casino and some 85 people were killed. Though the casino was rebuilt in 1981, Kerkorian sold it in 1985 to Bally Entertainment Corporation. The casino is now known as Bally's Las Vegas.

In 1993, Kerkorian opened a second MGM Grand. This one was even bigger than the first, with more than 5,000 rooms and multiple show venues. The MGM Grand Garden Arena hosts big-named concerts and sporting events. Originally, a theme park was included, but that was closed in 2000. A lion habitat was closed in 2012.

Such establishments operated in tents as well as formal buildings. Certain towns, like Deadwood, had not one but several gambling establishments—so many, for example, that the saloons went by numbers rather than formal names. Gambling and drinking gave the predominately male population something to do: a way to spend their money, pass the time, and potentially make some money. During this era, San Francisco, California, emerged as a major gambling center.

Near the end of the Old West era in the 1890s, those towns that survived became more law abiding and conservative. The mood of the nation swung back to its Puritan roots. Antigambling and temperance groups campaigned successfully for the prohibition of gambling and alcohol throughout the country.

### Las Vegas in the 20th Century

While more and more states throughout the nation outlawed gambling, Nevada decided to legalize the activity in 1931. In the same year, construction began on Hoover Dam. In anticipation of the surge in tourism and population growth in the area, Nevada promoted its nascent casino industry. Over the decades, Las Vegas became increasingly filled with casino nightclubs and casino luxury resorts. During the 1950s, the industry was greatly helped by the involvement of organized crime. Mobsters with money invested heavily in the newly constructed extravagant structures. In this decade and the next, the casinos catered to a well-dressed crowd with boundless glitz and impeccable service. Following a massive federal investigation into the role of organized crime in the industry, legitimate management of the gambling establishments was restored.

In the late 20th century, Las Vegas launched several new supersized casino-hotel combinations. These conglomerates featured casinos, luxury hotels, assorted restaurants, and shopping malls. No longer were casinos regarded as simple gambling establishments; they became attractions unto themselves. The formula swept across the city, resulting in jaw-dropping changes to the landscape. Happily, smaller, more intimate venues continued to operate.

### Beyond Las Vegas

After 1976, when New Jersey legalized gambling in certain areas, glittering new casinos emerged in Atlantic City, making the city the second most popular destination for gambling in the country. In the following decade, casinos began to proliferate everywhere, as states progressively legalized various forms of gaming in limited venues.

Casinos have multiplied on the Native American reservations, greatly contributing to the economies of many communities that had been historically impoverished (gambling was a popular activity with many tribes long before the arrival of Europeans in North America). Casinos also became popular on cruise ships and riverboats. The riverboats, whether docked or in transit, are popular in Iowa, Indiana, Louisiana, and Mississippi. Though casinos in Las Vegas and Atlantic City may be known for their opulence, casual attitudes and dress are the norm.

With the massive popularity of casinos and the abundance of facilities, gambling is now considered to be socially acceptable. However, in modern times gambling is recognized as being highly addictive for some people. Psychologists point to tragic cases of ruined lives and a descent into criminal behavior due to gamblers who are unable to walk away from the table.

### Images in Popular Culture

Casino movies have always been fashionable. These films run the gamut in terms of subject matter. The movies *Bugsy* (1991) and *Casino* (1995) pay homage to the casino's bygone mobster era. High-stakes heists drive the plot of movies such as *Ocean's Eleven* (2001) and its two sequels as well as the movie *21* (2008), about a group of MIT students who con casinos by way of a mathematical technique. The mature comedy, *The Hangover* (2009), follows the wild escapades of friends visiting Las Vegas for a bachelor party, reflects the mass appeal of 21st-century casino vacations.

### In Conclusion

Casinos have had a long history in America. Though gambling has been an activity enjoyed by communities since colonial times, actual casinos developed much later, emerging initially as the saloon and gambling establishments of the Old West. The modern casino took form in Nevada, developing into the multimillion-dollar industry that it is today. But the popular Nevada destination is no longer the only choice for gamblers. Casinos proliferate in states across the nation.

*See also* Atlantic City, New Jersey; Cruise Ships; Deadwood, South Dakota; Harvard University; Hoover Dam; Las Vegas, Nevada; Mississippi River; MIT; New Orleans, Louisiana; Old West; Saloons, Bars, and Taverns; San Francisco, California; Yale University

**The Rise of the Native American Casinos**

Large-scale gaming on Native American reservations began in the 1970s. Many reservations operated bingo halls and some built casinos by exerting their rights of this gaming industry. Some Native Americans felt that federal intervention was necessary to provide additional protection from state-imposed regulations. In 1988, the Indian Gaming Regulatory Act reinforced their right to operate gaming centers on reservations and ruled that states had no right to attempt to impose regulations on Native American gaming.

Since this ruling, Native American casinos have flourished, though the success of the casinos is often based on location. Remote reservations attract fewer visitors than reservations that are located closer to major cities and towns or near other popular attractions. Casinos have helped augment the economy, revitalize communities, and provide employment for Native Americans and non-Native Americans alike. For many Native American communities, the casinos have been a symbol of pride, dignity, and economic power.

**Further Reading**

Eisler, Kim Isaac. 2002. *Revenge of the Pequots: How a Small Native American Tribe Created the World's Most Profitable Casino*. Lincoln: University of Nebraska Press.

Mason, W. Dale. 2000. *Indian Gaming: Tribal Sovereignty and American Politics*. Norman: University of Oklahoma Press.

Schwartz, David G. 2006. *Roll the Bones: The History of Gambling*. New York: Gotham Books.

Schwartz, David G. 2003. *Suburban Xanadu: The Casino Resort on the Las Vegas Strip and Beyond*. New York: Routledge.

Thompson, William N. 2001. *Gambling in America: An Encyclopedia of History, Issues, and Society*. Santa Barbara, California: ABC-CLIO.

## Catalina Island

Catalina Island is a part of the Channel Islands located off the coast of California. The 76-square-mile island is located a mere 22 miles from the mainland (Sorensen 2010). Since the Spanish first arrived there in the middle of the 16th century, the island has attracted the interest of several waves of people who arrived in pursuit of profit-making ventures and beautiful getaways. In modern times, the island functions mostly as a home to a small population of residents and as a popular vacation destination. In sharp contrast to the busy, crowded mainland, Catalina Island offers a beautiful, natural respite for its residents and frequent visitors.

### Historical Perspectives

The Pimungans, the area's indigenous residents, lived in relative tranquility on the island they called Pimu until the first Spanish explorer, Juan Rodriguez Cabrillo, arrived on October 7, 1542. The Pimungans hunted and built canoes, which they used to navigate the turbulent channel to trade with other Native Americans on nearby islands or on the mainland. They lived peacefully for another two decades, until the arrival of the second Spanish explorer, Sebastian Viscaino, on November 24, 1602. Viscaino renamed the island after Saint Catherine, paying homage to the fact that he had arrived on the island on the eve of the titular Catholic holiday.

The tranquility of the island and among the people faded as the inevitable changes unfurled. The Spanish occupation of California saw the numbers of Native Americans dwindle, many dying from diseases that were introduced to the New World by the travelers. The Spanish established missions, converting members of the native population and making them work on their vast properties. Due to Spanish law, the Spanish did not enter into trade with foreigners. As a result, the lifestyle of the Pimungans was further altered.

Other changes came to the island as Spain, then Mexico, and finally the newborn nation of America claimed control of the area. In the 19th century, more foreigners arrived. Russians, Americans, and the Aleut, a tribe from Alaska hunted sea otters for their pelts. English and American smugglers came in the wake of Mexico's domination in 1820. The smugglers sold leather and tallow illegally to avoid the taxes Mexico imposed on the products and resources.

Mexico's rule ended after America's victory in the Mexican-American War (1846–1848). The signing of the Treaty of Guadalupe Hidalgo gave America present-day states such as California. In 1849, the discovery of gold in the state sparked the famed gold rush. Catalina Island experienced a rush of its own, as the island attracted silver prospectors as well as sheep and cattle ranchers, many of them squatters.

A few individuals, who had been awarded official land grants during Mexico's reign, were authorized to live on the island. The squatters were evicted in the years after America assumed control.

The squatters were not the only ones to depart the island. Over the century, the Pimungans migrated off the island to other islands and the mainland. By the end of the century, the island's new visitors—American tourists—arrived with their tents and their zest for vacations in exotic destinations.

In the 20th century, vacationers, along with filmmakers and their entourage of camera crews, makeup artists, producers, actors, and actresses, began their long association with the island. Their presence sparked the development of the island, with the construction of venues such as the Catalina Casino, the Tuna Club, the Green Pleasure Pier, and the Catalina Country Club and Golf Course.

The Catalina Casino, which was built in 1929, is an entertainment venue, not a gambling venue. The 12-story Art Deco building hosted Big Band music and lively dancing during the 1930s and 1940s (*Catalina Island Chamber of Commerce and Visitors Bureau*). The Tuna Club, established in 1898, catered to exclusive members such as President Theodore Roosevelt, war hero Winston Churchill, and performer Bing Crosby. William Wrigley Jr., who acquired the island in 1919, originally opened the Catalina Country Club & Golf Course in 1921 as the Chicago Cubs' spring training facility. Wrigley was a chewing gum magnate and owner of the Chicago Cubs. Green Pleasure Pier was built in the late 19th century. A second pier was built in 1909 after a storm destroyed the first one.

Prominent homes on the island include Wrigley's lavish home, built in 1921, and writer Zane Grey's house, built in 1926.

### Images in Popular Culture

The movie and film industry have deep roots on Catalina Island. Film activity was busiest during the silent film era to World War II (1941–1945). More than 225 films were filmed at on the island during those years (*Catalina Island Chamber of Commerce and Visitors Bureau*). Catalina was an ideal location for creating dramatic scenes for films like *Treasure Island* (1918), *Ben Hur* (1925), and *Mutiny on the Bounty* (1935).

Filming was prohibited during the war, but resumed at its end, though with markedly less activity. Nonetheless, the island was used as the setting for seminal films including *Jaws* (1974), the cult classic about a predatory shark that preys on beachgoers; *Waterworld* (1995), a film that takes place on an imaginative landless Earth; and *Amistad* (1997), the dramatic portrayal of real-life slave mutiny on the eponymously named ship.

### Contemporary Perspectives

In the 21st century, Catalina Island remains largely unchanged by modern-day sprawl and development. Most of the land is owned by the Santa Catalina Island Conservancy. The buffalo on the island descended from the bison that were used for the film *The Vanishing American* (1925). Avalon Bay, the island's main community, had 3,000 residents in 2010 (Sorensen 2010). The shores and the mountainous areas are mostly unobstructed by signs of contemporary civilization. Few roads meander across the landscape.

Many historic structures remain. The Casino Ballroom, for example, continues to operate for private gatherings, parties, and weddings. The Catalina Country Club & Golf Course now operates as the Catalina Island Country Club and is open to the public, but its famous baseball field is gone. Grey's home now functions as the Zane Grey Pueblo Hotel, and Wrigley Jr.'s home has been converted into the Inn on Mt. Ada.

### For Visitors

Catalina Island is visited by ordinary guests and celebrities alike. Popular attractions include the Avalon Museum, which chronicles the historical uses of the island. This museum is located inside the Avalon Casino. The Wrigley Memorial & Botanical Gardens is a 38-acre park that pays tribute to William Wrigley Jr. (Sorensen, 2010). The El Rancho Escondido, where horses are raised, is a popular tourist stop, as is Little Harbor, where vacationers visit for camping and hiking, and glass-bottom boat tours. Visitors to the island will be sure to notice that golf carts are used in lieu of cars for transportation.

*See also* Alaska; California

**Further Reading**

*Catalina Island.* http://catalina.com.

*Catalina Island Chamber of Commerce and Visitors Bureau.* http://www.catalinachamber.com.

*Catalina Island Conservancy.* http://www.catalinaconservancy.org.

*Catalina Island Museum.* http://www.catalinamuseum.org.

Pederson, Jeannine L. 2004. *Catalina Island.* Charleston, South Carolina: Arcadia.

Sorensen, AnneLise. 2010. *DK Eyewitness Travel Guide: California.* New York: DK Publishing.

## Cathedral of St. John the Divine

The Cathedral of St. John the Divine, also known as the Cathedral Church of Saint John the Divine, in the City and Diocese of New York, is a Christian church and the official bishop's seat. Generally, stone cathedrals built to castle-like proportions in ornate Gothic style are associated with Europe. However, Old world styles from England, Italy, and France were all the rage in America during the 18th and early 19th centuries. New York City, which saw a massive influx of European immigrants through Ellis Island, is home to many classic cathedrals. The Cathedral of St. John the Divine is among the most famous in the world, both for its architecture and its enormous size.

The construction of New York's famous cathedral began in 1892, and is considered to be "unfinished" to this day. At 121,000 square feet, 601 feet in length, and 232 feet in height (the height of the nave, the longitudinal area of the interior of the main entrance, is 124 feet), the building is immense, considered the fourth largest church in the world. But the cathedral is also known for its venerable age and its exquisite architecture, which incorporates Romanesque and Byzantine features into its primarily Gothic design. A place for worship, baptisms, weddings, concerts, and other events, the popularity of the cathedral and its modestly priced tours bears witness to its historical importance and structural beauty. Visitors are drawn by its age and grandeur, as well as its reputation as a living memorial to the art and architecture of an era long passed.

### Historical Perspectives

The origins of the Cathedral of St. John the Divine wind back nearly two centuries in time. First mentioned in 1928, the building of the great church crystallized into an official project after Bishop Horatio Potter received support from the Diocesan Convention of 1872. Subsequent support from the New York State legislature, which granted a charter in the following year, and mogul J. P. Morgan, who offered his financial support, made the project a reality. Bishop Potter's nephew, Bishop Henry Codman, a man with majestic expectations, would oversee the construction of the cathedral in its first phase. This began in 1888, when Heins and Lafarge won a competition for the contract, and property was acquired at the former site of the Leake and Watts Orphan Asylum. The land included 13 acres. The laying of the cornerstone took place on December 27, 1892, on St. John's Day.

The cathedral has undergone many changes from 1892 to the present. Originally, the plans featured a Romanesque and Byzantine design with a structure 520 in length and a conical spire. But in 1907, responsibilities for building and design were handed over to Ralph Adams Cram. Under Cram, the architectural style changed to Gothic. The cathedral was also lengthened an additional 81 feet.

Among the notable architectural marvels were the seven Chapels of the Tongues, completed in 1918. Each chapel features saints who represent the countries of the earliest major immigrant groups into Ellis

Cathedral of St. John the Divine in New York City. (Wangkun Jia/Dreamstime.com)

Island from seven places around the world: Denmark, Germany, Ireland and Scotland, Africa and Asia, France, Italy, and Spain. A model of the stained glass found in the Communications Bay, featuring a television to pay tribute to media support, went on display in 1921. The full expanse of the cathedral was finally opened on November 30, 1941, in a joyful celebration.

Construction halted for some three decades following the beginning of World War II (1941–1945), but it was still not considered complete, as plans for changes and renovation remained. Construction resumed in the 1970s and continues to the present. Indeed, following a fire in 2001, the Cathedral was closed for repairs until 2008.

## Highlights

The cathedral is most obviously known for the immense size of the building, commonly described as being two football fields long and tall enough to fit one of New York's most iconic structures, the

Statue of Liberty. Among the most notable features of the Cathedral are its central dome, many stained-glass windows, the stonework and carvings, and the Seven Chapels of the Tongues. Fascinating side-lights include the many dedications, such as to Holocaust and AIDS victims, the Peace Fountain, gardens, and organs, including the one known as "The Great Organ." The great west doors, also known as the "The Great Bronze Doors," measure 18 by 12 feet and feature biblical scenes. Peacocks reside on the grounds.

The Cathedral of St. John the Divine is more than a structure. Services were first held in a crypt in 1899. Currently, worshippers congregate in the cathedral proper, where services are held daily. Every fourth Saturday of the month, an AIDS Memorial Service is held. The Cathedral is host to numerous annual seasonal events, for example, for Thanksgiving, Christmas, and New Year. Sundry secular events, such as lectures, classical presentations, and other concerts, are also held.

### For Visitors

The general public may visit during specified days and times and for an admission fee, choosing from three tour options. The Highlight Tour provides an overview of the history and architecture of the cathedral, with stops at its most prominent features, such as its Great Bronze Doors, and an overview of services and programs offered. The Vertical Tour is suitable for the more adventurous and the slightly more athletic. Among the activities included in this tour are a 124-foot climb-up spiral staircases and an in-depth examination of the stained-glass windows. This tour concludes with a stunning view from the roof. Participants must be 12 years or older. The third tour option, the Spotlight Tour, features an array of talks centered on topics pertaining to the Cathedral. Most tours begin at the Cathedral's Visitor Center.

### In Conclusion

In the 21st century, the Cathedral of St. John the Divine stands tall in all its Gothic splendor amidst the numerous modern-day glass and metal structures that surround it. This clash of styles, living proof of the remarkable achievements of our ancestors, adds to the fascination of the cathedral, and keeps alive the narrative of America's boast that it can do anything.

*See also* Ellis Island; New York, New York; Statue of Liberty

### Further Reading

*The Cathedral of St. John the Divine*. http://www.stjohndivine.org/.

Dunlap, David W. 2004. *From Abyssinian to Zion: A guide to Manhattan's Houses of Worship*. New York: Columbia University Press.

Quirk, Howard E. 1993. *The Living Cathedral: St. John the Divine: A History and Guide*. New York: Crossroad.

*The Cathedral of St. John the Divine*. http://www.stjohndivine.org/.

## CBGB

CBGB was a music club located at 315 Bowery in Manhattan, New York. CBGB, which operated between 1973 and 2006, was originally a club showcasing country, bluegrass, and blues music. The subheading beneath the club's sign read OMFUG stood for "Other Music for Uplifting Gormandizers" (gormandiz-ers here was meant to imply people with a ravenous passion for music). As fate would have it, CBGB would become famously known, not for country, blues, or bluegrass, but rather for being the birth site of punk music. For this alone, CBGB had attained iconic status in American music history.

During its heyday, CBGB was one of few places punk enthusiasts could go, where punk and new wave bands like the Ramones, Television, the Patti Smith Group, and Blondie could perform. CBGB was the heart of an underground, transgressive music style that pulsed beneath the wave of mainstream venues where punk could not or would not take part.

### Historical Perspectives

Hilly Kristal founded CBGB in 1973 after a previous business located on the same site, Hilly's on the Bowery, foundered. CBGB did not appear to have the makings of a popular hangout. The building has been labeled "a dump" and "a dive" and has been described as "smelly." The restroom walls were notoriously plastered with graffiti. The building was inconspicuous save for the white façade with red lettering, and situated amid other grungy business establishments. When, on March 31, 1974, Kristal agreed to let a punk band, Television, perform, CBGB was in a financial slump. Though Kristal was no fan, the music—dubbed punk rock—struck a chord that reverberated with punk-enthused fans everywhere and lasted for decades.

CBGB eventually expanded to include a store, CBGB Fashions, and a café, which was later replaced with a second performance venue and an art gallery, CB's 313 Gallery. The Gallery and CBGB Fashions have since closed. The original CBGB closed in 2006 due to financial troubles.

While CBGB was in operation, the club provided the only venue in the city for live punk music. CBGB's unspectacular setting provided an appropriately unpretentious and unsterilized environment in which the rebellious, uninhibited subculture of punk could express itself.

### Cultural Distinctions

At the core of punk culture is a hard-edgedness. This is readily found in the chaotic pulse and frenetic screaming vocals of its music. Punk dancing is equally chaotic and sometimes aggressive, including flailing arms, rigorous jumping, and body slamming. The characteristic look of punk rockers includes ripped jeans, leather, multiple body piercings, tattoos, and unusual hair styles: cropped, spiky, or disarrayed in a motley of dyed colors. In the punk world, attitudes may be confrontational, surly, and irreverent. The music, the dress, and the attitude function as a mask for feelings of alienation, anger, and disregard for authority, social institutions, and social norms.

#### Hard-Drivin' Rock 'n' Roll

Punk or punk rock is a genre that exists on the fringes of traditional mainstream music, characterized by nontraditional melodic rhythms and sounds that are often referred to as edgy, abrasive, and dissonant. A driving beat accompanies vocals that are usually bellowed or screamed during designated sections of the song.

Punk has its beginnings in the cities of Detroit, Michigan, and New York, New York in the mid-1960s. At that time and for the ensuing decades, punk was largely an underground movement, attracting a highly unique subculture of people, whose attire, accessories, and makeup reflected the edginess of the music. Fans were attracted to the innovative techniques and uninhibited expressions of anger and discontent.

MC5 and the Stooges were among the punk-rock pioneers in Detroit. The Velvet Underground debuted in New York. In the 1970s, the movement established itself in well-known clubs, such as New York's CBGB and Max's Kansas City. The clubs nurtured a culture in which participants engaged in wild dancing styles. The music eventually began to spread internationally. The British are noted for starting hardcore punk and influencing the emergence of the new subgenre in America, performed by bands with colorful names such as The Misfits, Bad Brains, and the Dead Kennedys.

The 1980s and early 1990s saw the decline of punk music in America. New musical forms such as alternative and grunge replaced punk in popularity. Like punk, such genres were liked for their distinct and nontraditional sounds, though unlike punk, alternative and grunge tended to follow conventional melodic traditions.

### Images in Popular Culture

CBGB has appeared in the game *Guitar Hero: Warriors of Rock,* in the television series *The Simpsons* (1989–), and the Spike Lee movie *Summer of Sam* (1999). References to the club have appeared in the film *Staying Alive* (1983) and the Broadway musical *Rent*. In 2009, *Burning Down the House: The Story of CBGB* (2009), a documentary directed by Mandy Stein, premiered at the prestigious Tribeca Film Festival.

### In Conclusion

CBGB influenced not only punk rockers; the club made the leap into mainstream society and the world as a symbol of rebellious youth and edgy music. From obscurity, CBGB rose to take its place as a world-famous venue, an emblem for a radical music genre, and example of America's diverse cultural landscape.

***See also*** New York, New York

### Further Reading

Cogan, Brian. 2006. *Encyclopedia of Punk Music and Culture*. Westport, Connecticut: Greenwood Press.

Kristal, Hilly. 2005. *CBGB & OMFUG: Thirty Years from the Home of Underground Rock*. New York: Harry N. Abrams.

Salyers, Christopher D. 2006. *CBGB: Decades of Graffiti*. New York: Mark Batty Publishers.

## Central Park

Central Park is the first urban park built in America. Established in 1857 in the heart of Manhattan as New York City began its climb to becoming one of the foremost cities in America, Central Park remains legendary to this day. Each year, the Park hosts 25 million visitors, making it one of the most visited parks in the nation. Covering 843 acres, the park offers numerous things to do and see: lush green spaces, lakes and ponds, places for skateboarding, walking, jogging, and playing chess, monuments, playgrounds, and more. In 1963, it was designated a National Historic Landmark, and since 1980, it has flourished under the management of the Central Park Conservancy with additional support from the City, the New York City Department of Parks & Recreation, the New York City Police Department, and New York City Parks Enforcement Patrol. Central Park is a major tourist destination, but it is also, for many residents of New York City, an essential part of home, a familiar place to get away from it all. For children, it's a magical place filled with endless wonders.

### Historical Perspectives

New York City was still in its infancy when New Yorkers put out the call for a park. The Statue of Liberty did not yet majestically stand over New York Harbor; the Brooklyn Bridge had not yet joined Manhattan and Brooklyn. Residents such as poet William Cullen Bryant and landscape architect Andrew Jackson Downing made their desire known in 1844. Wealthy families, particularly those familiar with the famous green spaces of European cities, added their voices to the growing list of residents who believed the city needed a respite from increasing urbanization; some tranquil space for walking and spending time with family and friends or in solitude. Finally, in 1853, the New York legislature purchased 700 acres of land where the park (with an additional 143 acreage added) still lies to this day.

The construction of Central Park was an enormous project. Fortunately, the responsibility for the project was placed in exceptional hands. Key players included designers Frederick Law Olmsted and Calvert Vaux, architect Jacob Wrey Mould, master gardener Ignaz Anton Pilat, and engineer George Waring. For starters, the 1,600 residents of the area had to be moved. The ground itself required vigorous work, as nearly everything, including topsoil, trees, shrubs, and plants had to be transplanted from elsewhere, and the lakes and ponds had to be artificially created. The original park took 16 years to complete, plus an additional 3 years to complete the wall that surrounds it.

In its early years, the park greatly contributed to the development of New York City, drawing individuals and families to establish homes nearby, indirectly helping to attract businesses, which like the legendary Bloomingdale's, built nearby. For a period, Central Park lived up to its name, becoming central to the daily lives of New York society.

The Park's boom did not last. In the 20th century, Central Park experienced alternating periods of growth, decline, disuse, and crime until, in 1980, the City committed itself to ensuring the long-lasting success of the park.

### Maintenance

The Central Park Conservancy plays an instrumental role in maintaining the park. It also provides 90 percent of the park staff. Crews care for 250 acres, including the lawns, trees, lakes, flowers, benches, playgrounds, bridges, sculptures, and monuments. The City provides much of the financial support needed to maintain the park and its drives. The New York City Department of Parks & Recreation oversees user permits and events for the Park. The New York City Central Park Police Precinct and the New York City Parks Enforcement Patrol share the responsibility for patrolling the Park and ensuring safety.

### Images in Popular Culture

According to some accounts, Central Park has appeared in some 300 films, though others set the number at about 200. Either way, no other park in the nation appears in as many films as Central Park. The first film to feature Central Park, *Romeo and Juliet*, released in 1908. It was followed over the decades by movies such as *Taxi Driver* (1976), *Hair* (1980), *The Muppets Take Manhattan* (1984), *Wall Street* (1987), *When Harry Met Sally* (1989), *A Troll in Central Park* (1994), *Independence Day* (1996), *Serendipity* (2001), and *Enchanted* (2007).

### For Visitors

With six visitor centers and multiple guided tours, tourists have no problem navigating through the enormous park. The various sections of the park are known by different names: Central Park North, Central Park South, and Central Park West. The eastern side of the park is known by its street name, Fifth Avenue. For the intrepid adventurer, fun and sport can be found at every corner, aimed at both adults and children. Seasonal activities include swimming and ice-skating, volley ball, and rock climbing. Playgrounds, carousels, monuments,

#### Carousel Nostalgia

The carousel, or merry-go-round as it is often called in America, enjoyed its heyday during the early 20th century. Carousels have an ancient history; their direct modern decedents were created in Europe during the 17th century. In America, however, carousels developed into unique works of art. This exciting change actually increased their popularity around the world.

The first carousel to be built in America was in Hessville, Ohio, during the 1840s. The East Coast's most popular amusement park, Coney Island, constructed its first carousel in 1876. Since 1871, New York's Central Park has had four carousels. The current carousel, which was restored in the 1990s, features 57 colorful horses.

By the late 20th century, the popularity of carousels had dwindled. In the 21st century, America has only about 100 carousels; few survived the golden era. Modern carousels are made out of fiberglass rather than wood, reflecting little of the skilled artistic flair of true craftsmen. Still, carousels are treasured as nostalgic symbols of childhood and an older, simpler time.

and walking tracks are available most of the year. Among the popular places to visit are the Central Park Zoo, the Central Park Conservatory Garden, and a wildlife sanctuary. In summer, theatergoers and music lovers flock to Shakespeare in the park and concerts by the New York Philharmonic, the Metropolitan Opera, and many popular performers.

*See also* Bloomingdale's; Brooklyn Bridge; Fifth Avenue; New York, New York; Statue of Liberty

### Further Reading

Alvarez, Regina, Blonsky, Douglas, Horenstein, Sidney, and Rogers, Elizabeth Barlow. 2011. *The Ramble in Central Park: A Wilderness West of Fifth*. New York: Abberville Press.

Brawarsky, Sandee. 2002. *212 Views of Central Park: Experiencing New York City's Jewel from Every Angle*. New York, Stewart, Tabori & Chang.

*Central Park*. http://www.centralparknyc.org/.

Miller, Sara Cedar. 2003. *Central Park, An American Masterpiece: A Comprehensive History of the Nation's First Urban Park*. New York: Abrams with the Central Park Conservancy.

Miller, Sara Cedar. 2009. *Seeing Central Park: The Official Guide to the World's Greatest Urban Park*. New York: Abrams with the Central Park Conservancy.

Rosenzweig, Roy, and Blackmar, Elizabeth. 1994. *The Park and the People: A History of Central Park*. New York: H. Holt and Co.

## Cherokee Nation

The Cherokee Nation is one of three federally recognized Cherokee tribes. It also refers to the area in which many tribal members and the Cherokee government reside. Covering 66,000 acres in the northeastern part of the state of Oklahoma, the Cherokee Nation is the largest of the three recognized Cherokee tribes, and the second-largest Native American tribe in the United States. The Cherokee Nation is not a reservation. The Cherokee Nation enjoys self-governance and economic and cultural prosperity, successfully blending traditional culture and modern life. Into the 21st century, the Cherokee Nation is a place of beauty and vigor with many cultural, natural, and artistic attractions.

### Historical Perspectives

The Cherokee Nation traces its origins to the people who inhabited North America before the arrival of Europeans in the 15th and 16th centuries. Some scholars contend that the Cherokee, an Iroquoian-speaking people, may have migrated from the Great Lakes region before settling, during prehistoric times, in present-day Georgia, the Carolinas, and East Texas. Before contacting with Europeans, the Cherokee lived off the land, cultivating the food they needed for survival and practicing distinct forms of religion, dress, art, music, and dance.

But the Cherokee way of life changed drastically following the arrival and influence of Europeans (first contact occurred in the 16th century), culminating in the notorious period of forced migration as the Trail of Tears. Between 1838 and 1839, some 15,000 Cherokees were relocated into present-day Oklahoma, then known as "Indian Territory." As many as 4,000 died along the way.

Neither of the groups that later became known as the Eastern Band of Cherokee Indians and the United Keetoowah Band of Cherokee Indians took part in the Trail of Tears. Today, the Eastern Band of Cherokee Indians resides largely in North Carolina. The United Keetoowah Band, which voluntarily settled in Oklahoma before the Trail of Tears, has often clashed with the Cherokee Nation, which consists of the descendants of those Cherokee who were forcibly resettled.

**Cultural Distinctions**

Cultural differences, as well as rules by which the tribes are governed, distinguish the Cherokee Nation from the other Cherokee tribes. For example, admission into the Cherokee Nation is based on genealogy, which must be traced back to the list of names recorded by the Dawes Commission (created to dissolve the reservation system in favor of allotments) in the 1890s.

The Cherokee Nation's historical development also distinguishes it from other tribes and cultures in America. Within the land they were allotted in Oklahoma; a distinct economy, culture, and government were formed, starting with the adoption of a constitution in 1839. The Golden Age of the Cherokee Nation, between the 1840s and 1860s, saw the region experience notable economic growth. The first newspaper in the territory, *The Cherokee Messenger,* featuring English and Cherokee syllabaries, was established by a Cherokee man named Sequoyah in 1821. Town life buzzed around Tahlequah, which would become the capital of the Cherokee Nation. Businesses and schools were built, including two prestigious institutions, the Male and Female Seminaries.

**The Great Tragedy of the Trail of Tears**

For generations, the Cherokee inhabited lands in Georgia, Tennessee, Alabama, North Carolina, and Florida. However, American settlers eventually voiced their desire to claim these lands. In wholehearted support of the settlers' wishes, President Andrew Jackson advocated for and received authority for the removal when he signed the Indian Removal Act in 1830. Jackson set out to remove Native Americans from their coveted homelands in land designated as "Indian Territory" in present-day Oklahoma. He implemented the removal of the Native Americans by means of treaty and military force.

In 1838, the forced removal of the Cherokee occurred, despite the fact that the majority of the people objected to giving up their lands and protested what they perceived to be an unlawful treaty (the Treaty of Echota).

Over 20,000 Cherokee made the journey. It is estimated that over 4,000 died on the more than 1,000-mile trek. The loss of life as well as the cruel treatment to which the Cherokee were subjected to is an atrocity that will not be forgotten.

**Contemporary Perspectives**

Into the 21st century, the Cherokee Nation has experienced growth and development by blending old ways with new. Led by a tripartite government that includes a principal chief (executive power), tribal council (legislative power), and the Cherokee Nation Judicial Appeals Tribunal (judicial power), the Cherokee Nation enjoys great self-determination and sovereignty after centuries of dominance by the U.S. government. The tribe's prosperity is conspicuous. The number of buildings, hospitals, and venues for traditional and cultural events continues to increase. The place names, often in the Cherokee language, and traditional architecture of some of the buildings, reflect the undimmed Cherokee pride.

Those who reside within the area known as the Cherokee Nation, more than 70,000 of the 300,000 total number of Cherokee Nation citizens, reflect the tribes' successful blending of two worlds. Some residents embrace Christian religions; others follow traditional Cherokee belief systems. Traditional medicine men and women, though fewer in number, continue to play an important role in the mental, physical, and emotional health of many tribal members. Cultural festivals, dance, music, and artwork continue to be practiced and taught.

**Controversy**

In 2011, it was announced that the Cherokee Freedmen were being expelled from Cherokee Nation membership. The Cherokee Freedmen were descendents of African Americans who, before the Civil War

(1861–1864), had been slaves belonging to individual Cherokees, and had joined the Cherokee Nation upon gaining their freedom. This move by the Supreme Court of the Cherokee Nation upheld a 2007 vote to the same effect. The vote also expelled non–Native Americans.

This decision was immediately protested by individuals in the African American community as well as by the descendents of the Freedmen. Some Federal lawmakers believe this act is a civil rights violation. The Cherokee Nation, however, defended their decision as part of their right for self-determination and self-government.

**A Trailblazing Chief**

In 1985, Wilma Mankiller became the first woman to serve as the principal chief of the Cherokee Nation. Born in Tahlequah, Oklahoma, the capital of the Cherokee Nation, on November 18, 1945, Wilma Pearl Mankiller was raised in Mankiller Flats before moving to San Francisco, California, in the 1950s. Mankiller attended Skyline College and San Francisco State University. She earned a bachelor's degree in social sciences at Flaming Rainbow University in Oklahoma and took graduate courses at the University of Arkansas.

Inspired by demonstrations of Native American pride and resistance such as the protest staged on Alcatraz Island, Mankiller felt a strong desire to give back to her Native American community. Thus, in the 1970s, she returned to the Cherokee Nation. Initially, she worked for the tribal government as a planner and program developer. In 1983, she became the deputy chief of the Cherokee Nation. In 1985, she was named the tribe's principal chief, becoming the first woman to hold this position. After serving two terms, she resumed her work in activism, supporting causes such as health care and education.

During her lifetime, Mankiller lectured and penned such books as her autobiography, *Mankiller: A Chief and Her People* (1993) and *Every Day Is a Good Day: Reflections by Contemporary Indigenous Women* (2004). Mankiller died on April 6, 2010.

### Native Americans and Images in Popular Culture

Native Americans have had a problematic history in the American popular imagination, a fact that has severely affected how Native American tribes, such as the Cherokee Nation, are perceived. For many centuries, Native American cultures suffered extermination, oppression, discrimination, forced acculturation, and other atrocities. Negative or stereotypical images in American popular culture only underscore their precarious position in society.

Examples of this simplistic and demeaning portrayal abound in popular amusements, television shows, films, and sports. During the 19th and 20th centuries, Native Americans were either vilified or romanticized. Though Native Americans were often part of the Buffalo Bill's Wild West shows and other traveling acts and exhibits, they were either positioned as villains or were romanticized and exploited as the "noble savage." The so-called noble savage concept was credited to Jean-Jacques Rousseau in the 18th century.

Native Americans were often put on display as a form of entertainment at these Wild West shows. Yet they often either did not wear traditional clothing or wore clothing that did not denote their proper status and tribal affiliation. For example, the ubiquitous feathered "Chief headdress" worn by many Native Americans in the rodeo shows was in fact reproduced from the full eagle-feather war bonnet worn by the Lakota Sioux.

Museum collections of artifacts from Native American life and culture have also been a point of contention. Many decry the fact that museums have obtained and put on display artifacts belonging to the tribes (not to the museums) and feel that the exhibition of these artifacts treats both the everyday and the sacred items as mere historical or exotic objects.

In early films, America reflected its racial superiority and racist views in numerous black and white cowboy and Indian films. Reel after reel exist in which the struggle between perceived good (the white man) and bad (the Indian) culminate in inevitable victory for white America. All too often white actors in body paint portrayed Native Americans in films. For many generations, American children played out this disconcerting role in their everyday play.

Some critics assert that modern-day films depicting Native Americans are little improved. When Native Americans appear in films, they are usually depicted in romanticized historical ways, such as in *Dances with Wolves* (1990) and *Last of the Mohicans* (1992). Though these films have been widely praised, critics argue that the films continue to project Native Americans as subordinate to white men and restrict them to the nostalgia of early American history.

Evidence of ongoing controversial depictions of Native Americans can also be found in America's popular professional sports world. To this day, the Washington Redskins, a member of the National Football League since 1932, visibly display markers perceived as offensive by some Native American activists. The name "redskins," it is argued, has always been a disparaging term used to identify Native Americans. While some Native Americans could care less, activists find this, as well as logos and myriad appearances featuring the team's Native American mascot, equally offensive.

Progressive depictions of Native Americans, nevertheless, are evident. Wes Studi, a Cherokee born near Tahlequah, is one of the most prominent Native American actors in the American film industry. He played major roles in both films mentioned previously; but he has also transitioned to roles that do not limit him to playing Native Americans in historical times. In another step toward progress, independent films like *Smoke Signals* (1998) and the rare mainstream film *Thunder heart* (1992) have provided alternative and non glorified treatments of Native American life and culture in contemporary times.

### For Visitors

These days the Cherokee Nation offers modern images that resist and challenge old stereotypes and racist beliefs. A healthy and vital community, the Cherokee Nation offers many must-see sites and activities to residents and the general visiting public. The Cherokee Byways features 80 miles of sweeping natural beauty and attractions. At the Cherokee Heritage Center, visitors may tour outdoor museums and indoor exhibits and participate in educational programs. The Center also features a Trail of Tears Exhibit, while the Ancient Village and Outdoor Museum feature reproductions of traditional homes. Other popular stops are the Cherokee Casino in West Siloam Springs and the many bed and breakfasts and resorts to be found in the area. The Cherokee National Holiday occurs over Labor Day weekend and there is an annual film festival.

### In Conclusion

The Cherokee Nation has attained a safe and prosperous homeland despite great tragedies. Out of calamity, the tribe has forged triumph, while affirming their political independence and cultural heritage.

***See also*** Great Lakes; Texas

### Further Reading

Basel, Roberta. 2007. *Sequoyah: Inventor of Written Cherokee*. Minneapolis: Compass Point Books.

Birchfield, D.L. 2012. *Cherokee History and Culture*. New York: Gareth Stevens Publishing.

Ellingson, Terry. 2001. *The Myth of the Noble Savage*. Berkeley: University of California Press.

Mankiller, Wilma Pearl, and Wallis, Michael. 1993. *Mankiller: A Chief and Her People*. New York: St. Martin's Press.

Perdue, Theda, and Green, Michael D. 2007. *The Cherokee Nation and the Trail of Tears*. New York: Viking.

# Chicago, Illinois

Chicago is a major metropolis in the state of Illinois and the third largest city in the nation. Following the city's incorporation in 1837, Chicago grew rapidly, quickly becoming a symbol of American urbanization and progress. Today it is famous for its world-renowned buildings, legendary institutions, and influential residents. The city has had its share of troubles and tragedies, however, which have often made world news and contributed to the city's notoriety.

As other American cities compete for top spot in the nation, Chicago, with its population of 10 million, maintains its role as a major seat of history, culture, and industry. It's a place both historic and modern, showcasing classical architecture, magnificent skyscrapers, and an array of legendary streets and neighborhoods. Visitors flock to the city to pay homage to the Sears Tower, the Magnificent Mile, and the famous deep-dish pizza.

### Historical Perspectives

Native American tribes, like the Potawatomi, were the original inhabitants of the area, which they named *Checaugou,* meaning "wild onion" or "skunk cabbage." The name was gradually Americanized into *Chicago.* The first known Europeans associated with the area were Jacques Marquette, a French missionary, and Louis Jolliet, a French-Canadian explorer, who arrived in 1673. In 1779, Jean Baptiste Point du Sable, an African American trader, established the first permanent settlement. A treaty in 1795 gave the newly minted America a foothold in the region. But due to ongoing conflicts over the land, Chicago was not yet ripe for development. In 1833, the Native American tribes were removed from the area and relocated to reservations. In that same year, Chicago became a town, and by 1837 the town grew into a city.

Chicago officially became a city when its population eclipsed the 4,000 mark, after which its development was swift but not trouble free. In 1871, Chicago experienced a devastating event, the Great Chicago Fire, which is still talked about to this day. The fire started—no one knows how—in a shed and lasted 36 hours between October 8 and 10, resulting in the deaths of 300 people and the displacement of 100,000 or more residents.

Chicago inevitably rebounded and continued its remarkable growth. The Home Insurance Building, a nine-story structure designed by local architect William Le Baron Jenney and built in 1884, is known as the nation's first skyscraper. The acclaimed World's Columbian Exposition, also known as the World's Fair, took place in Chicago in 1893.

#### The Fire of the Century

Many cities and towns in the nation have been consumed by fire, but the fire that devastated Chicago, Illinois, in the summer of 1871 stands out as one of the most devastating fires in the nation's history.

Before the fire, Chicago was a bustling metropolis and one of the fastest growing cities in the nation. Though some buildings had been "fireproofed," 19th-century Chicago, as with any city in the nation, was ill-equipped to handle most fires. The fast moving and destructive blaze was helped by the fact that Chicago had been experiencing a particularly dry summer. The abundance of wooden structures in the city was another problem, as was the wind, which helped to feed the scorching flames.

No one knows exactly how the fire started on the evening of October 8. According to a legend that was turned into a song. Mrs. O'Leary lit a lantern in a shed that the family cow kicked over. Indeed, the fire did start in the vicinity of the barn owned by Patrick and Catherine O'Leary, but no one knows for sure whether the O'Leary's cow was actually to blame. The fire burned for two days before rain arrived and help the firefighters extinguish the flames. The fire devastated an area that was four miles long and one mile wide. Some 300 people were killed and thousands were left homeless. In total, more than 17,000 buildings were destroyed.

After the fire, Chicago worked quickly to rebuild in the process that came to be known as the "Great Rebuilding."

### Growth and Challenges

The rapid physical and cultural development of the region over the course of two centuries was made possible by the waves of immigrants sweeping across the nation. Many of the workers who helped construct Chicago's buildings, labored on the railroad and the Union Stock Yards and the meat, grain, and manufacturing industries established ethnic enclaves within the city. In the 1800s, immigrants from Ireland, Italy, Greece, Sweden, and Poland poured into the city. Later, throughout the 1900s, people arrived from Ukraine. Many Chinese also settled in the region, establishing businesses such as laundries and restaurants. African Americans from the South migrated to Chicago in distinct waves during the 1850s, the 1900s, and the 1940/1950s. Other groups, such as Hispanic Americans and Asians, also played an influential role in the city.

For a substantial part of Chicago's early existence, the very aspects that the city is celebrated for today—growth and diversity—were a source of contention and strife. Racial hostility among ethnic groups and aimed at ethnic groups by the dominant white culture produced daily tensions, scuffles, and riots. Rampant poverty and discrimination, particularly among immigrant groups, was a problem, and rights for workers and safe working conditions did not always grow concurrently with Chicago's rapid industrial development.

These issues prompted strikes and social reform. Hull House was created to help transition immigrants adjust to their new lives in America. This important institution was founded by Jane Addams and Ellen Gates Star in 1889. In the early 20th century, desperately needed meat-packing laws as well as the Food and Drug Administration were established as a result of Upton Sinclair's *The Jungle* (1906), a novel that exposed the deeply troublous life of immigrants and the heinous and unsanitary working conditions in Chicago. In the 1920s, during the prohibition years, the city saw the rise of infamous gangsters like Al Capone and criminals like John Dillinger.

Though black Chicagoans experienced a literary and cultural renaissance similar to the one in Harlem, New York, and the music (blues and jazz imported from the South), food, church, and community brought vigor to black life in the city, racism and poverty hit African Americans particularly hard. Riots in the 1940s underscored racial tensions. In the 1960s, civil rights leaders like Dr. Martin Luther King Jr. investigated conditions there and were astonished. Activist Jesse Jackson established special programs, such as Operation Breadbasket, to help alleviate some of the problems facing impoverished urban blacks. Though Chicago did not have the segregation and outright discriminatory laws found in the South, blacks still had to contend with racism and social, economic, and political oppression. Housing projects like Cabrini-Green, which was synonymous with crime, poverty, and hopelessness, became a symbol of urban blight.

### Contemporary Perspectives

Amid the problems and challenges of American city life, Chicago has found ways to address many of its problems and continue on its course toward advancement in the 21st century. Immigrant communities and African Americans have experienced incremental progress, and Chicago continues to be one of the most desirable places to live in the nation.

After a career that lasted from 1955 to 1976, Mayor Richard J. Daley has been followed by a series of notable successors, including Jane Byrne, the city's first female mayor, and Harold Washington, the city's first African American mayor. Chicago is proud to have been the starting point for the luminous careers of Oprah Winfrey, an African American woman, who rose to become one of the most influential people in the nation, and Barack Obama, the first African American president. After Obama became president, his long-time barber, Zariff, co-owner and barber of the Hyde Park Hair Salon in Chicago, continued to cut his hair. In the wake of the election win, Zariff, the salon, as well as the chair in which Obama sat became a local attraction. In 2010, Chicago-native Rahm Emanuel resigned as White House Chief of Staff to return to his native Chicago to run successfully for mayor.

> **Media Mogul**
>
> Oprah Winfrey is one of the most influential television personalities in the nation. Born in a small town Kosciusko, Mississippi, on January 29, 1954, Oprah Winfrey defied many odds to become a television and entertainment industry icon. In 1976 she became the host of the show *People Are Talking* in Baltimore, Maryland. This was a groundbreaking achievement, as she was one of only a handful of African American women given such a high-profile position in the television industry. Eight years later, she was offered a position as a host of the *A.M. Chicago* show and in 1986, Winfrey launched her national talk show in Chicago, which had a spectacular 25-year run and served as the platform that catapulted Winfrey to massive fame. Her show is credited with revolutionizing the talk show format and popularizing frank talk about personal topics and experiences.
>
> Winfrey became famous for her generosity, tirelessly engaging in philanthropic works. Loved and adored by her legion of fans, Winfrey has long held formidable powers of persuasion and influence. Guests marketing new products, books, or specialized knowledge were sure to profit from her association and endorsement. Winfrey's far-reaching success extended to her magazine, *O: The Oprah Magazine*, which debuted in 2000. In 2007, she opened the Oprah Winfrey Leadership Academy for Girls in South Africa. Since 2013, Winfrey has established her own television network, the Oprah Winfrey Network, also known by its acronym, OWN.

### Highlights

Chicago exudes efficiency as it maintains a world-renowned transportation system to accommodate its large population of residents and hoards of visitors. The city manages two busy airports: Midway and O'Hare. Midway was once the world's busiest airport. Today, O'Hare is the busier, ranking among the busiest airports in the nation. Buses, the L train (the local elevated subway system), and taxis run 24 hours, 7 days a week.

Chicago's downtown center is extensive, its towering skyscrapers contributing to its famous skyline. Among the notable attractions are the Museum of Science and Industry, the John G. Shedd Aquarium, the Willis Tower, the Magnificent Mile, the Navy Pier, the Millennium Park, the Adler Planetarium and Astronomy Museum, the Chicago Cultural Center, and the DuSable Museum of African American History. The Willis Tower, one of the world's tallest buildings, soars 1,454 feet into the sky. The Magnificent Mile features exclusive shops, such as those located in the eight-story Water Tower Place and Chicago Place, as well as the popular Hershey's Chicago. Hershey's Chicago is the largest of three Hershey's buildings, the other two being Hershey's Time Square in New York and the Hershey's Chocolate World in Pennsylvania.

Exquisite architecture proliferates in the city; famous architectural styles such as Gothic Revival, Richardsonian Romanesque, Queen Anne, the Chicago School, famed architect Frank Lloyd Wright's Prairie School, International Style, and Post-Modern abound. Chicago's newest addition, a giant sculpture of Marilyn Monroe in ethereal pastels, stands 26 feet tall in Pioneer Court on the Magnificent Mile (it will eventually be moved). The sculpture, created by Seward Johnson, was erected in the summer of 2011 and shows Monroe in one of her most famous poses, smiling as she holds down her billowing dress.

Chicago also has high-profile teams in the four major American sports. The city boasts two Major League Baseball teams: the Chicago Cubs, who play at Wrigley Field; and the Chicago White Sox, who play at U.S. Cellular Field. The Chicago Bears, a team in the National Football League, have won nine league championships and one Super Bowl to date. The Chicago Bulls of the National Basketball Association reigned supreme during Michael Jordan's spectacular basketball career in the 1980s and 1990s, winning six championships. The Chicago Blackhawks of the National Hockey League have won four Stanley Cups.

Chicago boasts many other iconic landmarks. Notable colleges and universities include the University of Chicago and Loyola University. The expansive Lake Michigan attracts summer visitors who sunbath along its beaches, and swim and boat in its waters. Due to a local law, Chicago's lakefront is free of development, so views of the lake remain unobstructed and accessible to runners, walkers, and skaters. Chicago also features several parks, theaters, bars and nightclubs, and diverse restaurants.

To this day, certain streets, sections, and neighborhoods in Chicago maintain a distinct identity. Ethnic festivals and restaurants serve Greek falafel, African American soul food, and Italian pasta dishes. Other famed Chicago culinary foods include hotdogs and deep-dish pizzas.

### The Bean

*The Bean*, formally known as the *Cloud Gate*, is a sculpture in Millennium Park in Chicago, Illinois. The surface of the sculpture is meant to look like liquid mercury but it is shaped like a kidney bean, hence its most popular name. Since it opened in 2004, the sculpture has rivaled Chicago landmarks such as the Navy Pier and Sears (Willis) Tower in terms of popularity. The Bean was built as part of an ongoing reclamation project that began in the late 1990s called Millennium Park that turned a dreary landscape comprising parking lots and railroad tracks into an award-winning green space situated between the downtown area and Lake Michigan.

Designed by artist Anish Kapoor, the Bean is more than 60 feet high. Its shiny surface is made of stainless steel that reflects the skyline. Visitors like to touch and take pictures of the sculpture. In the film *Source Code* (2011), the Bean makes a major appearance and functions as an important symbol in the futuristic movie.

### Images in Popular Culture

Chicago's colorful history is reflected in the teeming number of books, films, and television programs set in Chicago or based on legendary Chicago figures. Sinclair's *The Jungle,* set in Chicago, garnered international attention. Other influential books followed, such as Richard Wright's *Native Son* (1940) and Chicago-native Sandra Cisneros's *The House on Mango Street* (1984). Both novels narrated stories from the perspective of marginalized groups, African Americans and Latino Americans, respectively.

Chicago's most famous gangster, Al Capone, was a popular subject for many films, including *The Untouchables* (1987). Gangsters and hoodlumism featured as the central subject in countless movies, leading to the creation of a new genre, the gangster films, such as *Road to Perdition* (2002) and *Public Enemies* (2009). Black life in Chicago is explored in films such as *Soul Food* (1997) and *Barbershop* (2002). Romantic comedies that serve up Chicago views and themes on urban living and love are *My Best Friend's Wedding* (1997) and *The Break-Up* (2006). Other popular films include *The Blues Brothers* (1980) and *The Dark Knight* (2008).

Among the most famous television shows in American history, *The Oprah Winfrey Show* reigned supreme for 25 years, between 1986 and 2011, having an enormous impact on American society and the world. Popular plays such as *A Raisin in the Sun* and *Chicago,* the latter adapted as both a musical and an award-winning film (2002), appear to this day in theaters across the nation.

***See also*** Barbershops; Cabrini-Green Housing Project; Harlem; Hull House; Navy Pier; Sears Tower; Super Bowl; World's Fair; Wrigley Field

### Further Reading

Baldwin, Davarian L. 2007. *Chicago's New Negroes: Modernity, the Great Migration, and Black Urban Life*. Chapel Hill: University of North Carolina Press.

Gilfoyle, Timothy. 2006. *Millennium Park: Creating a Chicago Landmark*. Chicago: University of Chicago Press.

Holli, Melvin G., and Jones, Peter d' Alroy, eds. 1994. *Ethnic Chicago: A Multicultural Portrait*. Grand Rapids, Michigan: W.B. Eerdmans Publishing Company.

Keating, Ann Durkin. 2008. *Chicago Neighborhoods and Suburbs: A Historical Guide*. Chicago: University of Chicago Press.

Miller, Donald L. 1996. *City of the Century: The Epic of Chicago and the Making of America*. New York: Simon & Schuster.

Pacyga, Dominic A. 2009. *Chicago: A Biography*. Chicago: University of Chicago Press.

Swanson, Stevenson, ed. 1997. *Chicago Days: 150 Defining Moments in the Life of a Great City*. Chicago: Cantigny First Division Foundation.

## Chinatown

Chinatown is an ethnic enclave found in cities throughout the nation. The first Chinatown was founded in San Francisco, California, in 1850. Since then, Chinatowns have been an inseparable part of American society wherever Chinese immigrants have settled—in small towns, as well as in large metropolises like Chicago and New York City. Other notable Chinatowns are located in Honolulu, Hawaii; Las Vegas, Nevada; and Los Angeles, California.

Originally, Chinatowns were primarily made up of living places, since many Chinese were excluded from mainstream American life. In addition, Chinese communities provided security, familiarity, and support in an uncertain and hostile world, particularly during the 19th and a large portion of the 20th centuries. Over the years, Chinatowns have developed into tourist attractions; exotic places to go for non-Chinese to find trinkets, see Chinese architecture, and sample foods not found in mainstream America. But for Chinese Americans, especially those directly connected through family history, Chinatown provides a deeply meaningful connection, a shared memory, and an expression of the traditional way of life.

### Historical Perspectives: San Francisco and Los Angeles

Though the term "Chinatown" is used to describe enclaves of predominately Chinese ancestry, Chinatowns vary throughout the nation in sundry ways. Some are large, some are small. Some are impoverished or overcrowded slums; others are modern-looking and, therefore, more inviting. New Chinatowns emerge all the time, but it is the older Chinatowns and their interesting histories that attract inquisitive visitors. The history of Chinese Americans is entangled in tragedy, racism, and transcendence, and that is the true foundation of today's Chinatowns.

The Chinese migration to North America began with the gold rush in the West that began in 1848. The majority of Chinese arrived from Guangdong, lured by the discovery of gold. But their departure was also spurred by war, drought, and famine in their homeland. The Chinese called the Gold Rush *gum saan* or "gold mountain," and they called San Francisco *dai faw,* meaning big port.

The first Chinatown was founded in 1850. Two decades later, the Chinese population in America surged to 63,000. Even more Chinese arrived to help build the railroads. But the Chinese in America experienced racism and discrimination in California and other states to which they migrated. Laws were passed to forbid Chinese from owning property, voting, and participating in other freedoms enjoyed by mainstream white America. The Chinese were also subjected to verbal and physical hostility. Between 1882 and 1943, the Chinese Exclusion Act banned further migration of Chinese.

Oddly enough, racism played a role in the rebuilding of the San Francisco Chinatown and the construction of two Chinatowns in Los Angeles. Before the devastating earthquake hit in 1906, the San Francisco Chinatown wrestled with negative imagery. Perceived largely as an uninviting place, particularly owing to the depraved places, such as opium dens and prostitution houses, leaders in the community

View of the gates of Chinatown in Los Angeles, California, in June 2011. Chinatown in L.A. was established in the 19th century as a residential area of the city for Chinese immigrants who were imported as labor for building the railroads. (Gerry Boughan/Dreamstime.com)

decided to pay white architects to create a tourist-friendly Chinatown, complete with architecture based on the pagoda style. The architecture was based on a stereotypical look to project a positive, cheery, and more acceptable image to outsiders.

Between the 1920s and 1950s, Hollywood went to several Chinatowns in Los Angeles to film movies or to hire Chinese for movie roles and as extras. After the so-called Old Chinatown in Los Angeles was demolished in 1933, two more Chinatowns, China City and New Chinatown, took its place. Founded in 1938, these Chinatowns continue to be operated, largely for the enjoyment of Hollywood community and tourists. China City went to extremes by featuring rides and Chinese residents, children included, in traditional dress to heighten the effect of being in another world. In such spaces, China was commodified and marketed to visitors hungry to be a part of an unusual and excitingly different locale.

### Contemporary Perspectives

These days, tourism, to one extent or another, is an accepted part of most Chinatowns. For example, San Francisco's Chinatown is considered as popular as attractions like the Golden Gate Bridge and

Alcatraz. The Chinatown in Honolulu has experienced a renaissance, using community support to renovate dilapidated buildings and structures. Trinkets, T-shirts, and Chinese paraphernalia can be found at most enclaves. Visitors may be unaware of the schools, libraries, and offices that surround them, but in fact they are walking through a complex and a distinctly Chinese American culture that is expressed freely within the boundaries of Chinatown.

### Cultural Distinctions

The culture within American Chinatowns varies greatly by region, by city, and even by neighborhood. Most places are a blend of American and Chinese influences. At the heart of many Chinatowns are associations and organizations to aid the elderly and the continuing influx of Asian immigrants and schools that teach the Chinese language and writing to children. In some enclaves, Chinese, mostly Cantonese or Mandarin, is primarily spoken. At other enclaves, English is the primary language or both Chinese and English are spoken. The culture of Chinatowns is sustained by the bustling activity that centers on businesses, street vendors, produce markets, as well as schools and theaters. Special events, such as Chinese New Year, draw enormous crowds.

Although generations of Chinese have moved out of Chinatowns, these enclaves often remain an essential part of their daily lives and cultural traditions. To tourists, visiting Chinatown can be like visiting a foreign country. But for Chinese Americans, Chinatown is community, home, or an extension of home. Chinatown is where they find goods and produce imported from China and Hong Kong that are not sold elsewhere. Traditional foods are sold in Chinese-centered grocery stores and restaurants. Chinatown is where the elderly—silently and gracefully—can go through the motions of tai chi, a centuries-old form of exercise, and where youths gather around a bowl of noodles in a noodle shop. Chinatown is the place where relatives may still reside.

### Controversy

At various times over the 150 years of their existence, Chinatowns have often become isolated and therefore neglected sections of cities. Social problems, including poverty and crime, as well as stereotyping, have plagued many enclaves. Another problematic issue is the persistence of social perceptions that were established in the 1800s that label Chinatowns as inferior, dangerous, or mysterious spaces. Both perceptions ignore the richness and significance of Chinatowns as important places in American history and popular culture.

### Images in Popular Culture

From its first years to the present, the film industry has always represented Chinatowns in films. The enclaves have been commonly shown as places for non-Chinese to go for a good time, to experience a different world, and, more sinisterly,

#### *The Joy Luck Club*

*The Joy Luck Club* is a novel written by Amy Tan that was published in 1989. The novel, which emerged as a critical success, was especially notable because it brought attention to the achievements of Asian American women and their not oft-told stories. The novel narrates the lives of four immigrant women who regularly meet to play Mah Jong. They call themselves the Joy Luck Club. While the women play, it is evident that the game has a more important function than simple entertainment. During revealing conversations, the women talk about their lives and their American-born daughters. The book's phenomenal reception prompted the making of a film adaption, which was released in 1993.

Tan's intimate insights on the lives of immigrant women are reflective of her own experiences. Born on February 19, 1952, in Oakland, California, Tan is a second-generation Chinese American. Part of the inspiration for her first book, *The Joy Luck Club*, was her mother's hardships and challenges. Tan went on to author many other novels, such as *The Kitchen God's Wife* (1991) and *The Bonesetter's Daughter* (2000), as well as children's books and works of nonfiction.

to feed unlawful and immoral addictions. Going to Chinatowns to visit opium dens or prostitutes is a Hollywood cliché. The denizens of Chinatown are often used as silent backdrops indicating threat, or cast in docile and subservient roles. Chinatown gangs, another Hollywood staple, are always vicious and hostile, and are always martial arts experts. Depictions of Chinatowns on television are surprisingly rare.

As many critics have pointed out, stereotyping Chinatown as a place for illicit activity, replete with corruption and organized crime, paints a troubling and inaccurate picture. There is, however, a growing body of literature that provides accurate and well-balanced descriptions of these oldest ethnic enclaves in the nation.

### In Conclusion

Into the new millennium, Chinatowns still play a prominent role in newly arrived immigrants. The enclaves' ongoing cultural importance to generations of Chinese Americans who have moved into mainstream America underscores the relevancy of Chinatowns. For other visitors, Chinatowns promote cultural appreciation and understanding.

***See also*** Alcatraz; Bok Kai Temple; Chicago, Illinois; Golden Gate Bridge; Hawaii; Hollywood; Housing, Neighborhoods, and Enclaves; Las Vegas, Nevada; Los Angeles, California; New York, New York; Old West; Reservations; San Francisco, California

### Further Reading

Chang, Iris. 2003. *The Chinese in America: A Narrative History*. New York: Penguin Books.

Kwong, Peter. 1996. *The New Chinatown*. New York: Hill and Wang.

Kwong, Peter, and Miscevic, Dusanka. 2007. *Chinese America: The Untold Story of America's Oldest New Community*. New York: New Press.

Prasso, Sheridan. 2005. *The Asian Mystique: Dragon Ladies, Geisha Girls & Our Fantasies of the Exotic Orient*. New York: Public Affairs.

Tsui, Bonnie. 2009. *American Chinatown: A People's History of Five Neighborhoods*. New York: Free Press.

West, David. 2006. *Chasing Dragons: An Introduction to the Martial Arts Film*. New York: I.B. Tauris & Co.

Zhou, Min. 1995. *Chinatown: The Socioeconomic Potential of an Urban Enclave*. Philadelphia: Temple University Press.

## Chrysler Building

The Chrysler Building is an Art Deco skyscraper in New York City. This instantly recognizable building, completed in 1930, helps to define New York's iconic skyline. Conceived by Walter P. Chrysler, a titan in America's automobile industry, and designed by William Van Allen, the Chrysler Building is 1,045 feet tall. The building features multiple tiers; an extended, tier-less midsection; and an ornate top flourished with overlapping sunbursts that culminate in a 125-foot spire. Though the building was the tallest in the world for a mere 11 months, it remains one of America's most famous towers, an elegantly designed and unique icon that pays tribute to American achievement, industry, and ascent to modernity and power. The Chrysler Building was designated a National Historic Landmark in 1976.

### Historical Perspectives

When in 1928 construction began on the Chrysler Building, there was a fierce competition underway. Satiated with power and money, America's industrial barons battled with steel, mortar, and design schematics to build the tallest building in the world. Walter P. Chrysler, the founder of the

Chrysler Corporation, put his ambition and his own money into the construction of his corporation's new headquarters.

Lexington Avenue in Manhattan, the site Chrysler chose, was then on an upward trajectory toward its position as the beacon of American progress. The borough's growth was marked with both established and fresh new urban development: Central Park, the Brooklyn Bridge, and a subway system. Manhattan was already home to tall structures like Trinity Church, the New York World Building, the Metropolitan Life Tower, and the Bank of Manhattan Trust Building (now 40 Wall Street).

Chrysler's biggest rival was the Bank of Manhattan Trust Building, which, when it was finished, stood a staggering 925 feet high. In a calculated (and secret) move, the Chrysler Building was given a spire that rose more than 100 feet into the air, ensuring that the building would be ranked the tallest building in the world.

In the following year, the Chrysler Building was surpassed by another building—one that continues to this day to tower above the rest—the Empire State Building. Competition intensified in ensuing years as more buildings strained to outreach the other. As of 2011, the Chrysler Building was tied with the New York Times Building as the 3rd tallest building in New York City, the 7th tallest in the nation, and the 33rd tallest in the world.

### About the Site: Construction, Design, and Occupancy

Despite being eclipsed as the tallest building in the world, the Chrysler Building holds its own in terms of massiveness, elegance, and uniqueness. The construction cost Chrysler $20 million, an amount that then impressively demonstrated the automobile-industry magnate's monetary power. The building contains 32 elevators, 400,000 rivets, 3,826,000 white and dark gray bricks, 3,862 windows, 77 floors, and 29,962 tons of steel. The interior was lavishly decorated with marble floors, Art Deco and Egyptian-inspired art, and a ceiling fresco by Edward Trumbull entitled "Transport and Human Endeavor." Notable features of this structure include the crown featuring overlapping sunbursts, the spire lights added many years later to illuminate the top of the building, and gargoyles incorporating car shapes and parts on the building's exterior.

Embellishing traditional European-style cathedrals and structures with gargoyles and other mythical and fantastical creatures and animals was an ancient tradition. Chrysler and Van Allen, however, integrated uniquely American emblems, decorating the exterior of the building with eagles, metal hubcaps, radiator caps, Chrysler hood ornaments, and car fenders. By trading the symbols of old for the new, Chrysler underscored the role of America as a modern power, as well as America's powerful car industry.

For many years, sitting on the throne of this symbol of power was the Chrysler Corporation. Chrysler maintained its headquarters in the building between 1930 and the mid-1950s (today, headquarters are in Detroit). Other former residents of the building were the Cloud Club, which occupied several floors, and several broadcast stations. The public viewing gallery on the 71st floor has been closed to the public since 1945. As of 2008, 90 percent of the building is owned by the Abu Dhabi Investment Council; the remaining 10 percent is owned by Tishman Speyer Properties. Though Chrysler no longer owns the building, the building still bears the emblems of its legacy.

### About the Site: Symbols and Cultural Impact

The Chrysler name and the image of the Chrysler Building are synonymous with an epoch dominated by American corporations and business moguls. Chrysler stood for American company and positive American attributes such as success, quality, and power. The Chrysler name also stands for another all-American archetype, the self-made individual.

Chrysler is also associated with a golden era of American-made products that benefited the American people and the nation's economy. The corporation employed many Americans, providing steady income and a higher quality of life and contributing to America's economic wealth. The corporation endured despite the harrowing years of the Great Depression that came at the heels of the Chrysler Building's construction.

The name Chrysler is also inseparable from its famous product: the automobile. Thus, the tributes to the American car that embellish the Chrysler Building's exterior are more than decorations. They are symbols of what was once one of the most important products in the American way of life. The mass production of automobiles vaulted Americans out of the horse-and-buggy age and into the modern era. Cars gave Americans greater and more efficient mobility and opened pathways to new styles of living, ever-expanding highways and cities, roadside attractions, and drive-through eateries.

### Images in Popular Culture

In most any film or television programs set in New York City, one can discern from the skyscraper-laden skyline the familiar Chrysler Building. Most recently, in 2012, the building played a pivotal role in the third installment of the *Men in Black* series. In this science fiction film, Agent J, played by Will Smith, must jump from the towering building to time travel. Audiences get a close-up shot of one of the nation's most remarkable structures.

### In Conclusion

The Chrysler Building is more than an architectural marvel, it's a symbol of national pride and a memory of the days when America soared into modernity.

***See also*** Brooklyn Bridge; Cadillac Ranch; Carhenge; Central Park; Detroit, Michigan; Empire State Building; New York, New York; Subways

### Further Reading

Bascomb, Neal. 2004. *Higher: A Historic Race to the Sky and the Making of a City*. New York: Broadway.

Chrysler, Walter P., and Sparkes, Boyden. 1950. *Life of an American Workman*. New York: Dodd, Mead and Company.

Curcio, Vincent. 2001. *Chrysler: The Life and Times of an Automotive Genius*. New York: Oxford University Press.

Harris, Bill. 2002. *Five Hundred Buildings of New York*. New York: Black Dog & Leventhal Publishers.

Stravitz, David. 2002. *The Chrysler Building: Creating a New York Icon Day by Day*. New York: Princeton Architectural Press.

## Churchill Downs

Churchill Downs is a horse racing track in Louisville, Kentucky, where the most famous race in the nation, the Kentucky Derby, is held. Churchill Downs is noted for its centuries-old traditions, velvet green lawns, and gleaming horses. Churchill Downs maintains its hold on the national imagination as a place of high society, famous victories, and competitive betting. Churchill Downs brings it all together—the striking elegance of the facility, the awareness of social status, the visceral thrill of horse racing, and the electric ambience of the crowd—to create a popular American landmark.

### Historical Perspectives

Horse racing has been a popular pastime since ancient times in disparate parts of the world such as the Middle East, Asia, and northern Africa. As Europe was civilized, it too became enthralled with

Jockey Joel Rosario leads his horse, Orb, across the finish line to win the 139th Kentucky Derby horse race at Churchill Downs in Louisville, Kentucky on May 4, 2013. (AP Photo/David J. Phillip)

the sport. In England, where it became known as "the sport of kings," the popularity of horse racing bordered on the fanatical. English settlers eventually brought the sport to North America in the mid-1600s, and, not surprisingly, the sport took off in the New World too.

Before Kentucky became a state in 1792, its settlers established traditions that are present to this day. Thus Kentucky is known for its whiskey, bluegrass music, and beautiful horses and race tracks. The early horse races were amateur competitions that took place along common streets. The earliest racetracks were built in 1789. Many of these tracks foundered, but Kentucky has always been horse country, and the passion for racing kept the desire for good facilities alive.

Churchill Downs held its first races in Louisville, Kentucky, in 1875. The facility, not nearly as extensive or as formal as at present, but charming all the same, consisted of a main track, a porter's lodge, ticket offices, six stables, and a clubhouse on eight acres.

Churchill Downs' founder, Meriwether Lewis Clark Jr., was the grandson of William Clark of the famed Lewis and Clark expedition that took place between 1804 and 1806. The official name of the race track was originally the Louisville Jockey Club and Driving Park, but almost everyone referred to it as Churchill Downs, a name derived from the surname of Clark's two uncles, who leased him the property on which the track is located.

Over the years, Churchill Downs has hosted many different races—races of different lengths run by horses of different ages—but its most famous is the annual Kentucky Derby. Known as "the most exciting two minutes in sports," the Kentucky Derby is a one-and-a-quarter-mile race for three-year-old thoroughbreds. It occurs on the first Saturday in May each year.

### Highlights

Surviving financial crises, fires, and other catastrophes, Churchill Downs eventually clambered to the top of the list of America's foremost race tracks, beating out Belmont Park in New York, Hialeah in Florida, Santa Anita in California, and Pimlico in Maryland. Today's facility spans 147 acres and seats 50,000, but counting standing room, crowds can reach 150,000. These days Churchill Downs boasts practice tracks, high-tech stables, luxury suites, and the Kentucky Derby Museum.

Over the years, many variables have contributed to the success of Churchill Downs. Since its beginnings, Churchill Downs has hosted other events and activities, which helped it to remain busy year round. Churchill Down's trademark grandstand, adorned with twin spires, added style and distinctiveness to the facility. Placing the garland of roses on the Kentucky Derby winner and playing "My Old Kentucky home" became special traditions.

Recently, popular bands, including the Rolling Stones, the Police, and Bon Jovi, have drawn huge crowds during Derby Week and throughout the year. Though the track makes sure it stays relevant by including such new elements in its list of events, it will forever be remembered by its legends and the horses that ran and won the biggest race of the year.

### The Most Exciting Two Minutes in Sports

The Kentucky Derby is a one-and-a-quarter-mile horse race featuring some 20 competing thoroughbreds that takes place every year on the first Saturday in May as part of the two-week-long Kentucky Derby Festival in Louisville. First run in 1875, the race is billed as "The Most Exciting Two Minutes in Sports." Another popular name for the race is "The Run for the Roses," sonamed for the garland of roses that is draped over the winning horse. This tradition first appeared in 1896 with pink and white roses draped over the winning horse, Ben Brush. In 1904, the red rose became the race's official flower.

The Kentucky Derby is the most popular race run at Churchill Downs. It is the first race in the Triple Crown of Thoroughbreds (the Triple Crown for short). The other two are the Preakness Stakes, which is held at the Pimlico Race Course in Baltimore, Maryland, and the Belmont Stakes, which takes place at Belmont Park in Elmont, New York. The Preakness is the shortest of the three races at a mile and an eighth, and the Belmont is the longest at one and a half miles.

Winning horses of all three races are greatly esteemed. In 1973, Secretariat was the first Triple Crown winner in 25 years. Many tributes were paid to Secretariat, including his election to the U.S. Racing Hall of Fame in 1974 and the Kentucky Athletic Hall of Fame in 2007. Secretariat's likeness was added to a postage stamp in 1999; streets were named after him in Napa, California and Howell, New Jersey. Secretariat statues can be found at Belmont Park and Kentucky Horse Park. Secretariat was also immortalized in the titular film, released in 2010.

## Legendary Figures

The enduring mystique of Churchill Downs is augmented by its famous champions. The long line of championship horses, sleek with glossy coats, muscles rippling as they speed around the track, is like a genealogy of kings. Among the many famous horses that raced at Churchill Downs are Aristides, Secretariat, and Barbaro. Aristides won the first Kentucky Derby in 1875 and was immortalized in a statue in the courtyard at the facility. Secretariat, owned by Penny Chenery, one of the few prominent women in the sport, rose to fame in 1973 after winning the Triple Crown, a series of three thoroughbred horse races of differing lengths at different tracks, the first of which is the Kentucky Derby. Secretariat was the subject of an eponymous film in 2010. Barbaro, whose remains are interred at the entrance of Churchill Downs, died after shattering his leg in another race following his 2006 Kentucky Derby.

Isaac Murphy was one of many African American jockeys in the sport, which was one of the few professional American sports that allowed African Americans to participate before the mid-20th century. Murphy, who won a total of three Kentucky Derbies in 1884, 1890, and 1891, was the first inductee in the National Museum of Racing and Hall of Fame (a notable achievement in itself, considering individuals of color were historically admitted belatedly into their sports halls of fame).

## Controversy

Not long after the tragic death of Barbaro, Churchill Downs was rocked by another devastating event. In 2008, after participating in the Kentucky Derby, Eight Bells, a filly, sustained serious injuries and was euthanized. The news made headlines and provoked an avalanche of protest and scrutiny. Animal rights groups and public individuals denounced what they perceived to be abuses inflicted upon horses: euthanization and line breeding, a process that can result in deleterious health conditions and injuries caused by accidents sustained while racing or training.

> **Dress Hats, Crazy Hats, Fun Hats**
>
> Traditions abound at Churchill Downs, as well as during its most important race, the Kentucky Derby. One such tradition—hat wearing—has a long and sensational history. This tradition, which is most enthusiastically observed by women, began in the 1870s. Meriwether Lewis Clark Jr. (grandson of the legendary William Clark of the Lewis and Clark expedition), founder of the Kentucky Derby, started the tradition.
>
> Inspired by London's Epsom Derby and Paris' Grand Prix, Clark desired to add elegance and class to the race. In that era, places where individuals gambled and drank alcohol were not considered appropriate for women. However, Clark began to market his race as a place for the fashionable upper class. Women appeared front and center at the races, dressed in stylish clothes, shoes, and matching accessories. The centerpiece of this race-going costume was typically a dashing hat. The posh apparel of these finely dressed women was often referenced in newspaper articles.
>
> The fancy attire elevated the tone of the event, attracting moneyed visitors from home and abroad. Thus the custom continued down through the many decades. During the 1960s, women began wearing larger and more extravagant hats, as well as starting a trend for quirky hats, many in bright, flamboyant colors and prints. Some women have paid exorbitant prices for custom-made hats. In contemporary times, the style of hats varies greatly. While some wear elegant hats, others wear hats that are outlandish, enormous, and, above all, eye-catching.

Amid the negative press and protests, Churchill Downs responded with action. They implemented additional safety measures at their facility and took steps to prevent injuries to horses while training and racing. They also held a memorial service for Eight Bells. The filly's remains were interred outside the Kentucky Derby Museum. Also in honor of Eight Bells, a magnolia tree was planted and a race, the La Troienne Stakes, traditionally held on Derby Day, was renamed the Eight Belles Stakes.

### In Conclusion

Devastated but not destroyed by the tragedy of Eight Belles, Churchill Downs carries on its commitment to distinguished professional horse racing.

*See also* Bourbon Trail; California; Lewis and Clark Trail

### Further Reading

Brodowky, Pamela K., and Philbin, Tom. 2007. *Two Minutes to Glory: The Official History of the Kentucky Derby*. New York: Collins Publishers.

*Churchill Downs*. http://www.churchilldowns.com/.

Gatto, Kimberly. 2010. *Churchill Downs: America's Most Historic Racetrack*. Charleston, South Carolina: The History Press.

*National Museum and Racing Hall of Fame*. http://www.racingmuseum.org/.

Tweedy, Kate Cheney, and Ladin, Leeanne. 2011. *Secretariat's Meadow: The Land, the Family, the Legend*. Manakin-Sabot, Virginia: Dementi Milestone Publishing.

## Circus

A circus is a spectacular presentation of a variety of shows and exhibits, including acts featuring acrobats, animals, jugglers, and clowns. An ancient tradition, the actual term "circus" did not come into use until the 1780s in England. The first circus in the New World was held on April 3, 1793, in Philadelphia, Pennsylvania. It was organized by Scottish showman John Bill Ricketts. Ricketts was followed by others, such as J. Purdy Brown, P.T. Barnum (who dubbed his circus "The Greatest Show on Earth"), and the Ringling Brothers. Though its heyday (from the 1870s to the mid-20th century) is long over, the American circus has seen something of a resurgence since the 1970s. Today's circus incorporates cutting-edge technology and state-of-the-art props, appealing to new audiences with sophisticated tastes.

**Historical Perspectives**

A certain electric thrill fills the air as crowds stream under the Big Top, a term synonymous with the circus tent. The aroma of popcorn, the antics of clowns in makeup and brightly colored wigs playfully interacting with the crowds, and the intermittent sounds of animals are the sights and sounds associated with the circus. But this well-known image of the classic American circus performance did not appear overnight.

Humanity has long enjoyed both laughing at minor amusements and cheering large-scale spectacles. One can find similarities to the modern-day circus in ancient times. The clownish antics of the King's fool in various European courts and the exciting chariot races and animal exhibits that took place in Rome both foreshadow the circus as we know it.

During the early 18th century, horse-riding exhibits grew into a popular event on the east coast of America. These exhibits often included elements associated with the circus, such as riding tricks and the display of animals from distant lands. Exotic animals included the camel and the polar bear. In London, Philip Astley set up a large riding ring and a covered grandstand. His popular show, which debuted in 1768, featured trick riding, strong men, acrobatics, and a clown.

In 1782, English entrepreneurs Charles Didbin and Charles Hughes founded the Royal Circus in London in a permanent structure, giving birth to the term "circus." The Royal Circus was such a success that John Bill Ricketts decided to debut his own circus to American audiences. His show, which opened on April 3, 1793, took place in a white amphitheater Ricketts had constructed in Philadelphia, Pennsylvania, and is considered the first circus to perform in the nation. Audiences including President George Washington were riveted by the performances, which started with one-man equestrian acts and grew to include a tightrope walker and a juggling acrobat.

In the 19th century, the American circus expanded to include many new features. Mobility enabled circuses to travel to different locations. This was no easy task, but professional traveling circuses soon developed an efficient rhythm for loading and unloading their gear and supplies, including, depending on the type of circus, animals, costumes, makeup, and miscellaneous equipment. These groups primarily performed in towns on the East Coast. Popular features of the circus included a menagerie, which featured an array of animals such as horses, lions, bears, monkeys, and dogs. The human acts included acrobats, jugglers, and masterful equestrians.

Another innovation of the American circus in the 19th century was the tent. The tent, which would become one of the prominent symbols of the circus, was the innovation of J. Purdy Brown. In 1825, Brown used a tent so that performances would not be interrupted by inclement weather and so that they could be held later in the year. This resulted in greater profits for the circus.

Indeed, the circus was growing into a major industry that needed to be managed and operated with shrewd marketing zeal. Advertising grew, and bigger and more spectacular acts were created, such as the hair-raising act performed by Isaac A. Van Amburgh in the 1830s. Amburgh, an animal trainer, began putting his head and arm into the gaping jaws of a lion. As the circus grew bigger and more thrilling, it spread beyond the East Coast.

The next milestone in the history of the circus was the appearance of P. T. Barnum. Born Phineas Taylor Barnum on July 5, 1810 in Bethel, Connecticut, Barnum was one of the nation's most colorful and prominent showmen. He began his public career exhibiting an African American woman, Joice Heth, who he alleged was more than 160 years old. Though this untruth was found out, Barnum was not dissuaded from pursuing a career in entertainment.

In 1841, he opened Barnum's American Museum, which featured circus acts such as jugglers, glass blowers, performing fleas, Native American dancers, and dogs. He also incorporated curiosities and human oddities, such as the Feejee Mermaid and a man Barnum touted was the "Smallest Man in the World." General Tom Thumb, as he was known, was in actuality a little person. Barnum's exhibits, like those of the freak show era, which exhibited human deformities and extreme or out-of-the-ordinary physical features, drew curious crowds, though today's world would scorn such exploitive attractions.

In 1865, a fire destroyed Barnum's museum. Thinking he had left show business behind forever, Barnum went into politics. But after a brief stint as a Republican in the Connecticut legislature, Barnum was coaxed by Dan Castello and Cameron Coup into returning to the industry he had abandoned.

This three-person partnership launched Barnum's spectacular career. In 1871, they debuted the grandly named P.T. Barnum's Museum, Menagerie and Circus, International Zoological Garden, and Polytechnic Institute and Hippodrome. It was Barnum's name that reappeared on one fantastical show after the other. In 1872, they debuted a six-tent show named P.T. Barnum's Great Traveling Exposition and World's Fair. The show featured another creation that revolutionized the circus: the railroad circus train. The show on rails provided a highly efficient means of transporting the circus from place to place. Later, Barnum took his show to New York, where he entertained audiences at the Hippodrome, a structure that would later be used as the second site for the Madison Square Garden.

New Yorkers delighted in Barnum, as did everyone else in the nation. But Barnum was not the only major circus in the country. The Cooper & Bailey Circus was owned by James E. Cooper and James A. Bailey. Something that Cooper & Bailey had that Barnum did not was the American-born elephant named Columbia. In 1881, the rivals joined forces and became P.T. Barnum's Greatest Show on Earth, Howe's Great London Circus and Sanger's Royal British Menagerie. In the following year, they became known as the Barnum & Bailey's Greatest Show on the Earth, with Barnum getting top billing. In that same year, the showmen added a third ring, launching the custom of the three-ring circus. In a three-ring circus, three different acts are performed simultaneously. Compared to the one-show format, the three-show format appealed to more people.

After the death of Barnum in 1890 and Bailey in 1906, the circus was sold to Ringling Brothers. Under their helm, Barnum's famed circus show endures to this day as the Ringing Bros. and Barnum & Bailey Circus.

**The Era of the Freak Show**

Sideshows, which were also known as Freak Shows, were especially popular in America and England during the 19th century. The shows exhibited people from America and abroad with physical deformities and unusual medical conditions. Some individuals were exhibited simply because their ethnic features were unlike what the American public was accustomed to seeing. Naturally, to promote sensationalism, the showmen concocted extraordinary stories to explain and describe the individuals on exhibit.

American sideshows ran with considerable success from the 1820s to the 1940s. During this period, Americans were fascinated, at times horrified, by the display of human conditions. Men, women, and children streamed to the venues, which appeared separately or concurrently with local public gatherings such as fairs and circuses. According to the custom of the day, some exhibits were only accessible to men because of their graphic nature. Bearded women, conjoined twins, emaciated bodies, little people, so-called giants, and deformed faces were among the popular shows. The showmen themselves contributed to the excitement with their charismatic patter and presentations.

Billed as "human oddities" and "freaks of nature," the individuals on exhibit played a pivotal role in the sideshows. From a modern and enlightened perspective, that role was demoralizing and degrading. Contemporary critics also perceive the sideshows as exploitive. From another point of view, the sideshows provided a way to make a living for men, women, and children who, ostracized from general society, sometimes found in the sideshow a community to which they could belong.

### Contemporary Perspectives

The American circus hit hard economic times during the 1950s and 1960s. This period brought forth many changes in American society and culture. Circuses competed with a growing number and array of entertainment forms, such as television, vacation trips, amusement parks, and shopping malls.

A resurgence in interest in the circus occurred in the 1970s and continues in the present. Though the dazzle has been tempered, the circus has evolved to include different types of regional shows. State-of-the-art graphics incorporated into the presentations help to captivate modern audiences that are sophisticated than the audiences of the past.

**General Tom Thumb**

General Tom Thumb was one of the most successful human oddities of his era. Born Charles Sherwood Stratton on January 4, 1838, in Bridgeport, Connecticut, he was five years old and stood only 25 inches tall and weighed just 15 pounds when P.T. Barnum discovered him and convinced his parents to let him employ their son in his circus. Prior to Thumb's debut, Barnum heavily promoted his new sensation. He gave Stratton the name Tom Thumb after the English folk character, adding the title General for a bit of flair. Barnum also rigorously trained the child. A good study, Thumb transitioned masterfully into his new role as comedian and impersonator. Garbed in various costumes, such as a Scottish highlander and Napoleon Bonaparte, Thumb amused and captivated his audiences. Through the years, Thumb made an immense amount of money, became a worldwide celebrity, and developed a close relationship with Barnum.

On his first tour to England in 1844, he made a stop at Buckingham Palace, where he performed songs, danced, and did his popular impersonations for Queen Victoria and her family. In the 1850s, he toured the nation and Europe again. During adolescence, Thumb grew to a height of three feet. In the 1860s, he met Lavinia Warren, another small person who worked for Barnum. They married in Barnum fashion with news coverage and promotion on February 10, 1863, at Grace Church in New York City. On their honeymoon, President Abraham Lincoln invited them to the White House. Later in that decade, the couple went on a world tour. Thumb died in 1883 from a stroke. It is conjectured that his smallness could have been attributed to a growth hormone deficiency.

### Images in Popular Culture

Circus themes have been incorporated into popular musical performances in recent years. Britney Spears included traditional circus acts in her Circus Tour in 2009. In 2012, Madonna performed a circus-themed halftime show at Super Bowl XLVI, and Taylor Swift put on a circus-themed performance of her song "We are Never Ever Getting Back Together" at the MTV EMA in 2013 and the Grammys in 2013.

As one would expect, given its focus on exciting performances, the circus motif has also been used in a broad array of films featuring comedic, dramatic, and romantic themes. The classic *At the Circus* (1939) features the Marx Brothers, Groucho, Chico, and Harpo, in comedic situations in their effort to help save the circus from hooligans. *The Greatest Show on Earth* (1952), a fictional film, set in the Ringling Bros. and Barnum & Bailey Circus, is a serious drama that shows the enormous challenge of running a circus behind the surface of fun and extraordinary acts. The film *Water for Elephants* (2011) is a love story between a man and a woman who work for a circus.

Of the many circus archetypes, the clown is perhaps the most prominent. A fixture in circuses, clowns also appear in many other public and private venues. Though clowns are famously associated with children and whimsical fun, these circus favorites also conjure fear. This fear, which has its own name, coulrophobia, is reinforced by negative and frightening images, such as in the character Pennywise in horror author Stephen King's *It* (1986) and several horror films, of which *It* (1990) was one of the most chilling.

### In Conclusion

Though the circus is not an American invention, the nation greatly influenced its development into the three-ring events under the big top that audiences have come to expect. Thanks to the likes of

Barnum, Bailey, and the Ringling Brothers, the American circus endures as a timeless form of family entertainment.

*See also* Madison Square Garden; Philadelphia, Pennsylvania

### Further Reading

Barnum, Phineas T. 2000. *The Life of P.T. Barnum*. Urbana: University of Illinois Press.

Bogdan, Robert. 1988. *Freak Show: Presenting Human Oddities for Amusement and Profit*. Chicago: University of Chicago Press.

*Circus Federation*. http://www.circusfederation.org/.

Davis, Janet M. 2002. *The Circus Age: Culture & Society under the American Big Top*. Chapel Hill: University of North Carolina Press.

Weber, Susan, Ames, Kenneth L., and Wittmann, Matthew, eds. 2012. *The American Circus*. New York: Bard Graduate Center; Decorative Arts, Design History, Material Culture: New Haven, Connecticut; London, United Kingdom; Yale University Press.

## Cleveland-Lloyd Dinosaur Quarry

The Cleveland-Lloyd Dinosaur Quarry is an area designated for the excavation of dinosaur fossils. Located in a desert region, 30 miles south of Price, Utah, the famed site contains the largest source of fossils in the world. Africa, Asia, and Europe may have been inhabited by the oldest civilizations and richest sources of evidence of those worlds known to humanity but no place has yet to best Cleveland-Lloyd Dinosaur Quarry's magnificent abundance of dinosaur remains. This fact excites not just paleontologists. Adults and children alike are fascinated by prehistoric life and long to see evidence of the ancient giants and unusual creatures that once inhabited the earth. The quarry permits access to the general public for visits and tours, providing a once-in-a-lifetime view into the work of scientists and the hidden treasures from America's ancient landscape.

### Historical Perspectives

No one quite knows why, of all places, Utah holds such a rich deposit of paleontological animal life. Some paleontologists surmise that some unusually large river or lake deposit, earthquakes, or an extreme drought occurring at a waterhole are what caused so many remains to concentrate at the site. What is known is that the remains span 147 million years and were covered over, during those many years, by layers of water and material such as volcanic ash and mud. Erosion eventually whittled away the layers, making the mysteries below visible or at least easier to access.

The first known person to discover a fossil in this area was a sheepherder in the 1920s, sparking what would become one of the greatest discoveries in modern times. Once word spread that a dinosaur bone had been found, the scientists quickly followed. The University of Utah conducted the first dig in 1929, finding 500 dinosaur bones. Between 1939 and 1941, Princeton University headed a large research project at the site. During this time, the name, Cleveland-Lloyd Quarry, was bestowed on the site. "Cleveland" referred to the nearby city, and "Lloyd" was in honor of Malcolm Lloyd, who financed Princeton University's study. Since 1960, scientists from many institutions of higher learning and museums have collaborated. In 1966, the site was designated a National Natural Landmark.

### About the Site

Today, the primary denizens of Cleveland-Lloyd Quarry are scientists who have revealed, over time, an enormous array of discoveries. These discoveries included 30 complete skeletons, dinosaur eggs, and more than 15,000 fossil bones. Of the remains, two-thirds are derived from *Allosaurus*, a carnivore ranking among the largest that lived during the Jurassic period. Other remains come from plant-eating dinosaurs, such as the *Stegosaurus*, *Camarasaurus*, and *Camptosaurus*. Over all, some 14 dinosaur species have been found. Some of the remains are included in exhibits at the site; others are exhibited in museums around the world.

The small but information-packed visitor center at the BLM-managed Cleveland-Lloyd Dinosaur Quarry in Utah is dominated by a juvenile example of the 44 allosaurs who left their bones in this deposit. Many real bones are available for the visitors to touch and heft at this visitor center. (Eon Images)

### Popular Imagination

Dinosaurs, the main attraction at Cleveland-Lloyd Quarry, have appealed to the American popular imagination since they were first discovered. On television, the friendly pet Dino the Dinosaur cavorted with Fred and Wilma on the popular children's animation *The Flintstones* (1960–1966), and *Barney & Friends* (1992–) features a loveable giant purple singing dinosaur. Dino also appears in modern film adaptations of the *Flintstones* in 1994 and 2000. The mega blockbuster film series, *Jurassic Park* (1993, 1997, 2001), brings some of the most splendorous and terrifying images of dinosaurs to the big screen. Popular exhibits in museums, like the American Museum of Natural History, feature dinosaurs.

### For Visitors

Admission into the site is $5 for adults and free for children under 16. Spectacular activities can be witnessed during limited times of the year. A visitor center showcases many exhibits, including an *Allosaur* skeletal display and a *Stegosaur* wall mount. Visitors may tour the quarry and observe scientists actively recovering fossilized bones. Other tours include a Rock Walk Nature Trail and a hike to Raptor Point. Although camping is forbidden at the site (and visitors are prohibited from removing objects they may find), picnic tables are available for enjoying lunch. Attractions in the vicinity include cities and towns, state and national parks, and recreational and wilderness areas.

### In Conclusion

The desire to understand and experience the past is a deep-seated human need. The sight of dinosaur bones, bespeaking giant bodies and incredible lives, fires the imagination and gives us a glimpse of what life on planet Earth must have been like before humans walked its plains. Thus, a visit to see the wonderful dinosaurs of the Cleveland-Lloyd Quarry is another way in which we learn about ourselves.

***See also*** American Museum of Natural History; Cabazon Dinosaurs; Smithsonian Institution; State and National Parks

### Further Reading

"Cleveland-Lloyd Dinosaur Quarry." *Bureau of Land Management*. http://www.blm.gov/ut/st/en/fo/price/recreation/quarry.html.

Costa, Vincenzo. 1994. *Dinosaur Safari Guide*. Stillwater, Minnesota: Voyageur Press.

## Columbine High School

Columbine is a public high school in Columbine, Colorado. Prior to the nightmarish tragedy that unfolded there on April 20, 1999, Columbine was an archetypal American high school in the suburbs, little known to the nation or the world. But then two students terrorized students and faculty with guns and bombs, killing 12 students and 1 teacher on the school grounds. Though associated with none of the rampant social ills that trouble urban schools in the United States, Columbine's image in America is nonetheless marked with sadness, confusion, fear, and horror. In the aftermath, Columbine became a symbol of violence erupting in the midst of innocence.

### Historical Perspectives

Columbine High School was built in 1973. Its student teams were nicknamed the Rebels. In terms of demographics, the school is largely middle class and predominately white. Like any American high school, Columbine had its cliques and subcultures: Goths, honor students, jocks, and Christians. But it was, for all intents and purposes, a quiet school with normal everyday issues and mundane concerns—not at all the profile of a school that would be scarred by a heinous event.

### The Massacre

Columbine's place in American history changed on April 20, 1993. Two Columbine seniors, Eric Harris and Dylan Klebold, planted bombs in the school cafeteria and kitchen, but they did not ignite. Armed with a pistol, rifle, and two shot guns, and a duffel bag full of bombs, the two attackers terrorized students, faculty, and later, police inside and outside on the school grounds. They set bombs in their cars, but those, too, did not go off. At the end of 49 minutes of sheer terror, the two students turned their weapons on themselves and committed suicide. In total, 13 died and 24 were injured.

### The Aftermath

Fragments of the incident and its aftermath were captured on camera and replayed and recounted to the world on television and in countless newspapers, magazines, and websites. As the nation tried to make sense of what had gone wrong, many put the blame on the supposed ills of modern society: violent video games and music, the Internet, antidepressant drugs, bullying, and lenient gun control laws.

The fear and panic that this incident produced in the nation provoked a string of studies, research projects, and investigations to find ways to understand as well as to prevent school violence elsewhere. Among the erroneous explanations given for the Columbine Massacre was that the attack was carried out by bullied and antisocial students who deliberately targeted certain youths—Christians, African Americans, and athletes.

In the final analysis, however, experts claimed that the deeply troubled mental states of the killers were at the crux of the issue. The FBI, psychologists, and other mental-health experts pointed to the evidence, such as videos and journals left by the attackers, and interviews, to support their conclusions. What they discovered was that Harris and Klebold had planned the attack for a year, collecting and hiding an arsenal. Their intent was to wreak havoc, not on a select few, but on the many. Klebold was described by some reports as angry, depressive, and suicidal; Harris was reported as psychopathic, meaning that he had no empathy for others. Reports also allude to the fact that there were some signs of trouble (besides the alleged Internet sources and videos), such as bomb-making and stealing.

### Impact

The name "Columbine" casts a dark shadow on the public imagination. The name was brought up in subsequent violent rampages that have occurred on other American campuses, such as the Virginia Tech Massacre at Virginia Polytechnic Institute and State University in 2007. Columbine has, however, affected America in positive ways, such as prompting greater outreach programs and resources for students.

In the immediate aftermath of the massacre, Columbine underwent a remodeling project, replacing the library and cafeteria where most of the shooting had occurred, and adding memorial tributes throughout the school. The school reopened on August 16, 1999.

In 2007, the Columbine Memorial, located in Clement Park near the High School, was opened to the public as a way to pay tribute to the victims. Several books have been written about Columbine, and a motion picture and stage play are being developed. Thus Columbine takes its sad place in the American psyche as a warning against the horrors of incomprehensible violence.

*See also* Cyberspace; High School; Suburbia

### Further Reading

*Columbine Memorial*. http://www.columbinememorial.org/Overview.asp.

Cullen, Dave. 2009. *Columbine*. New York: Twelve.

Kass, Jeff. 2009. *Columbine: A True Crime Story, a Victim, the Killers, and the Nation's Search for Answers*. Denver: Ghost Road Press.

Lindholm, Marjorie, and Lindholm, Peggy. 2005. *A Columbine Survivor's Story*. Littleton, Colorado: Regenold Publishing Company.

Nimmo, Beth, Scott, Darrell, and Rabey, Steve. 2000. *Rachel's Tears: The Spiritual Journey of Columbine's Martyr Rachel Scott*. Nashville: Thomas Nelson.

## Comic-Con

Comic-Con is a fan-based convention that occurs in several cities throughout the nation. The most famous Comic-Con, which takes place in San Diego, California, is the birthplace of the massively popular event. From a modest start with 100 attendees to the current gatherings of more than 100,000, the San Diego Comic-Con, known formally as Comic-Con International: San Diego (CCI), has emerged as a phenomenon in the 21st century (*Comic-Con International: San Diego*). Comic-Cons around the country follow a similar format with distinctive embellishments depending on the city. Major attractions include autograph signings, celebrity panels, spaces for artists, comic books, and fans (costumed or not). Though some gatherings are smaller than others, the Comic-Con experience is highly prized by the nation's myriad fans of comic books and science fiction.

### Historical Perspectives

Fan conventions, as they are often called, may center around any number of related genres, such as science fiction, comic books, fantasy, and anime, which is a Japanese style comic form that has been embraced by Americans. The earliest conventions, which took place in the 1930s, were science fiction themed. The first Star Trek Convention, based on the popular *Star Trek* television and movie series that has since spanned five decades, took place in New York City on January 21 and 23 in 1972. During the early years, Star Trek conventions were little known outside of the so-called Trekkie subculture. Such gatherings attained some degree of notoriety over time, as outsiders regarded these gatherings mockingly. The boldest of the participants wore costumes paying homage to their favorite characters.

A legion of costumed fans poses outside the convention center during the San Diego International Comic-Con convention in July 2013. (Greg Amptman/Dreamstime.com)

Like the Star Trek Conventions, the Comic-Con Conventions began relatively quietly. The founders, Shel Dorf, Ken Krueger, and Richard Alf, coordinated the first of the Comic-Cons in San Diego on March 21, 1970, at the U.S. Grant Hotel. Though there were only 100 attendees, the founders were encouraged by the turnout and quickly set out to host another event that August.

Whereas the first event took place in one day, the second event lasted three days. Both events featured high-profile guests, like author Ray Bradbury, who attended the second event. At the second event, more than 300 people attended. Over time, the event changed location and grew in popularity. Today, the event sees a staggering number of attendees at the official site, the San Diego Convention Center. Because the event has grown, additional sites and more activities have been included to the program. To many Comic-Con fans, San Diego is the best, owing to its historical significance, size, and the high quality of its guests and programming.

**Expansion**

Currently, an ever-increasing number of cities across the country hold Comic-Con conventions. Following San Diego's lead, Chicago debuted its first convention in 1976. A few more cities were added to the list of convention holders in the 1990s. The 21st century has seen enormous growth in the number of cities organizing such conventions.

### The Event

The size and offerings at Comic-Con conventions vary. Prior to the convention, tickets are sold to the event for one or more days (conventions generally run three days). At the convention, many fans come dressed casually, perhaps sporting logos and pictures of related themes on their shirts or caps. Some fans come in costumes which range from simple to elaborate handmade or purchased costumes. Some costumed fans wear full makeup, including contacts in assorted colors. Accessories can range from robotic appendages to hulking alien prosthetics. The characters featured run the gamut from the classic to the obscure in comic books, books, film, television, and video games. Costumed attendees are often the center of attention and are stopped repeatedly for photo-ops with other fans.

The convention schedule teems with activities. Among the popular events are autograph signings and picture-taking (for a fee) with featured high-profile celebrities. Celebrities from movies past, present, and future often appear as guests in panels. In a separate area, fans commission artists for illustrations, buy books, action figures, posters, cups, and other souvenirs from vendors, and mingle with comic-book writers. Group events are scheduled into the evening, such as costume and karaoke contests.

### The Media Connection and the Fan-Based Convention

The increasing popularity and changing demographics of science fiction and comic-book fans have often been correlated to the media and its depictions of comic book, science fiction, and fantasy. With the advent of films in the 1920s, comic books in the 1940s, and television in the 1950s, science fiction, fantasy, and comic-book themes reached increasingly large and receptive audiences. Comic books in particular had a profound impact on American culture. For the first half of the 20th century, the individuals who read science fiction and comic books were a small and distinct subculture: mostly adolescent and young males.

Starting in the 1960s, technology in film and television helped to increase the popularity of science fiction. Though classics like the *Batman* (1966–1968) television series seem quirky by today's standards, the series was broadcast in color, which was at the time still a novelty for television audiences. Influential movies, such as the first three installments of *Star Wars* (1977, 1980, 1983) and *Superman* (1978), and hit television shows such as *The Six Million Dollar Man* (1974–1978) and *Wonder Woman* (1975–1979) had considerable impact on youth culture. A plethora of paraphernalia, figurines, dolls and accessories, coloring books, and lunch boxes were consumed by mainstream society in their wake.

The *Star Trek* franchise featured a series of space-themed television shows and movies from the 1960s to the present. In the early years, sci-fi buffs were still largely perceived as a peculiar group. During this period, conventions, science fiction or comic-con-based, had modest attendance numbers.

In the 1990s, the science fiction and comic-book genres began to experience new heights of technological and graphic brilliance. The popularity of the genre attracted a significant number of girls and women. The battery of new female action characters in film and television that appeared with increasing frequency coincided with the increasing number of female fans. Since the 1990s, comic-book heroes have made an enormous comeback in films, featuring such classic characters as the Hulk, Iron Man, Thor, the Avengers, Batman, and Superman in spectacular, realistic portrayals.

Against this backdrop, the Comic-Con conventions have soared to extraordinary heights of success, drawing both males and females in droves. Though the stigma of terms such as "nerd" and "geek" may still be attached to attendees of such gatherings, the stigma is largely gone, and the stereotype of the science fiction fan is no longer intrinsically negative.

### Images in Popular Culture

Comic-Con's prominence in mainstream society is reflected in the growing references to the convention in local media news, as well as on prime-time television shows such as *The Big Bang Theory* (2007–), which debuted amidst the new geek-is-in trend. The movie *Paul* (2011) starts out with two tourists from England starting their American road trip at the San Diego Comic-Con Convention before setting out to visit the major (alleged) alien hot spots in the nation.

### For Visitors

Buying tickets well before the scheduled convention is highly recommended. Due to the immense popularity of Comic-Con conventions, particularly in major cities such as San Diego and Seattle, tickets are often sold out early. Attendees should expect long lines, extraordinary costumes, and a genial atmosphere. All ages are represented; underage youth must be supervised by an adult. First-time attendees should note that Comic-Con conventions are not just for the die-hard fans, and a comprehensive knowledge of science fiction, fantasy, or comic books is not necessary to enjoy the experience. Visitors should bring cash in hand, cameras, and bottles of water.

***See also*** Chicago, Illinois; Seattle, Washington

### Further Reading

Bacon-Smith. 2000. *Science Fiction Culture*. Philadelphia: University of Pennsylvania Press.

*Comic-Con International: San Diego*. http://www.comic-con.org/.

Duncan, Randy, and Smith, Matthew J. 2009. *The Power of Comics: History, Form, and Culture*. New York: Continuum.

Roberts, Adam. 2007. *The History of Science Fiction*. Basingstoke: Palgrave Macmillan.

Salkowitz, Rob. 2012. *Comic-Con and the Business of Pop Culture: What the World's Wildest Trade Show Can Tell Us about the Future of Entertainment*. New York: McGraw-Hill.

Wright, Bradford W. 2001. *Comic Book Nation: The Transformation of Youth Culture in America*. Baltimore: Johns Hopkins University Press.

## Community Garden

A community garden is a section of land that is cultivated by members within a social group, commonly individuals who live within a residential area. Community gardens in America are the direct descendants of the Victory Gardens that emerged during World War I (1914–1918) and World War II (1941–1945). Though these gardens were generally abandoned in the years immediately following the end of World War II, public interest picked up again, particularly in urban environments, first in the 1970s and again in the 1990s. The popular appeal of these spaces has been varied. First, the emergence of such gardens was due to a response to economic issues and environmentalism trends as well as urban blight and feelings of alienation. Second, such gardens are a response to persuasive campaigns that advocate their many benefits, including fostering community, bolstering sustainability efforts, and providing a healthy food source for the community or other people in need.

### Historical Perspectives

Community gardens are not a new concept. So-called allotment gardens, an early form of community gardens, have existed in many European countries, such as England, Denmark, Germany, and Sweden, since the 18th century. In America, the concept of a communal system of living and ownership was a way of life prior to the arrival of the Europeans. In North Carolina, Moravian immigrants established the first community garden in Old Salem in 1759. During slavery times, communal plots for gardens among slaves were common.

In the late 19th century, Sir Ebenezer Howard, who lived in England, founded the garden city movement. He was not alone in his quest for a utopia. Books such as *Looking Backward: 2000–1887* (1888) by Edward Bellamy boldly depicted idyllic living environments—the antithesis of the increasingly urban environments of real life. Many sensitive critics of urbanization lamented the negative by-products of the bustling cityscape, with its economic disparities, pollution, and disregard for green spaces and efficient space management.

In 1898, Howard wrote a book of his own: *To-Morrow: A Peaceful Path to Real Reform.* The book was later titled *Garden Cities of To-morrow.* In this book, Howard revealed his ideas, designs, and vision of a self-sufficient environment comprising affordable residences, open spaces, and parks all contained within one neat area. In 1899, Howard organized the Garden City Association, which went on to help establish two garden cities in England: the Letchworth Garden City and Welwyn Garden City. Interest in Howard's Garden City eventually spread to other countries, including America, where garden-city-inspired neighborhoods were established in Massachusetts, New York, New Jersey, Maryland, Virginia, Tennessee, and California.

During the two world wars, America rallied behind the community garden movement that was spearheaded by the government. Food shortages were a major factor contributing to the emergence of public gardens. During World War I, the U.S. School Garden Army, a Bureau of Education program, promoted garden projects through public schools. During World War II, gardening was promoted as a way for Americans to support the war effort. Created by a sense of patriotic duty, the gardens helped address a need and boost morale and feelings of patriotism. Once the last war ended, most of the gardens were neglected, removed, or repurposed for some other use, either residential or commercial. During the financial crisis sparked by the Wall Street crash of 1929, community gardens were grown to help feed the nation.

### The 1970 Movement

The 1970s saw the flowering of a grassroots movement that began in the most urban environment in the nation: New York City. Urban blight, abandoned buildings, and empty lots defined the big city at the time. Communities were made up of strangers that barely spoke to one another, let alone mobilized in an effort to address an issue or a crisis.

In 1973, Liz Christy founded the Green Guerrillas, a nonprofit environmental group in New York. The organization committed itself to creating, promoting, and preserving urban gardens. Other individuals, like Karl Linn, helped spread community gardens to cities throughout the nation. This was no difficult task, for inflation, frustrations with urban living, and the rising popularity of environmentalism had impacted many in the nation. The community gardens were embraced as a viable answer to the crisis of urbanization.

### The 1990s to Present

The children of the 1970s, influenced by the generation before them, added to the number of individuals who were receptive and eager to take part in the environmental movement of the 1990s. A significant segment of the American population,

#### Farmers Markets

Farmers markets are not a new idea. The modern concept is often traced back to the 1970s.

Influenced by growing concerns about the environment and the desire for high quality and affordable produce, more and more individuals began to open farmers markets. Farmers markets fostered a sense of community and generated income for local farmers.

Beginning in the late 20th century, farmers markets experienced a revival. In addition to produce, vendors may represent local restaurants, jewelry makers, and sellers of specialty items such as soap, honey, knitted hats and scarves, and art work. Entertainers often perform at markets. Performances may include jazz or folk music, acoustic guitar, and even belly dances. Another trend associated with farmers markets involves restaurants that advertise the fact that they cook with produce from local farmers markets.

especially in the cities, was knowledgeable and concerned about national and global issues such as clear-cutting, acid rain, preservatives in food, and the rainforests in South America. Collecting rainwater in barrels, collecting food waste for compost, boycotting plastic products, and establishing community gardens all became popular ideas at liberal colleges, universities, and in the homes of the alumni of these institutions.

By the start of the 21st century, several crises helped to keep the surge in community gardens going. Al Gore's film *An Inconvenient Truth* (2006) intensified worries about humanity's perceived disastrous effect on the environment. The housing meltdown in 2008 triggered an avalanche of problems, one of which was the fact that many Americans lost their jobs. Anxiety over the environment and insecurities over how food was being grown (such as pesticide use and genetically modified food production), as well as ongoing money shortages compelled many individuals to find creative environmentally friendly ways to cut costs. Community gardens were a solution that made sense. Advocates stressed other benefits of community gardens, such as bringing the community together, beautifying the neighborhood, and bringing people back to nature. They contended that, in the fast-paced, artificially lit world of urban living, community gardens helped individuals to slow down and smell the roses.

### About Community Gardens

Community gardens are everywhere; some are many decades old or older, others have been established only recently or are still being planned. The culture of the community garden varies by location; gardens are influenced by the people who cultivate them, the founders who started them, and the environment in which they are located. Community gardens can be started by cities, schools, senior citizen homes, churches, agencies, nonprofit organizations, or the residents of a neighborhood. Oftentimes, it takes only one person to start the process; the rest will follow. Some community gardens feature straightforward individual allotments that are maintained by individuals or families. Others comprise one large garden maintained communally. The gardens may be embellished with artwork and folksy signs, or they may take on the appearance of a traditional garden found in another country. Community gardens may be small or large; they may be volunteer based or funded and supported by businesses, the city, or private individuals. The plot on which the garden is located may be owned publicly or privately. Highly organized programs such as New York's Green Thumb and Seattle's P-Patch Community Gardens have been operating since the 1970s. The American Community Gardening Association has been active since 1979.

Community gardens are not limited to urban neighborhoods. Community gardens are appearing increasingly on Native American reservations. Traditional foods are making a comeback in these gardens. In communities such as Chinatowns or neighborhoods with large Asian populations, community gardens have long supported the agricultural traditions of the residents. These gardens provide exercise and socialization for the elderly, many of whom work in the gardens. Intergenerational relationships develop, as the participation of youth grows. The produce that is grown helps supplement the diets of individuals who are often on fixed incomes. This produce is sometimes donated to homeless shelters or churches or sold at farmer's markets.

Community gardens are sometimes found in unexpected places. Rooftop gardening is popular in cities with limited access to green space. Gardening in barrels has also become a popular way to grow vegetables and flowers. Another out-of-the-ordinary space where a community garden has emerged is the White House, where First Lady Michelle Obama established a vegetable garden in 2009.

### In Conclusion

To say that community gardens have grown into a phenomenon is an understatement. Community gardens have been embraced and promoted by city officials, residents, and local businesses. They are showing up with greater frequency in towns and cities throughout the nation, transforming the historical image and appearance of the urban landscape, challenging paradigms, and mobilizing communities in support of an idealized lifestyle.

*See also* California; Chinatown; New York, New York; Seattle, Washington; White House

### Further Reading

Hou, Jeffrey, ed. 2010. *Insurgent Public Space: Guerrilla Urbanism and the Remaking of Contemporary Cities*. New York: Routledge.

Hou, Jeffrey, Johnson, Julie M., and Lawson, Laura J. 2009. *Greening Cities, Growing Communities: Learning from Seattle's Urban Community Gardens*. Washington, DC: Landscape Architecture Foundation in Association with University of Washington Press; Seattle & London.

Lawson, Laura J. 2005. *City Bountiful: A Century of Community Gardening in America*. Berkeley: University of California Press.

## Coney Island

Coney Island is a neighborhood and amusement park in New York City. Coney Island is most celebrated as America's one-time largest amusement park. Between 1880 and World War II (1941–1945), it lived up to its moniker as "the world's playground." It's famously known as a distinctly American world of colorful vendors, exciting entertainments, and beachside fun. People who grew up on Coney Island or who have childhood memories of holidays spent on the beach or at the amusement park at the legendary site refer to their experiences with notable nostalgia.

These days, Coney Island is a somewhat dimmer version of its greater, former self. The landscape has changed many times throughout its history, and many of the rides and buildings have vanished. Coney Island, however, refuses to disappear as a symbol in popular culture.

### Historical Perspectives

Coney Island's earliest inhabitants were Native American tribes. Exploration by white Europeans began in 1609 when Hendrik Hudson, who was employed by the Dutch East India Company, landed on Coney Island. The Dutch, who famously settled the New York City area, called the region Conyne Eylandt, meaning Rabbit Island. When the English took over the region, they translated the Danish name to Coney Island. For many years, rabbits flourished there, but development and human activity diminished their population.

The epic story of Coney Island's reign as an amusement park began in 1829, when the first of several hotels was constructed. In 1867, the hot dog was invented on Coney Island by a man named Charles Feltman. Popular attractions for the masses quickly followed, including a colossal structure, the Elephant Hotel. Improved transportation, such as railroads and the construction of the Brooklyn Bridge, accelerated the growth and popularity of the amusement park.

### Highlights

Coney Island eventually grew into a phenomenon. Extravagant hotels, fancy restaurants, and highbrow entertainment were located nearby for those who could afford it. Mature adults had their pick of edgier forms of entertainment, like drinking at the saloons, while most other Americans, including working-class immigrants, participated in the array of affordable family- friendly fun.

In 1916, Nathan's Famous Hot Dog Stand opened for business and started its annual hot-dog-eating contest, which has been held on the 4th of July every year since then. Besides food, candy, soda fountains,

View of the babbling brook at Luna Park on Coney Island, one of the nation's oldest amusement parks, in Brooklyn, New York, ca. 1903. (Library of Congress)

and sideshows, rides such as a steel Ferris wheel called the Wonder Wheel, a roller coaster called the Cyclone, and the Parachute Jump drew hoards of thrill seekers. All these rides are currently designated as New York City landmarks and listed on the National Register of Historic Places. The rides and attractions were individually owned and operated by several different amusement park entities that shared the park. These entities included Luna Park, which operated between 1903 and 1946; Dreamland, which operated between 1904 and 1911; Steeplechase Park, which operated between 1897 and 1964; and Astroland, which operated between 1962 and 2008.

Another feature of Coney Island was its stretch of beach property. The beach, some two-and-a-half miles long, drew enormous crowds in hot and humid New York summers. The beaches, salt-water pools, and bathhouses swelled with men, women, and children in bathing suits. Swimmers refreshed themselves in the Atlantic Ocean, while walkers promenaded the Riegelmann Boardwalk.

## Challenges

When the Great Depression of the 1920s hit and left many Americans penniless and homeless, Coney Island lowered its prices and stayed in operation. The Great Depression did not quench the spirit of Coney Island, but there were many factors that chipped away at the famous amusement park. After

World War II (1941–1945), many societal changes and local issues negatively impacted Coney Island. The mass use of automobiles and airplanes, the creation of new diversions and other competing amusement parks, such as Disney World, drew the crowds in other directions.

A succession of problems wore down the aging Coney Island: pollution, fires, the closure of Steeplechase Park in 1964, general neglect, disuse, decay, the deaths of long-time Coney Island workers, gang activity, and vandalism. These issues, plus the changing interests of the public, resulted in ongoing demolition, rebuilding, and relocation of various attractions. In the 1970s and 1980s, developers aspired to turn the property into housing developments or an Atlantic-City-style casino gambling resort. The plans were never put into effect.

### Contemporary Perspectives

Though no longer "the world's playground," Coney Island still generates plenty of thrills and excitement. Visitors flock to Deno's Wonder Wheel Amusement Park, the Cyclone Roller Coaster, the Beach and Boardwalk, McCullough's Kiddie Park, the Coney Island Museum, and the New York Aquarium. The Abe Star Rink offers hockey and ice-skating. MCU Park (formerly Key Span Park) features the minor league baseball team, the Brooklyn Cyclones.

The annual Mermaid Parade, BK Festival, and Seaside Summer Concerts are popular events that still bring in the crowds. Coney Island recently debuted new additions, such as Lunar Park, named after the original, in 2010 and the Scream Zone in 2011.

#### The Great American Roller Coaster

In its heyday, the roller coaster was the signature thrill ride at amusement parks across the nation.

The origins of the modern roller coaster can be traced back to Russia in the 17th century. The Russian Mountains was an attraction that allowed riders to slide down hills of ice on sleds. Such rides did not look like roller coasters as the public knows them today, but the concept is generally the same. France developed its own prototype in the early 19th century. They called the steel-wheeled rides that traveled on wood tracks, Les Montagnes Russes or the Russian Mountains.

There is considerable debate as to who built the first modern roller coaster in America. What historians do know is that in 1884, New York's Coney Island was the first to feature a roller coaster designed for public amusement. By the 1920s, the American roller coaster had entered its golden era, with rides proliferating throughout the country. This boom time lasted until the 1940s, when their popularity entered a period of decline that lasted until the 1960s.

The 1970s saw the resurgence of the roller coaster. In 1978, American Coaster Enthusiasts was founded. This and other organizations were dedicated to the preservation of the old, predominately wooden, structures. Alongside these efforts to conserve the roller coasters of yesteryear, new, larger, faster rides revitalized the popularity of the roller coaster.

Modern roller coasters are made of steel and strong modern construction materials. The new generation of mega coasters have drops that range from 200 to 299 feet. Giga coasters have drops that range from 300 to 399 feet, and the strata coaster have drops of 400 feet or more.

### Images in Popular Culture

Most recently, Coney Island turns up in the popular science fiction film *Men in Black 3* (2012). The grounds appear in wistful Technicolor fashion after Agent J, starring Will Smith, has traveled into the past to the year 1969. In a significant scene, the amusement park appears lively, full of people, motion, and fun.

### In Conclusion

Coney Island has weathered the challenges of time and shifting cultural preferences and has, in the new millennium, experienced new growth. This is a testament to the ongoing appeal of a certain mix of summer fun, thrilling rides, and good food in American culture.

*See also* Brooklyn Bridge; Casino; Disney World; New York, New York; Saloons, Bars, and Taverns; Soda Fountain

**Further Reading**

*Coney Island*. http://www.coneyisland.com/.

Denson, Charles. 2002. *Coney Island: Lost and Found*. Berkeley, California: Ten Speed Press.

Ierardi, Eric J. 2001. *Gravesend: The Home of Coney Island*. Charleston, South Carolina: Arcadia Publishing.

Immerso, Michael. 2002. *Coney Island: The People's Playground*. Piscataway, New Jersey: Rutgers University Press.

## Congo Square

Congo Square is an area in New Orleans, Louisiana. An important landmark in the history of African Americans, Congo Square was a gathering place for African descendants, enslaved and free, a site for celebrations, dances, and open markets in the antebellum South. Today, Congo Square is an important cultural landmark, as well as a popular center attracting local and national visitors. Congo Square was added to the National Register of Historic Places in 1993.

### Historical Perspectives

Before the arrival of European settlers, the area that includes present-day Congo Square was well known to Native Americans. The Quinipissa, Houma, and Tunicas who inhabited the region considered it a sacred place, as well as a site of celebration for the annual corn harvest. The arrival of Europeans in Louisiana set in motion the end of the Native American way of life and the start of a new world.

The French founded New Orleans in 1718. African descendants, both enslaved and free, arrived shortly thereafter. By the 1740s, Congo Square, though used for various purposes by different people, had become firmly established as the setting for weekly retreats. Slave life was rigorous and severely regimented. Free time was limited to quick meals and sleep to recover for the next day's toil. Because of religious beliefs, the French, and later the Spanish, allowed black slaves to have one day of respite a week: Sunday.

Thus on many Sunday afternoons, blacks congregated on the square. They numbered in the hundreds, sometimes thousands. The men and women danced, played music, and traded goods in open markets they set up for the occasion. A number of these dances were derived from their African heritage. The instruments they played, predominately handmade, included a mule's jawbone, gourd rattles, and the marimba. Eventually, the dances, songs, and instrumental music incorporated elements from French and American culture.

Following the occupation of Louisiana by Union forces during the Civil War (1861–1865), the jubilant voices, drumming, and rhythmic thump of dancers' feet faded. During the period of segregation in the South, Congo Square was known as Beauregard Square, and in one of many harsh ironies that appeared in the wake of the Civil War, African Americans were prohibited from going there. For more than 100 years, America forgot.

### Contemporary Perspectives

Then, in the 1980s, Congo Square, still officially known as Beauregard Square, was reborn. It began with the creation of the Louis Armstrong Park Complex, a tribute to the legendary African American blues performer. Within this complex, the area once known as Congo Square was reclaimed as a historic landmark.

The ground was covered with paved stones placed in a circular fashion. Water spouts were installed to cool children during the hot summer months. Benches and a 12-foot sculpture of Louis Armstrong were added, and the area was neatly landscaped.

The newly developed Congo Square was host to a series of new events by African descendants from a new century. There were small gatherings like weddings and picnics, and larger gatherings such as the New Orleans Jazz and Heritage Festival, a Juneteenth Celebration, the Congo Square International Festival, the Kwanzaa celebration, and the Louisiana Black Heritage Festival. Located nearby are the Morris F.X. Jeff Municipal Auditorium and the Mahalia Jackson Theater of Performing Arts. After Hurricane Katrina raged through New Orleans in 2005, Congo Square was once again used as a site for important cultural and social gatherings. One of the notable events that occurred there was the Congo Square Rhythms Festival in 2007.

### Impact on Popular Culture

Congo Square's influence on America has been vast, starting in the 18th century when the square was a popular dancing ground for enslaved and free blacks. Freddi Williams Evans, who authored *Congo Square: African Roots in New Orleans* (2011), asserts that the music of Congo Square inspired the development of jazz music and rock and roll. Dances performed there inspired popular dance forms, such as the Twist, the Shimmy, and the Congo Grind in the early 20th century. The legacy of Congo Square also inspired poets such as Langston Hughes and is paid homage to this day by musicians around the world.

***See also*** New Orleans, Louisiana

### Further Reading

Evans, Freddi Williams. 2011. *Congo Square: African Roots in New Orleans*. Lafayette: University of Louisiana at Lafayette Press.

Johnson, Jerah. 1995. *Congo Square in New Orleans*. New Orleans: Samuel Wilson, Jr. Publications Fund of the Louisiana Landmarks Society.

Stearns, Marshall, and Jean. 1994. *Jazz Dance: The Story of American Vernacular Dance*. Cambridge, Massachusetts: Da Capo Press.

Sublette, Ned. 2008. *The World that Made New Orleans: From Spanish Silver to Congo Square*. Chicago: Lawrence Hill Books.

## Coral Castle

Coral Castle is a roadside attraction off of U.S. 1 near Homestead, Florida. The attraction consists of an elaborate array of sculptures and monoliths. Though the famous residence is called Coral Castle, the structure is made from oolite. What is most unusual is the fact that a single man, Edward Leedskalnin, weighing only 120 pounds and allegedly only 5 feet tall, created Coral Castle himself, without the use of modern tools or technology.

The attraction, originally built in the 1920s, then moved and added to in the 1930s, is a spectacular sight to behold. But it's the mystery behind the attraction that draws the curious: How did Leedskalnin do it?

Coral Castle was added to the National Register of Historic Places in 1984.

### Historical Perspectives

Little is known about the Coral Castle's creator. He was born in 1887 in Iangubalene, Latvia. As a peasant, he worked in the fields and with animals, and learned stonemasonry. Under the oppressive rule of

Coral Castle, the creation of reclusive Edward Leedskalnin, who, using only hand tools, moved more than 1,100 tons of coral several miles, then sculpted them into a series of stone tributes to his wife. (Library of Congress)

Russia, many Latvians migrated to America. Leedskalnin was one of those who left, arriving on Ellis Island in 1912. He traveled through Canada, Washington, and Oregon before settling in Florida City, Florida, in 1923. At the time of his arrival in Florida, he was deathly ill from a possible lung illness he may have developed while working in the logging industry. Ruben Moser and his family helped nurse him back to health. Despite an ominous prognosis of six months to live, Leedskalnin survived another three decades.

In Florida City, Leedskalnin built his first rock attraction on a two acres lot. While living in a wood shack, he created a massive structure out of enormous pieces of oolitic limestone. The rock was white in color, smooth, and impossibly heavy, and yet Leedskalnin harvested the pieces himself using tools he made by hand. The process of construction was concealed, because he worked at night. No one knew how he was able to move the pieces from which he carved out rocking chairs and tables, moons, and planets. This first creation was called "Ed's Place," and Leedskalnin served as its tour guide and advertised to the general public in the late 1920s.

It was said that Leedskalnin, usually quiet and elusive, came to life during his tours. He happily showed everyone his creation: neighbors, youths, high school students, and strangers. He described each piece, though he was enigmatic when asked how he was able to build the various structures. His tools were no secret, but he insinuated that he had ancient knowledge, the kind that was used to build the Egyptian pyramids. He also liked to tell visitors that his creation was inspired by the love of a woman he referred to as Sweet Sixteen. He told many that this woman was Agnes Scuffs, a lost love from his home country.

In 1937, Leedskalnin purchased 10 acres in Homestead, Florida, and moved there, taking each piece of sculpture with him. He borrowed a truck and a tractor to make the move, but the owners of the vehicles observed little of how Leedskalnin loaded and unloaded the pieces. In Homestead, Leedskalnin added more structures to his growing complex, now working with coral stone of a darker hue and rougher texture. Soon there was a two-story tower in which he lived, a massive gate and wall, a barbecue area, telescope, and sun dial. He called this creation Rock Gate. By now, Leedskalnin was also a published author, having written two books: *A Book in Every Home* (1936) and *Magnetic Current* (1945). At this new site, Leedskalnin attracted more tourists. In 1951, he died from uremia.

### Contemporary Perspectives

In the 1950s, a man named Julius Levin bought the property, and the attraction became known as Coral Castle. Levin added a gift shop and an entry area. His advertisements, more lavish than those created by Coral Castle's original owner, featured beautiful models and artificially tinted coral rocks.

Not until Coral Castle came into the hands of Coral Castle, Inc. in 1981 did the attraction's popularity soar.

### Images in Popular Culture

Coral Castle has been used as a setting for a series of campy movies, such as *Wild Women of Wongo* (1958), *Nude on the Moon* (1961), and the film *Jimmy the Boy Wonder* (1966). In 1981, Coral Castle was featured on a popular television show *In Search Of* (1976–1982). Coral Castle and its creator inspired the song "Sweet Sixteen" by Billy Idol and a subsequent music video set at the site in 1986.

Leedskalnin and his creation were also the subject of magazine articles and, more recently, the Internet. Leedskalnin is considered by some to be somewhat of a modern-day mystery. Mystified, people wanted to uncover the secret of Leedskalnin's superhuman achievement. Some conjectured that he had the help of alien technology, that he had the ability to levitate objects or manipulate magnetic energy or the earth's alleged energy grids, or that he knew some esoteric ancient secret. Others assumed he simply knew how to manipulate the large stones utilizing ordinary techniques learned from his time working as a stonemason and a logger. But no one knows for sure.

### For Visitors

Today, Coral Castle has been expanded to include modern, tourist-friendly additions. Open seven days a week, visitors can park in a designated parking lot, visit the gift shop, and eat at the restaurant. Tour guides navigate visitors through the sculptures, explaining the history of the rock gate, the well, reading chairs, a Florida-shaped table, a moon fountain, throne and throne room, a sun couch, and a heart-shaped table.

***See also*** Ellis Island; High School

### Further Reading

*Coral Castle*. http://coralcastle.com/.

Leedskalnin, Edward. 2006. *Magnetic Current*. Minneapolis: Filiquarian Publishing.

Leedskalnin, Edward. 2010. *A Book in Every Home*. Cedar Lake, Michigan: Reada Classic.

McClure, Rusty, and Heffront, Jack. 2009. *Coral Castle: The Mystery of Ed Leedskalnin and His American Stonehenge*. City and state: Ternary Publishing.

## Corn Palace

The Corn Palace is popular tourist attraction and sports arena in Mitchell, South Dakota. Mitchell's economy was based on farming for centuries. Farms and golden fields of grain, mostly corn, are found near Mitchell, now one of the largest cities in South Dakota. The city's grandest creation, the Corn Palace, is touted as the "World's Only" facility of its kind.

Decorated by the fruits of the heartland's produce—corn and various grains and grasses—the Corn Palace is a lofty structure built in a Moorish Revival architectural style. The Corn Palace is an exposition of the region's cultural traditions, as well as a venue for such activities as popular concerts and sports events. A symbol of America's agricultural heritage and a venue for popular American amusements, the Corn Palace is not only a local sensation. It attracts more than 500,000 visitors from around the nation and the world each year.

Main Street view of the Corn Palace in Mitchell, South Dakota, in August 2007. The lavish building is an event venue, originally built in 1892 as an exhibition hall to showcase the state's agricultural offerings and rebuilt in 1921. Its distinctive domes and minarets, as well as the exterior murals made out of corn, continue to make the Corn Palace a must-see destination for tourists. (Americanspirit/Dreamstime.com)

### Historical Perspectives

The Corn Palace that stands today on Main Street is not the first of its kind in the nation. Similar structures in Plankinton and Sioux City, Iowa, for example, predate Mitchell's Corn Palace.

Inspired by these structures, the original Mitchell's palace was built in 1892 to celebrate the annual harvest, as well as to attract tourism and promote the city's growth. Known as the Corn Belt Exposition, the facility featured towers and turrets, dirt floors, and an exterior decorated in local grains and grasses. Entertainment at the site included such performing groups as dancers, juggling acts, and illustrious bands, such as legendary conductor John Phillips Sousa and his band. Because of the panic of 1893 and a severe drought, this facility stopped operating until 1900.

The Corn Belt Exposition changed its name and appearance in the 20th century, and in 1905 was renamed the Corn Palace Festival. This facility was built to make room for the rapidly growing crowds. The new structure showcased a Moorish design, with minarets and bulbous domes. Attendees enjoyed similar forms of entertainment to those that had been featured at the previous facility: bands, agricultural exhibits, and various entertainers. Both the first and second structures were made of wood and had dirt floors and no electricity.

The third palace, built in 1921 out of steel and concrete, was larger and featured a basketball arena. The fanciful turrets and towers were removed, but were replaced in 1937 and have remained ever since. This venue has attracted popular country-and-western singers and other entertainers.

All three incarnations of the Corn Palace have featured highly creative crop art on the exterior walls. This wonderful agrarian form of expression has reflected many themes over the years, such as international, local, and Native American–inspired.

### For Visitors

Today, the Corn Palace features a medley of activities. The Corn Palace Festival is a longstanding and popular event held in August each year. Other events and activities include the Corn Palace Stampede Rodeo, the Corn Palace Polka Festival, basketball games, and music concerts.

*See also* Main Street

### Further Reading

Anderson, Reuben. 2004. *Uniquely South Dakota*. Chicago: Heinemann Library.

Cerney, Jan. 2004. *Mitchell's Corn Palace*. Charleston, South Carolina: Arcadia Publishing.

*Corn Palace*. http://www.cornpalace.com/.

## Costco

Costco is large member warehouse club and one of the top retailers in the nation. Since its founding in 1983, Costco has popularized the concept of buying bulk and low prices without the glitz, selling its goods within monolithic warehouses across the globe. Costco offers its members a smorgasbord of products, many of them sold in jumbo sizes and large quantities at deep discounts. This strongly appeals to Costco's cardholders, who total over 60 million. Costco and other warehouse clubs have revolutionized the way Americans shop by offering never-ending big deals, enormous sizes, and large quantities.

### Historical Perspectives

The direct predecessor of Costco is Price Club. Price Club was founded in 1976 by Sol and Robert Price. Price Club was the original warehouse club, but it catered to businesses only. In 1982, Jeff Brotman and

Jim Sinegal collaborated to create a warehouse club for everyday people through a membership-based program. In 1983, the first Costco warehouse opened in Seattle, Washington. The concept took hold and spread quickly. Costco's major competitor, Sam's Club, another member-only warehouse club, opened that same year. As of 2011, Costco alone had more than 590 warehouses and 8 Costco Business Centers.

### Evolution of the American Shopping Experience

From the beginning, Costco was unlike the traditional American retailer and the common shopping experience. For centuries, the usual retailer was local and specialized, with the exception of general stores. The proprietor, customarily friendly and sociable, often knew customers by name. The cobbler made and sold shoes. The baker sold bread and pastries at the local bakery. The butcher cut, sliced, and packaged uncooked meats. The outdoor farmer's market featured garden-fresh produce and homemade products and came to life with the voices of venders marketing their wares and customers negotiating prices.

In the 20th century, stores grew more institutionalized, less folksy, and larger (though not yet Costco-sized), and prices skyrocketed as stores incorporated shinier floors, brighter lighting, and flashier displays. These stores also offered products, presented in aisles that were neatly stocked each day, with packaging that was more colorful, elaborate, and engaging than previously. Some stores paid exorbitantly for upscale designs, inside and out; such costs inevitably trickled down to customers.

Not so with Costco that broke the trend by caring not at all about appearance. Costco warehouses range from 73,000 to 205,000 square feet. The parking lots are also expansive. Visually, Costco looks, well, like a warehouse. It's boxy, plain, windowless, and concrete from top to bottom. Shelving in this facility is high, as high as 15 feet or more.

One of the benefits of a low-maintenance warehouse is that it keeps overhead costs low. By keeping things plain and simple, providing products in bulk, keeping the products on the pallets on which they arrive by delivery, and providing no plastic or paper bags at checkout, Costco keeps prices low. In addition, Costco does not offer a wide variety of brands for one product as many retailers do.

Customers can purchase most anything at Costco. Products include electronics, computers, food, produce, books, music, clothes, household items, toiletries, vitamins and supplements, pharmaceutical medicines, sporting goods, cosmetics, jewelry, furniture, meat, and baked goods, including the famous Costco jumbo-sized cupcakes. Costco is also one of the biggest wine sellers. Some locations offer additional services, such as hearing-aid centers, pharmacies, optometrists, photo processors, and gas stations. Some locations have food courts featuring popular treats such as hotdogs and 20-ounce drink for a mere $1.50 or a big slice of pizza. Interspersed through most warehouses are tasting booths, where shoppers can sample food items and other products.

The biggest distinction between Costco and other retailers is that Costco is membership based. Members are charged an annual fee. A membership card, with photo, must be presented at the entrance of every Costco building for every visit. Nonmembers are admitted as guests with members, and only members may make purchases. When exiting, members must show their receipts.

### Cultural Distinctions

For many Americans, Costco membership is a ticket into an exclusive guild. Often compared to an amusement park, Costco takes ordinary shopping to a new level for an already shopping-obsessed society. Sharon Zukin, in *Point of Purchase: How Shopping Changed American Culture* (2004), describes how shopping has become an intrinsic part of everyday American culture. People shop for every possible reason: special occasions, parties and celebrations, work-related events, personal and family consumption, boredom, social status, and addiction. Shopping fulfills social needs, personal wants, and imparts social status. It is common for many retailers to be open 24 hours a day, all-year long. Costco has restricted hours but is open seven days of the week, with an option to buy on their online website 24 hours a day. Shopping, especially in facilities such as Costco, epitomizes the concept of America as a land of plenty, where one can acquire anything, in any color, size, and flavor.

Indeed, Costco has most everything shoppers want and need. The large, spacious environment, impossibly tall shelving and a dizzying assortment of books, sweaters, socks, and other products create an almost festive feeling. Zukin points out that, in the late 1980s, Americans shopped more than they visited traditional attractions.

Some veteran shoppers take a professional approach to shopping. In his book *The Costco Experience: An Unofficial Survivor's Guide* (2003), Larry N. Gerston shares knowledge already used by experienced Costco shoppers. He stresses the importance of preparation, such as getting to know the best times to shop, writing down shopping lists before shopping, and determining what vehicle to take, the compact car or SUV, depending on shopping needs. He also recommends a scouting trip prior to shopping. The reasons he gives for this are many. Costco occasionally changes out some products and does not usually mark aisles with signage as most moderately sized retailers do. Also, as Gerston points out, Costco has no guides or visitor center. Though employees are available for questions and directions, they are frequently occupied with other work, leaving shoppers on their own to navigate through the facility.

Costco cardholders tend to be very familiar with the layout and have found creative ways to make the most of their time. For one thing, experienced Costco shoppers do not generally approach shopping as a leisurely stroll through the mall. Costco shoppers tend to be more deliberate. They dress in comfortable clothes and shoes best suited for copious amounts of walking and hard, concrete floor. Whether traveling by foot or by in-store vehicle, shoppers don't engage in a lot of casual conversation. Communication is largely limited to shopping and facilitated, in cases when shopping parties split up to expedite the process, by cell phones or walkie-talkies. Shoppers move adeptly in and out of aisles with monster-sized baskets and flatbed carts.

### Issues

Costco criticisms abound, despite the retailer's mass popularity. Some critics argue that large retailers like Costco hurt small and local businesses. Another argument is that Costco can sometimes reinforce the materialistic, excessive, wasteful, and heavy debt-carrying side of modern culture. Some members complain about long checkout lines, rude shoppers, and the sometimes frustrating and overwhelming process of navigating the warehouse. The impersonal nature of the interactions between shoppers and cashiers, and the bland environment of the warehouse are also criticized.

Some Americans turn their noses up at member warehouses like Costco, considering discounts and warehouse shopping and the people who shop there in a lesser class.

### Impact

Costco's impact in America and abroad is as deep as its competitive discounts. Many Internet blogs, such as Addictedtocostco.com and Ilovecostco.com, stand as virtual testimonials to the effect Costco has on the general public. With more than 590 warehouses in 40 states and Puerto Rico, and multiple warehouses in other countries, Costco has secured its place in the world market.

***See also*** The Mall; Seattle, Washington

### Further Reading

Berger, Arthur Asa. 2005. *Shop 'Til You Drop: Consumer Behavior and American Culture*. Lanham, Maryland: Rowman & Littlefield Publishers.

Gerston, Larry N. 2003. *The Costco Experience: An Unofficial Survivor's Guide*. New York: E-Reads.
Zukin, Sharon. 2004. *Point of Purchase: How Shopping Changed American Culture*. New York: Routledge.

## Cotton Club

The Cotton Club was a famous nightclub in Harlem, New York. During a spectacular existence that spanned nearly two decades in the early 20th century, it was a place of glittering talent showcasing African American bands, singers, comedians, dancers, and musicals. Notable Cotton Club performers included illustrious band leaders Duke Ellington and Cab Calloway, Ethel Waters, Lena Horne, and Bill Robinson. To this day, the Cotton Club's name invokes the magic of a storied era and a legendary people, time, and place. In its day, the club captured the imagination with its star-quality ambience and kaleidoscope of black entertainers.

However, behind the scenes of this entertainment wonderland located in the heart of New York City was a world affected by racism and gang culture.

### The Legendary Lena Horne

Lena Horne was a singer and an actress known for her exceptional beauty and poignant voice. Horne was born on June 30, 1917, in Brooklyn, New York. Lorne's childhood was filled with difficulties as she was shuttled from home to home. She lived with her grandparents until they died, then with family and friends, and sometimes with her mother, Edna Louise Horne, who attempted to find steady employment. During Horne's adolescence, she lived in New York with her mother and stepfather.

At the age of 16, Horne dropped out of high school and began performing at the Cotton Club in Harlem. She went on to perform with the Noble Sissle Society Orchestra and on Broadway. The Charlie Barnet Orchestra, a white swing band, became one of the first groups to integrate when Horne was hired to sing with the band. Though the band supported her, the racism Horne experienced while on tour prompted her to leave the band. Through the 1940s, Horne captivated audiences in nightclubs in New York.

After moving to Hollywood, Horne enjoyed success in a string of films during the 1940s. She is best known for *Cabin in the Sky* (1943) and *Stormy Weather* (1943). Lesser known is Horne's membership in the leftist organization, the Progressive Citizens of America, and participation in the civil rights movement. For her leftist views, she was blacklisted in Hollywood for a period during the 1950s. Horne died on May 9, 2010.

### Historical Perspectives

Harlem was at the nexus of an African American population boom that occurred in the wake of World War I (1917–1918) in New York City. The population consisted of a medley of local well-to-do blacks already established in New York and the arrival of working-class migrants from the South in search of work and opportunity. A rich life rapidly formed there, attracting intellectuals, poets, writers, jazz musicians, and performers and giving rise to the fabled Harlem Renaissance. Word quickly spread by mouth, black newspapers, and other means that Harlem was the place to be, prompting yet further growth and development.

By the 1920s, Harlem had also attracted the attention of whites. This was sparked largely by the growing popularity of jazz among white audiences. Due to the strong economic conditions in the nation following the war, whites had a great deal of money to spend, and they went to Harlem to spend it, despite the historical tendency of whites, blacks, and other ethnicities to stay within their own neighborhoods.

Gang leaders capitalized on Harlem's popularity in the white community, as well as the opportunity to sell beer and other alcoholic beverages that were outlawed during Prohibition. Owney Madden, an infamous gang leader, established the Cotton Club in 1923, thus ushering in an era unrivaled by any other nightclub in Harlem. Decorated with a jungle-inspired motif and stylish accessories, the

Cotton Club was known not only for its fine ambience but its vivacious late-night entertainment.

## Highlights

Elegance, exciting performances, as well as a glamorous clientele made for a winning formula. Cotton Club regulars included lavishly dressed gangsters, socialites, and high-profile patrons. Patrons indulged in illicit drinking and dined on an array of options on the Cotton Club menu, such as ethnic food, including Chinese cuisine and soul food, as well as conventional fine-dining fare. Gifted set and costume designers, song writers, and choreographers produced one-to-two-hour Broadway-style shows featuring all-black dancers, such as its Cotton Club Girls and later the Cotton Club Boys, musical numbers by the band, and songs. Many acts featured the latest and greatest dance moves. Among the most notable musical shows was the "Stormy Weather Show." Band leaders ranged from the flashy and charismatic Cab Calloway to the debonair Jimmy Lunceford.

Stars were born at the Cotton Club. Cab Calloway, over the course of his long career, inspired a new vernacular called jive talk and influenced flamboyant fashion trends. Lena Horne, the elegant actress and singer, started out at the Cotton Club in her teens and then went on to appear in black and white films featuring predominately African American casts in the 1930s. Horne continued to appear in movies and television programs into the 1990s.

### The Hi De Ho Man

Cab Calloway was a dancer, singer, and band leader. Born Cabell Calloway III on December 25, 1907, in Rochester, New York, Calloway is remembered as a groundbreaking talent, introducing his trademark skat singing to mainstream audiences. Skat is described as a way of singing with a string of spontaneous sounds rather than words. Calloway is also well known for his dashing and confident style.

Calloway began his career in Chicago, Illinois, before moving to New York, where he was hired to work at the famous Cotton Club. He and his orchestra reigned supreme during the 1930s. Major hit songs included "Minnie the Moocher," which was released in 1931. He appeared in many films, such as *The Big Broadcast* (1932), *The Singing Kid* (1936), and *Stormy Weather* (1943). He also recorded musical short films like *Cab Calloway's Hi-De-Ho* (1934) and *Cab Calloway's Jitterbug Party* (1935).

Every bit the charismatic entertainer, Calloway's influence was far-reaching. Many African American men straightened their hair to emulate his silky hairstyle and acquired zoot suits, considered the epitome of coolness, and which were popularly worn by Calloway. His music influenced blacks and whites as the jazz era flourished through the 1930s. In the 1950s, he worked on projects such as the award-winning musical *Porgy and Bess*. In 1979, he appeared in the movie *The Blues Brothers*. Calloway died on November 18, 1994.

The Cotton Club maintained its appeal through difficult and desperate times. It appeared unaffected by the Great Depression that rocked American society in the 1930s. It avoided tax troubles and the controversial character of its owners. While Harlem reeled under increasing poverty and racial tension, and New York society at large was jolted by periods of mob violence, the Cotton Club stayed on top.

The club also maintained its popularity when, in 1936, it moved to Broadway. The move was prompted by an increasing lack of interest at its original site. The Harlem Renaissance lost momentum as the 1930s progressed, and also lost its appeal to whites. By 1940, the Cotton Club's end had come. Jim Haskins, the author of *The Cotton Club* (1994), believes that the main reason for the Cotton Club's demise was that it fell out of fashion with its white patrons.

## Issues

Madden's club was, during its lifetime, an undisputed success, but critics, then and now, recognized the problems lying beneath the glittering surface. For one, only whites were admitted to the Cotton Club and, later, when a few blacks were allowed to attend they had to be fair-skinned. This was not an isolated rule.

Many clubs in Harlem and elsewhere were segregated by race. For many blacks and whites alike, this was a bitter rule reflecting the racial strife that prevailed in American society. For some blacks, they preferred going to African-American-only venues and were not interested in patronizing the Cotton Club.

Other discriminatory practices and issues troubled critics. Only light-skinned women, no older than 21, were allowed to join the club's exclusive Cotton Club Girls, and they were subjected to overwork and inferior conditions, such as the use of only one restroom and a cramped dressing room. Critics protested that performing for white spectators was demeaning and objectifying. They felt that the venue culturally and economically exploited black talent. This issue was complicated by the fact that white interest contributed greatly to the club's acclaim and the extraordinary careers of the men and women who worked there and approached their work with sincere pleasure and professionalism.

### Images in Popular Culture

The legacy of the men and women entertainers and the club they performed at can be found in the numerous works about Harlem and its important places and people, as well as the musical *Bubbling Brown Sugar* (1976) and film *The Cotton Club* (1984). The film is deemed a historically and culturally important movie that retells the story of a gripping period of black life in America, exposes the reality of the times, and presents spectacular performances by African Americans nearly a half century after the closure of an American icon.

***See also*** Broadway; Harlem; New York, New York

### Further Reading

Downey, Patrick. 2004. *Gangster City: The History of the New York Underworld 1900–1940*. Fort Lee, New Jersey: Barricade Books.

Gavin, James. 2009. *Stormy Weather: The Life of Lena Horne*. New York: Atria Books.

Haskins, Jim. 1994. *The Cotton Club*. New York: Hippocrene Books.

Huggins, Nathan Irvin. 2007. *Harlem Renaissance*. Oxford, New York: Oxford University Press.

Lewis, David Levering. 1997. *When Harlem Was in Vogue*. New York: Penguin Books.

Locke, Alain, ed. 1999. *The New Negro: Voices of the Harlem Renaissance*. New York: Touchstone.

Shipton, Alyn. 2010. *Hi-De-Ho: The Life of Cab Calloway*. Oxford, New York: Oxford University Press.

## Country Music Hall of Fame

The Country Music Hall of Fame is located in Nashville, Tennessee. Halls of Fame play an important role in American society, commemorating legendary men and women who epitomize the best in a particular field. The Country Music Hall of Fame celebrates the rich heritage of country-and-western music. "Country-and-western," or simply "country" music, has its roots in homespun music created on faded wooden porches, inside homely living spaces, and in backyard gatherings and dance halls in rural areas. Singers, accompanied by guitar, banjo, fiddle, and harmonica, sang lyrics that frequently told of heartache and woe, themes that run deep in America's rural heritage. One of America's most popular music genres, the story of country music and its legendary performers is chronicled in the Country Music Hall of Fame and Museum.

### Historical Perspectives

In 1961, some four decades after country music appeared in America's commercial music industry, the Country Music Association began recognizing the giants of the industry. The first inductees

View of the Country Music Hall of Fame and Museum in Nashville, Tennessee. The museum opened in 1961 and preserves the evolving history and traditions of country music. (Sean Pavone/Dreamstime.com)

were Jimmie Rodgers, Fred Rose, and Hank Williams. Their likenesses and brief bibliographies were etched on bronze plaques and put on display in the Tennessee State Museum, where they remained until 1967.

In 1964, the Country Music Foundation was formed by the state of Tennessee, the hometown of many a rising country-and-western stars. This foundation serves as the governing body of the Country Music Hall of Fame and Museum, which opened in 1967 in Nashville's Music Row. In 2001, the Country Music Hall of Fame and Museum moved to its new location in downtown Nashville.

### About the Site

The new Country Music Hall of Fame building is extraordinary. Its decor combines a musical theme with symbols from Americana. Seen from the sky, the building is shaped like a bass clef. Windows are shaped like piano keys, and the northwest corner of the building protrudes like a 1950s Cadillac tail fin. Inside, the building houses many treasures, such as the bronze plaques of all its inductees.

As of 2011, there were 115 inductees. Noteworthy inductees include the first woman inductee, Kitty Wells, the Queen of Country music, who was inducted in 1976, and the first African American inductee, Charley Pride, who was inducted in 2000. Historically, African Americans were not generally associated with country music, and were not, until many decades later, included in the hall of fame, reflecting the slow progress of America's inclusion of minorities in predominately white institutions.

The building also holds many artifacts, such as costumes, instruments, automobiles, photographs, video clips, and recorded music. The Country Music Hall of Fame and Museum also features the museum store and a restaurant.

### For Visitors

Visitors may access the museum daily from 9: 00 to 5: 00 P.M. Tours are offered within the museum and to the RCA Studio B, which produced some of country's greatest hits between 1957 and 1977. Visitors may also see the museum-owned-and-operated Hatch Show Print, a print shop that specializes in printing posters. Live music and autograph signings are also on tap in the museum store.

***See also*** Appalachia; Nashville, Tennessee

### Further Reading

*Country Music Hall of Fame*. www.countrymusichalloffame.com.

Escott, Colin. 2004. *Hank Williams: The Biography*. New York: Little, Brown and Company.

Kingsbury, Paul, McCall, Michael, and Rumble, John W., eds. 2012. *The Encyclopedia of Country Music: The Ultimate Guide to the Music Compiled by the Staff of the Country Music Hall of Fame and Museum*. New York: Oxford University Press.

Lynn, Loretta, and Vecsey, George. 1996. *Loretta Lynn: Coal Miner's Daughter*. New York: Da Capo Press.

Pride, Charley, and Henderson, Jim. 1994. *Pride: The Charley Pride Story*. New York: W. Morrow.

## Crater Lake

Crater Lake, located in southern Oregon, is the deepest lake in the nation. Famous for its mesmerizing deep blue waters most apparent during the summer months, as well as its depth of 1,943 feet at the deepest portion of the lake, Crater Lake is a local and national treasure (*Crater Lake National Trust Park*). The lake was formed some 7,700 years ago as a result of the eruption of Mt. Mazama, followed by years of snow and rain accumulation in the caldera of the volcano. Today, the lake is a popular tourist attraction, visited by locals and guests from across the nation and abroad. Tourists are inspired by the lake's beauty and attracted by the opportunities for exploration and outdoor activities.

### Historical Perspectives

The Klamath lived in the area of present-day Oregon and were there when Mt. Mazama erupted. They explained the spectacular event through dramatic legends involving two deities, Skell, the sky god, and Llao, the god of the underworld (depending on the narrator, the deities may be referred to as spirits or chiefs). The fight that flared between the two deities resulted in the destruction of Llao's home, Mt. Mazama, as well as the formation of the lake. The area within the vicinity of the lake was commonly used by Native Americans for vision quests, which often function as a rite of passage for youth. During the vision quests, youth spend time alone, sometimes undertaking special tests and awaiting visitation by a spirit guide and the experience of a profound vision that is unique to each person. The goals of the visions may include challenging one's courage and seeking to find one's spirit guide.

According to geological history, the fight that occurred between Skell and Llao was a volcanic eruption. The lake, serene, tranquil, and in a deep blue color, was eventually visited by the first non-Natives in the 1850s when John Wesley Hillman, Henry Klippel, and Isaac Skeeters lingered in the area in search of gold. They found the lake instead, calling it simply the Deep Blue Lake, and then went on their way.

More than a decade later, William Gladstone Steel visited the lake. This visit, in 1885, had a lasting impact on the area. Indeed, Steel was named the "Father of Crater Lake National Park" as a result of his life's work to preserve the area for posterity and save the beautiful space from human development and industry. In 1886, Steel and several geologists explored and surveyed the area. While there, Steel named some of the lake's most notable landmarks. He named Wizard Island, one of the two islands on the lake. The other island was named Phantom Ship. He also named Llao Rock, a precipice that is nearly 2,000 feet high (*Crater Lake Institute*). After several years of campaigning, President Theodore Roosevelt signed into law the Crater Lake National Park Act on May 22, 1902.

### For Visitors

Seeing the nation's deepest lake is a lure in itself; however, there is much else to see in and around the park. The 33-mile drive around the lake includes scenic stops and points of interest. Cliffs and pine, fir, and hemlock trees make up the scenery. Wildlife includes deer, eagles, and hawks, which are occasionally spotted. Black bears and bobcats also live in the area. During the summer, visitors enjoy the wildflowers in bloom. Activities in the summer are endless, as visitors popularly hike, bike, camp, and fish. The fish are not native to the area but were added to the lake at various times between 1888 and 1941. In the winter, the roads are usually closed due to snow, but activities such as snowmobiling provide amusement. Lodging may be found inside or outside the park; two visitor centers provide information for visitors. Visitors should determine if permits are needed during their visit.

Additional attractions, such as the Oregon Caves National Monument, the Rogue River National Forest, and the Lava Beds National Monument, are located outside the park.

***See also*** Grand Canyon; Great Lakes; Meteor Crater

### Further Reading

Brinkley, Douglas. 2009. *The Wilderness Warrior: Theodore Roosevelt and the Crusade for America*. New York: HarperCollins.

*Crater Lake Institute*. http://www.craterlakeinstitute.com/.

*Crater Lake National Trust Park*. http://craterlaketrust.org/.

Harmon, Rick. 2002. *Crater Lake National Park: A History*. Corvallis: Oregon State University Press.

## Crazy Horse Memorial

The Crazy Horse Memorial, a tribute to a Native American hero, is located on Thunderhead Mountain in the Black Hills of South Dakota. Work on the sculpture began in 1948 and is yet to be completed. Neither has a deadline for completion been determined. The massive sculpture depicting Crazy Horse on his horse, pointing into the distance, is expected to be, when completed, the largest mountain sculpture in the world. The memorial is projected to stand 563 feet tall and 641 feet long. This arresting memorial is one of several attractions located at the Crazy Horse Memorial, created to honor Native American culture. The memorial draws 1 million visitors each year.

### Historical Perspectives

Crazy Horse is believed to have been born into the Oglala Lakota tribe in 1845. In stories, legends, and memories from those who knew him, Crazy Horse was described as a generous man and a skilled warrior-leader faithful to the ways of his people. Early on, he showed bravery in battles against enemy tribes. In the 1860s, Crazy Horse was thrust into battles against a more formidable foe: the U.S. Federal Government. At stake was his tribe's physical and cultural survival. Other tribes had lost the fight; many had been massacred; others forced to give up their traditional ways and live on reservations with inferior resources. Crazy Horse fought in several battles, most notably the Battle at Rosebud Creek, during the Great Sioux War of 1876–1877, which delayed Brigadier General George Crook and his men from going to the aid of General George A. Custer.Scholars believe this contributed to Custer's infamous demise at

The giant sculpted face of Crazy Horse gazes out over the South Dakota's Black Hills near Custer in August 2010. (AP Photo/Dirk Lammers)

the Battle of Little Bighorn. In 1877, Crazy Horse was killed at Fort Robinson, Nebraska. Accounts of his death vary. According to Thomas Powers's book, *The Killing of Crazy Horse* (2010), Crazy Horse died from a bayonet wound inflicted by a soldier as Crazy Horse attempted to resist arrest.

In the 1940s, Henry Standing Bear, a Lakota elder, wrote to Polish-American sculptor Korczak Ziolkowski, who had contributed to the famous sculpture of four presidents at Mount Rushmore. In his letter, Standing Bear expressed his desire to create a memorial to pay homage to a Native American hero. Native Americans had long been marginalized in American society; a memorial to Crazy Horse would be a powerful statement, underscoring the richness of Native American history and its heroes, and would stand as a symbol of cultural pride. Ziolkowski agreed to the project, moving to the Black Hills and committing to the work until the end of his life in 1982.

**About the Site: The Memorial**

The memorial stands on Thunderhead Mountain in the Black Hills, a place considered sacred to the Lakota. The land was acquired through the Crazy Horse Memorial Foundation, a private nonprofit organization. All monies used toward this project have since been derived by charitable donations from individuals, corporations, admission fees, and sales made at the site.

Once the property was acquired, Ziolkowski set to work. Mountain sculpting, an arduous process, involves mountain blasting and many careful hours of carving to the specifications of the design. The design is not, as visitors might expect, an exact representation of Crazy Horse. It is believed that Crazy Horse refused to be photographed, though some claim to own photographs and a drawing of him. Ziolkowski's design is thus an artist's concept of Crazy Horse. In this image, Crazy Horse is depicted pointing with his left hand in response to the question posed to him in real life, "where are your lands now?" The statement, "My lands are where my dead lie buried," is attributed to Crazy Horse. Since 1948, the work on the Crazy Horse Memorial has moved slowly and steadily forward. When completed, the memorial will be 563 feet high and 641 feet long, many times larger than the Mount Rushmore sculpture, located several miles away.

The Crazy Horse sculpture was only part of Ziolkowski's grand vision. He planned such projects as a poem carved in the mountain, a museum, the American Indian University and Medical Training Center, and a visitor complex. Today, with the help of many individuals, including Ziolkowski's surviving wife and children, the memorial has developed considerably. As of early 2011, Crazy Horse's head had been completed and work had begun on the top of his arm and his horse's head.

### For Visitors and Students

Though much work remains on the actual sculpture, the memorial is immensely popular, and a great deal of Ziolkowski's plan has been implemented. Activities at the memorial include viewing the intermittent blasts that occur on the mountain, and the Volksmarch, an organized hike to the sculpture that occurs on a weekend in June. Other features at the memorial include a welcome center, the Indian Museum of North America, the Native American Educational and Cultural Center, Korczak's studio and home, Laughing Water Restaurant, and a gift shop. In 2010, the Indian University of North America was founded at the Crazy Horse Memorial. The university currently provides several programs, including a 10-week-long summer program to prepare students for college and promote Native American culture and traditions.

### Controversy

Some descendants of Crazy Horse have criticized the memorial organizers because they were not consulted about the project and had not given their consent. Others oppose the memorial, contending that disrupting the natural beauty of the mountain desecrates the sacred land and that the memorial exploits Native American culture.

Thus, on the one hand, the Crazy Horse Memorial is deemed irreverent, and on the other, it is celebrated worldwide as a place of learning and cultural preservation. Though these unreconciled positions persist, workers at the memorial carry on with their labor.

***See also*** Mount Rushmore

### Further Reading

*Crazy Horse Memorial*. http://crazyhorsememorial.org/.

Powers, Thomas. 2010. *The Killing of Crazy Horse*. New York: Alfred A. Knopf.

Sandoz, Mari. 2008. *Crazy Horse: The Strange Man of the Oglalas*. Lincoln: University of Nebraska Press.

## Cruise Ships

Cruise ships take passengers on extended voyages to popular destinations, sometimes making stops at interesting locales. Since their emergence in the 20th century, cruise ships have experienced spectacular growth and transformation. Compared to the passenger ships of the early years, today's ships transport more people than ever—millions of Americans each year—are bigger in size, and feature delights that surpass the imagination. The endless array of activities, comfort, and excitement aboard these mega giants of the sea have made cruising a destination in itself, with the occasional port of call sometimes serving as secondary bonuses. This, along with the affordability of the experience, has made cruise ships an American obsession.

## Historical Perspectives

Invention helped give life to the cruise ship industry. Thomas Newcomer's invention of the steam engine in 1712 provided speed to the once laboriously slow-going ships. The first ship designed for passengers was the Prinzessin Victoria Luise, built by the American Hamburg Company in 1900. The ship was 406 feet long and 52 feet wide. Cruise ships were not only purpose built but often converted from ships that were used for other purposes. Many countries, including England, France, Italy, Germany, and America, participated in the passenger ship industry.

Passenger ships transported two types of passenger: the wealthy and the poor and working class. While the latter tended to travel aboard the passenger ship bound to a singular destination, the wealthy could afford the luxury of staying aboard ship, traveling to a number of places. For a vacation experience, passenger ships catered to the affluent, who enjoyed opulent dining rooms, attentive service, live classical music, and fine lodging. The poor often brought their own food to sustain them during the journey or went without and amused themselves with their own folk music. Underscoring class differences, the ships delineated sections of the ship for each group.

By the 1960s, competition from the airplane industry had made passenger ships, meaning those ships used primarily for transporting passengers from one place to another, virtually obsolete. Indeed, most passenger ships had by that time been converted to cruise ships and were pursuing America's fast-growing middle class. The advantage cruise ships have over planes is that they not only serve as transport to a vacation destination but offer bountiful on board pleasures and activities that rival a popular metropolis or Las Vegascasino hotel.

## Contemporary Perspectives

The major cruise lines, owned and operated by international companies, often target groups such as singles or ethnic communities or offer a variety of themed cruises. Top cruise lines include Carnival Cruise Lines, which currently has the largest fleet in the world, and Royal Caribbean International, which operates the largest ship in the industry. Disney, which began in animation and moved on to operate a chain of world-famous theme parks and resorts, also has its own cruise line. Because of the immense popularity of cruising, Americans can depart from any one of dozens of busy centers along the nation's coast. From the West Coast, cruise ships go to Alaska, Canada, Mexico, and Hawaii. From the East Coast, they travel to the Caribbean, Canada, and Europe.

The ships are enormous. The *Allure of the Seas*, operated by Royal Caribbean International, was ranked the largest ship in 2011. Its length is 1,187 feet, and it holds a maximum capacity of 6,360 passengers. Unlike the passenger ships of the past, today's cruise ships have all the modern amenities: air conditioning, heat, and plumbing. The average cruise ship's appointments include indoor and outdoor swimming pools, gyms and fitness centers, multiple dining and entertainment areas, casinos, shops, restaurants, lounges, spas, and lodging for passengers and crew. Cruise ships have attained legendary status for their entertainment and expansive buffets.

### Issues

Since the first ship set sail across the ocean, safety has been a concern, and this is one thing that has not changed. Despite modern improvements that have made cruise ships run better and smoother than in the past, accidents, large or small, caused by human error, technical malfunctions, storms, or other events, can happen. The sinking of the *Titanic* is one of the most notorious tragedies in history. On April 15, 1912, the passenger liner sank after striking an iceberg while traveling from England to New York City. Less than half of the 2,224 passengers survived the disaster. On January 12, 2012, the *Costa Concordia,* an Italian cruise ship, capsized off the coast of Tuscany. Reports show that the captain may have caused the accident when he attempted a steering maneuver. The accident has been compared to that of the *Titanic,* though the loss of life was much less (as of January 22, 13 passengers have reportedly died with 20 passengers still missing). The ship was carrying 4,200 passengers at the time of the accident.

Waste is another issue that entangles cruise ships in controversy. The statistics, put out by an organization called Oceana, are grim. Every year ships dump into the world's oceans many thousands of gallons of waste in the form of sewage from toilets, sinks, galleys, and showers. Waste also comes from garbage, chemicals, and bilge water.

Critics like Jonny Finity, whose article "Overboard?: The Environmental and Cultural Impact of Cruises" was published in 2009 on a travel website called Matador Network, objected to the exploitive nature of the relationship between cruise ship passengers and local cultures visited by passengers at ports of call. Cultural exploitation can go both ways. As some perceive it, exploitive behavior is exhibited when individuals disingenuously play the role of a tourist attraction, sell items displayed as authentic when they are not, and beg tourists for money. Attitudes toward and treatment of locals based on disparaging stereotypes or perceptions that impoverished locals are inferior, further complicate intercultural relations.

### Images in Popular Culture

Between 1977 and 1986, the television show *The Love Boat* enthralled viewers. Every episode, interspersed with comedy and real-life stories, featured the possibility of love gained or love lost. Love and tragedy comingle in the multiple Academy Award–winning blockbuster, the *Titanic* (1997). *The Poseidon Adventure* (1972) and its remake, *Poseidon* (2006), capitalize on humanity's deepest fears against a backdrop of nonstop action and impossible situations that disrupt the gaiety of a seemingly ordinary ocean liner cruise.

### In Conclusion

For most passengers, vacationing on a cruise ship is not a frightful or dreadful event, and thoughts of calamity rarely surface. Cruise ship vacations are an extravaganza of fun, relaxation, and excitement, providing opportunities for Americans to escape the monotony and cares of everyday life.

*See also* Academy Awards (Oscars); Alaska; Casino; Gyms and Fitness Clubs; Hawaii; Las Vegas, Nevada; New York, New York; Transcontinental Railroad

### Further Reading

Dawson, Philip S. 2003. *Cruise Ships: An Evolution in Design.* London, United Kingdom: Conway Maritime Press.

Klein, Ross A. 2002. *Cruise Ship Blues: The Underside of the Cruise Ship Industry.* Gabriola Island, British Columbia: New Society Publishers.

Quartermaine, Peter, and Peter, Bruce. 2006. *Cruise: Identity, Design and Culture.* New York: Rizzoli.

## Crystal Cathedral

The Crystal Cathedral is a church located in Garden Grove, California. Spanning some 40 acres, and including multiple structures and facilities composed of glass and stainless steel, tranquil gardens, fountains, trees, and sculptures, the Crystal Cathedral bears little resemblance to either the iconic steepled Main Street church or the lofty stone European-style cathedral. The church is noted for its stunning beauty and as one of the first churches built studio-ready for television broadcast. The over 10,000 members and millions of viewers of the weekly *Hour of Power* program speak to the popularity of the church as a place of worship. The buildings' grandeur attracts even more attention as a popular tourist destination.

### Historical Perspectives

The founder of the Crystal Cathedral, Dr. Robert H. Schuller, arrived with his young family in Garden Grove California in 1955. His innovative thinking led to several unique places for his congregation to worship and to conduct church-related activities. For example, with no church available in the area, Schuller held the first service of the Garden Grove Community Church of the Reformed Church in America in a drive-in. Shortly thereafter, a chapel was constructed several miles away. For the next five years, two morning services were held, one at each site. The congregation grew steadily, but the strain of maintaining two services at different sites impelled Schuller to conceive another plan for their next church building, the first of several new structures built on the property.

### Construction and Development

The property of the Crystal Cathedral was developed over a span of five decades. The first project, designed by Richard Neutra, comprised several single-story buildings, such as a fellowship hall and other facilities for the ministry office and other activities. (Today, these buildings have been repurposed for other uses. For example, the fellowship hall now serves as an art gallery.) In 1961, the Neutra Sanctuary was completed. This structure, open and spacious, provides views of the new Fountains of the 12 Disciples. Members and visitors sit in the indoor auditorium, in the garden, or listened to sermons from inside their cars in the outdoor drive-in. From all three locations, members and visitors could watch Schuller as he gave weekly sermons.

Interior view of the Crystal Cathedral in Garden Grove, California. (Library of Congress)

The next structure that was constructed was the Tower of Hope, also designed by Neutra. Completed in 1968, the tower stands 13 stories high and is topped by a neon cross that emblazons the night sky. The building was originally intended to hold church offices, a 24-hour suicide and crisis prevention hotline, and the notable "Chapel in the Sky." It offers breathtaking views through its glass elevators. Two years after the construction of this building, the church broadcast its first "Hour of Power," the still-running television program.

In 1980, the church's namesake, the Crystal Cathedral, was finished. Designed by Philip Johnson, the Crystal Cathedral is an all-glass angular structure that serves as the congregation's main auditorium. The 120-foot-tall, 414-foot-long, and 207-foot-wide building also has immense 90-foot-tall doors that are kept open during services. The auditorium features an indoor fountain and an enormous organ, as well as what is believed to be the nation's first interior Jumbotron screen. The Jumbotron allows everyone in the congregation in this immense space to see the preacher. In addition to church services, large public and private events are held in the Crystal Cathedral including the annual "Glory of Christmas" and the "Glory of Easter."

The Crystal Cathedral building was followed by more structures. Designed by Philip Johnson, the Crystal Cathedral Spire was completed in 1990. The spires of the colossal structure reach jaggedly upward to 236 feet. They are composed of stainless steel that reflects the magnificent natural lights and colors that are ever changing throughout the day and seasons. This structure has a 52-bell carillon named in honor of Schuller's wife, Arvella Schuller. At the bottom of the spire is the Mary Hood Chapel, open for individual prayer 24 hours a day. In that same year, a Family Life Center was added to the grounds some distance away from the sites' main structures. In 2002, the Welcome Center, designed by Richard Meier, was completed. It comprises a medley of circular and angular shapes and straight lines and is made from stainless steel. A glass elevator traveling four floors connects a lobby, a food court area, the Evelyn and Frank Freed Theater, and a museum that documents the history of the church.

### Evolution of the Church Building

Churches have changed significantly over the centuries. Originally, early Christians met in each other's homes. From these humble beginnings came purpose-built church buildings, which evolved into colossal wood or stone structures. Amazing castle-like churches built hundreds of years ago still exist in Europe. In America, the plain and modest wood-framed church in all its architectural variety existed alongside European-inspired cathedrals.

In the 20th century, modern church buildings as well as megachurches increased in number across the country. It is not uncommon for churches like the Crystal Cathedral to have membership in the thousands and tens of thousands. Lakewood Church has held top ranking for largest membership for several years. In 2007, the church had 47,000 members.

As the megachurches became bigger and more elaborate, some incorporated gym facilities, housing for the elderly, schools for youth, and colleges. Some, like the Crystal Cathedral, broadcast religious programs the world over. Television has made possible the growth of believers who do not worship in church buildings but worship via religious programming from their homes.

### Issues

The spectacular rise of the megachurches is not without its critics. Many have complained that large churches are impersonal and factory-like. The megachurches have tried to counter this by offering smaller-sized church services and small-group bible classes and activities. But other issues are not so easily addressed.

Other critics have publicized their censure of megachurches in books and other publications. For example, among the many points made in the book *Pagan Christianity?: Exploring the Roots of Our Church Practices* (2008) by Frank Viola and George Barna is that church buildings—whether large or small—absorb the church's energy and resources in ways that might be better utilized in other ways, such as in providing for the various needs of the church community and community at large.

The expense of church buildings can be an overwhelming issue. Though many churches are able to afford the exorbitant price of construction with the help of donors and membership contributions, often without debt, the financial strain of maintenance, repair, and other church expenses can be too much to bear.

Another issue that concerns some critics about large and expensive church buildings is related to appearances. Some critics argue that large modern church buildings reflect an ostentatious, materialistic, and a highly institutionalized society, and that these modern structures have departed from the simple, unpretentious churches that dominated America in bygone days.

In a shocking turn of events, the Crystal Cathedral succumbed to the weight of its financial commitments and filed for bankruptcy in 2010 and, in 2011, was sold to the Catholic Diocese of Orange. Currently, Crystal Cathedral meets at Shepherd's Grove.

*See also* California; Gyms and Fitness Clubs; Main Street; Megachurch

### Further Reading

Chiat, Marilyn J. 1997. *America's Religious Architecture: Sacred Places for Every Community.* New York: John Wiley & Sons.

Kieckhefer, Richard. 2004. *Theology in Stone: Church Architecture from Byzantium to Berkeley.* New York: Oxford University Press.

Loveland, Anne C., and Wheeler, Otis B. 2003. *From Meetinghouse to Megachurch: A Material and Cultural History.* Columbia: University of Missouri Press.

Schuller, Robert H. 2005. *A Place of Beauty a Joy Forever.* Garden Grove, California: Crystal Cathedral Ministries.

Sheperd's Grove. http://www.shepherdsgrove.org/about/.

## Cubicle

A cubicle is a small workspace designed to make the most efficient use of an office area. Composed of plain partitions, a desktop, and shelving, cubicles do not generate national headlines in prime-time news, but they are pervasive in the American workplace and are thus a component of the daily lives of the American workforce. Cubicles are accessories of the modern world, ones that are often associated with ergonomic hazards and the dreariness and ordinariness of everyday work life. Still, workers have found a variety of ways to make the most of cubicles. Love or hate them, cubicles have made an impact on American culture.

### Historical Perspectives

A few million years ago, humanity moved, labored, and explored within the unconfined spaces of the natural environment. This environment boasted sunshine, fresh air, and, in most cases, boundless open spaces. With the exception of wild animals, precarious landscapes and conditions, such as thick impenetrable woods, steep mountains, and intermittent famine times, life then, compared to now, has often been idealized. From today's perspective, the goal of life seemed simple: to survive.

Many years after most of humanity put away its spears and gathering baskets, the modern world became preoccupied with ways to optimize the bottom line, that is, to find the most efficient ways to make and keep more profits. Another prominent issue involved finding ways to manage change. Businesses are constantly changing, in many ways faster than the evolutionary process of humanity's ancestors. In 1968, Robert Propst, a professor of fine arts at the University of Colorado, created the cubicle, ushering forth a new and enduring artifact for American businesses and corporations. Other cubicle developers, such as Herman Miller's Glenn M. Walters, made substantial contributions to the concept of the cubicle.

### Use and Design

Inexpensive and designed to adapt to ongoing business changes, cubicles are designed to create an optimally efficient space. In most any business, employees come and go for countless reasons, creating a need for a malleable work space. Cubicles can be taken down, set up, and moved to most any location with relative ease. The panel walls, usually five to six feet tall, provide space for pinning up notes, calendars, and other items. Because cubicles take up little room, more employees can fit into one area in an office than in traditional spaces that utilize standard desks or office rooms. Better than open office spaces, the cubicle provides not only privacy but compact and adequate storage for computers, paperwork, files, and manuals.

### Cultural Distinctions

As the debate rages on among researchers over how efficient cubicles have proven to be, the cubicle has been firmly established as the definitive modern American workspace with its own unique culture. This culture is in part defined by what happens in the cubicle and how the cubicle is used. Cubicles can be a place of solitary, detached, and monotonous work. They can also be a place of drama. Strife and assorted crises play out within cubicles in personal telephone conversations and between coworkers. Gossiping, complaining, and other forms of conversation regularly occur. Internet usage, particularly on social networking sites like Facebook, and games are popular ways employees pass their break times and lunch hour. Instant messaging and emailing also provide ways in which coworkers maintain social contact with one another and the world.

To break up the monotony of cubicle life, pranks and decorations are rife in many workplaces. Popular cubicle pranks include attaching sticky notes or plastic wrap-over items inside cubicles, including staplers, computer monitors, chairs, and everything in between. Cubicle decorating is viewed as more socially acceptable than cubicle pranks, though the latter are often enthusiastically enjoyed by all. Decorating cubicles with balloons and streamers for birthdays and other special events is often accompanied by celebratory cards, cakes, or department potlucks.

Cubicle decorating as an everyday custom is widely practiced and fulfills many functions. Cubicle decorations are an outward expression of individuality and creativity and add spark to the otherwise drab gray or tan wall panels. Depending on company rules, the decorations can range from the conservative to the outright obnoxious. Popular decorations include animal or cartoon-character motifs and feng-shui designs. Some employees bring the outdoors to their cubicle spaces with plants and natural sunlight lamps. Pictures of island getaways permit employees visual escape; photographs of spouses and children help provide work motivation.

### Issues

Cubicles may be boring or fun, depending on what employees make of them and the general ambience of the work environment; but in general, cubicles bear a negative connotation in American society. Terms like "cubicle dweller" and "cubicle farm" underscore the dehumanizing effect of cubicle life. Other complaints are that employees are prohibited from getting natural sunlight if they are not positioned by windows. Employees get little exercise and experience common work-related issues such as weight gain, wrist and back pain, and neck and shoulder strain. Privacy is often elusive; coworkers with disruptive habits such as talking loudly or eating foods that are malodorous in their cubicles are cases in point. It is hard to argue that life without sunshine, mobility, and natural space is harmful to the physical and emotional health of humans.

### Solutions

While cubicles remain a popular workspace configuration for many businesses around the world, other companies and individuals are trying out alternatives. Fed up with traditional work environments, some individuals are trading cubicles for working in the outdoors. A growing number of employers are allowing their employees to work from home or other satellite locations. Businesses like the multibillion-dollar dotcom company Google have created spaces, albeit expensively made, that break out of the norm of the boxy, plain cubicle space, incorporating many types of work spaces designed in bright, appealing colors with contemporary accessories and furniture. Many of these spaces are open and encourage teamwork and group collaboration; others accommodate solo work. But despite the migration of workers to other work spaces, cubicles are not vanishing any time soon.

### Images in Popular Culture

Books and articles on cubicle etiquette and survival abound. Scott Adams examines cubicle life in the famous comic strip *Dilbert,* striking chords with and the funny bones of millions of cubicle workers. The television show, *The Drew Carey Show* (1995–2004) features workers in cubicles. The film *Office Space* (1999) offers comedic commentary on the high-stress life in a cubicle farm in a software company. In movies like *The Matrix* (1999), *The Incredibles* (2004), *Wanted* (2008), and *Red* (2010), the protagonists are transported from drab, colorless, unsatisfying cubicle lives to exciting, meaningful, and action-packed lives.

### In Conclusion

Cubicles have permeated both business and popular American culture. Often represented as an undesirable and negative by-product of modern living, the ubiquitous cubicle is among the most prominent symbols of contemporary American society.

*See also* Facebook

### Further Reading

Franz, David. 2008. "The Moral Life of Cubicles." *New Atlantis* 19: 132–129.

Musser, George. 2009. "The Origin of Cubicles and the Open-Plan Office" *Scientific American* August 17.

Propst, Robert. 1986. *The Office: A Facility Based on Change*. Zeeland, Michigan: H. Miller.

Thompson, James F. 2007. *The Cubicle Survival Guide: Keeping Your Cool in the Least Hospitable Environment on Earth.* New York: Villard.

## Cyberspace

Cyberspace is a term to describe any abstract realm of electronic communication. Since the 1980s, the term has been popularly associated with the Internet. Unlike a physical space, cyberspace refers to spaces where people (called "users" in computer jargon) exist electronically through the medium of the computer, smartphone, tablet, or any other technological device. Entrance into this world is accessed, not by a key or a door, but by the tap of a button; the inputting of a username and password. Once in cyberspace, users navigate a limitless number of virtual spaces and engage in equally limitless activities.

The creation of cyberspace has revolutionized the concept of "place," as well as human interaction and exploration. For example, place, in cyberspace, is neither fixed nor tangible. Individuals, no longer bound by the limitation of physical space and distance can converge electronically from nearly any point on the planet. In cyberspace, users may create and experience spaces and activities that emulate many of the experiences as activities in physical places. Examples of cyberspaces include chat rooms, message boards and forums, virtual worlds, social network sites, general and business websites, and specialized virtual communities.

Cyberspace has permeated everyday life and culture in the 21st century. Indeed, cyberspace preoccupies the lives of many users who have become increasingly dependent upon cyberspace for socialization, communication, entertainment, emotional support, and personal expression. Users also conduct business and engage in education in cyberspace.

### Historical Perspectives

Cyberspace, as it is applied to the Internet or the World Wide Web, has its origins in the 1950s. In 1958, President Dwight D. Eisenhower established the Advanced Research Projects Agency (ARPA) to further the development of technology and science for applications in the military, space exploration, and related industries. ARPANET, which emerged out of ARPA (now known as DARPA, the Defense Advanced Research Projects Agency), was established in 1969. ARPANET is a computer network wherein users can exchange information and communication among different computers. ARPANET brought together the high-powered minds of scientists and computer wizards from the federal government and universities such as MIT, UCLA, and the Stanford Research Institute. Other countries also made contributions. In 1965, Larry Roberts at MIT directed the first network experiment wherein two computers successfully talked to each other. On October 29, 1969, Charley Kline, a UCLA student programmer, sent the first message on ARPANET from Boelter Hall to a host computer at Stanford Research Institute.

ARPANET spread nationally and globally, stimulating additional development, thus setting the foundation for cyberspace as it is known today. In the 1970s, the concept of "email," the electronic sending of messages, was born. In the following decade, IBM built the world's first personal computer. (Over the ensuing years, companies such as Apple Inc. and Microsoft would rise to dominate the computer and technology market, producing personal computers, laptops, smart phones, and other high-tech devices that support cyberspace environments.) In 1984, William Gibson coined the term "cyberspace" in his book *Neuromancer* (1984). By the 1990s, computer technology and cyberspace had permeated the military, business, government, schools, and the private life of millions.

### Places in Cyberspace

What makes cyberspace limitless is the fact that any user can create a space, either from scratch or by co-opting an existing template. This explains why there are so many and varied environments in cyberspace. Beginning in the 1990s, message boards, forums, and chat rooms on the Internet became popular spaces. Email also was widely used. In these spaces, individuals connect with friends, family members, acquaintances, coworkers, and strangers across the globe. On message boards, users are drawn together by specific subjects and interests. Examples include industry-related chat rooms or forums (message boards) revolving around divorce, single parenting, sports, music, and subculture groups, such as rockers and Trekkies. Lively interaction occurs, where individuals can access any number of threads, organized by subject matter, interest, or demographic. Typed messages allow users to communicate with other users in real time or whenever the user is free.

Online users come and go at any time; many users visit their favorite chat rooms and message boards several times a day. Users adopt one or more user names, which may combine actual names, hobbies, songs, and interests. Users identify themselves with a brief description, which may or may not include actual contact information, of their interests. While many users in chat rooms participate in lively conversations, others merely observe the conversations as they take place. Users may also invite other users to communicate one-on-one in private.

Another type of cyberspace, popular with gamers, is the virtual world. Virtual worlds are defined as interactive simulated environments accessed by multiple users. In virtual worlds, users often create avatars, computerized identities that may or may not be designed to look like the user, and interact with other users in real time. For example, in the popular 3D virtual world, Second Life, users create imaginative environments, select avatars that may or may not be depicted in human form. Via their avatar, users travel to a variety of places and interact with other users. World of Warcraft is a popular virtual game world combining fantasy and virtual interactions with other users.

Social networks and online communities are, as of this writing, all the rage in cyberspace. Examples of widely used social network sites include Facebook, Tumblr, Pinterest, Google+, and Twitter. In Facebook, users create pages that include postings of personal news, pictures and videos for sharing with a network of friends or with the public. Privacy settings allow users to control who can view their information. Friends can be added and removed from a user's network.

Sometimes cyberspace replaces real-life places and activities. For example, rather than going to bricks and mortar stores (to use cyberspace jargon), users may shop on websites. In lieu of reading actual magazines and newspapers, users increasingly receive information through online news sites. Instead of watching television and movies via traditional television sets and movie theaters, many users view programs and films that stream through the Internet. Other real-life activities that can be experienced through this medium are churchgoing, obtaining educational certificates and degrees, dating, and finding employment.

Online communities are as diverse and plentiful as the interests of the users on the Internet. These communities may include businesses and organizations such as churches, clubs, museums, libraries, and academic institutions such as schools, colleges, and universities. Other online communities may form around topics, such as life experiences, hobbies, politics, activism, and charity work.

### Issues

Needless to say, sociologists, entrepreneurs, and users all have worries and complaints about cyberspace. One issue that concerns users and critics is privacy. Lack of privacy or inconsistent and weak privacy settings expose user information to others, such as employers and companies that may collect information for marketing or other means. Other online issues, such as trolling, defined as antisocial activity with the intention of creating strife or theft, explicit images, and excessive self-disclosure have cast a negative shadow over cyberspace. Some users and nonusers lament the fact that cyberspace is superseding face-to-face or, even voice-to-voice, interactions.

These issues are compounded by the dangers that have been associated with the phenomenon. Cyber stalking, cyberbullying, and cyber predators, for example, have threatened the safety of and resulted in fatal consequences for some users. Such issues have resulted in crimes against victims and fatalities. Cyberbullying has emerged into a pervasive issue among the nation's youth, affecting one in three youths ("Cyber Bulling Statistics"). The issue involves bullying, harassment, as well as rumormongering through texting, emailing, and social networking sites. In extreme cases, cyberbullying has resulted in suicides.

### In Conclusion

Cyberspace has created a new type of place, a virtual place, in society. Whereas socialization before cyberspace meant engaging with others in a real environment, socialization can now often be carried out through virtual spaces using technological devices. Tourism, entertainment, and businesses have also been impacted as evident in commercials and radio advertisements that incorporate Facebook accounts and website addresses. Even when individuals do participate in activities in the real world, those experiences are often incorporated or shared in cyberspace. The ramifications of this phenomenon are easily observed, as real-life industries, such as news publications and booksellers, have struggled to compete with cyberspace.

***See also*** Apple Inc.; Facebook; Microsoft; MIT

## Further Reading

"Cyber Bullying Statistics." *Bullying Statistics.* http://www.bullyingstatistics.org/content/cyber-bullying-statistics.html.

Dasgupta, Subhasish, ed. 2006. *Encyclopedia of Virtual Communities and Technologies.* Hershey, Pennsylvania: Idea Group Reference.

Papacharissi, Zizi, ed. 2011. *A Networked Self: Identity, Community and Culture on Social Network Sites.* New York: Routledge.

Rheingold, Howard. 2000. *The Virtual Community: Homesteading on the Electronic Frontier.* Cambridge, Massachusetts: MIT Press.

Song, Felicia Wu. 2009. *Virtual Communities: Bowling Alone, Online Together.* New York: Peter Lang.

# D

## Daytona Beach, Florida

Daytona Beach, a city on the East Coast of Florida, is synonymous with auto racing. There, locals and tourists will find the Daytona International Speedway, which was constructed in 1958, and the headquarters of NASCAR, the National Association for Stock Car Auto Racing. Millions of race-car fans flood Daytona Beach each year during the race season, which starts in February. The thrill of the fast cars, the adoration of the legendary drivers, and the lure of the grandest of spectator sports combine to make Daytona Beach one of the most popular destinations in Florida.

### Historical Perspectives

When Daytona Beach was incorporated in 1876, the city was remote and undeveloped. The area's most alluring features were the 23-mile stretches of impeccably smooth beaches with an uncommonly hard surface and a solitary hotel, Hotel Ormond, which was built in 1888. Desiring to bring more business to the hotel, the managers, Joseph Price and John Anderson, hosted the city's first official beach race in 1903. The early races attracted drivers from America and abroad. The drivers were men of wealth who could afford the luxury of car ownership. Women did not begin racing there until 1941 when an all-women's race was held and were not allowed to race alongside men until 1949.

Daytona's early race-car drivers were not what they are now. Drivers were amateurs. They wore formal attire on race days. In general, races were not a competition between drivers or cars to the finish line but rather a test of the speed limitations of their automobiles. Henry Segrave, a notable driver of the early years in Daytona's history, was the first driver to reach 200 miles per hour on the beach. He set this record in 1928 with a speed of 207.55 miles per hour.

Daytona's early racing history was not without challenges and setbacks. Racing was not always as popular among Americans as it is today, and financing was difficult to come by. Equally troublesome was the fact that the beach was a temperamental location for auto racing: sporadic storms, changing tide schedules, and the shifting sands made the course inconsistent. But following the establishment of NASCAR and the construction of a modern race track, racing at Daytona Beach survived and flourished.

### NASCAR

NASCAR was founded at a meeting in Daytona Beach in 1947. A total of 35 men, including Bill France, who is credited as the founding father of NASCAR, attended that meeting. NASCAR plays a leadership role in creating race tracks and sanctioning races throughout North America. Headquartered in Daytona Beach, NASCAR's first official race, a beach race, occurred in 1948 in Daytona.

Martin Truex Jr. and Mark Martin lead the field in the first lap at of the Daytona 500 at the Daytona International Speedway in Florida on February 15, 2009. (Walter Arce/Dreamstime.com)

Ten years later, Daytona saw its last beach race and ushered a new era of modern automobile racing at the Daytona International Speedway.

**Daytona International Speedway**

Construction on the new race track at Daytona International Speedway began in 1957 and was completed in time for its first official race in 1959. The Daytona International Speedway was the fastest track for stock-car racing until the Talladega Superspeedway opened in Alabama in 1969. In the late 1990s, lights were installed around the track. Premium seating for spectators offers vantage points of the start and finish line and the pits, or turns one and four and the super stretch. Regular spectators have terrific views of most of the 2.5 miles of paved track.

Today, the track hosts several annual events. The largest attraction, the Daytona 500, culminates a series of races, such as the Koni Sports Car Challenge and the Rolex 24 at Daytona, that occur during Speed weeks. Other races at other times of the year include the AMA Superbike Championship and AMA Super cross championship for motorcycles.

Today's races are big-time events. Long gone are the amateur drivers. Professional drivers compete for large winnings, wear uniforms, and drive high-performance cars plastered with sponsor logos and racing numbers. Drivers have attained celebrity status equal to the biggest sports stars, appearing in popular news stories on television, in print, and on the Internet.

The Daytona 500, the speedway's most prestigious race, is an extravaganza that melds tradition and full-throttle extravaganza. The event features a pre-race concert by a popular entertainer, prayer, the singing of the national anthem, the race, and intense media coverage.

### Legendary Figures

Champions of Daytona include Richard Petty, Mario Andretti, Dale Earnhardt, and his son Dale Earnhardt Jr. In 2012, Danica Patrick, the third woman to start the Daytona 500, finished 38th out of 43 racers after being involved in a crash on the second lap. (The first two women to race the Daytona 500 were Janet Guthrie in 1977 and 1980 and Shawna Robinson in 2002).

### Images in Popular Culture

Though racing is avidly watched on television and featured in video games, films most vividly reflect America's adoration for fast cars and fast drivers through their dramatization and depiction of drivers as heroes or antiheroes. As with cowboys, soldiers, and other heroic archetypes, race-car drivers are venerated in American society. Classic films include *Grand Prix* (1966), winner of three Academy Awards, featuring an American driver competing in international racing. *Le Mans* (1971) follows American driver played by Steve McQueen as he competes in the demanding Le Mans 24-hour race. *American Graffiti* (1973) an iconic coming-of-age movie, commemorates the era of street racing and classic American cars in early 1960s America. *Days of Thunder* (1990), based on the life of race car driver Tim Richmond, stars Tom Cruise racing towards NASCAR victory. Other racing films, such as the *Fast and the Furious* series (2001, 2003, 2006, 2009, 2011), sensationalize the underworld of illegal car racing, *Talladega Nights: The Ballad of Ricky Bobby* (2006) parodies racing stars and the industry, and *Cars* (2006, 2011), a popular animation, features a lighthearted comedy of talking automobiles and protagonist Lightning McQueen's quest for racing victory.

### In Conclusion

Throughout the years, the array of both serious dramas and comedies underscores the esteem of car racing in America, and its reoccurring popular American theme of rising to the top amid adversity and mayhem. Daytona Beach has also prevailed against adversity and withstood the test of time, setting the precedent for the best and fastest in the race car industry.

***See also*** Academy Awards (Oscars)

### Further Reading

*Daytona Beach*. www.daytonabeach.com/.

Humpy, Wheeler, and Golenbock, Peter. 2010. *Growing up NASCAR: Racing's Most Outrageous Promoter*. Minneapolis: MBI Publishing Company.

Lazarus, Bill. 2004. *The Sands of Time: A Century of Racing in Daytona Beach*. Champaign, Illinois: Sports Publishing LLC.

Pierce, Daniel S. 2010. *Real NASCAR: White Lightning, Red Clay, and Big Bill France*. Chapel Hill: University of North Carolina Press.

Punnett, Dick. 2008. *Beach Racers: Daytona before NASCAR*. Gainesville: University Press of Florida.

Waltrip, Michael, and Henican, Ellis. 2011. *In the Blink of an Eye: Dale, Daytona, and the Day That Changed Everything*. New York: Hyperion.

# Deadwood, South Dakota

Deadwood is a small city nestled in the northern reaches of the Black Hills in South Dakota. Established in 1876, Deadwood will always be best remembered as a nefarious town of the Wild West. Deadwood, along with many other towns on the road west, was established by the multitude of fortune seekers who were swept up and carried away by the feverish rush for gold. The town, with its bevy of bawdy and lascivious forms of entertainment—saloons, gambling houses, and brothels—provided the backdrop for an array of colorful residents and visitors with equally lively sounding monikers, such as Wild Bill Hickok and Calamity Jane. Today, tourists, numbering in the millions, are also drawn to Deadwood, not for gold or adventure, but to see and experience a remnant of America's wild and rugged heritage.

### The Law Man

Seth Bullock is most famously known as a lawman in the notorious town of Deadwood. Born on July 23, 1849, in Ontario, Canada, Bullock arrived in the United States during the late 1860s. In 1870, he lived in Helena, Montana, where he worked as a grocer. He was soon selected to become a member of the Montana legislature, and served in the Territorial Senate in 1871 and 1872. In 1873, he was appointed to be a sheriff in Lewis and Clark County, Montana.

Like many entrepreneurs, Bullock knew that the discovery of gold in the Black Hill would bring forth a need for businesses to support the population. Bullock and his hardware-store partner, Sol Star, moved to Deadwood in 1876. However, businesses were not all that the town of Deadwood needed! Deadwood experienced recurring bouts of violence, as did many frontier towns of the day. Bullock was soon made sheriff of the town. As the town's daring sheriff, Bullock brought order to the town.

Bullock continued to live a productive life. In the latter part of the century, he helped found the city of Belle Fourche, South Dakota. He got involved in ranching and investing. In 1884, he was hired as a deputy U.S. marshall. After his hardware store burned down in 1894, he and Star built the town's first luxury hotel in its place.

In 1898, Bullock joined the Rough Riders, a volunteer regiment under the command of Theodore Roosevelt that fought in the Spanish–American War. In 1919, he established a monument for his friend, former president Roosevelt, on Sheep Mountain (now known as Mount Roosevelt). Bullock died the same year and was buried at Deadwood's Mount Moriah Cemetery. The hotel he built with Sol Star continues to operate as the Bullock Hotel.

### Historical Perspectives

To the Lakota Sioux that lived in the region, the Black Hills were sacred; the land was also essential for hunting and gathering food. In 1868, the U.S. government established the Treaty of Fort Laramie, which added the Black Hills to the Sioux Reservation. Once gold was discovered in the 1870s, no one, including the U.S. military, could keep the hordes of hungry fortune seekers at bay.

Like prairie flowers in spring time, Deadwood bloomed with life. At first, prospectors set up tents and rough-hewn cabins; next came wood buildings (which were replaced by brick structures following a destructive fire in 1879), Main Street, and then a multitude of homes and services for the rough and rowdy residents. In 1877, residents constructed 75 saloons, a number that does not include the many gambling houses, brothels, and theaters. In addition to drinking and gambling, denizens participated in assorted activities, such as boxing, cockfighting, and dog fighting. On any given day, brawls, gunfights, and volatile confrontations took place in the open street. Murders occurred frequently; punishment was rare. The law arrived slowly, starting with the establishment of Deadwood's first sheriff, Seth Bullock (Bullock's other claim-to-fame was his instrumental role in founding Yellowstone National Park).

Deadwood was not all violence and rambunctious living. It boasted reputable theaters, an opera house, and a church. For many years, Deadwood's Chinatown was the center of a self-sustaining and thriving community. The Chinese were lured to the West, like the majority of the population in Deadwood, by the promise of gold. The Chinatowns of the West also provided some defense against the often harsh and racist world that lay beyond its boundaries.

### Legendary Figures

Many legendary individuals passed through or settled in Deadwood during its heyday. Nat Love, an African American cowboy, was a former slave who named himself "Deadwood Dick" and penned an animated autobiography, *The Life and Adventures of Nat Love* (1876). Wyatt Earp, a lawman and sharp shooter, and Buffalo Bill Cody, a showman, spent time in Deadwood. Earp, however, is mostly associated with the O.K. Corral, where he participated in a legendary shootout against the Clantons in Tombstone, Arizona.

Other Deadwood legends include Wild Bill Hickok, born James Butler Hickok, and Calamity Jane, born Martha Jane Canary Burke. Hickok had an illustrious career as a scout, soldier, detective, and lawman. He came to Deadwood in 1876, at the age of 39, in search of gold, but spent much of his time playing cards. Not long after his arrival, he was shot in the head and murdered by Jack McCall while playing poker in the No. 10 Saloon. Hickok left behind a reputation that has yet to fade. Calamity Jane, who dressed like a man and sometimes passed for one to get work, frequented the saloons and reveled as hard and talked as rough as the predominately male patrons. Like Deadwood Dick and others, she wrote a memoir, *The Life and Adventures of Calamity Jane by Herself* (1896). Calamity Jane, reputedly six feet tall, was one of only a few rough and tough women amid the sea of males. For most of Deadwood's early history, the ratio of males to females was startling: 200 males for every female.

### Contemporary Perspectives

Many factors contributed to Deadwood's transformation from wild frontier town to respectable city. Bullock played a major role in civilizing Deadwood. By 1885, gun fighting was a thing of the past, and, in 1890, the railroad arrived. With each passing decade, Deadwood moved further away from its notorious past.

### Images in Popular Culture

Deadwood, the subject of many books and films, fiction and nonfiction, has secured a place as a mainstay in popular culture. Treasured literature includes writings by the stalwart and swashbuckling men and women on the frontier. Dime novels of the late 19th and early 20th century sensationalized gunfights, men and women gunfighters, and the perilous lifestyle on the frontier. Western movies were popular from the earliest days of American cinema at the end of the 19th century and continued to thrive as a genre into the latter half of the 20th century. In more recent years, Deadwood returned to the public consciousness in the profanity-laced, widely watched HBO television series *Deadwood* (2004–2006). The characters in the series were based on and inspired by true events and real people as well as myths that are larger than life. This series, as well as the town, bear witness to America's love affair with the Wild West in general and, more specifically, a town called Deadwood.

### For Visitors

Today's Deadwood is largely a tourist attraction. Though its population is small (less than 1,300), the town is popular for its many modern gambling venues and tributes to its past. In 1964, the city was designated a National Historic Landmark. Some of the old structures, such as the hotels and saloons, have been restored; reenactments of confrontations between gunslingers occur throughout the day. A popular reenactment replays the murder of Wild Bill Hickok at Old Style Saloon No. 10. Tourists may pan for gold or visit Mt. Moriah Cemetery, the final resting place for more than 3,000 people.

***See also*** Chinatown; Crazy Horse Memorial; Main Street; Old West; Saloons, Bars, and Taverns; Yellowstone National Park

### Further Reading

Ames, John. 2004. *The Real Deadwood: True Life Histories of Wild Bill Hickok, Calamity Jane, Outlaw Towns, and Other Characters of the Lawless West*. New York: Chamberlain Bros.

Bennett, Estelline. 2001. *Old Deadwood Days: The Real Wild West of My Childhood*. Torrington, Wyoming: The Narrative Press.

Matheson, Richard. 2009. *The Memoirs of Wild Bill Hickok*. New York: Forge Books.

McLaird, James D. 2012. *Calamity Jane: The Woman and the Legend*. Norman: University of Oklahoma Press.

Schlissel, Lillian. 1995. *Black Frontiers: A History of African American Heroes in the Old West*. New York: Simon & Schuster.

Wolff, David A. 2009. *Seth Bullock: Black Hills Lawman*. Pierre: South Dakota State Historical Society.

## Dealey Plaza

Dealey Plaza is a city park located in Dallas, Texas. It will forever be remembered as the place where President John F. Kennedy was assassinated in 1963. Several acres of the area have been preserved in commemoration. Many of the buildings, structures, as well as the light fixtures on the city streets are the same as they were at the time of Kennedy's murder. Seminal landmarks at Dealey Plaza include the Texas School Book Depository, where the Sixth Floor Museum was established on the sixth and seventh floors of the building, the grassy knoll, the triple underpass beneath the railroad bridge, and the John F. Kennedy Memorial. The Dealey Plaza Historic District, which was declared a National Historic Landmark in 1993, draws hundreds of thousands of visitors each year, all desiring to witness the location of a great tragedy in American history.

### Historical Perspectives

Funded by President Franklin Roosevelt's Works Project Administration program, Dealey Plaza was constructed in 1940. Located on 411 Elm Street, the plaza is situated on the west end of downtown Dallas and marks the birthplace of the city. The plaza features colonnades, buildings, an underpass beneath a railroad bridge, and a grassy knoll. A bronze statue of George Bannerman Dealey, the plaza's namesake, was installed after Dealey's death in 1946. Dealey was a newspaper publisher and prominent leader in the community.

In 1963, the city hummed with excitement. Local news reports broadcast the upcoming visit of America's 35th president, who planned to make an appearance in a motorcade en route to the Dallas Trade Mart. Kennedy was well loved by many Americans. Youthful and known as a man of the people, Kennedy and his glamorous wife, Jacqueline, were perceived by the public as American royalty. Kennedy was praised for his supportive role in the struggle for civil rights that dominated national news and events in the 1960s. He helped break new ground in bringing about the elimination of discriminatory laws that denied equality for blacks and fueled the culture of racism in parts of the nation.

### The Assassination

On November 22, 1963, President Kennedy entered Dealey Plaza riding in an uncovered presidential limousine in a motorcade. Kennedy and his wife sat in the backseat. Texas governor John Connally and his wife Nellie sat in the front. Many exuberant spectators milled around Dealey Plaza to catch once-in-a-lifetime glimpse of the president. Just as the limousine passed the Texas School Book Depository, where the grassy knoll loomed above its occupants, shots were fired. The president was hit by rifle fire in the upper back and, fatally, in the back of his head. The governor and a spectator were also hit by gunfire, but survived. A preliminary investigation identified Lee Harvey Oswald as the shooter, but he was murdered by Jack Ruby before the end of the investigation. Numerous investigations followed, showing that some information had not been disclosed, and that Oswald may not have acted alone. Since then, conspiracy theories have abounded, including allegations of a government cover-up. Through it all, the shock and horror of Kennedy's death reverberated across the nation.

### Images in Popular Culture

Due to the preponderance of images, actual and reimagined, of Kennedy's assassination at Dealey Plaza in the news, on television, in documentaries, and in popular films, Dealey Plaza is widely recognizable. Notable films that examine Kennedy's assassination include *JFK* (1991), *In the Line of Fire* (1993), and *Watchmen* (2009), a film based on a graphic novel. The films all dramatize the assassination itself, as well as raise theories and offer speculation, sometimes imaginatively, as to who killed Kennedy.

### For Visitors

Dealey Plaza contains many structures and locations that are associated with the Kennedy's assassination. Visitors explore the grassy knoll, which appears in amateur film recordings and photographs taken at the time of the assassination and is considered by conspiracy theorists to be the location of a second shooter. An X marks the spot where Kennedy was shot. In 1970, the John F. Kennedy Memorial Plaza was completed. It features a cubical cenotaph, 30 feet high and 50 by 50 feet wide, designed by Phillip Johnson. The memorial is located one block from Dealey Plaza. A museum, opened in 1989, resides on the sixth and seventh floors of the red-brick building that was originally the home of the Texas School Book Depository (Oswald fired his shots at the president from the sixth floor of this building). The Sixth Floor Museum, as it is called, features exhibits, a reading room, artifacts, and special programs. Across from the museum are the Museum Store and Café.

### In Summary

Resolution of the mystery that surrounds Kennedy's murder remains elusive in the 21st century. But America has not forgotten. The year 2013 marks 50 years since Kennedy's shocking death. While downtown Dallas bustles with pedestrians, thousands of visitors go to Dealey Plaza to pay homage to the martyred president and bear witness to a tragic and world-changing event in America's history.

***See also*** Arlington National Cemetery; John F. Kennedy Center for Performing Arts; Kennedy Space Center; Texas

### Further Reading

Bradford, Sarah. 2000. *America's Queen: The Life of Jacqueline Kennedy Onassis.* New York: Viking Press.

Douglass, James W. 2008. *JFK and the Unspeakable: Why He Died and Why It Matters.* New York: Touchstone.

Fetzer, James H. 2000. *Murder in Dealey Plaza: What We Know Now That We Didn't Know Then.* Chicago: Catfeet Press; Emeryville, California: Distributed by Publishers Group West.

*John F. Kennedy Presidential Library and Museum.* http://www.jfklibrary.org/.

*The Sixth Floor Museum at Dealey Plaza.* http://www.jfk.org/.

## Detroit, Michigan

Detroit is a city in Michigan, a northern state that is cradled by the Great Lakes. Dubbed the Motor City, Detroit is widely recognized as the center of America's automobile manufacturing industry. The city is also the birthplace of the illustrious Motown Record Corporation, a major producer of African American music. In its brightest days, Detroit was a major metropolis, thriving with financial success and a trailblazer within the music industry. Detroit was a place where American industry boomed and life was rigorous and optimistic. There, American ideals of taking pride in making an honest living, good old-fashioned hard work, and a solid family life were held dear, a fact that made many thousands anxious to settle in Detroit.

Today's Detroit, however, struggles to rise from many years of decay and economic crisis. The steady stream of newcomers to the city has waned substantially, as many middle-class Detroiters have deserted their homes in search of a better life.

### Historical Perspectives

The European development of Detroit began in 1701. On July 24 of that year, French explorer Antoine de La Mothe, Sieur de Cadillac, arrived in the region and established Fort Pontchartrain de Détroit.

Abandoned home in Brush Park in Detroit, Michigan, on December 2, 2013. Once a thriving metropolis, the city's downward spiral was sorely evident when, in mid-2013, Detroit filed the largest municipal bankruptcy case in American history due to a debt as high as $20 billion. (AP Photo/Carlos Osorio)

For many years, the fort was used as a trading center between Europeans and local Native Americans. In 1760, during the French and Indian War (1754–1763), the British obtained the land on which the fort was built. In 1783, this land changed hands again when the British lost to the Americans in the American War of Independence (1775–1783). In time, Detroit developed in the usual way of many American cities, drawing first builders, then laborers, and finally the affluent.

### Automobile Industry

Detroit's growth as the Motor City began in the 1920s. The automobile industry, including the three giants, General Motors, Chrysler, and Ford, established headquarters in the city. These corporations, as well as other automobile-industry-related businesses, were responsible for Detroit's explosive population growth and the transformation of the city's landscape. As factories went up, houses were constructed for workers, many of them hailing from distant parts of the nation and the world, such as Canada, England, Scotland, Mexico, and Ireland. After the flow of immigrants into America was stopped by legislation during World War I (1939–1945), the influx of transplants to Detroit consisted mostly of African Americans from the South. Although African Americans experienced racism and discrimination in housing and in the workplace, Detroit offered many more opportunities than did the South. A substantial black middle class soon rose up in the city.

Many African Americans, as well as other Americans historically excluded from the wealthier classes, were able to build an idyllic life in safe neighborhoods where they could own their own homes (in other major cities, housing was largely limited to crowded tenements). Detroit workers received incomes that permitted recreational excursions to restaurants, clothing shops, and entertainment venues. Detroit's population surged to 2 million in the 1950s, the same decade that saw the flowering of Motown.

### Motown

The Motown Record Corporation ushered forth an unprecedented era in American music. Founded in 1959 by Berry Gordy, the African American–owned record corporation produced music by the likes of The Miracles, The Marvelettes, The Temptations, Smokey Robinson, Stevie Wonder, and Marvin Gaye. Motown's brightest years occurred during the 1960s, when its music was considered fresh and new and had not yet been eclipsed by the changing tastes of ensuing decades.

### Crisis

Many factors contributed to the downward spiral of America's Motor City. In the 1960s, racial tensions boiled over into a riot when police officers raided a nightclub and attempted to arrest African Americans who had gathered to welcome home two Vietnam veterans. The violence and rampage that ensued in the black community was a spontaneous reaction in response not solely to the raid on the nightclub but to years of systemic racism experienced by the African American community as well as to disparities within that community. In the wake of this violence, whites fled Detroit in large droves. Known as white flight, the mass exodus of whites totaled 67,000 in 1967. This was to be the first of several major departures by whites from the city.

Detroit's economic and social institutions began to unravel at the seams. In the following decades, prompted by the construction of new highways, many businesses, including major automobile factories, moved to surrounding suburbs. Only those who could afford the move migrated with their jobs. Many minorities were left out of this migration. Their numbers added to Detroit's staggering unemployment rate.

Other factors accelerated the crisis in Detroit. Labor disputes, competition from international companies, such as the carmakers in Japan, and oil shortages in the 1970s and 1980s contributed to the hardships of Detroit's automobile industry. In the 1990s, many workers were replaced by new technologies that automated traditional human labor. Major corporations in Detroit faced uncertain futures following the economic crisis that occurred in the industry between 2008 and 2010. These factors contributed to the devastation of the once-thriving and heavily populated metropolis.

All these issues combined to result in a deeply troubled city. Where proud buildings and healthy neighborhoods once stood, crumbling store fronts, dilapidated structures, and boarded up homes appeared. Schools suffered academically and crime soared. The denizens of Detroit steadily fled to places with stronger economies, healthier infrastructures, and more employment opportunities.

### Contemporary Perspectives

In late 2011, President Barack Obama announced that America's major car companies were making comebacks. Economic resurgence within the nation's automobile industry and the efforts of city officials have contributed to Detroit's slow resurrection. But as of early 2012, Detroit remains embattled. Detroiters are still fleeing, taking with them memories of prosperous times, thriving employment, secure neighborhoods, and white picket fences. They leave behind the poor and destitute and a stricken all-American city whose future remains uncertain.

*See also* Carhenge; Chrysler Building; Great Lakes; Motown; Suburbia

### Further Reading

Austin, Dan, and Doerr, Sean. 2010. *Lost Detroit: Stories behind the Motor City's Majestic Ruins.* Charleston, South Carolina: The History Press.

Bak, Richard. 2011. *Detroit land: A Collection of Movers, Shakers, Lost Souls and History Makers from Detroit's Past.* Detroit: Wayne State University Press.

Carlisle, John. 2011. *313: Life in the Motor City.* Charleston, South Carolina: The History Press.

Heitmann, John. 2009. *The Automobile and American Life.* Jefferson, North Carolina: McFarland & Company.

## Disney World

Walt Disney World, known formerly as Walt Disney World Resort, is an entertainment resort in Lake Buena Vista, Florida, near Orlando. Founded by film director, animator, and creator of the Disney phenomenon, Walt Disney, Disney World opened in 1971, nearly two decades after the original theme park, Disneyland, opened in Anaheim, California. Disney World debuted with the Magic Kingdom theme park. The resort now features three other theme parks, including EPCOT (Experimental Prototype Community of Tomorrow), Hollywood Studios, and Animal Kingdom as well as many other attractions.

Regarded as the world's most popular family destination, Disney World pays tribute to world cultures as well as American fairy tales, history, and culture. Like Disneyland, Disney World is a place of magic and fun.

### Historical Perspectives

Disneyland, which opened in California in 1955, was only the beginning of Walt Disney's commitment to build entertainment venues that would bring innocence, wonder, and entertainment to Americans of all ages. But once Disneyland was completed, the land surrounding the park was rapidly developed by hotels and other businesses not representative of the Disney name. This prevented Disney from expanding his park.

With no room for growth in Anaheim, California, Disney decided to develop an additional park elsewhere. He wanted the new park to differ from Disneyland and to expand Disney's presence in a different part of the country. Eventually, Disney acquired 43 square miles in a tranquil and rustic area in Florida, a state located on the opposite coast. In a tragic turn of events, Disney died from cancer in 1966 before seeing his dream come to fruition. Roy Disney, who had worked beside his brother Walt for many years, inherited the project.

Disney World opened, with great fanfare, on October 1, 1971.

### About the Site

Disney World is currently helmed by Robert Iger, the CEO of the Walt Disney Company. The Walt Disney Company oversees the Disney legacy, which includes multiple ventures in film, television, consumer products, and a cruise line, as well as the parks and resorts.

The Disney World Resort features many activities for individuals of all ages. Magic Kingdom features Cinderella's Castle, a colossal 190-foot castle embellished with spires, turrets, and its own storybook moat (Cinderella is a popular Disney character based on the classic fairy tale). The park also comprises several themed lands (including some of the most popular from Disneyland), such as Main Street USA, Adventure land, Frontier land, Liberty Square, Fantasy Land, and Tomorrow land.

Other attractions were added later. The park's centerpiece, Spaceship Earth, which hovers at the park's entrance, is a futuristic-looking sphere 518.1 feet in circumference that is raised 18 feet off the ground by pylons. The EPCOT theme park was added to the park in 1982. EPCOT includes two main attractions: Future World and World Showcase. Guests watch shows based on technological innovations at Future World. Eleven countries are represented in the Pavilions in the World Showcase.

The later added attractions, Hollywood Studios and Animal Kingdom, debuted in 1989 and 1998, respectively. Hollywood Studios comprises six attractions, including Hollywood Boulevard, Echo Lake, Streets of America, Animation Courtyard, Pixar Place, and Sunset Boulevard. This park also features thrilling rides and performances. Animal Kingdom hosts a medley of amusements, rides, animals, and attractions within seven areas, including Oasis, Discovery Island, Camp Minnie-Mickey, Africa, Rafiki's Planet Watch, Asia, and Dinoland USA.

Theme parks are not the only entertainment in Disney World. Guests enjoy golfing, shopping, and going to water parks. Accommodations include campgrounds and an array of themed Disney World resorts. Disney World's Pleasure Island, located in the downtown area, is a hotspot for nightclubs, dance clubs, restaurants, and other entertainment.

### In Conclusion

Universally known, devotedly visited by Americans from diverse walks of life and regions for over 40 years, Disney World is true Americana. It is a place that is synonymous with wholesome entertainment and thrills, the premier family vacation destination.

***See also*** California; Cruise Ships; Hollywood; Main Street

### Further Reading

Gabler, Neal. 2007. *Walt Disney: The Triumph of the American Imagination*. New York: Vintage Books.

Thomas, Bob. 1998. *Building a Company: Roy O. Disney and the Creation of an Entertainment Empire*. New York: Hyperion.

*The Walt Disney Company*. http://thewaltdisneycompany.com/.

# Disneyland

Disneyland, hailed as the "The Happiest Place on Earth," is a theme park in Anaheim, California. Officially known as Disneyland Park, the popular attraction, featuring rides, lively characters, fantastical realms, and sensational entertainment, opened to the public in 1955. Since then, Disneyland has endeared itself to the hearts of the world by entertaining some 600 million and counting. No other park has permeated the American imagination quite like this one; few other parks have so pointedly and expansively captured the essence of American popular culture, myth, lore, history, and heritage. Disneyland looms large in the American psyche as a place of gaiety, adventure, and enchantment.

## Historical Perspectives

Americans were very familiar with the name "Disney" long before Disneyland opened in 1955. Walt Disney, the founder and face of the Disney phenomenon (along with his less-visible brother Roy), had already gained fame as an animated-movie maker. His films, beginning in the 1920s, featured animated characters such as Alice, of *Alice in Wonderland* fame, Mickey Mouse, and Snow White.

The first of many popular Disney television productions, *Disneyland,* debuted on October 27, 1954. The move to television was a strategic one. Disney felt it was good business to adapt to the changing times, which meant accepting the new technology even though television was not well received by America's film industry. The move enabled Disney to reach a larger audience than ever before as television became a staple for America's growing middle class. Television also provided the funding to turn Disney's concept of a family-friendly theme park into a reality (the construction of the theme park totaled $17 million).

Disneyland's grand but rocky opening took place on July 18, 1955. The weather was hot and there were more in attendance than had been invited, leading to unhappiness among the attendees. But Disney never looked back, and the park's fame and popularity have endured for more than a half century. Other attractions, such as Walt Disney World in Florida and other theme parks outside the country, in Tokyo, Paris, France, and Hong Kong have made sure that the Disney name is known throughout the world.

## About the Site

Disneyland comprises several themed areas, sometimes referred to as lands or realms. The most recognizable part of the theme park is the ethereal Sleeping Beauty Castle. Guests begin their journey at the entrance of the park at Main Street, USA and then travel to other lands. The original lands included Main Street USA, Adventure land, Frontier land, Fantasy land, and Tomorrow land. New Orleans Square, Critter Country, and Toontown were added later.

Various set shows and activities enhance the Disney experience. Wandering Disney characters (costumed Disney staff) such as Mickey Mouse, Minnie Mouse, Goofy, and Snow White enthrall guests. Fireworks exploding above the Sleeping Beauty Castle, the Disneyland Band plays, and parades also add to the festive, magical ambience of the park. Disneyland also offers numerous shops and restaurants.

## Popular Rides

Some guests go to Disneyland primarily to enjoy the rides, which cater to preschoolers on up. Guests can keep it safe by taking a trip through Mickey's House or ramp it up with a flying adventure on Peter Pan's flight. Splash Mountain is a thrilling half-mile adventure through several drops climaxing in a 52-foot,

45-degree, 40-mile-per-hour, stomach-churning drop. Splash Mountain is based on the American folk characters Brer Rabbit and his archenemies Brer Fox and Brer Bear. Dozens of other rides keep up the excitement and thrill for Disneyland guests.

### Themes

Many of the realms and the characters and activities that appear within them center on Disney's exploration of the fundamental themes, symbols, and images found in American history. As a tribute to the traditional American Main Street, Disneyland features a replica wherein guests are transported back in time to Disney's Main Street, USA. This Main Street includes objects and places that were integral to the nostalgic American town: a train station, town square, city hall, a horse-drawn streetcar, and shops.

Other themes are derived from American mythology, literature, and films that paint rosy and imaginative portraits of America's past and future. In Adventure land, guests experience escapades in attractions based on Indiana Jones, the heroic archeologist of a popular film series. Tarzan, the muscle-bound jungle dweller who appeared first in an American novel and then in film and on television, is represented in a Disneyland attraction. In Frontier land, Disney pays homage to the fabled Old West. Here, guests visit Native American villages, ride the Mark Twain Riverboat, and watch an Old West show. In Tomorrow land, guests experience futuristic rides, battles, and a Michael Jackson film called *Captain EO*.

### For Visitors

Disney designed his place of wonder for people of all ages, but affording the trip can require some savvy planning. Special offers, packages, and passes help defray the costs of making the excursion to Disneyland. The trip may include airfare, car rental, accommodations at a Disney Resort Hotel, food, admission, and souvenirs. Millions of American and international tourists have made the journey. For some, the visit is a rite of passage; for others it is an essential event. Either way, the trip to Disneyland has come to embody the quintessential American vacation.

***See also*** California; Disney World; Main Street; Old West

### Further Reading

Gabler, Neal. 2006. *Walt Disney: The Triumph of the American Imagination*. New York: Alfred A Knopf.

Jackson, Kathy Merlock, and West, Mark I., eds. 2011. *Disneyland and Culture: Essay son the Parks and Their Influence*. Jefferson, North Carolina: McFarland & Company, Inc.

Lindquist, Jack, and Combs, Melinda J. 2010. *In Service to the Mouse: My Unexpected Journey to Becoming Disneyland's First President*. Orange, California: Never land Media and Chapman University Press.

## Dodge City, Kansas

Dodge City, located in Kansas, was founded during the period of the American Old West (ca. 1830–1920). For most Americans, the city conjures images of the wild frontier, of gun slinging desperados and bronco-riding cowboys. These images do not stray far from reality, for Dodge City attracted all manner of archetypal Western characters. Many were rugged hunters seeking to make money in the buffalo trade. Cowboys and restless drifters also passed through town. Heroic lawmen performed the ominous duty of enforcing law and order. Long after the West has faded into American history, tourists continue to swarm the city, drawn by both the historical record and the sensationalized tales of the town.

Scene outside the successful Wright Beverly store in Dodge City, Kansas, ca. 1883. (AP/Wide World Photos)

### Historical Perspectives

Dodge City was settled in 1872 on the great open spaces of the plains. The area was originally inhabited by Native Americans, and, starting in the 1840s, several U.S. forts had been built nearby. In those days, wildlife was plentiful, and buffalo moved across the plains in thick, massive herds. The settlement, situated near famous byways such as the Santa Fe and Chisholm Trails, grew rapidly.

Dodge City occupied an ideal location for those occupations peculiar to the Old West such as buffalo hunting and trading and, later, cattle herding. Hunters from hither and yon for a while made a good living selling the rich brown hides and the bones of the bison. But hunting soon decimated the herds. By 1875, with the buffalo nearly extinct, the era of the cowboy was in full swing. The cowboys, like the buffalo hunters before them, eked out an impressive income driving cattle along the trails to Dodge City.

### Cultural Distinctions

The Wild West was replete with towns and cities that had a reputation for what was called at the time "wickedness." Situated in remote areas, far removed from long-established cities and law enforcement, the Old West was a place known for uninhibited opportunity—legal or otherwise. Lascivious recreation in the form of prostitution, gambling, and heavy drinking in saloons was plentiful.

Dodge City was no different. In the early part of the city's history, lawlessness was rampant. With the arrival of the lawmen, things began to change. Wyatt Earp, a famous lawman, was famous for "cleaning up" Dodge City. Laws were established that delineated the north side of the railroad track for respectable businesses and activities. To the south of the railroad tracks, ne'er-do-wells and lawless men indulged in activities of ill repute.

Dodge City, however, always was more than a symbol of wickedness. To the hunters, cowboys, soldiers, and businessmen and women who lived in the city or passed through, Dodge City was an important nucleus, a stopping point for victuals and rest, relaxation, and entertainment, a bustling center of human activity.

### The Close of an Era

Once the cattle drives stopped, prompted by devastating winters, Dodge City, the thriving Western town, was no more. The memory of it, however, lived on in popular dime novels, biographies, folk songs, Wild West shows, rodeos, movies, and on television.

### Images in Popular Culture

Vivid images and tales of the Wild West entered the popular culture contemporaneously in the form of paintings, photography, and dime novels. Americans were captivated by the mystique of gun-toting heroes, the beauty and thrill of the open range, and the rigors of Spartan living. Outlaws, whether condemned as irredeemable or romanticized as misunderstood, were the stuff of high drama.

In the 20th century, the bravery of Wyatt Earp was immortalized in *Wyatt Earp: Frontier Marshal* (1931), in a 1950s television series and in other renditions. Dodge City was the subject of a long-running radio show in the 1950s and a television series called *Gun smoke*, an American favorite that ran on television from 1955 to 1975. Dodge City was the setting of several films, such as *Dodge City* (1939), *The Gunfight at Dodge City* (1959), *Cheyenne Autumn* (1964), and *Wyatt Earp* (1964).

### For Visitors

Twenty-first century Dodge City has little in common with the images its name inspires. Though home to less than 30,000 individuals, the city has morphed into a traditional American town with modern amenities and structures, neighborhoods, a police station, public schools, a Walmart, and ethnic and fast-food restaurants.

Modern amenities, notwithstanding, many historic sites and Old West–themed attractions can still be found. Historic landmarks include El Capitan, a bronze Texas Longhorn steer that pays homage to the cattle drives and a bronze statue of Wyatt Earp, and a major thoroughfare is also named after Earp. The Boot Hill Museum houses artifacts and exhibits featuring the Long branch Saloon, Boot Hill Cemetery, the American Buffalo, and Nomadic Indians. Other attractions include the Cowboy Hall of Fame, shows, and a reenactment of the Boot Hill Gunfighters shooting it out on Front Street. Downtown Dodge City features tours, shops, and other attractions for visitors.

*See also* Great Plains; National Frontiers Trails Museum; Old West; Saloons, Bars, and Taverns; Texas; Walmart

### Further Reading

*Boot Hill Museum and Front Street.* http://www.boothill.org/.

Masterson, Bat. 1995. *Famous Gunfighters of the Western Frontier: Wyatt Earp, Doc Holliday, Luke Short and Others.* Silverthorne, Colorado: Vista Books.

Roberts, Gary L. 2006. *Doc Holliday: The Life and Legend.* Hoboken, New Jersey: John Wiley & Sons.

Shilling berg, William B. 2009. *Dodge City: The Early Years, 1872–1886.* Norman, Oklahoma: Arthur H. Clark Co.

Vestal, Stanley. 1952. *Dodge City: Queen of Cow Towns: "The Wickedest Little City in America," 1887–1886.* New York: Harper & Row.

## Dollywood

Dollywood is a theme park in Pigeon Forge, Tennessee. Dollywood features blockbuster rides, star-studded performances, festivals, and other attractions. The theme park focuses on cultural traditions native to the region, such as bluegrass and country-and-western music, arts and crafts, southern cuisine, and other important symbols of rural heritage. Dollywood also imparts modern twists to old traditions and incorporates multicultural themes and activities. The theme park's principal owner, legendary country-and-western singer Dolly Parton, lends her star power and enthusiasm to the theme park that bears her name.

### Historical Perspectives

Rebel Railroad was the original name of the theme park situated in the Smoky Mountain town of Pigeon Forge, Tennessee. Build in 1961 by the Robins Brothers, the Rebel Railroad featured such attractions as a simulated Confederate steam train, a saloon, blacksmith shop, and Civil War (1861–1864) battle reenactments. After undergoing several name and ownership changes, the park became Dollywood in 1986. The park is owned by Dolly Parton, a native Tennessean, and the Herschend Family Entertainment Company.

Born in 1946, Dolly Parton began her spectacular singing career in the 1960s. Her fame quickly spread beyond the bounds of the country music subculture, as she was embraced by mainstream music with hits such as "Islands in the Stream," released in 1983 as a duet with Kenny Rogers. Parton also ventured successfully into television and film. She starred in nationally acclaimed movies such as *9 to 5* (1980), *Steel Magnolias* (1989), and *Joyful Noise* (2012).

### Highlights

Under its new ownership, the 150 acres of Dollywood underwent major reconstruction, which took place over the course of many years. The park includes 10 themed areas, including Show street, River town Junction, the Country Fair, Jukebox Junction, Owen's Farm, and Adventures in Imagination. The themed areas feature rides, music, museums, and other attractions, many of which include fundamental aspects of southern life and traditions. Themes that pay homage to the musical, cultural, and rural traditions of the region's people appear throughout. Rivertown Junction, for example, consists of attractions such as the Tennessee Mountain Home, the Back Porch Theater, and the Smoky Mountain River Rampage whitewater rafting ride. The mountain home, back porch, and Smoky Mountain River motifs all

The Tennessee Mountain Home is a replica of Dolly Parton's childhood home, located at her amusement park, Dollywood, in Pigeon Forge, Tennessee. (AP/Wide World Photos)

represent fundamental aspects of country living in the region. More than two dozen rides, including six roller coasters, are located at the park.

Dollywood's many festivals are also grounded in southern heritage. The Festival of Nations explores cultures from around the world. The Barbeque and Bluegrass festival invites visitors to immerse themselves in traditional southern cuisine and music. The National Southern Gospel and Harvest Celebration showcases gospel music, handmade crafts, and harvest-time recipes. Smoky Mountain Christmas is a timeless tradition.

Southern cuisine, an important tradition in the region, is taken very seriously at Dollywood. Visitors pick from many dining options, though the park is famous for its high-fat and meat-laden southern delights. BBQ, pork rinds, kettle corn, and ham and beans with cornbread are also favorite food options. But Dolly also caters to modern dietary trends, offering diabetic, gluten-free, and vegetarian options.

In addition to the rides, attractions, and festivals, Dollywood operates the Dollywood's Splash Country and Dixie Stampede dinner theaters.

### In Conclusion

Despite the fact that the park is based on a culture that has historically been regarded as on object of derision and contempt, Dollywood has achieved national acclaim. At Dollywood, diversity, as well as the culture of the region, is celebrated. Importantly, the region's heritage—the music, the food, and other traditions—is presented with a deep-seated pride that is many generations strong.

*See also* Appalachia; Great Smoky Mountains; Nashville, Tennessee

### Further Reading

*Dollywood*. http://www.dollywood.com.

Miller, Stephen. 2009. *Smart Blonde: Dolly Parton*. London: Omnibus Press.

Parton, Dolly. 1994. *Dolly: My Life and Other Unfinished Business*. New York: HarperCollins.

Samuelson, Dale, and Yegoiants, Wendy. 2001. *The American Amusement Park*. Minneapolis: MBI Publishing.

Stanley, Summer L. 2010. *Gatlinburg: With Pigeon Forge, Sevierville, and the Smokies*. New York: Channel Lake.

## Dormitory

A dormitory is a small room designed primarily for sleeping, offering limited amenities. The term may also refer to the building that contains such rooms. Dormitories, also called dorms or residence halls, play a significant role in the life of the American college or university student. For incoming freshmen in particular, dormitories serve as a transition from adolescence to young adulthood, from a state of dependence to greater independence. Lifelong friendships are forged and vivid memories are created in the dorm, all contributing to the archetypal college experience.

### Structure

Dorms have long been incorporated into places of higher learning, but they do not all look the same. American colleges and universities may have several dorms spread throughout the campus. The style of the dorm buildings varies from traditional brick rectangular structures to tall, modern works of architectural wonder. Some campus dorms have themes, such as the arts, a foreign language, or the outdoors, to attract residents with shared interests. Dorm rooms range from single to multiple-person occupancy.

The traditional dorm room contains a bed, desk, and a closet. Restrooms and showers are customarily situated elsewhere on each floor of the building. In lieu of a kitchen and dining area in the dorm, colleges and universities offer one or more separate dining facilities on campus.

### Cultural Distinctions

Though unoccupied dorms appear to be spartan and in highly institutionalized places, they typically contain a cornucopia of cultural artifacts. Dorm culture is specific to the year, the institution, the dorm, and the residents who live there and thus changes dramatically from year to year.

Institutions try to set the tone for the culture of their dormitories. Conservative institutions, for example, are more likely to separate dormitories by gender. Such institutions may appoint individuals to monitor the dormitories. These individuals oversee the residents and enforce rules and regulations, such as curfews for residents and guests. At some institutions, men and women are not allowed to visit each others' dorm rooms.

On the other side of the spectrum, more liberal institutions permit residents much greater freedom. On these campuses, coed dormitories, by floor or room, are a popular option. The role of resident assistants (RAs) is less intrusive. RAs organize voluntary social activities and meetings and are available to help provide additional security and support to residents. Dorm residents may come and go without curfews, entertain guests at will, and host social gatherings.

Other factors influence the culture of the dorm. Decades ago, dorm rooms were limited to sleeping and late-night talks between roommates. Additional activities, such as movie watching, typing papers, and dining, took place in lecture halls, theaters, libraries, computer labs, and campus dining facilities. Today's dorms are heavily influenced by the technology boom, which makes it possible to carry out many of these activities within the small dorm-room space. Students furnish their dorms with miniature refrigerators and microwaves and utilize cell phones, smart phones, laptop computers, flat screen televisions, and many other gadgets and devices. Facebook allows physically isolated individuals to gather together in one virtual space.

### Functions

Dorms serve many functions on the typical college campus. They provide easy access to classes, campus events, and other resources for all students. For those students who come from great distances—different states or countries—dorms are essential as living spaces away from home. Dorms allow students to fully immerse themselves into campus life. They also provide opportunities to build relationships with classmates, to expose students to others with diverse backgrounds, and to experience greater independence within the safety of the campus grounds.

### Other Options

Dorms are most often associated with underclass students, especially freshmen, who are sometimes required or strongly encouraged to live on campus for their first year. Larger campuses may offer dorms that cater to older students in graduate school or students with spouses and children. The dorm is not the first choice for everyone.

Many colleges provide alternatives to the traditional dormitory for upper-class men and women. Fraternities and sororities offer members exclusive dormitories. Off-campus apartments, studios, and houses are preferred by some students. Though these housing options are still located near campus, they are viewed as less institutionalized and more conducive to an independent lifestyle. Many students, by their second year in college, feel they have grown out of dormitory-style campus housing and opt for off-campus housing offered by the institution or by private individuals in nearby towns.

### Images in Popular Culture

College life is a popular theme in American films and is also seen, though less frequently, on television. *Higher Learning* (1995) is a film that examines racism, love, sex, and other issues on a college campus. *Scream 2* (1997) incorporates the slasher film genre within the setting of a college campus. In *The Social Network* (2010), the dorm scenes provide both drama and comedy as the protagonist develops a new social network on the Internet. A popular Internet comedy film, *Dorm Life* (2008–2009) parodies the lives of college students in dorm floor 5 South.

Dorm life has also been featured in popular television series such as *Felicity* (1998–2002) and *A Different World* (1987–1993), set in a fictional historically black college. In these shows, dorm scenes show characters grappling with life as well as enjoying light moments with roommates. The appearance of dorms in popular media reflects the significance of dorm life in American culture.

### In Conclusion

Though dorm life is a transitory experience that may last for only one year in the life of a student, dorms help facilitate the exploration of identity, friendships, and love, and the building of shared cultural experiences and memories.

***See also*** Cubicle; Facebook; HBCUs

**Further Reading**

DeVillers, Julia. 2006. *The College Dorm Survival Guide: How to Survive and Thrive in Your New Home Away from Home.* New York: Three Rivers Press.

Moffatt, Michael. 1989. *Coming of Age in New Jersey: College and American Culture.* New Brunswick, New Jersey: Rutgers University Press.

Nathan, Rebekah. 2005. *My Freshman Year: What a Professor Learned by Becoming a Student.* Ithaca, New York: Cornell University Press.

## Drive-In Theaters

The drive-in theater is a venue in which motion pictures are shown on large outdoor screens and viewed by individuals sitting inside their automobiles. Founded in 1933 by Richard Hollings head in Camden, New Jersey, the drive-in grew to be a fixture in American culture and society. Over time, drive-ins became increasingly spectacular as technological improvements were made, more appealing movies

Actor Charlton Heston as Moses looms large onscreen in the *The Ten Commandments* at a drive-in movie theater, with a lovely nighttime cityscape as its backdrop, in August 1958. (Time & Life Pictures/Getty Images)

were shown, and additional attractions, such as playgrounds, were incorporated into the experience. The golden era of the drive-in theater lasted through the 1970s, after which their popularity began to decline. This was due in part to the invention of videos and video rentals, which permitted families to enjoy movies from the comfort of the home for less cost. Recently, drive-in theaters have undergone a resurgence in some cities and towns, though their popularity is nowhere near that of the drive-ins of yesteryear.

### Historical Perspectives

Since the early days of the 20th century, when silent films were all the rage, America has been in love with the movies. For some four decades, the indoor movie theater was the only choice for movie viewing, as television sets and video recording devices were the stuff of science fiction. Early movie goers were astounded by the "magic" of movies, which were stored on reels and played on a projector. Though actors moved jerkily across the screen, silently mouthing their words, with subtitles on black backgrounds inserted into the action to explain what they were saying, the movies were a sensation. When the talkies emerged in the early 1930s, moviegoers had even more to be excited about.

Richard Hollings head claimed to be inspired by his mother in his determination to create an outdoor movie experience. Mrs. Hollings head reportedly could sit comfortably enough in a car but not in the seats at the movie theater. Hollings head tinkered with his invention at home until it met his standards. He experimented with sound, adverse weather, and car spacing to create the perfect outdoor movie experience.

Hollings head opened his Park-In Theaters, Inc. in 1933. The sound was less than ideal. Patrons to his theater sometimes struggled with the low volume—but they still showed up. Word spread, and others, excited about the new concept and wanting to experience it for themselves, arrived. Before long, other entrepreneurs across the nation started their own drive-ins.

### Evolution

In 1934, the next three drive-ins opened: Shankweiler's Auto Park in Orefield, Pennsylvania, Drive-In Short Reel Theater in Galveston, Texas, and Pico in Los Angeles, California. Another dozen appeared before 1940 in Massachusetts, Ohio, Rhode Island, Florida, Michigan, New York, and Maine. Massachusetts had four drive-ins, the most in the country. The drive-in boom began in the wake of World War II (1941–1945) and lasted through the 1970s. This growth was paralleled in many other countries.

Several factors contributed to the drive-in's popularity. Most notably, the new sound system allowed the sound track to be picked up by car radios, making movie watching outdoors much more appealing. The addition of concession stands, restaurants, and amusements such as playgrounds, miniature trains, boat rides, animal shows, miniature golf, and pony rides made drive-ins the ideal destination for couples with children. Societal developments, such as the rise of the middle class, disposable incomes, leisure time, and the automobile culture, left Americans seeking for activities to engage in. Going to the drive-in became one of the top activities for families, especially on Friday nights or on the weekend.

With the rising popularity of the drive-in, some owners invested in bigger facilities to keep up with demand. Such drive-ins accommodated up to 3,000 cars. One of the biggest drive-ins was the All-Weather Drive-In in Copiague, New York. This drive-in boasted heating and air-conditioning as well as a cafeteria, a playground, and a shuttle train to transport its customers across the site. Other large drive-ins were in Detroit, Michigan; Lufkin, Texas; and Melville, New York; and Long Beach, California.

### Cultural Perspectives and Distinctions

The people who went to the drive-ins varied depending on the type of movies that were shown. For many years, families with children were the primary patrons. Later, as movies for adults became more widespread, drive-ins were popularly enjoyed by couples, particularly adolescents going on dates. Movie watching was only one aspect of the drive-in's appeal. Moviegoers enjoyed watching the movies in the privacy of their vehicles. The concessions also augmented the experience, as moviegoers feasted on popcorn and other snacks. At some drive-ins, patrons had to leave their cars and walk to the concession building to purchase snacks; at others, customers were served at their cars. For teenagers, the privacy afforded by the cloak of darkness, the private automobile, and the fact that they were commonly not chaperoned gave rise to the drive-in becoming a popular spot to "make-out."

### Decline

Rising inflation, as well as the aforementioned factors, resulted in the decline of the drive-in. Video rentals, in particular, transformed the private home into the preferred recreational space. From the comfort of home, families and children made their own popcorn and watched movies whenever they felt like it, rather than at set movie theater times. Over time, the number and variety of offerings at the movie rental stores provided families with an overwhelming assortment of films for adults, children, and the entire family. Movie rentals were especially popular for sleepovers, where any number of youth could watch a movie together, without being limited by the number of seats in the car. In another shift, cable TV, such as HBO, Showtime, and Cinemax, featured movies all day long.

In the 1980s, many drive-ins closed, while only a few new ones opened. Many of the closed drive-ins were simply abandoned. Some were turned into flea markets, with the enormous drive-in screens still visible but unused.

The 1990s saw a revival on a small scale, allowing new generations of families to enjoy the novel experience of going to the local drive-in. Some drive-ins added multiple screens, hoping to entice larger crowds. Such marketing efforts were successful.

### Contemporary Perspectives

The revival of drive-ins in the 1990s did not spark an all-out resurgence across the nation. Indeed, even indoor movie theaters have been closing in record numbers in the 21st century. Increased competition from even easier rental businesses, such as Netflix and Red Box, vie for the public's attention. Netflix, founded in 1997, offers unlimited numbers of DVDs that are mailed out to customers as well as the opportunity to stream movies via the Internet. Founded in 2002, Red Box allows customers to rent videos from automated retail kiosks located at many stores for a nominal fee and then return them the next day or later. Another new trend, the cable television series, has diverted the attention of the public from traditional movies.

### In Conclusion

In an era that has seen a marked decrease in traditional movie watching, the drive-in has emerged as a recreational activity from the past. For those who fondly remember the experience, the drive-in is treasured for its nostalgic value. For those who have discovered the drive-in for the first time, the experience is deemed a novelty amid the dizzying array of more sophisticated ways in which to watch movies.

***See also*** Detroit, Michigan; Los Angeles, California

## Further Reading

Heitmann, John A. 2009. *The Automobile and American Life*. Jefferson, North Carolina: McFarland & Co.

McKeon, Elizabeth, and Everett, Linda. 1998. *Cinema under the Stars: America's Love Affair with the Drive-In Movie Theater*. Nashville: Cumberland House.

Sanders, Don, and Susan. 2000. *Drive-in Movie Memories*. Middleton, New Hampshire: Carriage House.

Segrave, Kerry. 1992. *Drive-In Theaters: A History from Their Inception in 1933*. Jefferson, North Carolina: McFarland & Co.

# E

## El Morro National Monument

El Morro, which means "the headland" in Spanish, is a 200-foot sandstone bluff in New Mexico. This national monument is a popular camping destination, offering scenic trails and desert terrain under open skies. More than this, El Morro is popularly known for the peculiar history that is inscribed on its walls. Tourists travel from far and wide to see the remnants of ancient graffiti carved into the surface of El Morro. The people who left these enduring markings include the ancestors of the present-day Pueblo Indians, who lived on top of El Morro, Spanish explorers and missionaries, and American immigrants moving westward.

Today, no one is allowed to write on the rock, but anyone can view the marks left by the diverse peoples who collectively, over the centuries, documented the history of North America.

### Historical Perspectives

The ancestors of the modern Pueblo Indians lived in villages below El Morro and also built a pueblo a top the rock structure. The center of life for these people was the cool, refreshing waterhole located at the base of the bluff—the only source of water for many miles. While living there, the people drew symbols, animals, creatures, and other undecipherable objects on the rock. The meanings of most of these markings, known as petroglyphs, have been lost over time. By the beginning of the 15th century, the Pueblo Indians were gone.

The Spanish were the next group to leave inscriptions on El Morro. The first recognizable inscription was made in 1605 by Don Juan de Oñate. He was one of many Spaniards who visited the area during the period of Spanish exploration and conquest that occurred over a period of two centuries. Many of the Spanish inscriptions began with "Por acqui paso," meaning "He passed by here." Other marks varied. Inscriptions included names, dates, and brief explanations of why the writer had come to the region. At least one person carved a poem into the rock. The inscriptions were written by men of assorted occupations, such as governors, leaders of armies, and priests.

Though Mexico claimed the region that includes present-day Texas, New Mexico, and parts of California and Arizona between 1821 and 1846, no Mexicans left their markings on El Morro. But a group of American pioneers, who braved the journey to the West Coast in 1858 following the end of the war with Mexico, did. The journey was brutal for the 26 people in the wagon trail. The travelers struggled with the merciless desert heat, lack of water, and violent clashes with Native Americans. Yet all 26 individuals signed their names on the cliff walls, marking their arrival for posterity.

### For Visitors

The El Morro National Monument is open year round except during times of inclement weather. For a small fee, individuals can venture along the two-mile trail that passes by the ancient watering hole and the inscriptions on the rock wall. From the top of the bluff are spectacular views of the Zuni mountains, volcanic craters, and the El Morro Valley. The trail also overlooks the ruins of the ancient pueblo. Other facilities at the monument include guided hikes, a visitor center, a picnic area, and camp grounds.

*See also* California; 5 Pointz; National Frontiers Trails Museum; Texas

### Further Reading

"El Morro."*National Park Service*. http://www.nps.gov/elmo/index.htm.

Murphy, Dan. 2003. *El Morro National Monument*. Tucson, Arizona: Western National Parks Association.

Noble, David Grant, and Woodburry, Richard B., eds. 1993. *Zuni and El Morro Past and Present*. Santa Fe, New Mexico: Ancient City Press.

## Eldridge Street Synagogue

The Eldridge Street Synagogue is a Jewish house of worship in Manhattan, New York. Built in 1887, the synagogue, a richly ornate structure, was for many decades the center of eastern European Jewish life and culture in the Lower East Side of New York City. A steady exodus of Jews from this section of the city to surrounding boroughs in the 1940s and beyond resulted in a dramatic decrease in the membership of the once-popular synagogue and the eventual decay of the building. Renewed interest in the synagogue, beginning in the 1970s, prompted its restoration. In 1996, the Eldridge Street Synagogue became a National Historic Landmark.

In the 21st century, the synagogue stands as a spectacular architectural edifice, a place for sacred gatherings for modern-day worshippers, the site of the Museum at Eldridge Street as well as a historical landmark that honors America's past and diversity.

### Historical Perspectives

The Jews came from Russia, Romania, and other parts of Eastern Europe in search of religious freedom and opportunity. Between the late 19th century and early 20th century, millions of Jews from this region of the world arrived in America. Most settled in the Lower East Side of Manhattan, where they formed a tight-knit community, sharing customs, languages, and religious beliefs. Many of the Eastern European Jews followed an orthodox form of the Jewish faith. In the early years, worship took place in rented buildings, halls, storefronts, attics in homes, rooms above noisy saloons, and churches. By the late 1880s, Jewish congregations throughout the city had accumulated enough money to build synagogues, such as the Eldridge Street Synagogue.

### About the Structure

Construction on the Eldridge Street Synagogue began in 1887 and was completed the following year at a cost of $91,907.61. The sandy-colored structure was built in the Gothic, Romanesque, and Moorish styles, but the Moorish style is what stands out most prominently. The façade includes a large rose window with 12 rondelles, which symbolize the 12 tribes of Israel, and horseshoe arches, which give the building its distinctive Moorish style. A Star of David, a motif carved numerous times on the exterior of the building,

The interior of the Eldridge Street Synagogue on the Lower East Side of Manhattan on June 6, 2010. (Sean Pavone/Dreamstime.com)

crowns the synagogue. Notable interior features include an ark that displays the Ten Commandments, a 50-foot barrel-vaulted ceiling from which hangs a Victorian brass chandelier, a 3,060-square-foot sanctuary, and stained glass windows.

**Cultural Distinctions**

The Eldridge Street Synagogue helped preserve the religious practices and beliefs of the new immigrants and their descendants. The synagogue also supported the cultural heritage of Eastern European Jews. In the years that followed the construction of the synagogue, the surrounding neighborhood was dominated by Eastern European Jews. Jewish businesses dotted the major thoroughfares. Tenements squeezed tightly together provided lodging for the working class and impoverished. The more affluent families, many of whom were successful business owners, lived in lofty homes. But at the Eldridge Street Synagogue, the wealthy members and the poor worshipped together.

Members of the synagogue continued to uphold their long-held traditions even as they adapted to life in America. At that time, only men could purchase or rent seats within the synagogue. Women and men entered at separate entryways. The women sat in the balcony, and the men worshipped in the main sanctuary. Services were held on Saturdays, a day referred to as the Sabbath, which, in Judaism, is a day for rest and religious observance. Eldridge Street brought congregants, family, and community together, not only for worship, but for communal events such as weddings, bar mitzvahs, and meetings. Congregants also pooled their resources and money together to fund community projects and to provide financial assistance to Jews in other parts of the world.

The popularity of the Eldridge Street Synagogue waned following World War II (1941–1945). The 1940s saw a mass exodus from the cities to suburbia all over America. Eastern European Jews in Manhattan were no exception. The poverty and overcrowded tenements gave many residents cause to find new homes elsewhere. Though the congregation paid off the last of its bulky mortgage in 1944, the synagogue fell into disrepair, and membership numbers continued to decline. In the 1950s, services were restricted to a smaller section of the synagogue, and the sanctuary was closed. Eventually, the neighborhood, once a thriving hub of European American Jewish life, was transformed into a bustling Chinatown.

### Revival

The renaissance of the Eldridge Street Synagogue was brought about by the efforts of people who recognized the historical, cultural, and religious importance of the synagogue. In the 1970s, Gerard Wolfe established the Friends of Eldridge Street and instituted tours of the synagogue. Roberta Brandes Gratz and William Joseph son established the Eldridge Street Project which implemented plans to restore the synagogue to its former beauty. Renovations were completed in 2007.

### For Visitors

The Eldridge Street Synagogue holds weekly Sabbath and Holiday services. The Museum is open Sunday through Friday and features tours, discussions, and special events. Visitors who attend the Museum events and tours learn about the synagogue's history, architecture, and religious traditions.

***See also*** Bar Mitzvah/Bat Mitzvah; Chinatown; Ellis Island; New York, New York; Weddings

### Further Reading

Bortniker, Larry, Gratz, Roberta Brandes, and Dimun, Bonnie. 2011. *Beyond the Façade: A Synagogue, A Restoration; A Legacy: The Museum at Eldridge Street*. London: Scala Publishers.

Diner, Hasia R. 2000. *Lower East Side Memories: A Jewish Place in America*. Princeton, New Jersey: Princeton University Press.

*Eldridge Street Synagogue*. http://www.eldridgestreet.org/.

Mendelsohn, Joyce. 2009. *The Lower East Side Remembered and Revisited: A History and Guide to a Legendary New York Neighborhood*. New York: Columbia University Press.

Polland, Annie. 2009. *Landmark of the Spirit: The Eldridge Street Synagogue*. New Haven, Connecticut: Yale University Press.

## Ellis Island

Ellis Island, located in New York Harbor, is famous for the immigration station that once operated there. Between 1892 and 1924, this immigration center saw the arrival of some 12 million immigrants. These immigrants, mostly from Europe, came to America for many reasons; however, religious, political, and economic oppression spurred much of the migration. To these immigrants, America represented a haven of limitless opportunity and freedom. Stories abound of immigrants who found contentment, happiness, and success in their new homeland. America too was indelibly affected by their arrival and subsequent proliferation. Although the immigration station closed in 1954, Ellis Island will forever be a national symbol of hope and opportunity, a testament to a period in history that transformed the American identity.

### Historical Perspectives

Local Native Americans called the tiny island (less than three acres) "Koshk" or Gull Island. After the arrival of the Europeans, the island was occupied first by the Dutch and then by the English. In 1785, Samuel Ellis, the island's namesake, purchased the island. It was later sold to the state of New York and then to the federal government, which used it as a fort and an ammunitions depot. Starting in 1855, the island was home to an immigration station called Castle Garden. But by 1890, it was clear that the station was too small to handle the growing numbers of immigrants.

The Ellis Island Immigration Center was the government's response to the growing need for a larger space to receive the suddenly enormous waves of immigrants. The first building opened in 1892 and welcomed its first immigrant, a teenager named Annie Moore, who hailed from Ireland. For being "first," Moore was gifted with a $10 gold piece. The two-story structure was poorly constructed, however, and in 1897, the building was destroyed by a kitchen fire. The subsequent building and complex, comprising dormitories, hospitals, a bath house, kitchens, and other facilities, opened in 1900. Later, the size of the island was expanded to 27.5 acres by the addition of landfill.

### Immigration Station

Ellis Island, though known today as a place of great import replete with emotional meaning, was in its heyday an antiseptic and impersonal place. Immigrants from various European countries, such as Ireland, Italy, and Germany, arrived on Ellis Island by ferry. Each day, thousands were funneled along lines for inspection and questioning by various doctors, officials, and inspectors. The immigrants who did not pass various cursory exams regarding mental and physical health were not allowed to enter the United States.

Of the millions who came to America, two percent were deported back to their native countries. During the early history of the station, immigrants were denied admission if officials perceived an issue that would cause them to be an economic burden to the country or threatened the health of the nation's genetic pool. Later, immigration was heavily restricted by legislative laws and quotas. Some immigrants, like the Chinese, were for a time denied admission into the United States simply because of their race.

For the immigrants who were allowed to stay in America, life was an assortment of struggles, tragedies, happiness, and success. Some immigrants were victims of racism, violence, and poverty. Others eked out a decent living in ethnic enclaves or transitioned into mainstream America. Many others, whether as immigrants or descendants of immigrants, pursued and claimed ambitious careers in assorted fields such as politics, science, film, business, and architecture.

### Detainment

After 20 busy years, Ellis Island's dominance as an immigration station began to fade. By the 1930s, immigration had significantly decreased, largely due to the passage of stricter legislation limiting the number of immigrants allowed to enter the United States. During and after World War II (1941–1945), the federal government found additional uses for the station. Controversially, the government identified certain groups as potential or actual threats to the country and detained individuals from these groups on Ellis Island. Japanese, Italians, Germans, Communists, and Fascists all suffered this indignity. In 1954, Ellis Island closed, ending an era. Disuse and neglect caused the facilities to deteriorate with the passage of time.

### Museum

Nearly four decades after Ellis Island closed its doors, a museum was established within the main building of the immigration station. The Ellis Island Immigration Museum pays homage to the history and memory of the immigration center. The museum includes tours, exhibits, and resources for individuals to research family members who had passed through Ellis Island. The exhibits include numerous artifacts, oral histories, photographs, and displays. Other popular features include the American Family Immigration History Center, the American Immigrant Wall of Honor, Journeys: The Peopling of America Center, 1550–1890, The American Flag of Faces, and a documentary titled *Island of Hope, Island of Tears.*

The museum and the station that stands on Ellis Island are important national icons. Together they bring to life the memory of an integral time in American history and are a symbol of hope, optimism, and transformation.

### Impact

The influence of the waves of immigrants who streamed through Ellis Island or other gateways is immeasurable. Today, nearly half the population of American has roots abroad. Statues, streets, parks, and buildings bare the likenesses and the names of men and women who immigrated to America. Popular foods, television sitcoms, and films also reflect the influence of immigration.

From the moment they set foot on American soil, immigrants achieved enormous fame. Italian bodybuilder Charles Atlas was idolized by early-20th-century boys and inspired the early American fitness craze. Russian cosmetician Max Factor is to this day a prominent name in the makeup industry. Poet Claude McCay, who hailed from Jamaica, made enduring contributions to American literature. Movie producer Samuel Goldwin came from Poland. Famous telephone inventor Alexander Graham Bell came from Scotland, and world-known scientist Albert Einstein came from Germany. Irish immigrant Charles E. Logue built Boston's celebrated Fenway Park. Other famous immigrants include steel magnate Andrew Carnegie, former secretary of state Madeleine Albright, actors Bob Hope and Arnold Schwarzenegger, singer Gloria Estefan, and guitarists Eddie Van Halen and Carlos Santana. Without its diversity of race and ethnicity, America would be only a shadow of what it is today.

***See also*** Fenway Park; Statue of Liberty

### Further Reading

Brownstone, David M., Franck, Irene M., and Brownstone, Douglass. 2003. *Island of Hope, Island of Tears: The Story of Those Who Entered the New World through Ellis Island—In Their Words.* New York: Metro Books.

Cannato, Vincent J. 2010. *American Passage: The History of Ellis Island.* New York: Harper Perennial.

*Castle Garden.* http://www.castlegarden.org/.

*The Statue of Liberty—Ellis Island Foundation.* http://www.ellisisland.org/default.asp.

## Empire State Building

The Empire State Building, erected in 1931, was once the tallest building in the world. Towering 1,250 feet and dwarfing the many other skyscrapers of New York City, the structure has since been surpassed in height by several buildings, but it has not lost the status it occupies in the American imagination. The building pays homage to American drive, daring, and the desire to stretch the limits of human aspiration, innovation, and skill.

The structure has received numerous accolades. In 1955, the American Society of Civil Engineers selected the Empire State Building as one of the greatest engineering achievements in the nation's history. The building has been added to the State and National Register of Historic Places and declared a National Historic Landmark. In 2007, the building was awarded the title "America's Favorite Architecture." The structure's fame and world renown make it a top tourist attraction, as well as a local and national icon.

### Historical Perspectives

The Eiffel Tower in Paris, France, was the world's tallest building for many decades. Built in 1889, the structure stood 984 feet tall. Compared to Europe, America at that time was a young, bustling nation. New cities were springing up every where, especially along the eastern coast, to accommodate the booming population. In the early 20th century, the era of the American skyscraper began. New York's Metropolitan Life Tower, built in 1909, was 700 feet high. Its construction triggered a race among American industry magnates and business moguls to build ever taller, more magnificent buildings. New York City and Chicago led the charge with the largest number of the tallest structures in America.

New York's John Jakob Raskob, former vice president of General Motors, was one such magnate who got caught up in the fever to build skyscrapers. Raskob is thus responsible for building of the Empire State Building. Construction on the building began in March 1930, the same year that the illustrious 1,046-foot Chrysler Building was completed in New York. The Empire State Building was built on land where the Waldorf Astoria once stood. Shreve, Lamb, and Harmon were the architects. The construction involved 3,000 laborers and, when completed, included two observatories, one on the 86th floor and another on the 102nd floor. The building contained 103 floors, 10 million bricks, 1,872 steps, and 73 elevators. A 203-foot broadcast tower distinctly topped the monolith.

### Contemporary Perspectives

New additions and features have been added to the Empire State Building over the years. For example, in 1976, colored floodlights were added, so that the tower could be lit with assorted colors during special occasions. On Earth Day and St. Patrick's Day, the tower lights are green. On President's Day, the lights are red, white, and blue. In honor of Valentine's Day, the lights are red, pink, and white.

Since 1978, runners have taken to the stairs of the Empire State Building for the annual Empire State Building (ESB) Run-up. Since 1994, contestants have vied for the opportunity to wed at the Empire State Building on Valentine's Day. In the new millennium, amid growing concerns about humanity's impact on the environment, the Empire State Building has undergone changes to make the structure more eco-friendly and sustainable. This progressive project includes finding ways to increase recycling and energy efficiency, reduce water usage, and incorporate environmentally friendly products.

### Images in Popular Culture

According to the Empire State Building website, the building has appeared in more than 250 films. King Kong clinging to the Empire State Building is an iconic scene in the eponymous films of 1933 and 2005 (the former World Trade Center, not the Empire State Building, was at the center of action in the film that was released in 1976). The Empire State Building shows up in other box-office hits such as *Taxi Driver* (1976), *Superman II* (1980), *When Harry Met Sally* (1989), *Sleepless in Seattle* (1993), and *Independence Day* (1996).

### For Visitors

The exterior view of the Empire State Building is recognizable the world over, but visitors are privileged to explore firsthand the interior of this iconic landmark. (The building is not solely a tourist attraction; the Empire State Building also rents office space with enviable views of the city and features eateries, banks, and other businesses.) The Empire State Building also features a visitor's center and a sustainability exhibit on the second floor. Ticket purchases provide visitors access to the 86th and 102nd floor observatories for expansive views of the city. The 80th floor features a permanent exhibit on the construction of the building and a gift shop.

*See also* Chicago, Illinois; Chrysler Building; New York, New York; Waldorf Astoria

**Further Reading**

Bascomb, Neal. 2003. *Higher: A Historic Race to the Sky and the Making of a City*. New York: Doubleday.

*The Empire State Building*. http://www.esbnyc.com/.

Stichweh, Dirk. 2009. *New York Skyscrapers*. New York: Prestel.

Tauranac, John. 2012. *The Empire State Building: The Making of a Landmark*. New York: St. Martin's Griffin.

Willis, Carol, ed. 1998. *Building the Empire State*. New York: W.W. Norton in Association with the Sky scraper Museum.

## Everglades

The Everglades, also known as the Everglades National Park, are a large marshy area that provides habitat for abundant natural wildlife and plant life and supplies freshwater to much of the state. This wilderness area covers 1.5 million acres in the southernmost part of Florida. Early America saw the natural environment, with its endless acres of marshes and alligators, as unappealing and a problem that should be fixed. Today, the Everglades are viewed as a place to be preserved and cherished. Popular the world-over with tourists, adventurists, photographers, animal lovers, and environmentalists, the Everglades provide a unique glimpse into a remote and engaging but, nonetheless, threatened world. Efforts to protect and restore the health of the Everglades are a contentious issue in contemporary times.

### About the Site

Viewed from above, the Everglades appear as a vast area of water and saw grass with watery lanes winding around green islands of various sizes. The main features of this boundless region are pinelands, mangroves, swamps, and tropical hardwood hammocks (islands that rise a few feet above the water level). The shallow waters of the Everglades flow sluggishly from the Kissimmee River in Orlando to Lake Okeechobee and into the Gulf of Mexico. The Everglades support over a thousand species of plants, birds such as egrets, herons, and eagles, and animals such as crocodiles, Florida panthers, and snakes.

### Historical Perspectives

Some 15,000 years ago, the first known humans arrived in the Everglades. Their descendants, such as the Calusa and Tequesta, developed distinct cultures and ruled over vast empires. The Seminoles next occupied south Florida, but their population was decimated by war with the U.S. government and they were forced to live on reservations. Only a small remnant refused to leave their homeland.

Beginning in the late 19th century, land developers and politicians became consumed with the desire to drain the Everglades. The general opinion was that the great Everglades were a vast wasteland that should be put to good use. Over time, canals and levees were constructed to reroute the flow of water. The newly developed land was used for agricultural purposes and eventually for living spaces and an airport. The effects of this intrusion into the ways of nature were scoffed at or ignored.

### Contemporary Perspectives

However, draining the Everglades affected the environment in troubling ways. The land mass of the Everglades drastically reduced: once it was twice as the size that it is today. Diverting the water from its natural course significantly decreased the amount of water the plant and animal life received every year, eventually affecting the availability of water far to the north. The smaller habitat and reduced water supply drastically reduced the bird population and contributed to the critical situation that exists in the region today.

Other issues threaten the Everglades. Nonindigenous plants such as the Brazilian pepper tree and animals such as the python threaten the environment's natural plant and animal life. Pollution causes problems such as mercury toxicity, which has greatly affected the fish population and the fishermen who depend on them for a living. Natural disasters such as hurricanes wreak havoc on the land.

Recognizing the importance of the area was the critical first step to recovery. In 1947, the Everglades became the first national park to protect an ecological system. Efforts to "save the Everglades" have brought much-needed support to the region. The park's precarious environmental situation attracts international attention. But programs to monitor the health of the region's various habitats and plans to restore the original water flow struggle in the face of the powerful land development industry.

### Images in Popular Culture

The Everglades have an uncommon beauty, but it is also a mysterious place where danger lurks just beneath the surface of the shallow waters or high above in the dark leafy trees. With no signposts among the complex watery thoroughfares and only one main road in and out, the Everglades are an ideal setting for a novel, a comic book, or a movie. Indeed, the Everglades provide a fascinating backdrop for many novels, as well as for a fight between the Lizard and Spiderman in the popular comic book series. Movies such as *Attack of the Giant Leeches* (1959) and *Mega Python vs. Gatoroid* (2011) depict the Everglades as a place where frightening monsters reside.

But it is the image of the Everglades as an endangered natural space that predominates in today's world. A common subject of television and film documentaries as well as magazines, the plight of the Everglades have been seen around the world through the camera lens. The images produce amazement as well as concern, helping to expose the plight of the nation's natural spaces and the need to protect and preserve them.

***See also*** State and National Parks

### Further Reading

Brown, Loren G. 1993. *Totch: A Life in the Everglades*. Gainesville: The University Press of Florida.

Goss, James P. 2000. *Pop Culture Florida*. Sarasota, Florida: Pineapple Press.

Kras, Sara Louise. 2010. *The Everglades*. Tarrytown, New York: Marshall Cavendish.

*The Seminole Tribe of Florida*. http://www.semtribe.com/.

Simmons, Glen, and Ogden, Laura. 2010. *Gladesmen: Gator Hunters, Moonshiners, and Skiffers*. Gainesville: The University Press of Florida.

## Extraterrestrial Highway

The Extraterrestrial Highway is a 98-mile stretch of road linking Crystal Springs and Warm Springs in the state of Nevada. The highway is not traveled much by local commuter traffic. The travelers who do appear on the route are more often than not seeking unidentified flying objects, otherwise known as UFOs. Allegedly, UFO sightings are common on the Extraterrestrial Highway. Tourists hope for glimpses of mysterious aircraft but also enjoy stops at local UFO- and extraterrestrial-related attractions along the route, most notably in the town of Rachel, famous for the Little A'Le'Inn bar and restaurant and the mystifying Area 51, a secret military base.

A sign marks Nevada Route 375 as the Extraterrestrial Highway, a road that leads to Rachel and the infamous Area 51. (Emattil/Dreamstime.com)

**Historical Perspectives**

The Extraterrestrial Highway was originally named State Route 375. The highway is remote, and the surrounding landscape encompasses miles of brush and dessert terrain. Wildlife shows itself intermittently. Few residents travel the road, as nearby towns, like Rachel, are sparsely populated. The location of the highway is ideal for the secret base, Area 51, where new aircraft and weapons are reportedly tested. Unmarked Humvees and warning signs near the base add to the secretive ambience.

Public interest in Area 51 was sparked in large part by Bob Lazar, a government worker at the secret base. Lazar claimed that the government was reverse engineering extraterrestrial aircraft. In the wake of this claim, others reported that they had seen strange lights and aircraft moving in unnatural ways in the Nevada night sky. Capitalizing on the public attention, the Nevada Commission on Tourism changed the name of the nearby highway to the Extraterrestrial Highway. The public dedication ceremony was attended by stars from the blockbuster *Independence Day* (1996). Curious tourists from all over the world began to put the Extraterrestrial Highway on their lists of favorite destinations.

### For Visitors

Not even the locals are convinced that the UFO allegations are true. Many are convinced that what the conspiracy theorists and alien aficionados call UFOs are human-made aircraft not yet released to the public. Still, the visitors come, sometimes alone and sometimes with a tour guide. Popular tours stop at the Little A'Le'Inn bar and restaurant, which heavily promotes the alien craze with themed foods like the Alien Burger with Cheese, books, and other paraphernalia. Unauthorized guests are not permitted beyond the Area 51 boundary; however, this restriction does not prevent tourists from flocking to the perimeter fence to gaze upon the fabled property. Another popular destination is the black mail box, where UFO sightings—or government aircraft, depending on one's belief—are alleged to occur most frequently.

*See also* Area 51

### Further Reading

Birnes, William J. 2010. *Aliens in America: A UFO Hunter's Guide to Extraterrestrial Hotspots across the U.S.* Avon, Massachusetts: Adams Media.

Holm, Matthew, and Follett, Jonathan. 2006. *Highway: An American UFO Journey*. Hudson, New York: Toadspittle Hill Productions.

# F

## Facebook

Facebook is a social-networking website that has taken the 21st century by storm. Launched in 2004, Facebook now has nearly 800 million visitors (called users) around the world. America, with some 157 million users, tops the list. To date, all users are adults, as children have not yet been allowed to join. Companies, organizations, and other professional agencies have also made the leap to the popular social-networking site. Facebook's popularity is fueled by public interest in communicating virtually with friends, relatives, coworkers, and friends with similar interests. This virtual gathering place allows users to post their thoughts, share photos, videos, and details of their lives, and to keep track of hundreds of friends. Companies benefit from the limitless exposure their products and services receive.

### Historical Perspectives

Facebook was developed in a dormitory in Harvard University in Cambridge, Massachusetts, by Mark Zuckerberg in 2003. Zuckerberg was then a sophomore and a computer science major. A contradictory account has it that Zuckerberg's Facebook (formerly the Facebook) was influenced by a similar project called Connect U, one that Zuckerberg was allegedly contracted to create by twin brothers, Cameron and Tyler Winklevoss. Facebook caused an immediate sensation with its users, who were originally limited to Harvard students. Soon, Facebook expanded to include other colleges, universities, and organizations.

In 2004, Zuckerberg dropped out of college and was joined by his dorm mates, Dustin Moskovitz and Chris Hughes, in a move to Palo Alto, California, also known as Silicon Valley. In California, Zuckerberg set about growing his new company. However, in that same year, the Winklevoss brothers sued Zuckerberg, alleging that he had stolen their idea. In 2008, Facebook settled out of court for $65 million. Unscathed by the lawsuit, Facebook has emerged as a worldwide phenomenon of the digital age.

### About the Site

Individuals must set up an account with Facebook in order to access the website. The account is free (Facebook receives its revenue primarily from advertisements that appear on the site), and allows users to set up their own page. From there, users input profile information that may include personal information such as job, school, interests, gender, religion, contact information, and event relationship status. Users can write message and post photos and videos in sections called the news feed or the wall, and also on the walls of friends. The design of the site itself is simple. Photos and other embellishments added by users personalize each page. The friends section contains a list of users which allows to view the user's Facebook page. Friends can be added or deleted at any time. Privacy settings allow users to control who can view their page and what information can be viewed by the public. Users also have the option of hiding their presence on Facebook altogether so that their name does not appear in a general search.

### Cultural Distinctions

Facebook is a cultural phenomenon, the latest in a series of long-distance communication tools. Messenger, letters, telegraph, telephone, email, cell phones, and texting have all had their day in the sun, but none offer the cocktail of applications that has allowed Facebook to take the world by storm. Facebook has helped foster a unique social experience, one that allows users to create or be a part of any community of their liking, immediately, no matter where they are.

Communities are formed by users who make and accept friend requests or join groups. Facebook groups consist of individuals with shared hobbies and interests or with connections to the same geographical location. Some users restrict their friends to those who are an integral part of their lives, such as family members, church members, close friends, school mates, assorted interest groups, and coworkers. Others, less discreet, invite friends and accept friend requests from individuals they may know casually or not at all.

The individual users are the stars of their virtual space. User posts include daily happenings, thoughts, and personal experiences. Oftentimes, Facebook becomes a forum for gossip or updates about breakups, make-ups, scandals, awards and promotions, and charitable events. Users commonly share photos such as ordinary pictures of vacations, weddings, baby showers, pets, children, meals, or themselves. Sometimes the information and the photos shared on Facebook go beyond the limits of propriety, modesty, and discretion, bringing embarrassment of varying degrees upon the very real head of the virtual user.

The Facebook experience has also fueled certain questionable trends, such as snooping (or Facebook stalking, as it is sometimes called) or trying to garner social status by collecting ridiculous numbers of friends they do not know. Critics of the virtual life worry that users prefer Facebook to real-life experiences or that they may view real-life events simply as opportunities to post pictures, commentary, and personal entries.

### Issues

Criticism has surfaced alongside the praise of the Facebook phenomenon. News reports have linked inappropriate Facebook posts and photos to employment firings. Some allege that Facebook has contributed to divorces, family feuds, and dissolved friendships. News reports warn that Facebook pages have been used by attorneys, insurance companies, and other entities to the detriment of users. Cyberbullying on Facebook has been shown to cause enormous problems, the extent of which is undetermined. Critics also argue that Facebook has helped to create a society of information overexposure and narcissism. Others lament the lost art of traditional personal interaction via telephone and letter, and point out that the consequences of living vicariously through Internet experiences are unknown.

Notwithstanding the mounting railings against Facebook and the committed individuals who refuse to open Facebook accounts or who close their accounts after a period of usage, proponents argue that Facebook has benefited the society in many ways. Facebook has helped to connect and reunite the world, as well as old friends and distant family members. In Egypt, Facebook provided a vehicle for organizing a successful protest against an oppressive government. Facebook also provides a welcome conduit for the support of philanthropic organizations and charities.

### Images in Popular Culture

Though Facebook is not used by everyone, it is difficult to avoid its impact. Most promotional campaigns today, including companies that sell products and services, television shows, and movies, advertise

Facebook addresses. Retail stores encourage customers to "friend" them or "like" them on Facebook. Facebook is often brought up in everyday conversation and when individuals meet one another for the first time. Rather than exchange phone numbers or email addresses, individuals are encouraged to look one another up on Facebook.

In 2010, Facebook made its way to the heart of American popular culture by becoming the central theme of a major film. The movie, *The Social Network,* told the story of the creation of Facebook. It was not, however, created or promoted by Mark Zuckerberg or his corporation. The film was based on the book *The Accidental Billionaires* (2009) by Ben Mezrich, which delves into the controversy surrounding Zuckerberg and the origins of Facebook. Though Zuckerberg was critical of the film, *The Social Network* grossed over 200 million at the box office.

***See also*** California; Cyberspace; Dormitory; Harvard University; Silicon Valley; Weddings

### Further Reading

Bauerlein, Mark, ed. 2011. *The Digital Divide: Arguments for and against Facebook, Google, Texting, and the Age of Social Networking*. New York: Jeremy P. Tarcher.

Kirkpatrick, David. 2010. *The Facebook Effect: The Inside Story of the Company That Is Connecting the World*. New York: Simon & Schuster.

Livingston, Jessica. 2008. *Founders at Work: Stories of Startups' Early Days*. Berkeley, California: Apress.

## Fallingwater

Fallingwater is the name of the famous home that was built on top of a waterfall near Pittsburgh, Pennsylvania, on property owned by the Kaufmann family. Designed and furnished by the world famous architect, Frank Lloyd Wright, the house was constructed from 1936 to 1938, and the guest house was completed in 1939. At the time of its completion, the world was astonished by the innovative creativity of Wright's concept and design.

The house was utilized by the Kaufmanns until 1963, when it was entrusted to the Western Pennsylvania Conservancy. In 1966, the house was declared a National Historic Landmark. Today, the remarkable home is open to the public for tours. The nearby barn, which was utilized by Edgar Kaufmann as part of a dairy farm, has been repurposed with the architecture carefully preserved for use as a meeting space and for gatherings such as weddings.

The historical and architectural importance, as well as the striking beauty of Fallingwater, has enticed more than 4 million visitors since its opening to the public in 1964 (*Fallingwater*).

### Historical Perspectives

Edgar Kaufmann and his wife, Liliane, owned Kaufmann's Department Store in Pittsburgh. While they lived in Pittsburgh, they frequently escaped to the mountains. Their desire to retreat permanently to the mountains prompted their plans to move to the site where they owned a summer camp, which included a cabin with no electricity and no running water. Frank Lloyd Wright, asked to design the home, envisioned a grand home like no other. He completed his design in 1935.

### Frank Lloyd Wright

Frank Lloyd Wright is one of the most famous architects in the nation. Born on June 8, 1867, in Richland Center, Wisconsin, he started his career in architecture in Chicago, Illinois, in the late 19th century. It was there that Wright designed his legendary home and studio in Oak Park, constructed in 1888–98. It was in Oak Park that Wright conceived his prairie-style architecture. The structures that were built in this style

Fallingwater, a house in in Mill Run, Pennsylvania, designed by Frank Lloyd Wright, is on Smithsonian magazine's list of 28 Places to Visit Before You Die. It was designated a National Historic Landmark in 1966. (Edwin Verin/Dreamstime.com)

were characteristically long and low to the ground. Another trademark of Wright's was the harmonious blending of the structures within their environment. His prolific architectural career included designing famous structures, such as homes, churches, skyscrapers, and hotels, in America and abroad. Many structures, such as the prairie-style Robie House, are in Chicago. Completed in 1910, the Park Inn Hotel, in Mason City, Iowa, was the last hotel that Wright designed. The famed Guggenheim Museum, which opened to the public in 1959, is located in New York City. In that same year, on April 9, Wright died, leaving behind a spectacular legacy.

### Construction, Use, and Reuse

After the construction of Fallingwater in 1938, the Kaufmanns and their son, Edgar Kaufmann Jr., moved in. Their home's most unusual feature was its location on top of a waterfall. The house had been made so that the tranquil sound of water could be heard in the house. The house included furnishings designed by Wright, as well as spacious windows, a hearth made with boulders quarried from the local environment, and balconies. Wright's penchant for Japanese themes played subtly in the design of the house. The house also featured a carport, servants' quarters, and a guest house with a pool.

Not far from the home, a barn that had been a part of a late-19th-century family farm known as Tissue Farm, which was owned by farmer Ross Tissue, was purchased by Kaufmann. In 1940, he expanded the barn so that it included a milking parlor for his cows. The Kaufmanns lived at Fallingwater until their deaths in the 1950s. Their son, who lived until 1989, entrusted the property to the Western Pennsylvania Conservancy in 1963.

While Fallingwater endures as a popular tourist destination, the barn has been repurposed for other uses. The barn now comprises the following main features: the fireplace room, the threshing floor, the courtyard, and the amphitheater, which are rented out to the public.

The fireplace room was originally the milking parlor. The main feature in this room is its stone fireplace. This room is equipped with modern features to accommodate modern technological devices. The threshing room, which features rustic beams and maple flooring, is now also used as a meeting space and for social gatherings. In keeping with the authenticity of this space, this room is not equipped with heating or air-conditioning. The outdoor areas, including the courtyard and amphitheater, are promoted as ideal settings for weddings. The courtyard features a flagstone patio and elegant staircase and a trellis sheathed with wisteria.

### Images in Popular Culture

At the time that Fallingwater was constructed, the public perceived it as a modern-day marvel. In 1938, the house was featured on the cover of *Time* magazine. Touted as a masterpiece in architecture and interior design by several of Wright's contemporaries, Fallingwater not only rekindled Wright's popularity but created a public sensation. The nation had never before witnessed a creation that transcended the imagination in terms of innovative architecture and bold placement in nature.

### For Visitors

Visitors to Fallingwater are treated to a special experience, as the house is the only house designed by Wright where the original furnishings, artwork, and setting have been preserved. Visitors may rent space at the nearby barn for meetings and social gatherings. Lodging, though not built over a waterfall, is available in the vicinity.

***See also*** Barns; Cabin; Chicago, Illinois; New York, New York; Summer Camp; Weddings

### Further Reading

*Fallingwater*. http://www.fallingwater.org.

Waggoner, Lynda S. 1996. *Fallingwater: Frank Lloyd Wright's Romance with Nature*. Pennsylvania Conservancy; New York: Universe.

Wright, Frank Lloyd. 1946. *An Autobiography*. London: Faber & Faber.

## Fenway Park

Fenway Park is the nation's oldest baseball stadium. Located in Boston, Massachusetts, and home of the Boston Red Sox, the stadium, though small in size, stands out from the rest. Amid the sea of modern, state-of-the art facilities, Fenway Park, which opened in 1911, retains much of its original appearance and features, though renovations over the years have added modern facilities for both players and spectators.

The size and age of the stadium in no way detract from Fenway. Indeed, these qualities seem to add to the stadium's appeal. To Boston fans, the stadium is hallowed ground; a structure that honors the history of a revered all-American pastime. The stadium is deemed, as the saying goes, "America's Most Beloved Ballpark." More than 100 years after it first opened its gates, visitors are attracted from near and far to experience the quintessential American game in the old-fashioned ambience of Fenway Park.

### Historical Perspectives

The Red Sox, first known as the Americans, originally played in a wooden ballpark, the Huntington Avenue Grounds. Not to be outdone by the newer and grander ball parks that were being built throughout the nation, John Taylor, the team's owner, decided to construct a new stadium. The fiercely patriotic Irish American city leaders took special pride in the fact that the new stadium, Fenway Park, was built by Charles E. Logue, a successful Irish American contractor. Logue had come to America in 1881 when he was 23 years old. By the time he took on the construction of Fenway Park, he had already accumulated an impressive resume. In 1890, he started the Charles Logue Building Company (the company continues to operate today as Logue Engineering) and built part of the Boston College campus and several Catholic churches in the area.

Fenway Park, however, is Logue's most celebrated accomplishment. Visitors were delighted with Fenway when it opened on April 20, 1912, after just one year of construction. Mayor John F. Fitzgerald threw out the first pitch on opening day. The ballpark, with its brick façade and short left field fence, originally sat 27,000 on wooden bleachers. Not everyone had an ideal view, and the ballpark had only one level of seating. But these drawbacks mattered little to the fans, as the Red Sox were victorious over the Yankees (known then as the New York Highlanders). Over the years, Fenway Park hosted many events in addition to baseball, such as the Irish sports games, and in 1944, former president Franklin D. Roosevelt's last campaign speech.

### Contemporary Perspectives

Substantial renovation and additions to the park began as early as the 1930s and continue today. In 1934, Fenway received its first scoreboard. In 1946, a second tier of seats was added. More seats have been added in recent years, bringing Fenway's seating capacity up to its current 37,000—a number that still pales in comparison to the capacity of most other major league baseball stadiums. Other recent renovations include a modernized food area, additional restrooms, and some high-tech flourishes such as the high-definition video displays that are fixtures in modern baseball stadiums across the nation.

Fenway Park has many notable features. On display throughout the stadium are relics of the stadium's past and visual tributes to the history-making events that have occurred there. The park's most famous feature, the 37-foot left-field wall, has been part of the stadium since the beginning. Once simply dubbed the Wall, fans began to refer to the structure as the Green Monster after it was painted green. Seats were recently added above the Green Monster, increasing the thrill and excitement for fans hoping for a chance to catch a home-run ball. The so-called red seat is located in section 42, row 37, seat 21. This seat was painted red to mark the spot where, in 1946, Red Sox player Ted Williams hit the longest home run ever hit in Fenway.

### Images in Popular Culture

Baseball films have had a long history in American cinema. The genre captures the nation's adoration of the game and its heroes, and the magical place—the stadium—in which their heroes play it out on the field. Fenway Park takes the limelight in popular films such as *Field of Dreams* (1989), *Fever Pitch* (2005), *The Town* (2010), and *Ted* (2012). A documentary, *Inside Fenway Park: An Icon at 100,* marked the ballpark's centennial. Now entering its second century of existence, Fenway Park, a historic icon for baseball lovers everywhere, is still going strong.

### For Visitors

Visitors may experience Fenway Park in and out of the baseball season. Visitors may view the stadium while touring Boston's Irish Heritage Trail or while participating in an official Fenway Park walking tour. Of course the best way to see the stadium during the season, which lasts from April through September, is to take in a baseball game. Visitors also attend music concerts performed by popular artists at the stadium or rent space for weddings, corporate events, and other special occasions.

In 2012, visitors to Fenway Park were treated to a once-in-lifetime event. April 20, 2012, marked Fenway Park's well-publicized centennial. Celebrations featured sentimental appearances of more than 200 former Red Sox players. Caroline Kennedy, John Fitzgerald's great-granddaughter, threw out the first pitch. Wearing throwback uniforms, the Red Sox and the Yankees, who had played in the stadium's first-ever game, battled it out again. The Red Sox, however, did not win this time around. The extraordinary occasion was memorialized with a commemorative DVD titled *Fenway Park: 100 Years as the Heart of Red Sox Nation* (2012) and books, such as *Fenway Park: The Centennial: 100 Years of Red Sox Baseball* (2012), as well as *Sports Illustrated Fenway: A Fascinating First Century* (2012).

***See also*** Baseball Hall of Fame; Boston, Massachusetts

### Further Reading

Frommer, Harvey. 2011. *Remembering Fenway Park: An Oral and Narrative History of the Home of the Boston Red Sox*. New York: Stewart, Tabori & Chang.

Powers, John, and Driscoll, Ron. 2012. *Fenway Park: A Salute to the Coolest, Cruelest, Longest-Running Major League Baseball Stadium in America*. Philadelphia: Running Press.

## Fifth Avenue

Fifth Avenue is a 12.6-mile-long street in the borough of Manhattan in New York City. The storied avenue extends from Washington Square Park to the Harlem River. Since the late 1800s, the thoroughfare has been associated with the rich and famous. In the beginning, it served predominately as an affluent residential area. Today, the street is populated with upscale retailers, historic residences, parks, museums, historic churches, and many other popular attractions and landmarks that appeal to shoppers, sightseers, and local city dwellers. Visitors are also drawn by the aura of haute culture and luxury that still emanates from this major thoroughfare.

### Historical Perspectives

Washington Square Park, on the southern end of Fifth Avenue, was a potter's field during the late 1700s and early 1800s. The area was developed as a neighborhood for New York City's aristocrats during the Gilded Age (1860s to 1890s). The Gilded Age marked a period of economic and industrial growth and prosperity in the nation. During this period, New York's wealthiest settled in mansions and fine homes along Fifth Avenue in the vicinity of Washington Square Park. Washington Square Park, encompassing nearly 10 acres, opened in 1871.

On the cusp of the new century, the commercial development of ritzy Fifth Avenue gained momentum. The first building constructed in the area was the Astoria Hotel (the original Waldorf Astoria building), which opened in 1893. In 1906, the flagship department store, B. Altman and Company, was built on Fifth Avenue and 34th Street. Growth spurred on the migration of the city's upper-class residents to neighborhoods nearer Central Park. Eventually, fancy shops, boutiques, stores, restaurants, hotels, and other places subsumed the opulent residential neighborhood and the street itself.

### Contemporary Highlights

The Fifth Avenue that is known today is not exclusive to the well-to-do. The affordability of automobiles, the accessibility of mass transportation, and the growth of America's middle class have all contributed to the mainstreaming of this once elite area. Though premier shopping and high fashion largely define the avenue, the arterial buzzes with tourists and locals of diverse economic backgrounds, all eager to indulge in the assorted delights that Fifth Avenue has to offer.

### Washington Square Park to 59th street

From the south, Washington Square Park, now a part of Greenwich Village, is surrounded by residential homes. Many buildings in the area have been acquired or built by New York University. Traveling northward along Fifth Avenue, visitors reach the heart of the street's hub, a mix of mainstream stores and elite shops peppered with historic landmarks. Prominent places in this area include Coach, Kenneth Cole, Saks Fifth Avenue, St. Patrick's Cathedral, Gianni Versace, Cartier, the Museum of Modern Art, the American Folk Art Museum, Elizabeth Arden, the Disney Store, Giorgio Armani, Escada, Trump Tower, Gucci, Tiffany and Company, Niketown, Louis Vuitton, Chanel, Christian Dior, the Apple Store,

> **Saks**
>
> Saks, known formally as Saks Fifth Avenue, is a luxury department store chain. The company was founded in 1924 by Horace Saks and Bernard Gimbel. The name of the company combined the name of the store's predecessor, Saks & Company (founded by Horace Saks and his family), and the legendary street on which the flagship store and headquarters were built. Bernard Gimbel was a member of the family-owned multimillion dollar company, Gimbel Brothers, or Gimbel's.
>
> Soon after Saks opened, it became a local sensation, a place where high society and the famous flocked to buy the latest fashions, inspired and acquired from around the world. The retailer brought to the city an elegance and worldliness that would soon become known the world over. Expansion was inevitable. Though considered a chain, Saks maintains its exclusivity by limiting the number and location of its stores to only the most desirable cities.
>
> Today, Saks continues to be a status symbol, specializing in high fashion, handbags, shoes, jewelry, and cosmetics. Saks's prominence has greatly influenced popular culture. A sign of that is the fact that the store makes an appearance in the animated film *Shrek 2* (2004) as Saxon Fifth Avenue. Comedian and actor Steve Martin published a love story, *Shop Girl* (2000), that was adapted into a film released in 2005. In the book, Mirabelle Buttersfield, the protagonist, is a salesperson at Neiman Marcus in Beverly Hills, California. In the film, Mirabelle (Claire Danes) is a salesperson at Saks Fifth Avenue in Beverly Hills.

and the Grand Army Plaza. Many of these famous businesses are located along Fifth Avenue or a short distance away on neighboring streets. Notable streets near Fifth Avenue include Madison Avenue and Park Avenue to the east and the legendary Broadway to the west.

### Other Landmarks

Notable landmarks along Fifth Avenue include Rockefeller Center, the New York Public Library, and many of the mighty skyscrapers for which New York City is famous. Rockefeller Center, which opened in 1939, is an expansive commercial complex built on 22 acres. Located at Fifth Avenue and 42nd street, the New York Public Library is a stately historic building that opened in 1911. A number of New York's trademark skyscrapers, such as the GE Building, the Olympic Tower, Trump Tower, the Sony Building, and the Empire State Building, soar above Fifth Avenue's busy thoroughfare. The GE Building was erected in 1933 and stands 850 feet. The Olympic tower was completed in 1976 and is 620 feet tall. The Trump Tower, opened in 1983, rises 663 feet in the air. In the following year, the Sony Building, 647 feet tall, opened. Until the forthcoming One World Trade Center is completed, the Empire State Building is New York's tallest building. Erected in 1931, the Empire State Building is 1,452 feet from street level to the top of its antenna spire.

### 59th to 110th Streets

Central Park and the Museum Mile occupy either side of the avenue between 59th and 110th. Central Park, spanning the full distance between these streets, was established in 1857. The popular park is over 800 acres in size. The so-called Museum Mile, which runs from 82th to 105th streets, includes the Metropolitan Museum of Art, the Goethe-Institut New York, Neue Galerie New York, Solomon R. Guggenheim Museum, National Academy Museum and School of Fine Arts, Cooper-Hewitt, National Design Museum, Smithsonian Institution, the Jewish Museum, Museum of the City of New York, El Museo Del Barrio, and the forthcoming Museum for African Art.

### Beyond Central Park

From Central Park, Fifth Avenue traverses two famous neighborhoods: Harlem, which comprised mostly African American residents since the 1920s, and Spanish Harlem. The area is also the home of the Marcus Garvey Park, so-named after an African American leader who immigrated to the United States from Jamaica in 1916. Between 1918 and 1927, Garvey mobilized a spectacular movement through his organization, the Universal Negro Improvement Association, from his headquarters in Harlem.

### Images in Popular Culture

From the 1900s to contemporary times, Fifth Avenue, a symbol of affluence and privilege, has inspired literature, films, and more. *The Age of Innocence* (1920), a novel by Edith Wharton, describes the life and culture of the exorbitantly rich within the setting of this exclusive street. Candace Bushnell explores Fifth Avenue in modernity in her book *One Fifth Avenue* (2008). Sam Wasson's *New York Times* best seller *Fifth Avenue, 5 A.M.: Audrey Hepburn, Breakfast at Tiffany's, and the Dawn of the Modern Woman* (2010) delves into the life of fashion-setting actress Audrey Hepburn and the making of the classic film *Breakfast at Tiffany's* (1961). Christopher Smith's popular thrillers, the Fifth Avenue series, include *Fifth Avenue* (2010), *Running of the Bulls* (2011), and *From Manhattan with Love* (2011).

Among the classic films that feature the avenue is the comedy *It Happened on Fifth Avenue* (1947), which tells the tale of a homeless man who lives in a mansion with friends and the home's owners on Fifth Avenue. Other films with notable scenes set on Fifth Avenue include *Breakfast at Tiffany's* (1961), *Ghostbusters* (1984), *Six Degrees of Separation* (1993), *Ransom* (1996), *Meet Joe Black* (1998), *13 Going On 30* (2004), and *The Sorcerer's Apprentice* (2010). Many other films include camera shots of legendary buildings and landmarks situated on Fifth Avenue.

In the late 1990s, Elizabeth Arden created the popular Fifth Avenue perfume, a scent intended to convey sophistication and a sense of affluence to mainstream women. An ongoing tradition for which Fifth Avenue is known across the nation is the massive and highly publicized annual parades, such as the St. Patrick's Day Parade, Macy's Thanksgiving Day Parade, and the Puerto Rican Day Parade.

**The Age of Innocence**

*The Age of Innocence* is a time-honored novel that was written by Edith Wharton in 1920. The novel won the 1921 Pulitzer Prize for Fiction, a first for a woman. The award was a milestone for a time when women were largely marginalized in society.

Wharton (1862–1937) was born Edith New bold Jones into a wealthy New York family on January 24, 1862. After marrying Edward Wharton, a banker, in 1885, she embarked on a career of her own—writing. By the time *The Age of Innocence* was published, Wharton had written nearly a dozen novels and was divorced (her marriage dissolved in 1913). In all, Wharton wrote 11 collections of stories and 16 novels. *The Age of Innocence* explores love and upper-class society in late-19-century New York. The book is celebrated for its extraordinary insights into life in one of the most formative eras in America's history.

The novel spawned many adaptations. In 1924, a silent film version was released. In 1928, the novel appeared as a play on Broadway, and in 1934, a new movie adaption with sound was released. In 1993, audiences thronged to the movie theaters once again. This film yielded a Golden Globe Award for Winona Ryder, who was cast as May Welland Archer, and an Academy Award for costume design.

***See also*** Apple Inc.; Broadway; Central Park; Empire State Building; Greenwich Village; Harlem; Macy's Thanksgiving Day Parade; Metropolitan Museum of Art; New York, New York; New York Public Library; Niketown; Rockefeller Center; Smithsonian Institution; Spanish Harlem; Tiffany & Company; Trump Tower; Waldorf Astoria

### Further Reading

Homberger, Eric. 2008. *New York City: A Cultural History*. Northampton, Massachusetts: Interlink Books.

Patterson, Jerry E. 1998. *Fifth Avenue: The Best Address*. New York: Rizzoli.

Simon, Kate. 1978. *Fifth Avenue: A Very Social History*. New York: Harcourt.

## Fire Island

Fire Island is a barrier island near Long Island in New York City. The popular getaway destination is bounded by the Atlantic Ocean and bays such as the Great South Bay. The island, 32 miles long and less than 1 mile wide, has no paved roads and the majority of its land is protected from future development. Access to the island is limited to ferries, boats, and seaplanes. This tranquil and isolated enclave has a small permanent resident population, but visitors come to commune with nature and to enjoy the many activities offered by the island. Fire Island, which hosts more than 800,000 visitors each year, is indeed a haven for those who want to get back to nature and escape the busyness of modern life.

### Historical Perspectives

No one is exactly sure where the name Fire Island came from. The earliest inhabitants, the Secatogues, called it "Sictem Hackey," meaning the Land of the Secatogues. Since the arrival of the Europeans, the island has been used in various ways. In the mid-1600s, Fire Island was a whaling station. In 1825, the Fire Island Lighthouse was built. In the 1950s, the island's popularity as a vacation spot emerged. Though predominately used by East Coasters, Fire Island is a popular getaway destination for both celebrities and ordinary tourists from all over.

### Highlights

Fire Island is home to residential villages, resort communities, hotels, recreational opportunities, scenic beaches, and other natural sites. There are 17 resort communities. Each community has its own personality and provides different activities. Cherry Grove and Fire Island Pines are popular resorts designated for lesbian, gay, bisexual, and transgender (LGBT) communities. Davis Park is popular with families and boat lovers. Parties, dancing, clubs, and bars are found in Kismet. Shoppers enjoy Fair Harbor, a downtown district that offers a food market, shops, and a celebrated restaurant, Le Dock. Ocean Beach, comprising 600 homes, features nostalgic thoroughfares and stores. Other activities on the island, fun for individuals of all ages, include boating, sailing, tennis, biking, clamming, swimming, surfing, hiking, fishing, and camping. An important historic landmark, the Fire Island Lighthouse, has been refitted as a museum for visitors.

The occasional song, popular fiction novel, or television reference to Fire Island often plays heavily on the gay culture found on the island. In fact, the island caters to all Americans as a popular place for vacations, summer retreats, and weekend getaways.

***See also*** New York, New York

### Further Reading

*Fire Island*. http://www.fireisland.com/.

Rich, Jason R. 2010. *Insiders' Guide to Long Island*. Guilford, Connecticut: Morris Book Publishing.

Whitehouse, Jack. 2011. *Fire Island: Heroes & Villains on Long Island's Wild Shore*. Charleston, South Carolina: The History Press.

## Fisherman's Wharf

Fisherman's Wharf is a historic pier and popular attraction in San Francisco, California. California has two wharfs by the same name. One is located in Monterey, California. The other one, San Francisco's Fisherman's Wharf, is the more widely known. Located amid many famous city landmarks, Fisherman's Wharf is a singularly popular draw, welcoming millions of tourists each year while still operating as a pier for commercial crabbers and fishermen—descendants of generations of men and women who have worked in these businesses. The wharf is a living memorial of California's history as well

Pier 39 at Fisherman's Wharf in San Francisco California. (Jerryway/Dreamstime.com)

as a place where people go to experience a unique environment and see the sites for which northern California is famous.

**Historical Perspectives**

More than a century ago, Italian immigrants from Genoa and Sicily settled into the San Francisco area. Many of these hardy souls came from a long line of fishermen who fished along the coasts of Italy. In the New World, they continued to make their living fishing off Fisherman's Wharf. In the early years, feluccas, sailboats like those in Italy, were docked along the wharf at dusk and taken out at dawn for a day's hard labor. It was the fisherman's lot to navigate the waters in the hope of returning to the pier with a hardy bounty. These immigrant fishermen were known for their ability to navigate by interpreting subtle signs they observed in nature and for singing, with gusto, opera songs from their boats.

Tourists did not come to the wharf until the 1950s, after which the wharf morphed into the popular tourist attraction it is today.

**Contemporary Perspectives**

The fishermen who fish at Fisherman's Wharf in the new millennium are descendants of the wharf's original denizens. But much has changed. Fishermen share the pier with tourists and modern shops.

They now operate modern boats, and the once profuse supply of crabs has dwindled considerably. Crabbers must go out further and search deeper to find crabs.

### For Visitors

From end to end, Fisherman's Wharf brims with many exciting attractions. The arterial streets are Jefferson and Embarcadero. Tourists flock to watch the fishermen on the pier and to read the plaques that tell the wharf's history. The wharf also features shopping venues like Pier 39, Ghirardelli Square, museums, restaurants, and crab stands. Fisherman's Wharf also features a historic trolley line and a red fire engine. Tourists may ride the fire engine while touring the area. From Pier 33 at Fisherman's Wharf, they may take a ferry ride to the infamous Alcatraz Island. Fisherman's Wharf is in the vicinity of other iconic California places, such as the Golden Gate Bridge and Chinatown.

***See also*** Alcatraz; California; Chinatown; Golden Gate Bridge; San Francisco, California

### Further Reading

Baccari, Alessandro, Jr. 2006. *San Francisco's Fisherman's Wharf.* Charleston, South Carolina: Arcadia Publishing.

Fichera, Sebastian. 2011. *Italy on the Pacific: San Francisco's Italian Americans.* New York: Palgrave Macmillan.

*Fisherman's Wharf.* http://www.fishermanswharf.org/.

Pierce, J. Kingston. 2009. *Yesterday and Today: San Francisco.* Chicago: West Side Publishing.

## 5 Pointz

5 Pointz is an aerosol art center and outdoor art exhibit in Long Island City, New York. The center is known by many names, including its formal moniker, 5 Pointz Aerosol Art Center, "The Institute of Higher Burnin'," and the Graffiti Mecca. Both celebrated and criticized, 5 Pointz is known around the globe for the edgy and high-energy graffiti artwork splashed across the face of the exterior of the building. The center is popular with artists, individuals from the hip-hop urban community with which graffiti is inextricably linked, and local supporters who recognize it as a place that confers prestige and pride to a controversial art form and subculture.

### Historical Perspectives

Graffiti as it is known today sprang up in the American inner cities, with Philadelphia, Pennsylvania, credited as its birthplace. But graffiti has appeared in disparate forms in all other countries and earlier periods in history. Examples include ancient graffiti in Rome, Pompeii, and Egypt. Inscription Rock at El Morroin New Mexico displays ancient markings and signatures. In the early 20 century, gangs indicated their presence in and claims on certain neighbors in American cities with markings and symbols splashed on buildings and other landmarks.

However, the graffiti that made its debut in the late 1960s was like no other. The markings began as so-called name tags. Youth in Philadelphia started painting their street names on buildings and then subway cars—not to identify with gangs but as a way of expressing themselves, to appropriate status, and for entertainment. Name tagging eventually spread to other cities, notably New York City.

Name tagging was eventually followed by character drawings: widely recognizable images from popular culture, like cartoon characters, as well as original creations. Styles such as bubble letters and extravagant, multicolored creations proliferated. New tools to create the graffiti were employed, and graffiti art evolved into full-blown murals.

In time, graffiti became a pervasive symbol of the city, one that was, however, stigmatized more often than not. Graffiti was considered a blight on the city landscape. City leaders denounced the brazen

Five Pointz, considered a graffiti mecca in Queens, New York City, is an outdoor exhibit space featuring numerous graffiti artists. (Sean Pavone/Dreamstime.com)

activity as vandalism. City governments and property owners paid large sums of money to clean graffiti from billboards, signs, and the walls of buildings. The markings, no matter how artistic, were associated with juvenile delinquency, rebelliousness, and gang activity, generating fear and disapproval among the general public. Graffiti, after all, was an unlawful act when private or public property was used as a canvas. No one seemed to notice that the graffiti artists were not customarily affiliated with gangs, nor did their work involve aggressive confrontations or violence against the public.

### Cultural Distinctions

Hip-hop and graffiti developed alongside one another. Since the late 1960s, the predominately African Americans and Hispanic youth living in urban communities across the country have shared a heritage that includes street jargon, street names, break dancing, rap music, and hip-hop attire. Hip-hop culture, particularly since the 1990s, has increasingly generated mainstream acceptance and popularity.

Graffiti has slowly emerged as a legitimate art form and now commonly appears in mainstream culture. Designs appear on clothing, advertisements, and literally anything that has a graphic element. Commissioned graffiti artists create elaborate designs on buildings. Graffiti has been a popular subject in books and magazines and has been displayed in galleries and museums. Today, graffiti is often described as street art, aerosol art, or spray can art.

### About the Site

The 200,000-square-foot factory known today as 5 Pointz originated in 1993 as the Phun Phactory. From the start, the factory was used as a place to promote graffiti as an art form. In doing so, in the process the managers, hoped to help provide a solution for youth vandalism in the city. In 2001, Jonathan Cohen founded 5 Pointz at the factory. The name pays homage to the five boroughs in New York City. Cohen is also the center's curator.

Cohen's center has achieved substantial popularity within the world of graffiti and hip-hop. Artists from around the world vie for the opportunity to exhibit their work in the outdoor space. Graffiti is exhibited on more than 350 murals. Inside the building are some 200 artist studios. Both graffiti and hip-hop artists, who regularly perform at 5 Pointz, celebrate the subculture of the urban centers of the nation.

The center's popularity notwithstanding, 5 Pointz faces possible eradication. Urban developers seek to replace the building with upscale condos and other businesses. The community is conflicted between those who contend that 5 Pointz provides a positive outlet for youth expression and individuals who still perceive graffiti negatively.

### Controversy

Though graffiti has gained significant mainstream acceptance, the art form's detractors have not gone away. Critics protest that graffiti is not a true art form and denounce its formal exhibition in museums and elsewhere, contending with distressing oversimplification that such museums may even encourage vandalism. Others argue that graffiti is an outdated phenomenon that no longer has a place in the 21st century.

### Images in Popular Culture

Graffiti's depiction in film mirrors the controversy that it provokes in real life. In the 1980s, a plethora of hip-hop films attempted to portray hip-hop culture as a genuine way of life and art form. The films present the major aspects of hip-hop culture—break dancing, community, and graffiti—in a positive light. Notable films include *Wild Style* (1983), *Breakin'* (1984), and *Krush Groove* (1985). In contemporary films, graffiti often appears negatively in the *mis-en-scene* of cop, gang, or tough city movies, intended to add to the sense of danger and anxiety in the urban landscape. 5 Pointz plays a critical role in the climactic magic trick in the film, *Now You See Me* (2013).

### In Conclusion

Admired or despised, American graffiti has managed to survive and spread across the continent. New generations of youth and young adults have embraced the style. While places such as 5 Pointz try to funnel the artistic energy behind the graffiti into a positive and respectable movement, such venues are beleaguered by financial pressures and harsh critics.

### For Visitors

5 Pointz is open for individual tours, group tours, and corporate team-building opportunities. The organization encourages visits especially from school, college, university, and art students. Many graffiti

pieces are located at the site. Special shows are put on at different locations. Classes are available for interested persons. Graffiti artists must contact the organization regarding permission to paint art work for display.

*See also* El Morro National Monument; New York, New York; Subways

**Further Reading**

Chalfant, Henry, and Prigoff, James. 1987. *Spraycan Art*. New York: Thames and Hudson.

Cooper, Martha, and Chalfant, Henry. 1984. *Subway Art*. New York: Holt, Rinehart, and Winston.

Felisbret, Eric. 2009. *Graffiti New York*. New York: Abrams.

*5 Pointz*. http://5ptz.com/graff/.

Gastman, Roger, and Neelon, Caleb. 2010. *The History of American Graffiti*. New York: Harper Design.

## Florida Keys

The Florida Keys is an archipelago located at the southern tip of the state of Florida, extending in a southwesterly direction. The 1,700 islands, which stretch from the islands of Key Largo to the north to Key West to the south, are classified as the upper keys, the middle keys, the lower keys, and the outlying islands. Both Key Largo, located closest to Florida, and Key West, situated closest to Cuba, are popular island destinations. The exotic, tropical environment, the gorgeous natural habitat of plants, land mammals, and marine animals, and the plentiful outdoor-based activities attract many. Its blend of laid-back ease, multicultural influences, and modern-day comforts place the Keys high on the list of popular seaside tourist retreats. For many others, island life is home.

### Historical Perspectives

Though Spanish explorer Juan Ponce de Leon discovered the Florida Keys in 1521, he and his crew were not the first humans in the area. The islands were inhabited by indigenous communities such as the Vescayo, the Matecumbese, and later the Calusa. The islands were also visited intermittently by ships hurled ashore by storms or rough waters. Hurricanes regularly blasted the islands with tumultuous winds and rain.

In the 1700s, Bahamians immigrated to the islands. Pirates also came ashore, but they were permanently removed by the American Navy in the early 1800s. Despite Spanish and British claims, Florida, including the Keys, became a U.S. territory as a result of the Adams-Onis Treaty in 1819.

In the following year, a significant settlement emerged on the island of Key West. The deepwater port attracted a productive trading industry. Residents fished, salvaged shipwrecks, and grew produce such as melons, pineapples, and coconuts. The wreckage was not only sold to buyers off the island but purchased and used by residents in their own homes. Other profitable industries were sponge cultivation and shark processing. Getting around to other islands, even to the Florida mainland, was cumbersome, as islanders depended solely upon boats for transportation.

In the 20th century, island life was transformed by the arrival of the railroad. Henry Flagler, the president of the Florida East Coast Railroad, laid track from the mainland across several islands down to Key West. The railroad was completed in 1912. Other developments included the opening of public schools and the construction of roads to accommodate automobiles. After the railroad was destroyed by a hurricane in 1935, the Overseas Highway was built, facilitating greater traffic to and from the mainland and helping to keep islanders connected to the rest of the nation.

### Earnest Hemingway and Key West

Key West, the southernmost island in the archipelago, is also the most developed. Even in the 1920s and 1930s, when the famous author Ernest Hemingway lived there, Key West provided tourists and residents with interesting venues for dining and entertainment.

Hemingway, who was born in the ordinary small town of Oak Park, Illinois, in 1899, filled his adult life with the unusual and extraordinary. He went to Europe while serving in World War I (1914–1918) and was an expatriate in Paris during the 1920s. Other travels took him to such locales as Africa, Spain, and Cuba. From 1928 to 1939, Hemingway and his wife, Pauline, lived in Key West. Their stay began unintentionally, when Hemingway was delayed in Key West after leaving Havana, Cuba. He stayed at the Trevor and Morris Apartments, and was instantly enamored with the place. He and his family soon settled in a Spanish colonial villa. While in Key West, Hemingway frequented and made friends at Sloppy Joe's Bar (now Captain Tony's Saloon) and ate meals at Mrs. Rhoda Baker's Electric Kitchen. Hemingway wrote prolifically in his writing studio, publishing such seminal works as *The Green Hills of Africa* (1935) and *For Whom the Bell Tolls* (1940). His novel *To Have and to Have Not* (1937) is set in Key West and Cuba.

### Contemporary Issues

Major issues in the island paradise of the Keys include drug smuggling and conservation. Drug smuggling, which involved illegal substances such as cocaine and marijuana, proliferated beginning in the 1970s. A roadblock and an inspection point were finally established by the U.S. Border Patrol at the roads connecting the Florida Keys to the mainland in 1982. Residents protested profusely, contending that such obstructions were a blatant disregard to their U.S. citizenship, and the checkpoint and roadblock were removed. However, law enforcement continues to monitor, investigate, and apprehend drug smugglers in the Keys through such agencies as the Coast Guard.

The issue of conservation has mobilized environmentalists and scientists. Areas prohibiting activities that pose a danger to the environment have been established. For example, Pennekamp Park was established in 1959. Other areas, such as Key Largo National Marine Sanctuary, founded in 1976, and Looe Key National Marine Sanctuary, founded in 1981, prohibit such activities as spear fishing and coral collecting.

Other challenges to the environment include oil spills and off-shore drilling, which residents fear may result in oil spillage. As of yet, no solution has been reached in this matter. Cleanup in response to accidental oil spills has been the only recourse.

### Images in Popular Culture

Hemingway was not the only artist to be inspired by the Keys. In 1988, the Beach Boys, a group that was famous for their California surf songs, released the song "Kokomo." The song's title pays tribute to the name of a fictional island "off the Florida Keys," and the lyrics make references to several islands, including Key Largo. The song paints a vivid picture of a romantic paradise, as the singer tries to entice the object of his love to run away with him. The song was played often on the radio and was featured on the soundtrack of the popular movie, *Cocktail* (1988), about a bartender who moves from New York City to Jamaica.

The Keys reappeared in the limelight when a 64-year-old swimmer named Diana Nyad made history. In 2013, the New York–born Nyad became the first person to swim from Havana, Cuba, to Key West without using a shark cage for protection.

### For Visitors

With so many islands to visit, tourists and residents can indulge in countless amusements. Coral reef scuba diving and snorkeling are popular activities. At the Key West Shipwreck Museum, visitors explore the history of one of Key West's most profitable early wrecking industries. Visitors also enjoy exploring two historic homes: the Hemingway House and Museum and the Harry S. Truman Little White House. Former president Truman maintained a home in Key West in 1946. In Key Largo, patrons dine on Cuban food in the restaurant called Marlin. The Florida Keys History of Diving Museum is located in Islamorada. Visitors can interact with dolphins at the Hawks Cay Resort.

*See also* California; New York, New York

### Further Reading

Kerstein, Robert J. 2012. *Key West on the Edge: Inventing the Conch Republic*. Gainesville: University Press of Florida.

McIver, Stuart B. 1993. *Hemingway's Key West*. Sarasota, Florida: Pineapple Press.

Ogle, Maureen. 2003. *Key West: History of an Island of Dreams*. Gainesville: University Press of Florida.

Scott, Chris. 2004. *Endangered and Threatened Animals of Florida and Their Habitats*. Austin: University of Texas Press.

Williams, Joy. 1987. *The Florida Keys: A History & Guide*. New York: Random House.

## Folk Festival

The folk festival is a type of popular event that is evidence of America's cultural diversity. Such festivals celebrate the richness and importance of everyday life and activities that are often not represented in, or have been historically denigrated by mainstream society. Folk life encompasses music, dance, food, stories, and other traditions. Folk festivals may involve a single tradition or a combination of many. Commonly an annual three-day event that occurs over a weekend, folk festivals, also known as folk music festivals, or by other similar terms, are an integral part of American culture and life across the county. These festivals are known for generating enthusiasm and popular participation. They appeal to those who embrace cultural traditions, their own as well as those that are new and unfamiliar.

### Historical Perspectives

The folk festival in America has a long history, beginning in the 19th century. With the coming of immigrants from distant lands, immigrant communities, like the Germans, Swedish, and other groups, put on festivals to maintain their connection with their native culture and to transfer cultural traditions to younger generations. Dancing, music making, and the display of traditional clothes and cuisine were standard fare at these early festivals.

In subsequent decades, interest in folk culture grew. Folklorists scavenged rural communities and ethnic enclaves to document old songs, dances, and stories in an effort to save what they believed to be endangered cultures. Many prominent folklorists, such as Jean Bell Thomas, were influential in starting new festivals. Thomas founded the American Folk Song Festival in Kentucky in 1930. In this era, the hillbilly identity, emanating from Appalachia and other mountain communities, grew in popularity. Fiddle contests and rural festivals emerged throughout the South. Other major folk festivals, such as the National Folk Festival in St. Louis, Missouri, followed. Many of these festivals focused on a single culture and some disregarded other cultures all together. For example, in the South, though African Americans greatly influenced the nation's music, they were not allowed to perform at certain festivals.

With the mainstreaming of folk music on American radio and television, folk festivals increased in popularity and in scope. The 1950s and 1960s were an important era for these festivals, ushering forth a period of greater tolerance and appreciation for and inclusiveness of different cultures within the context of the festivals. Festivals took place in cities, on college and university campuses, and in rural locations across the country. Performances were held indoors or outdoors and showcased nationally known celebrities alongside local performers in assorted genres of music and dance. They represented various cultures such as Native American, African American, Greek, Italian, German, rural communities, as well as the hippy subcultures wherein the American folk tradition ran strong.

### Contemporary Perspectives

Whether indoors or outdoors, on the East Coast or West, today's folk festivals carry on the legacy of cultural preservation, appreciation, and sharing in an atmosphere that is jovial and casual. However, critics argue that some modern-day festivals have lost much of their folksy charm. One complaint concerns the increasing commercialization of the events, which is evidenced by the numerous vendors selling wares and products that do not reflect folk culture or are premanufactured en mass in factories. Some argue that big-name bands and performers that produce popular music take the attention away from the local artists and performers who represent genuine folk culture.

Attendance at folk festivals remains high, a testament to the fact that folk traditions are an enduring phenomenon. Into the 21st century, these events will continue to commemorate the culture and diversity of the American people.

***See also*** Appalachia

### Further Reading

*American Folk Festival*. http://www.americanfolkfestival.com/.

Cohen, Ronald D. 2008. *A History of Folk Music Festivals in the United States: Feasts of Musical Celebration*. Lanham, Maryland: Scarecrow Press.

*National Folk Festival*. http://www.nationalfolkfestival.com/.

*Smithsonian Folk Festival*. http://www.festival.si.edu/.

## Folsom State Prison

Folsom State Prison is located in Folsom, California. Situated at the end of a meandering road with green lawns and trees on either side, Folsom's granite entryway and expansive complex loom ominously above the visitor. Folsom, the second oldest prison in the state, and the first prison to have electricity, is infamously known as a violent and dangerous place. In terms of the national imagination, Folsom epitomizes the archetypal prison experience, complete with hardened criminals, chilling violence, escapes, and dreary maximum-security cells. Since the facility was established in 1880, the prison has generated both fear and fascination, insuring its reputation as a notorious national landmark.

### Historical Perspectives

The original facility was built by convicts at the abandoned Stony Bar mining camp near the American River. The prison, comprising two cell blocks, opened its doors the summer of 1880. Each cell was designed to hold two occupants, who slept behind an iron door with only a 10 × 3 inch opening for air. The prison had neither plumbing nor electricity.

In subsequent decades, Folsom underwent many changes. Some buildings were added; others were repurposed. The prison eventually included new cell blocks, a post office, a dining room that doubled as a movie theater, homes for prison workers, a hospital, a tower for the prison armory, a wall enclosing 41 acres that extended 30 feet above the ground and 15 feet below ground, a chapel, a cemetery, a firehouse, and an administration building. The facility also operated a prison farm, a prison powerhouse, and a sewage disposal plant.

Behind Folsom's walls, prison life was a mix of social activities and danger. Folsom housed the nation's most notorious criminals: cold-blooded killers, robbers, gangsters, and other lawbreakers. Between 1884 and 1929, women were also admitted to Folsom. (Fast forwarding into the 1970s, notorious serial killer Charles Manson was a resident from 1972 to 1976, as Folsom was the only prison at the time equipped to handle inmates of his notoriety).

Violent confrontations among inmates and between inmates and staff made headlines. Folsom also had more than its share of brazen escape attempts. In 1893, gunfire exploded in the air between guards and escapees Anthony Dalton, Henry Wilson, Frank Williams, Charles Abbott, George Sontag, and Charles Smith. Three convicts died that day. In 1914, Frank Creeks won only two days of freedom after violently escaping from Folsom. During the escape, he killed a night sergeant, John Drewry, and shot the leg of a guard, Frank Maher, in the yard tower. Maher later died from infection from the wound. Creeks was apprehended after only a few days and later hung. Another attempted escape, which occurred in 1932, ended in a fatal miscalculation. Inmate Carl Reese tried to escape in a makeshift diving helmet by way of the nearby canal, but when he opened his valve for air, he drowned, as the mechanism was not long enough. Prison escapes continued intermittently into the new millennium.

Especially difficult prisoners, like those who tried to escape, were forced to wear the ball and chain, a contraption that shackled an inmate to a ball weighing some 25 or 30 pounds. Early inmates wore the so-called Oregon boot, a heavy foot-brace that prevented inmates from running. To restrain difficult inmates, a straitjacket referred to as "Susie's Corset" was used. Punishment was meted out by hanging inmates by rings against the wall or solitary. Hanging was the form of execution carried out at the prison.

The violence and severity of life in Folsom was offset in part by prison activities. Life was more than forced labor and bland meals (beans were a standard menu item). Folsom inmates learned trades, like barbering, and took courses in various subjects. Some inmates learned how to read for the first time in their lives. Inmates also played

### The Man in Black

Johnny Cash was a musician who rose from poverty to stardom. He was Nicknamed "The Man in Black" because of the trademark all-black outfits that he wore during performances. Cash was born John Cash on February 26, 1932, in Kingsland, Arkansas, one of seven children born to his sharecropper parents. Cash was surrounded by music. Family members constantly sang or played instruments. The workers in the field sang to lessen the strain of their labor.

After graduating from high school in 1950, Cash joined the U.S. Air Force. In 1954, he was discharged from the Air Force and though he worked as a salesman, music remained a priority. He formed a group called Johnny Cash and the Tennessee Two, later known as the Tennessee Three. The group performed a fusion of blues and country-and-western music. Cash's group released "Hey Porter" in 1955. Other songs followed, including "So Doggone Lonesome," "Folsom Prison Blues," and his career-altering "I Walk the Line."

Cash moved to Ventura, California, and worked under a new record label, Columbia Records. Alleged drug and alcohol use were among the problems that prompted Cash's wife to divorce him in 1966. Cash descended into a life of chaos, underscored by a forest fire he accidentally started in Tennessee.

But Cash did another about face and sobered up. In 1968, he met singer June Carter who had a tremendous career of her own, dancing, singing solo and with Cash, and acting. Cash's career flourished as the host of his own television show, *The Johnny Cash Show* (1969–1971) and as a singer. He was inducted into the Rock and Roll Hall of Fame in 1992. In 2003, he recorded his last album. Cash died on September 12, 2003. Cash's life was portrayed in the film *Walk the Line* (2005).

volleyball and baseball, and boxed. They played instruments in the prison orchestra and served as deejays for the Folsom radio station.

### Contemporary Perspectives

In contemporary times, Folsom has modernized considerably. The population has swelled from just under 2,000 in the early years to over 5,000. The current facility consists of the old Folsom and the new Folsom. The new Folsom, which opened in 1986, includes dormitories and larger cells for inmates convicted of lesser crimes and several modernized buildings. The names of officers who have died in the line of duty at the prison are memorialized on a black marble monument.

### Images in Popular Culture

Prison films are a staple of the American film history. Usually hard and gritty, these films provide a glimpse of life behind prison walls for those lucky but curious individuals who stay out of trouble. Folsom has been the setting for a number of popular prison films such as *Inside the Walls of Folsom Prison* (1951), *Riot in Cell Block II* (1953), *Reprieve* (1962), and made-for-television films *The Jericho Mile* (1979), *The Outlaws* (1982), and *Another 48 Hours* (1982). Other films include *Diggstown* (1992), *American Me* (1992), *Heat* (1995), and *Walk the Line* (2005).

Folsom also inspired prominent country singer Johnny Cash. Cash paid homage to the prison when, inspired by *Inside the Walls of Folsom Prison,* he released the ballad "Folsom Prison Blues" in 1955. The song narrated the fictional crimes of a Folsom inmate. Cash also recorded *At Folsom Prison,* a live album, at the prison in 1968.

### For Visitors

The Folsom Prison Museum is located off Prison Road in Folsom, California. It offers tours, historical information, artifacts, exhibits, as well as a gift shop. Museum exhibits cover the gamut of life in prison from assorted points of view, notorious escapes, riots, and violence. The museum also keeps alive the memory of Johnny Cash, who forever memorialized the prison in song.

***See also*** California; Dormitory

### Further Reading

Brown, Jim. 2008. *Images of America: Folsom Prison.* Charleston, South Carolina: Arcadia Publishing.

*Folsom Prison Museum.* http://www.folsomprisonmuseum.org/.

Sharrer, Nan Nichols, and Sharrer, Ward. 1979. *Escape from Folsom Prison: The True Story of William Jennings Bryan Burke as Told to Nan Nichols Sharrer.* Sacramento, California: Nichols-Sharrer Enterprises.

Streissguth, Michael. 2005. *Cash at Folsom Prison: The Making of a Masterpiece.* Cambridge, Massachusetts: Da Capo Press.

## Football Hall of Fame

The Football Hall of Fame is a museum that pays tribute to professional football players and the game that is labeled "America's favorite sport." The museum opened in 1963 in a 19,000-square-foot facility in Canton, Ohio. Thanks to ongoing expansion, it now occupies some 118,000 square feet. Further expansion, which includes a new main entrance and grand lobby and expanded spaces for events, were completed in time for the museum's 50th anniversary in 2013.

The spectacular growth of the Football Hall of Fame speaks of the sport's enormous appeal in American society. The museum is a shrine to all things football, particularly to the millions who love the

The NFL Football Hall of Fame in Canton, Ohio, in July 2003. (Wisconsinart/Dreamstime.com)

game, have made heroes of its players, and who devotedly follow their favorite teams as they battle one another in this uniquely American sport.

**Historical Perspectives**

No one knows exactly how American football began. Football historians generally agree that the game has its roots in the English game of rugby, but its direct origins are found in America. Football is believed to be a descendant of the game played at Harvard University, then known as Harvard College, in the late 1800s. The sport was later refined and shaped by Walter Camp, who is considered the father of American football. In 1920, the American Professional Football Association was formed. The association's name changed to the National Football League the following year.

In the 1920s, American football took off and has continued to grow in popularity over the years. Unlike traditional "foot" games, like soccer, the American game permits players to hold and throw the ball. Its most infamous feature is the full-contact tackle. In the early years, deaths due to violent plays and a lack of or insufficient safety gear were not uncommon. Today, the sport is heavily monitored, and players wear gear to protect their bodies. But bodily harm due to the effects of such an aggressive sport remains a contemporary issue that the league struggles to manage. Gear includes helmets, mouthpieces, shoulder pads, knee, thigh, hip, and tailbone pads, cleats, and other accessories. The gear, the uniform (jerseys with numbers and spandex pants), and the traditionally large bodies of the players give football players their distinctive look.

By 1960, as televised games increased the sport's popularity, it became clear that the sport had to have its own Hall of Fame, a fixture in American society. In 1962, Canton, Ohio, won the bid as the location for the Football Hall of Fame. Canton has played a major role in the legacy of football. The American Professional Football Association (now the NFL) was founded there. It was also home to one of the earliest teams, the Canton Bulldogs.

The first inductees into the Football Hall of Fame in 1963 were Sammy Baugh, Bert Bell, Joseph Carr, Dutch Clark, Harold Grange, George Halas, Mel Hein, Pete Henry, Carl Hubbard, Don Hutson, Earl Lambeau, Tim Mara, George Preston Marshall, John McNally, Bronko Nagurski, Ernie Nevers, and Jim Thorpe.

**The Father of American Football**

Walter Camp, known as the Father of American Football, was born on April 7, 1859, in New Britain, Connecticut. While attending Yale College, Camp played football, which was not yet the game we know today. After graduating from Yale in 1880, he pursued a medicine career at Yale Medical School. But sports, not medicine, would occupy his adult life. In 1888, he served as general athletic director, head advisory football coach, and chairman of the Yale football committee. In that same year, he married Alice Graham Sumner. They had two children. He created a fitness routine he called the "Daily Dozen," which he used in a program for training Army and Navy soldiers. Thanks to a fascinated news media, the Daily Dozen became a sensation with the public.

Camp went on to enjoy success in multiple fields. His writing career produced nearly 30 books, more than 200 magazine and newspaper articles, all of which were primarily about football. Camp also made contributions to American football rulebooks and helped foster the development of the sport.

His writing career, as well as his hands-on work in football, made Camp one of the foremost and definitive voices in the sport's history. Along with writing and refining America's most popular game, Camp served as president, treasurer, and general manager of the New Haven Clock Company. He died on March 14, 1925.

### Selection Process

Each year four to seven inductees are chosen. These inductees may include not only football players, but owners and coaches who have made outstanding contributions to the sport. The inductees are chosen by a 44 member selection committee. Enshrinement of the inductees is celebrated over a 10-day festival. Inductees, a current total of 275, are immortalized by bronze busts and touch-screen kiosks in the *Hall of Fame Gallery,* located inside the Football Hall of Fame Museum.

### Cultural Distinctions

Football—watching it on television, betting on it, buying memorabilia, tailgating, and yes, actually going to games—has permeated all levels of American society. Though it is a traditionally male-dominated activity, it is seeing an increase in interest by women and girls. Madden NFL, a popular NFL-sponsored video game series, is popular with individuals of all ages. During the football season, fans watch games on television or in-person in jam-packed, state-of-the-art stadiums and regularly sport the football regalia of their favorite teams. Fans also follow the game on the Internet. The annual Super Bowl brings together friends and family to watch the end-of-the-season match up of the best two teams of the year on the largest HD TV screen available.

Football also permeates the everyday conversation of Americans. Gridiron talk is not isolated to any one place or to a specific demographic. Unlike certain historically diversifying topics, such as politics or religion, Americans go out of their way to energetically talk football. Football talk takes place at work, on buses, in cubicles, in airports, in gyms and fitness clubs—literally anywhere people come together. Football talk crosses traditional boundaries of race, region, and age, underscoring the unifying nature of the sport.

### For Visitors

The Football Hall of Fame offers a spectacular rendering of the history of the game along with its legendary players and greatest moments. The museum features several floors of exhibits. The *Hall of Fame*

*Gallery* displays the bronze busts and detailed information on the inductees. The exhibition rotunda provides the early history of game. Other exhibits include the *Pro Football Adventure Room*, the *Moments, Memories and Mementos* Gallery, and the *Lamar Hunt Super Bowl Gallery*. Other areas of interest include the museum store, and the archives and information center.

***See also*** Cubicle; Gyms and Fitness Clubs; Super Bowl

### Further Reading

Bernstein, Mark F. 2001. *Football: The Ivy League Origins of an American Obsession*. Philadelphia: University of Pennsylvania Press.

Murray, Jim, Schechter, Gabriel and Leifer, Neil. 2011. *Guts and Glory: The Golden Age of Football, 1958–1978*. New York: Taschen.

*Pro Football Hall of Fame*. http://www.profootballhof.com/default.aspx.

## Ford's Theatre

Ford's Theatre is where President Abraham Lincoln was assassinated on April 14, 1865. While watching the performance *Our American Cousin*, Lincoln was shot by John Wilkes Booth. Lincoln died the next day. From that moment on, Ford's Theatre would forever be known for the tragedy that occurred there. Today, the theater features a museum and a learning center to commemorate the memory of Lincoln. Theatrical performances are still staged there.

### Historical Perspectives

In 1833, a church was constructed by the First Baptist Church of Washington. Then known as the "Tenth Street Baptist Church," the church was eventually vacated in 1859 when the members merged with the Fourth Baptist Church. In 1861, John T. Ford leased the building and then rented it to George Christy, who named the theater "The George Christy Opera House."

In the following year, Ford renovated the building, removing the pews and installing a proper stage and seating fit for a theatrical venue. The newly christened "Ford's Athenaeum" was a success, but it was badly damaged by a fire shortly after. Ford constructed a new building in 1863, naming this one "Ford's New Theatre." The renovated theater seated 2,400 and had two tiers of balconies. Ford's Theatre rapidly became a local success story. Tourists visited during their travels to the nation's capital. The nation's 16th president, Abraham Lincoln, made several visits. Ironically, he attended a performance, *The Marble Heart*, which featured John Wilkes Booth, his future assassin.

### Abraham Lincoln

Born in Kentucky on February 12, 1809, Abraham Lincoln was one of the nation's most prominent presidents. Tall and gangly, Lincoln rose from life on a farm to military captain in the Black Hawk War (1832). The Black Hawk War was one of several wars between the Americans and the Native Americans on the frontier. Preexisting tensions between the Native Americans, who were friendly with the British and disgruntled over territorial issues, and the Americans contributed to this brief but violent confrontation.

After the war, Lincoln practiced law and entered politics, becoming a member of the Illinois State legislature between 1834 and 1840 and of the United States House of Representatives in 1846. In 1861, he became president of the United States. Shortly thereafter, the Civil War (1861–1865) erupted, a war which saw the emancipation of slaves, and, at the war's end, the reunification of the North and South.

### John Wilkes Booth

Booth was born near Bel Air, Maryland, on May 10, 1838. Much younger than Lincoln and known for his comeliness, Booth was raised on a farm that used slave labor. After the Civil War broke out, Booth served as a secret agent on the Confederate side. In the wake of the war, he resumed his acting career, which he had begun as a teenager. In doing so, Booth followed in the footsteps of his father, Junius Brutus Booth, who had been an actor.

The younger Booth's successful life and career did not distract him from his inner discontentment—devotion to Confederacy causes and the belief that the war was not over—which he transferred upon Lincoln. After he and several others failed in an attempt to kidnap the president, on April 14, 1865, he decided instead to confront the president in a brazen and violent manner.

#### *April 14, 1864*

Going to Ford's Theatre was a welcome diversion for the president and his wife, Mary Todd Lincoln. On April 14, Lincoln, Mary, and some guests sat in the Presidential Box to watch another performance at the popular venue. During an intermission, Lincoln's bodyguard left to get a drink in the lobby. Act 3 Scene 2 of the performance had just begun when Booth approached Lincoln's box, raised his gun, aimed and shot Lincoln in the back of his head. Pandemonium ensued. Lincoln was rushed across the street to the Petersen House, and Booth managed to flee the scene. The nation's president died the following morning.

### Aftermath

The nation mourned the death of Lincoln as news spread of his assassination. As for Booth, he immediately went into hiding in a barn at a farm. After his location was discovered, he was shot and killed as authorities attempted to apprehend him.

The name Ford's Theatre entered the national imagination as a synonym for assassination as well as national tragedy of the worst type. Following Lincoln's death, Ford attempted to carry on the operation of the theater. But after threats to burn down the venue, Ford leased the theater to the government. Later, Congress purchased the building, converting it to office space. However, the building could not support the new residents, and so it collapsed in 1893.

After years as a warehouse followed by disuse and abandonment, the Department of the Interior took over the building in 1931, utilizing it as the "Lincoln Museum." In 1933, the National Park Service (NPS) took over management of the museum. The NPS also acquired the Petersen House. Since then, the house has operated as a historical house museum.

In 1968, Ford's Theatre was recognized as a National Historic Site and underwent renovations. The building was also reopened as an active theater. After closing for renovations in 2007, Ford's Theatre reopened in 2009. Notable guests at the opening events were President Barrack Obama and First Lady Michelle Obama. The new theater was outfitted with new seats and a modern sound system. Exhibit space was also incorporated into the venue.

### For Visitors

The modern-day Ford's Theatre is more than a stage for theatrical performances. The theater serves as a museum and an educational center, which debuted in 2012. Two floors of exhibit space feature artifacts from and information about the life, death, and legacy of Lincoln. The Center for Education and Leadership, which is located next to the Petersen House Museum, features workshops, programs, and a distance-learning lab. The Petersen House, which was owned by a German tailor named William A. Petersen, is a three-story red brick townhouse. Inside, a recreation of the home at the time of Lincoln's death is open to the public for viewing.

***See also*** Barns; Washington, D.C.

**Further Reading**

*Ford's Theatre*. http://www.fordstheatre.org/.

McPherson, James M. 2009. *Abraham Lincoln*. Oxford, England; New York: Oxford University Press.

O'Reilly, Bill. 2011. *Killing Lincoln: The Shocking Assassination That Changed America Forever*. New York: Henry Holt and Co.

Titone, Nora. 2010. *My Thoughts Be Bloody: The Bitter Rivalry between Edwin and John Wilkes Booth That Led to an American Tragedy*. New York: Free Press.

## Forks, Washington

Forks is located on the Olympic Peninsula in Washington State. The town is named for its geological location at the forks of the Calawah, Soleduck, and Bogachiel rivers. The former logging town, nestled in a heavily forested area and situated near the rivers and the Pacific Ocean, receives the most rainfall of any place in the contiguous United States.

Small towns will always hold a special place in the national imagination. Forks, like any American small town, is a reminder of simpler times. It inspires nostalgia and generates curiosity, especially for the majority of individuals in America who live in larger towns and sophisticated cities. Forks's added appeal is that the town attracts outdoor enthusiasts who enjoy hiking, camping, panning for gold, and other outdoor activities.

### Historical Perspectives

The open terrain upon which Forks is built was created by the Quileutes, Native Americans who burned the land to spur on the growth of plants that attracted the deer and elk that they hunted. White settlers arrived in the 1870s; in the ensuing decade, the Quileutes were removed from their traditional homeland and transferred to a reservation in La Push, 12 miles away.

The new residents established several industries in Forks. Farmers grew such crops as grain, hops, hay, and oats and engaged in dairy farming. Gold mining also took place in the area. Logging, a prominent occupation in Washington, became a major industry. By 1945, when Forks was incorporated, the town and its residents had achieved visible signs of prosperity and growth. The logging business thrived until the 1980s, when the industry throughout the state declined.

### Contemporary Perspectives

Into the new millennium, Forks remains a small town. It has a comparatively modest number of services, but the pharmacy, hardware store, banks, hospital, medical center and clinic, library, restaurants, and outdoor-oriented retailers provide enough comforts to sustain life in a 21st century town. Educational facilities include an alternative school, and elementary, middle, and high schools. For more options, residents can travel to the closest city, Port Angeles, about 46 miles away.

### Images in Popular Culture

Forks is the setting of the popular *Twilight* series (2008, 2010, 2011, 2012), which consists of four books written by Stephenie Meyer. Meyer chose Forks because it was the rainiest place in the United States. The local American Indian tribe and its legends also served as inspiration for Meyer's novels. The series follows the protagonist, Bella Swan, an adolescent who moves to Forks, Washington, to live with her father. She and a resident vampire named Edward fall in love. Jacob, a member of the Quileute tribe and a werewolf, is another major character in the books. According to Quileute legend, the tribe was created from wolves.

**Team Edward or Team Jacob?**

The *Twilight* saga comprises four novels written by Stephenie Meyer. The novels are *Twilight* (2005), *New Moon* (2006), *Eclipse* (2007), and *Breaking Dawn* (2008). The series follows the life of Bella Swan, who moves from Arizona to Forks, Washington, to live with her father and attend the local high school. Swan falls for another high school student, Edward Cullen, who is actually a 100-plus-year-old vampire posing as a human. The drama of the story revolves around the conflict between Edward and Jacob, a member of the local Quileute tribe in La Push who also happens to be able to shapeshift into a wolf. The relationship between vampires and wolves has historically been hostile. Exacerbating these tensions is the fact that the two characters vie for Bella's affections. Even bigger problems loom as the love affair between Bella and Edward grows stronger, and she insists upon becoming a vampire so they can share eternal love. Amid the drama, an evil threat challenges Bella's safety.

Since the publication of the first book in the series, the *Twilight* books have amassed an enormous following, rivaling the phenomenon caused by the British *Harry Potter* book series. The primary *Twilight* audience is young and adolescent girls, as well as adult women. During the *Twilight* craze, Team Edward and Team Jacob T-shirts were worn by adoring fans.

Excursions to Forks, Washington, started a tourist boom in the usually sleepy former lumber town. Fans flooded the theaters when *The Twilight Saga* film series was released. Bearing the same names as the books themselves, the films were released in 2008, 2009, 2010, with the last installment appearing in two parts, in 2011 and 2012.

The books and films that followed caused a massive surge of interest in Forks. Until then, the town's main claim to fame was as a popular recreational destination. Today, many retailers and tourist operations have capitalized on Forks's madness, attracting droves of visitors of all ages to the town.

### For Visitors

Forks offers an assortment of activities for visitors. Visitors enjoy local restaurants and cafés for food and ice cream and learn about the history of the town at the Forks Timber Museum. Nearby are resorts and endless trails for hiking and exploring. The rivers and ocean provide the opportunity for water sports such as kayaking, fishing, and surfing. Nearby Sol Duc Hot Springs offer warm pools, scenic views of towering hills swathed in dense forests, camping, and nature watching.

*Twilight* fans have their pick of activities and sights. Fans can take pictures of the red 1956 Chevy truck, the same color, make, and model that Bella drove in the movies. Tourists may also see the outside of the private residence that was used as Bella and her father's home in the movies and Forks High School, where Bella and Edward attended school. Tourists can dine at Bella Italia, the restaurant where Bella and Edward went on their first date, go to the beach where the wolves had their meetings, and participate in the annual Stephenie Meyer Day/Bella's Birthday Weekend, which takes place the weekend closest to September 13. Forks T-shirts and other *Twilight* paraphernalia can be purchased at numerous locations.

***See also*** High School

### Further Reading

Cook, Chris. 2009. *Twilight Territory: A Fan's Guide to Forks and LaPush*. Forks, Washington: Olympic View Publishing.
Forks Timber Museum, Burtness, Larry, and Cook, Chris. 2011. *Forks*. Charleston, South Carolina: Arcadia Publishing.
"La Push Quileute Tribe, La Push, Washington." *Forks-Web*. http://www.forks-web.com/fg/quileute.htm.
*Stephenie Meyer*. http://www.stepheniemeyer.com.

## Fort Hood

Fort Hood is an army base located near Killeen, Texas. It is one of more than 200 military bases situated throughout the United Sates. Each base is operated by one of the five armed services: army, navy, air force, marines, and coast guard. Fort Hood, also known as "The Great Place," is among the largest active-duty armored posts in the United States. The facility covers 340 square miles. Population-wise, Fort Hood is second to Fort Bragg. For soldiers and their families as well as base personnel, some of them civilian, Fort Hood is a self-sufficient, tightly managed world of its own. Visits to such facilities as are open to the public or to special events provide a rare glimpse into military life.

### Historical Perspectives

Fort Hood, originally known as Camp Hood, was named after Confederate General John Bell Hood. Camp Hood was founded in 1942 on 108,000 acres that had previously been used as farmland by some 300 families. The initial purpose of Camp Hood was to test and store military weapons and tank destroyers during World War II (1941–1945). Eight years later, after the base was established, Camp Hood's name was changed to Fort Hood, and the base was transformed into a permanent installation.

### About the Site

Larger and more complex than a neighborhood, yet not exactly a city, Fort Hood is a place where more than 50,000 soldiers work, train, live, and recreate. Other denizens of the base include the dependents, the term used to refer to the spouses and children of the soldiers, and the civilian personnel who work on the base. The installation comprises three main sections, the cantonment area (temporary quarters for troops also known as the Main Post), West Fort Hood, and North Fort Hood. The base is also home to a commissary and stores, restaurants, a library, fitness centers, a golf course, movie theater, schools, housing for families, dormitories or barracks for single soldiers, airfields, and many other facilities necessary for the support of the base as well as the soldiers and their families. Individuals who work on the base and are not military personnel are referred to as civilians. Not all soldiers live on base. Married soldiers are provided a special allowance for living off-base if they so choose.

### Cultural Distinctions

The life and culture at most military installations are similar. Residents are bound by shared experiences and knowledge, a strong support network, and a pronounced culture of order and uniformity. Unlike most American neighborhoods, college campuses, and other communities, the population on military bases shares a singular commonality that brings many different people together under one organization: the military industrial complex. The base is managed by the military and operated primarily to support military activities, soldiers, and their families. In this environment, common experiences include familiarity with military terminology and acronyms, such as those used to distinguish facilities on the base, and the transitory life of soldiers and their families, who receive orders to new assignments at different locations every few years.

Within this environment, the people who live and work on military bases are brought close together through a strong network of resources provided by the base. The base provides most of the same recreational activities and entertainment that can be found off-base (in nearby cities), such as movie theaters, fast-food restaurants, nightclubs, fitness centers and gyms, obviating the need for individuals to go elsewhere. Additional resources, such as classes, support groups, programs, and centers, located on base provide support to soldiers, spouses, youth, and retirees on a wide range of needs and issues. Fort Hood features many such programs, including the Army Community Service and the Family Advocacy Program. This self-contained and supportive environment helps to foster the military's uniform identity and community.

Indeed, the military identity and the base community are above all, uniform. As any visitor to a military base can attest, uniformity, as well as structure, is at the heart of the military life. Rules and regulations govern all aspects of life. While on duty, soldiers are required to wear uniforms. Men sport closely shaved haircuts; women customarily cut their hair short or wear their hair in a bun when in uniform. Overgrown lawns will not be found on Fort Hood or any other base; streets are neat and tidy, homes tend to look identical, row after row, and the various facilities are unadorned and institutionalized in appearance.

At the same time, military bases are famous for their diversity. On one block in any given neighborhood or in any office space, you will find individuals who hail from many different states and countries. The exposure to different regional and international cultures helps nurture mutual acceptance, appreciation, and intercultural sharing.

### Tragedy

Tragedy on the level that struck Fort Hood in 2009 rarely occurs. In that year, on November 5, a U.S. Army Major and psychiatrist named Nidal Malik Hasan went on a shooting rampage in the Soldiers Readiness Center, killing 13 and injuring many others. In the aftermath, Fort Hood strove to restore the base to normalcy and to find answers to the questions raised by this shocking event.

Tragedy struck again on April 2, 2014, when Army Specialist Ivan Lopez shot and killed three people on the base. During the shooting spree, 16 individuals were injured. The shooting ended when Lopez took his own life with a self-inflicted gunshot. The tragedy has generated discussions and concerns about the mental health of soldiers and gun control laws.

### Images in Popular Culture

From battlefields and warships to boot camps and prisoners of war, military themes are commonplace in American films and television programming. Military bases play a prominent role in movies such as *The General's Daughter* (1999), where warrant officers uncover the mystery of a murder of an army captain, the daughter of a base commander. *Army Wives* (2007–), which airs on cable television's Lifetime TV channel, follows the day-to-day lives of four military wives.

### For Visitors

Since 2001, Fort Hood has no longer been considered an open post. Due to the September 11 attack on the World Trade Center in New York in that year, many military installations became closed posts. As a result, civilian access to the post is more severely restricted than before. Still, visitors with proper identification are allowed passes to tour the base. Attractions and public events include the base's two museums and the annual Independence Day Celebration.

***See also*** Dormitory; Gyms and Fitness Clubs; Texas

### Further Reading

Baker, Anni P. 2008. *Life in the U.S. Armed Forces: (Not) Just Another Job.* Westport, Connecticut: Praeger Security International.

Cooley, Alexander. 2008. *Base Politics: Democratic Change and the U.S. Military Overseas.* Ithaca, New York: Cornell University Press.

*Fort Hood.* http://www.hood.army.mil/.

## Fort Knox

Fort Knox is a highly secured government depository in Kentucky. The official name of the depository is the United States Bullion Depository, but it known by the name of the nearby Fort Knox military installation.

Exterior view of the United States Gold Bullion Depository at Fort Knox. (Department of Defense)

Because much of America's gold is stored there, the fortress has entered English vernacular to refer to anything that is locked-down securely and impenetrable. Though the government and the military disclose few details about the facility, Fort Knox nonetheless occupies a prominent place in the public imagination.

**Historical Perspectives**

Fort Knox was created originally to meet the pressing need to store the abundance of gold the Federal Reserve purchased from American citizens as a result of Executive Order 6102, put into effect by President Franklin D. Roosevelt in 1933. U.S. coins were originally made from gold, silver, and copper. This watershed order took gold out of circulation throughout the nation; U.S. coins would no longer be made out of gold. Construction on the facility began in 1936 at a cost of $560,000, with the depository opening the following year.

The facility's primary purpose is to guard that portion of the nation's gold reserves that are stored within its walls. The United States's gold reserves are stored at several other locations, such as the Philadelphia Mint, the Denver Mint, the West Point Bullion Depository, and the San Francisco Assay Office. Other treasures, such as the Declaration of Independence and the Constitution, have been kept temporarily inside the impenetrable fortress.

**About the Site**

Unlike many famous national landmarks, Fort Knox is an unadorned, blocky 105-foot by 121-foot structure that stands 42 feet above the ground. The outside of the building is made of granite lined with concrete.

The flashiest part of the exterior is the marble entrance, which features the words "United States Depository" and the seal of the Department of the Treasury. The depository also boasts a steel fence, guards, a two-story basement, an attic, high-tech surveillance and exhaustive security measures, and the infamous vault, wherein the gold reserves are stored. The nearby military installation provides additional security, if necessary.

### The Vault

The gold vault resides behind a door that weights more than 20 tons. Several combinations, parts of which are known by select members of the staff, must be dialed to unlock the vault. Inside, 147.3 million ounces of gold is preserved in the form of bars. Some of the bars were made from pure gold; others were made from melting gold coins.

### Images in Popular Culture

The secretiveness of Fort Knox has not stopped the public from imagining what it is like inside and creating sensational stories about the facility. Over the years, Fort Knox has been featured in many popular movies and television series. The attempted gold heist from Fort Knox is a popular plot in movies such as *Behind the Headlines* (1937) and *Goldfinger* (1964), a film adapted from a James Bond novel, and in the animation *Pinky and the Brain* (1995–1998). In *Battlefield Earth* (2000), gold is taken from Fort Knox to give to aliens who have come to earth on a quest for the precious metal.

In reality, Fort Knox remains impenetrable to this day. No attempts have been made by anyone to break into the facility.

### For Visitors

No public tours are available at Fort Knox—with one exception. In 1974, 100 reporters and a dozen congressmen were permitted a glimpse into the vault to prove that, despite rumors, the vault was not empty.

Despite the inaccessibility of Fort Knox, a trip to the vicinity has much to offer. Popular places to go and events to attend include the General George Patton Museum, the Kentucky Derby, Churchill Downs, the Kentucky State Fair, the Schmidt Museum of Coca-Cola, Squire Boone Caverns, and the Native American Heritage Museum.

***See also*** Churchill Downs

### Further Reading

*Fort Knox*. http://www.knox.army.mil/.

Kempf, Gary. 2004. *The Land before Fort Knox*. Charleston, South Carolina: Arcadia Publishing.

Rector, Matthew D. 2005. *The United States Army at Fort Knox*. Charleston, South Carolina: Arcadia Publishing.

## Fort Lauderdale, Florida

Fort Lauderdale is a city located on the southern coast of Florida, the southeast-most state of the nation. Covering 33 square miles, including more than 7 miles of sunny beaches on the Atlantic Ocean, Fort Lauderdale is famous as a destination for college students during spring break. Its warm weather and bountiful attractions make the city a popular American vacation for travelers of all ages throughout the year.

### Historical Perspectives

The Fort Lauderdale of today took more than two centuries to create. The region's earliest Native American inhabitants settled in the region and sustained life through hunting, gathering roots and herbs, and fishing in the major freshwater source, the New River, which flowed from the Everglades. Their descendants, the Tequesta Indians, so-named by the Spanish explorers, made the region their home for many years until, following the arrival of Europeans, the population was devastated by violence and disease.

While Florida changed hands between the Spanish, the British, and the Spanish again during the 18th century, a small number of settlers made their way to the Fort Lauderdale area. The first communities were made up of the families of Captain Joseph and Rachel Robbins and Charles and Frankee Lewis.

After the United States took control of Florida in 1821, the region saw the emergence of a New River settlement. Two prominent individuals of this settlement were William Cooley, who established a prosperous arrowroot factory, and Richard Fitzpatrick, who owned a plantation. Black slaves were brought to the region to work on the land. Native Americans also worked on the thriving settlement. Conflict between the Seminoles and the U.S. government resulted in three major wars, known as the Seminole Wars (1814–1819, 1835–1842, and 1855–1858) and the emergence of Fort Lauderdale.

### Military Occupation

The U.S. Army built Fort Lauderdale in 1838. It was named after Major William Lauderdale, who took part in the military pursuit of the Seminoles living in southern Florida. Though the Seminole Wars did not end until 1858, the military abandoned the fort in 1842.

### Settlements

Though the fort had been abandoned, the population of the nearby settlement that continued to be known as Fort Lauderdale continued to grow. Construction of a road and the establishment of several Houses of Refuge, which were constructed to provide aid to ocean castaways, spurred development.

Starting in the late 1890s, a new trend took America buy storm, as individuals, mostly the wealthy, were caught up in the feverish pursuit of outdoor adventure. Thousands departed their homes for fun and adventure in America's rugged wilderness areas. Fishing and boating were popular activities of these outdoor enthusiasts. The more adventurous endured, in the name of "fun," the sweltering and humid climate and the abundance of insects that permeated the swamp lands around Fort Lauderdale.

Most 19th-century individuals found this region, as well as the nearby Everglades, not fit for human habitation. But enough found the area tolerable to settle permanently, and to find ways to deal with the inhospitable climate. More settlers were brought into Fort Lauderdale by the new railway that was completed around 1895. A popular store owned by Frank Stranahan was a major hub. A school was built to accommodate the first generation of native residents of Fort Lauderdale.

The denizens of this growing city were whites, Seminoles, and African Americans. The African Americans, most of them from the Bahamas and the South, built their community east of the railway tracks. They owned businesses, built homes, their own school, and the first black church in Fort Lauderdale: Piney Grove Missionary Baptist Church.

### Incorporation

After Fort Lauderdale was incorporated in 1911, the city experienced many changes and underwent many improvements that added to the downtown that sprawled modestly along its main thoroughfare, Brickell Avenue. A stretch of highway was extended through Fort Lauderdale, easing the journey for travelers who came by automobile. A local real-estate craze made residents wealthy. New homes, roads, and neighborhoods, public facilities, hotels, and outdoor attractions sprang up on once undeveloped land. Of the three major communities that had settled in Fort Lauderdale, the African Americans and Seminoles received the least benefit from the city's growth. In fact, their situation worsened as formal laws segregating blacks from whites were enacted, and the Seminoles were forced to live on a reservation (in 1957, Hollywood Reservation was established as the Seminole headquarters). A naval air station was established in Fort Lauderdale during World War II (1941–1945). Following the war, Fort Lauderdale's population growth soared. The residents enjoyed new technology such as air-conditioning and an airport.

### Spring Break Revelry

Fort Lauderdale's reputation as a college spring-break town began in the first half of the 20th century. The city's reputation as a seasonal haven for college students started with the establishment of the Fort Lauderdale Casino Pool in 1928. In 1935, the lavish facility hosted the Collegiate Aquatic Forum, a popular event with local and out-of-state college students, which continues to this day. In 1953, city leaders invited college students throughout the nation to enjoy their city. Some 10,000 students responded.

Since the 1950s, college beach parties in Fort Lauderdale have become a fixture. The parties bring money and national attention, as well as woes, to the city. Locals bemoan the boisterous days and nights and the havoc that some college students cause. Well into the 21st century, the parties show little signs of letup.

### Contemporary Perspectives

The city of Fort Lauderdale has come a long way from its days as a remote and mosquito-bitten enclave. Though urban problems and racism persist, Fort Lauderdale's historically marginalized communities, the African Americans and the Seminoles, have attained considerable achievements. African Americans no longer contend with brazen discriminatory laws, and the Seminoles are thriving. The city itself continues to develop, with venues for the arts, upscale shopping districts, and contemporary structures.

### Images in Popular Culture

The popularity of Fort Lauderdale has ensured the city plenty of appearances in film and television. During the silent film era, Fort Lauderdale attracted directors who wanted to capture its exotic landscape. Films such as *Spring of the Year* (1917) and *Idol Dancer* (1919) were set in Fort Lauderdale. The real-life young adult obsession with Fort Lauderdale spring-break getaways inspired the novel and film *Where the Boys Are* (1960). Other films, including *Caddyshack* (1980), *Donnie Brasco* (1997), and *Marley & Me* (2008), were also filmed in Fort Lauderdale.

### For Visitors

Fort Lauderdale is not only for spring breakers. Tourism in Fort Lauderdale draws adults and families year-round. Sandy beaches, spas, restaurants, museums, nightclubs, casinos, and sightseeing cruises and tours are popular attractions.

***See also*** Casino; Everglades

### Further Reading

Bramson, Seth H. 2011. *The Greatest Railroad Story Ever Told: Henry Flagler & the Florida East Coast Railway's Key West Extension*. Charleston, South Carolina: The History Press.

Brickell, Beth. 2011. *William and Mary Brickell: Founders of Miami and Florida*. Charleston, South Carolina: The History Press.

Gillis, Susan. 2004. *Fort Lauderdale: The Venice of America*. Charleston, South Carolina: Arcadia Publishing.

Kersey, Harry A. 2003. *The Stranahans of Florida: A Pioneer Family of New River*. Gainesville: University Press of Florida.

*The Seminole Tribe of Florida*. http://www.semtribe.com/.

Work, Deborah. 2001. *My Soul Is a Witness: A History of Black Fort Lauderdale*. Virginian Beach, Virginia: Donning Company.

## French Quarter

The French Quarter refers to a famous neighborhood, encompassing some 90 blocks, in New Orleans, Louisiana. Founded in 1718, the French Quarter, also known as Vieux Carré (Old Square) or simply the Quarter, has a storied and decadent past. In the early years, the neighborhood generated notoriety from its flamboyant establishments and lively personalities. The lavish ballrooms and hotels, cafes and restaurants, gambling houses, taverns, and brothels that lined the heavily trafficked streets catered to refined society, everyday laborers, and rogues alike.

Then, as now, the French Quarter shimmers with an aura of excitement and enticement. Hosting a bevy of eclectic venues such as voodoo shops, nightclubs, strip clubs, bars, numerous festivals, and restaurants, the French Quarter is a popular destination for visitors of all kinds who want to take a walk on the wild side.

### Historical Perspectives

Originally founded in 1718 by the French Canadian Jean Baptiste Bienville, the French Quarter was heavily influenced by French culture and traditions. Many streets were named after French royalty; the buildings reflected French architectural styles; and the population was mainly Catholic. French Creoles were a by-product of the French influence in Louisiana. French Creole is a term used to classify the offspring of two racial groups: French and European descendants (white Creoles), or French and African descendants (black Creoles). The population of African descendants in Louisiana included slaves and free blacks. The white Creoles and the black Creoles lived in communities separated by race and social status. Within the community of African descendants, status was based on an individual's economic standing, free status (as opposed to slave status), education, and skin complexion (light skin color was preferred over dark skin color).

The French Quarter during this period was defined by the spirited individuals who lived or visited the area. The nearby Mississippi River brought a steady stream of thieves, ruffians, and prostitutes to those notorious venues built along the river.

The year 1762 ended France's reign in Louisiana, as France transferred control of the area to Spain. Spain thus played a prominent role in development of the French Quarter, especially after two destructive fires (occurring in 1788 and 1794) destroyed the majority of the buildings that had been built during France's rule. As a result, the French Quarter is peppered with Spanish architectural styles, such as pastel-colored buildings, wrought iron balconies, and courtyards.

In 1803, the Spanish sold Louisiana to the United States. At the time, New Orleans was considered a city of high-fashion, sophistication, and modernity. Its refined culture coexisted with the French Quarter's infamous locales and scandalous reputation. The change to U.S. rule meant little to the French Quarter, which continued to entertain locals and visitors with theaters and ballrooms, saloons, gambling halls, and brothels.

### Cultural Distinctions

In addition to French and Spanish, African influences also played a part in the cultural development of the region, contributing to the creation of unique music, language, religious beliefs, practices, and traditions. For example, the African descendants integrated their indigenous religion with Catholicism, producing voodoo. French, Spanish, and African blends contributed to the making of Creole food and music. Mardi Gras, the world-famous festival, incorporates African and French Catholic traditions. Some cultural traditions and practices, however, remained within isolated communities.

### Post–Civil War

The Civil War (1861–1865) devastated most of the southern states, including Louisiana and its famed French Quarter. Riddled with neglect and disrepair and wracked by economic woes, the French Quarter was no longer the place of rich opulence it once had been, becoming instead a place of increasingly tattered and worn Old World charm that attracted ever-more bohemian residents.

The 1930s brought forth a period of revitalization, and efforts to preserve historical buildings in the French Quarter began in earnest. The Vieux Carré Commission, established in 1936, helped the French Quarter maintain its historic architecture. New buildings and venues featured local cuisine, voodoo shops, jazz, and adult entertainment. Famous writers such as Tennessee Williams, William Faulkner, and Ernest Hemingway were drawn to the French Quarter, where they found inspiration for their work.

### Contemporary Perspectives

Today, tourists flock in large numbers to the French Quarter. Still a neighborhood that seems never to sleep, the famous streets of the French Quarter, such as the famous Bourbon Street, feature unusual trinkets and paraphernalia, music, savory food, and delights for families and adults. The largest festival in the region, Mardi Gras, is known for grand processions, colorful glass beads, rowdy parties, fun, and masquerades throughout the Quarter. The old-style architecture gives visitors to this southern city the feel of being in another century and country.

### Issues

The popular image of the French Quarter is problematic for some. Critics argue that the neighborhood has become excessively touristy and that the culture of the region has become a commodity to be packaged and sold to eager tourists in such places as bars, souvenir shops, and restaurants. Other critics oppose the fact that the French Quarter is depicted predominately as a place of decadence and immorality, denying the Quarter's authentic history and culture.

*See also* Bourbon Street; Cajun Country; Mardi Gras; Mississippi River; New Orleans, Louisiana; Saloons, Bars, and Taverns

### Further Reading

Asbury, Herbert. 1936. *The French Quarter: An Informal History of the New Orleans Underworld*. New York: Alfred A. Knopf.

Ellis, Scott S. 2010. *Madame Vieux Carré: The French Quarter in the Twentieth Century*. Jackson: University Press of Mississippi.

Hirsch, Arnold R., and Logsdon, Joseph, eds. 1992. *Creole New Orleans: Race and Americanization*. Baton Rouge: University of Louisiana Press.

McKinney, Louise. 2006. *New Orleans: A Cultural History*. New York: Oxford University Press.

Vogt, Lloyd. 2002. *Historic Buildings of the French Quarter*. Gretna, Louisiana: Pelican Publishing.